Springer Series in Media Industries

The media industries constitute an important sector of national and transnational economies; not only do they contribute significantly to the GDP of a country, they also serve cultural, political, and societal functions. Production conditions and the production output of the media industries are as much a result of their economic, cultural, political and societal environment as an influence on these spheres of life.

The series features research that considers this duality, and it focuses on the influencing factors that shape the structures and output of the media industry on all levels. This includes research on the macroeconomic level of media markets and industries, including policies and regulations; research on the organizational level of managerial decision-making and challenges; as well as research on the individual level of media workers. We welcome transnational and interdisciplinary perspectives.

The disciplines, approaches and theories applied may include (but are not limited to): media economics; political economy; media and creative industries studies; media policy studies; media management; organizational cultural theories; technology, creative and innovation theories; media and communication studies; audience and consumer theories; critical cultural media studies; professional cultural theories; and social psychology. All volumes in the series are peer-reviewed.

Series Editors:
M. Bjørn von Rimscha, Johannes Gutenberg University, Mainz, Germany
Ulrike Rohn, Tallinn University, Estonia

Advisory Editors:
Michel Clement, University Hamburg, Germany
Stuart Cunningham, Queensland University of Technology, Australia
Ethel Pis Diez, University Austral, Argentina
Gillian Doyle, University of Glasgow, United Kingdom
Tom Evens, Gent University, Belgium
Terry Flew, Queensland University of Technology, Australia
Gregory Ferell Lowe, Northwestern University, Qatar
Richard Gershon, Wester Michigan University, USA
Min Hang, Tsinghua University, China
Mónica Herrero, University of Navarra, Spain
David Hesmondalgh, University of Leeds, United Kingdom
Indrek Ibrus, Tallinn University, Estonia
Rita Järventie-Thesleff, Aalto University, Finland
Amanda Lotz, University of Michigan, USA
Paul McDonald, King's College, United Kingdom
Philip Napoli, Duke University, USA
Hele Sjøvaag, University of Stavanger, Norway
Petr Szczepanik, Charles University, Czech Republic
Patrick Vonderau, Stockholm University, Sweden
Steve Wildman, University of Colorado, USA

More information about this series at http://www.springer.com/series/16062

Petr Szczepanik · Pavel Zahrádka ·
Jakub Macek · Paul Stepan
Editors

Digital Peripheries

The Online Circulation of Audiovisual
Content from the Small Market Perspective

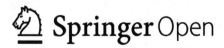

Editors
Petr Szczepanik
Film Studies Department
Charles University
Prague, Czech Republic

Jakub Macek
Department of Media Studies
and Journalism
Masaryk University
Brno, Czech Republic

Pavel Zahrádka
Department of Theater and Film Studies
Palacký University Olomouc
Olomouc, Czech Republic

Paul Stepan
FOKUS—Institute for Cultural
and Media Economics
Vienna, Austria

ISSN 2523-3882   ISSN 2523-3890   (electronic)
Springer Series in Media Industries
ISBN 978-3-030-44849-3   ISBN 978-3-030-44850-9   (eBook)
https://doi.org/10.1007/978-3-030-44850-9

This Springer imprint is published by the registered company Springer Nature Switzerland AG
The registered company address is: Gewerbestrasse 11, 6330 Cham, Switzerland

Contents

Editors and Contributors

About the Editors

Petr Szczepanik is Associate Professor at Charles University, Prague, Czech Republic. His current research focuses on East-Central European screen industries, production cultures and public service media in the Internet era. His historical research on the state-socialist mode of film production was published in the book "Behind the Screen: Inside European Production Culture" (Palgrave, co-edited with Patrick Vonderau, 2013).

Pavel Zahrádka currently works at the Department of Theatre, Film and Media Studies, Palacký University Olomouc, Czech Republic. Dr. Zahrádka's research focuses on the impact of the European Commission's Digital Single Market strategy on the Czech audiovisual industry, Internet piracy, ethics and aesthetics.

Jakub Macek currently works as a chair of the Department of Media Studies and Journalism, Masaryk University, Czech Republic. Dr. Macek's research fields involve social science, communication and media. His current projects are focused on convergent media audiences, on the role of media in societal polarization and on trust in media.

Paul Stepan teaches cultural economics, economics of copyright and economics of cultural and creative industries at the University for Music and Performing Arts Vienna, Austria, and at Palacký University Olomouc, Czech Republic. His research focuses on the impact of digitization on the cultural and media sector in general with emphasis on the film industry.

Contributors

Marcin Adamczak Department of Anthropology and Cultural Studies, Adam Mickiewicz University in Poznań, Poznań, Poland

Petr Bilík Department of Theater and Film Studies, Faculty of Arts, Palacký University, Olomouc, Czech Republic

Daniël Biltereyst Ghent University, Gent, Belgium

Karen Donders Imec-SMIT, Vrije Universiteit Brussel, Brussel, Belgium

Christian Handke Erasmus University Rotterdam, Rotterdam, The Netherlands

Tae-Sik Kim Department of Media Studies and Journalism, Faculty of Social Studies, Masaryk University, Brno, Czech Republic

Rudolf Leška University of Finance and Administration, Prague, Czech Republic

Ramon Lobato School of Media and Communication, Digital Ethnography Research Centre, RMIT University, Melbourne, VIC, Australia

Jakub Macek Department of Media Studies and Journalism, Faculty of Social Studies, Masaryk University, Brno, Czech Republic

Philippe Meers University of Antwerp, Antwerpen, Belgium

Lydia Papadimitriou Liverpool John Moores University, Liverpool, UK

Radim Polčák Faculty of Law, Institute of Law and Technology, Masaryk University, Brno, Czech Republic

Tim Raats Imec-SMIT, Vrije Universiteit Brussel, Brussel, Belgium

Julia Reda Berkman Klein Center for Internet & Society, Harvard University, Cambridge, MA, USA

Aram Sinnreich School of Communication, American University, Washington D.C., USA

Petr Szczepanik Film Studies Department, Faculty of Arts, Charles University, Prague, Czech Republic

Aleit Veenstra University of Antwerp, Antwerpen, Belgium

Ira Wagman School of Journalism and Communication, Carleton University, Ottawa, ON, Canada

Pavel Zahrádka Department of Theater and Film Studies, Faculty of Arts, Palacký University, Olomouc, Czech Republic

List of Figures

List of Tables

Chapter 1
Introduction: Theorizing Digital Peripheries

Petr Szczepanik, Pavel Zahrádka, and Jakub Macek

1.1 Globalization and Digitalization from the Perspective of the Small and the Peripheral

The global reach of online platforms and services as well as the globally synchronized flows of audiovisual content might suggest that the global media market is now fully integrated. This book argues contrariwise that the global digital market is far from united and that national borders, center-periphery hierarchies and differences in scale still matter, and perhaps they matter even more than in the analog broadcast era. Indeed, if we live in the era of "post-globalization" (Flew 2018), its defining features include consumers' continuing gravitation toward local content as well as national governments' continuing primacy in the supranational regulation of multinational media corporations and the Internet in general (Michalis 2016). To formulate the central claim of the book more radically: as material processes, the digitalization and globalization of audiovisual distribution actually take place through the work of negotiating borders, peripheral positions, differences in scale, cultural distances and all the "friction" that comes with them (Tsing 2005). The epistemological starting point of this book is that to understand the internal workings of the global digital market in the era of the "return of the state" (Flew et al. 2016) and of populist nationalisms, we need to start from the local barriers and places remote from the global

P. Szczepanik (✉)
Filozofická fakulta Univerzity Karlovy, nám. Jana Palacha 1/2, 116 38 Paha, Czech Republic
e-mail: Petr.Szczepanik@ff.cuni.cz

P. Zahrádka
Department of Theater and Film Studies, Faculty of Arts, Palacký University, Křížkovského 10, 771 47 Olomouc, Czech Republic
e-mail: pavel.zahradka@upmedia.cz

J. Macek
Faculty of Social Studies, Masaryk University, Jostova 10, 602 00 Brno, Czech Republic
e-mail: jmacek@fss.muni.cz

© The Author(s) 2020
P. Szczepanik et al. (eds.), *Digital Peripheries*, Springer Series in Media Industries,
https://doi.org/10.1007/978-3-030-44850-9_1

1

"media capitals" (Curtin 2009): peripheries that seem to slow down, be disconnected from, or even block digital flows across borders; peripheries that look toward the center but do not connect with one another through audiovisual exchange unless they are part of the same region or target diasporas.

This book does not aim to address exhaustively all aspects of unevenness in cross-border audiovisual circulation and all types of small and peripheral media markets. Rather, it takes as its point of departure primarily the region of Central and Eastern Europe (CEE), and especially the so-called Visegrad countries, and expands in scope to other European and non-European cases of smallness and peripherality, such as Belgium, Greece and Canada. The advantage of starting with CEE is that it not only connects small sizes and peripheral positions, but also that it opens a new perspective on the EU media and cultural policymaking debates, in which this particular region has remained surprisingly underrepresented. Our focus on CEE, part of the former Eastern Bloc, also provides a fresh perspective on globalization. Having been drawn into the Western media economy only recently, the region remains affected by political and industrial legacies of state socialism while still tending to some degree to approach transnational media as something foreign and imported. With the recent surge in nationalism, illiberalism and the politicization of media in some of the CEE countries and with its status, at the same time, as a key growth market for transnational online services (Ampere Analysis 2019), the region offers an illustrative case for studying the post-globalization tendencies in both industry practice and media policymaking (see Imre 2019). However, we chose not to frame the book's geographic focus as "post-socialist," not only because many of the chapters discuss Western European or non-European markets, but also because the concept imposes a restrictive epistemology that defines the present in terms of one historical rupture (the collapse of state-socialist regimes) and privileges a "territorial notion of space as bounded container" (Müller 2019: 538), while instead we seek to identify links and continuities, similarities and differences across various cases of the small and the peripheral.

Economic literature has drawn many distinctions between different groups of the CEE post-socialist economies, some of which have become successful and complex exporters. While they all emerged from the periphery of the capitalist world system (or from the "socialist core") after 1989, they have since developed different forms of capitalism and might be divided into clusters of "semi-core," "semi-periphery" and "periphery" in terms of international economic integration, with Visegrad states and Slovenia being attributed a "semi-core" profile (Bohle and Greskovits 2012: 44–48).[1] When looking at media industries more specifically, the CEE countries have certainly become an important part of the global value chain in some sectors, with Budapest and Prague, for example, being busy exporters of film and TV production services (Stachowiak and Stryjakiewicz 2018), but they have not become successful

---

[1]Greskovits (2008: 23) groups the new EU members into the "semi-core" consisting of "complex manufacturing exporters" (the so-called Visegrad states and Slovenia) and the "semi-periphery" of "basic manufacturing exporters" (the Baltic states and southeast Europe), while reserving the category of "periphery" for the "resource-intensive exporters" among ex-Soviet Union republics (Kazakhstan, Azerbaijan, Uzbekistan).

exporters of domestic audiovisual works,[2] which qualifies them as peripheries in this specific field (or "peripheries of the center" when looking at the EU from the outside). This is well documented in the current literature on cross-border circulation of films in Europe, which identifies as the center of the economic and cultural power in the EU film industry the "West European big five" (the UK, France, Germany, Italy and Spain). These biggest producing countries (and especially the UK and France) clearly dominate in all categories of successfully traveling films (big-budget blockbusters, middle-brow and art house, in Andrew Higson's terminology) and in all distribution windows including video on demand (VOD). While films from several small EU states still perform quite well in terms of the average international audience per title (e.g., Belgium, Denmark and Sweden), the CEE region demonstrates a disproportionately weaker market performance and CEE productions attract less critical acclaim and festival awards (Higson 2018; Holdaway and Scaglioni 2018; Grece 2017; Olsberg 2019; Ji.hlava IDFF 2019). In this book, we do not aspire to contribute to the discussions about regional economic development as such, and instead we stick to the simplified categories of "small" and "peripheral" media markets as perceived from the perspective of cross-border audiovisual flows, global online distribution services, cultural consumption and EU media policymaking (Fig. 1.1).

Below, we will first trace academic debates on small and peripheral media markets and reflect on whether and how their concepts can be used to study the uneven impacts of transnational online distribution on those markets. In the fourth section, we provide an example of a new typology of digital peripheries that offers a more dynamic way to group media markets according to their changing position in the new distribution ecosystem dominated and co-constituted by transnational VOD services

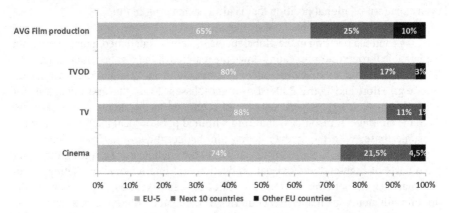

Fig. 1.1 Core/Semi-periphery/Periphery hierarchy in the cross-border circulation of EU nonnational films, comparing country clusters for film production and exports in theaters, TV and transactional VOD, in % of total titles exported. (*Source* Grece 2017: 11) (Most of the 11 CEE Member States fall into the "Other EU" cluster)

---

[2]With the significant exception of pornography, which, however, falls beyond the scope of this volume.

and platforms. The fifth section transposes the key concerns of these media industry debates about peripherality and the impacts of US-based media into the EU policy discourse on barriers in the European digital market, and focuses more closely on the conflicting interests related to territorial barriers within the European audiovisual market.

1.2   Scale Matters

The most obvious and universal factor of uneven integration in global flows of audiovisual content is differences in market scale. The existing literature on small media markets agrees that scale involves qualitative differences in terms of internal structure, position in transnational production networks and flows, and cultural relationships with bigger neighbors. If we take the European Union as an example, the current communication studies literature on small media markets usually chooses population as the basic characteristic, with the thresholds distinguishing the small EU countries from the big, and the very small ones, ranging from the former (population over 18–20 million) to the latter (population below 100,000 inhabitants); this positions 18–19 countries (or approximately 70% of the EU states and about 30% of the EU total population) in the small-market category (Trappel 2014: 240). Of course, other criteria should supplement population size, including general classifications such as GDP and the surface area, as well as more specific characteristics such as the volume of media industries based in the territory. Moreover, market size is not absolute or fixed, but always a relative, dynamic concept, implying a dependent, dominated, or even subaltern relational position that is always changing in time.

What is important for this book is the widely shared perception that the internal workings and the position in the global media system of small media markets are not explainable through simply scaling down the features of the big, hegemonic markets. Small markets' quantitative differences have structural and qualitative consequences (see, e.g., Hjört and Petrie 2007; Lowe and Nissen 2011) that are impactful, for example, on their export performance. In economic terms, small countries suffer from the shortage of resources, and from a limited pool of local talent and a narrow consumer base. With the median fiction film budget three times lower than in the large EU economies (EAO 2019: 12), and with the challenges of covering the larger fixed costs of high-end audiovisual production and international marketing, small EU countries cannot benefit from economies of scale like their larger counterparts do. Film financing in smaller EU countries, if compared with larger markets, relies more on direct public funding and less on presales, which further decreases their export potential (Fontaine 2019: 12). Moreover, small nations' cultural products tend to be perceived as too culturally specific, which activates the mechanisms of so-called cultural discount and inhibits their cultural export potential, especially to larger import markets. Eventually, media industries from small countries end up being more dependent on media content imports and public subsidies, while simultaneously being more vulnerable to foreign takeovers (Jones 2014; McElroy et al. 2018; Alaveras et al. 2018). The dependency on imported products and services applies even more to those small countries which share the same language with (or have a language similar to) a larger neighbor (e.g., Austria or Slovakia).

One of the most developed theoretical debates about small media systems currently pertains to their role in supranational regulation and policies aimed at supporting cross-border circulation and protecting cultural diversity. The small EU countries—despite being overrepresented in EU institutions—lack political leverage over international regulatory bodies and are reactive rather than proactive in regulatory decision-making processes that do not seem to be of the highest economic priority to them. This is why the EU's media and cultural policy initiatives tend to reflect the needs of larger countries. Smaller states, conscious of their competitive disadvantages, react by introducing protectionist measures to preserve local media production, to use media for promoting national identity and to defend their markets from foreign competition and takeovers, rather than adopting competitive, free-market and pro-export strategies. Small-market scale, especially in countries with large neighbors that share the same language, makes cultural diversity—a key goal of EU policy-making—difficult to achieve, due to small niche audience groups and the high costs of premium content that prevent local legacy media players from competing with transnational VOD services (Puppis et al. 2009; Trappel 2014). Although the number of films produced per capita tends to be higher in small countries due to the increased weight of public funding in smaller markets (Poort et al. 2019: 62–63), the less diversified economic structure and limited competition (linked with a smaller number of producers and distributors) result in a lower variety of products, with the cultural needs of certain groups of consumers (e.g., cultural or language minorities) remaining unmet.

An even more dynamic strand of small media systems research centers on broadcasting and especially public service media as crucial institutions for sustaining small nations' cultural identities and public spheres. Small countries tend to have relatively expensive and strong public service media that play a key role in domestic audiovisual production, and at the same time adopt more mainstream, populist programming than public service broadcasters in larger countries (Iosifidis 2007; Lowe and Nissen 2011; Raats et al. 2016).[3] Future research will have to tackle the challenges small countries face from transnational VOD services and online platforms, as well as the strategies their public service media can employ to survive in this new, highly competitive environment without eroding their public mission (McElroy and Noonan 2018; Donders 2019).

The key question this book asks is not about the essential features of small media markets per se, but rather about the way they are adopting new distribution technologies and practices, how they are approached by transnational online services and EU policymaking, and how they react to these initiatives. Moreover, to grasp

---

[3]See also the international research network "Television from Small Nations," https://smallnationstv.org, hosted by the Centre for the Study of Media and Culture in Small Nations at the University of South Wales, https://culture.research.southwales.ac.uk.

the obvious complexity of the topic, one of the sections of the book focuses specifically on small-market and peripheral-market audiences. This enables us to address the problem of the impact of digitalization and globalization within the audiovisual sector with respect to changing consumer habits and the spread of transnational culture due to migration and cross-border digital transmissions (see Kim's chapter in this volume). Instead of projecting unidirectional models of power, this edited volume focuses on players and processes between the global and the local: how global giants increasingly act as gatekeepers within local media ecosystems, and how local institutions and firms navigate the forces of globalization?

1.3   Renewed Debate on Cultural Flows and Center-Periphery Hierarchies

At the outset, it is important for us to clarify our terminology, starting with what separates small and peripheral countries according to the definitions utilized herein. The key difference between the small and the peripheral is in the emphasis of the latter concept on relationships with the center, usually defined by different forms of distance and dependency. Social sciences literature on center-periphery hierarchies usually draws upon the structuralist theories of the 1950s to the 1980s (such as dependency theory, Wallersteinian world-systems theory, neo-Marxist critiques of the international division of labor or cultural imperialism debates) designed to explain uneven development and inequality in the system of world capitalism by analyzing the impacts of historical patterns of uneven international exchange that sustain the dependence of the periphery on the core. Although criticized and revised from both economic and culturalist positions many times since, the center/periphery or core/semi-periphery/periphery model maintains its explanatory power when applied to culture and media in the era of globalization—historical flows of novels from the core to the semi-periphery and then periphery (exemplified by the "three Europes") in a literary world-system (Moretti 1998: 173), the economic geography of spatial "clusters" of cultural producers and workers (Scott 2006), the new international division of cultural labor (Miller et al. 2005), international television trade (Sinclair et al. 1996) and on a more general level, the political economy of the "world media order" with the domination by the USA and the four largest Anglo-American markets being gradually lessened by the boom of Chinese, Japanese and South Korean media economies that, since the late 1990s, have been "tilting the center of gravity of global media decisively toward Asia" (Winseck 2011: 38).

Film studies have an especially long tradition of tracing, criticizing and relativizing Hollywood's impact on national and regional cinemas over the world, often understood as being defined by their competition with, adherence to, or resistance to Hollywood, in both economic and cultural terms (Guback 1969; Thompson 1985; Nagib 2006; Crane 2014). At the same time, the discipline has long been engaged in attempting to escape the center-periphery binaries of the US-centered or Eurocentric views, celebrating peripheral and hybrid forms of filmmaking or movie-going, and attempting to de-Westernize thinking about film cultures by proposing alternative "third," "transnational" or "polycentric" models of approaching world cinema (see, e.g., Andrew 2006; Iordanova et al. 2010; Nagib et al. 2012).

The debates of the 1990s and 2000s regarding cultural globalization tended to dismiss center-periphery hierarchies and one-directional flow paradigms on both theoretical and empirical grounds, replacing them with multi-directional models and emphasizing processes of cultural hybridization. However, it seems that some key elements of the original models—issues of media concentration, unequal cultural power, shifting macro-level hierarchies and the direction of global media flows—are on the comeback, especially in the study of global digital media and regulation therein (Iordache et al. 2018). In the era of "post-globalization" (Flew 2018), VOD distribution and Internet television attract special attention in these renewed debates as vehicles of "programming from afar," inspiring a renaissance of the cultural imperialism critique and consequent cultural protectionism in the "discourses that shape policy and practice" (Lobato 2018: 216). International outrage was stoked when, in January 2019, the president of the Canadian public service broadcaster CBC compared Netflix to the British Empire, calling for Canada "to be wary of the negative effects of cultural imperialism" (Houpt and Robertson 2019). Looking at the current European debate over the Digital Single Market and cross-border circulation of audiovisual content, and putting it in the historical context of European media governance, it seems that the same anxiety about US cultural imperialism has been a key driver of EU media and cultural policymaking since at least the 1989 Television without Frontiers directive that introduced quotas for European content.

However, agreement on the dimensions and parameters of center-periphery dynamics is elusive. For example, Larissa Buchholz distinguished between three modes of cross-border cultural centrality: "(a) geographic centers of cultural mediation, (b) the dominance of a country's cultural/media products in the global marketplace, or (c) a country's position in the global flow and trade of symbolic goods" (Buchholz 2018: 19). But one of the important parameters missing in this typology is the power of a country to define the rules of the game, i.e., to impose national regulations and to influence supranational initiatives to regulate cross-border circulation of cultural products and services, such as the European Commission's Digital Single Market strategy discussed in this book. Moreover, the way multinational corporations are themselves creating their own world-systems of core/semi-periphery/periphery hierarchies by approaching different markets differently—based on their own criteria that may diverge from a country's position in international trade—is also omitted by this typology.

While small markets generally tend to be marginalized, some small countries' screen industries have managed to overcome the disadvantages of their small scale. Although the small scale limits the exportability of local content, not all small countries are automatically peripheral in the sense of their marginal position in global networks and flows. Consider Denmark and Poland: While the former (population 6 million) exports its films and TV drama successfully, the latter (38 million) ranks among the least efficient cinema exporters in the EU (Grece 2017: 94). Or compare the Czech Republic and Austria in terms of their relationships with neighboring countries: While the only foreign market where Czech content can be exported without dubbing or subtitling is Slovakia, one of the smallest markets in the EU, Austrian producers can target both German and Swiss markets.

This book presumes that online distribution redefines "periphery" and makes it—at least for the moment—more visible rather than merging it with the center. One way to identify digital peripheries is to chart unequal outgoing transnational flows of audiovisual content. Although this seems to be difficult due to the lack of data from online services, regular and steadily improving reporting by the European Audiovisual Observatory on VOD catalogs makes this at least proximately possible. The following map of films circulating across borders on TVOD indicates that Central and Eastern Europe lag not just behind the big five EU markets, but also behind the smaller West and North European countries (Fig. 1.2).

Some peripheral countries show surprisingly high levels of preference for, and shares of, local production and services in their domestic markets. The Czech Republic and Poland rank among the EU markets with the highest theatrical market share for domestic productions (Kanzler and Simone 2019: 34, 40) and have the highest audience share of their respective public service broadcasters among new EU Member States (Schneeberger 2019: 33). This success suggests that small scale and a periphery position might have the advantage of allowing for a closer, more intimate relationship between local producers and their audiences as well as national policymakers (Jones 2014: 10). This, however, does not apply to all small markets

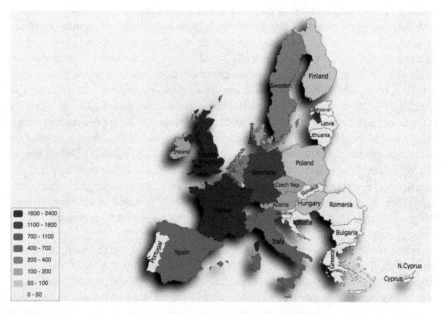

Fig. 1.2 An example of visualizing "digital peripheries" in the EU on-demand market: single film titles available in at least one other EU country in October 2016 on TVOD. *Source* Grece 2017: 60

(see below), and it also does not translate into stronger exports, despite the new opportunities of online distribution (Grece 2017).

"Peripheral" also refers to a country's lack of globally recognizable brands. In the attention economy, stars, franchises and awards play key roles as facilitators of cross-border circulation. Most peripheries lack strong brands, especially if their industries focus primarily on domestic audiences, such as in the case of the Czech Republic. Some peripheral countries are able to create a temporary splash with film auteurs and "new waves," but these are often target festival juries more than global consumer markets. For example, Romania and Hungary are countries with a very low national market share of their domestic productions in theatrical distribution (Kanzler and Simone 2019: 40–41) as well as a low-audience share of their respective public service broadcasters (Schneeberger 2019: 33) and weak total exports (Grece 2017), but their brands are relatively well recognized in the global film festival circuit. These examples suggest that there are at least two different dynamics of centrality and peripherality, which translate into two different logics of change in the center-periphery hierarchies: Gains in field-specific symbolic capital (such as festival awards) do not necessarily correspond with a country's gains in economic capital, i.e., successful exports of commercially oriented products. At the same time, the small Nordic countries, especially Denmark, have been able to develop an institutional environment supporting export-oriented commercial production (such as Scandi noir), and at the same time create global art house brands (such as Lars von Trier), and as such, have been able to transcend periphery status in terms of both symbolic and economic capital (Bondebjerg and Redvall 2015). Seen from this perspective, small-scale production might actually drive innovation, while domestic success might paradoxically hinder international ambitions.

Last but not least, the center-periphery hierarchy in media production does not automatically translate into a hierarchy in terms of transnational distribution control. While some peripheries gradually transformed into semi-peripheries, regional centers of production or even into media capitals competing with Hollywood (e.g., Mumbai and Seoul), cross-border distribution channels in Europe, especially in the field of digital distribution, have largely remained under the control of US-based studios, VOD services and platforms of the FAANG group (Facebook, Amazon, Apple, Netflix and Google).

Another way to draw a map of digital peripheries could be based on how global services such as Netflix and Amazon Prime treat different territories in terms of localization, acquisition of local content and (increasingly) original local content production. Such a map would be strikingly similar to the map depicting the scope of outgoing cross-border flows. For example, Netflix territorial catalogs in Central and Eastern Europe, until 2019, included virtually no local titles (this changed in the second half of 2019, especially in Poland and the Czech Republic), while already in 2017 they offered between 3 and 4% of local content in the Netherlands, Denmark and Austria (Grece 2019: 120). While Netflix has—since its "global switchover" in 2016—produced dozens of "originals" in Western Europe, including some small countries such as Belgium and the Netherlands, it has almost totally ignored the CEE region, labeling only one Hungarian feature film (*On Body and Soul*), one Romanian feature film (*Oh Ramona*) and one Polish series (*1983*) as "Netflix Original," plus co-funding one Czech feature (*Milada*) without explicitly labeling it as an original production as such. The "Netflaxes" graph pictured below is an example of how these Netflix catalog data might be used to group peripheral markets in a new way.[4]

1.4   Evolving Systemic Relations of Media Markets: Toward a New Typology of Digital Peripheries

The expansion of transnational VOD services opens a new opportunity for creating comparative typologies to study media systems of different sizes and in different positions in the European and global fields. It has been repeatedly noted that the most influential comparative typology of media systems in communication studies, proposed by Daniel C. Hallin and Paolo Mancini (2004), cannot be directly applied in studying media industries in their full complexity. Not only does it limit its scope to Western Europe and North America, but, moreover, it focuses on the role and ownership of news media and as such it addresses exclusively the interrelations between media and political systems. There have been attempts to broaden and rework the three types of media systems formulated by Hallin and Mancini (namely the polarized pluralist, democratic corporatist and liberal system), so the typology would be able to capture specificities of the post-socialist countries of Central and Eastern Europe, some of whose media systems have recently been going through processes of intense politicization (see, e.g., Dobek-Ostrowska (2019), or Herrero et al. (2017), the latter dividing the CEE media systems into eastern, central and northern clusters). At the same time, some of the CEE media systems, namely the Baltic states, Slovenia and the Czech Republic, have been characterized as "semi-core" rather than (semi-)peripheral in terms of "the ability of the media to supply and support the stability of the political sphere and the skills of its actors, whether decision-makers or citizens, with reliable and balanced information" (Greskovits 2015: 68). But even these attempts at revising the systems typology to capture the EU peripheries deal only with news media and not with media production or (cross-border) distribution in a broader sense. They draw on explanatory variables (such as the strength of political parallelism, public service broadcasting, press freedom and foreign ownership) that come with only a limited ability to explain variations beyond the field of news media, i.e., in entertainment industries, audiovisual markets and their relationships. Therefore, a typology that would be able to address globalizing audiovisual markets is urgently needed—an as yet missing tool for the size-sensitive comparative analysis of media industries and their interrelations, consisting of different groupings of hegemonic centers and peripheries.

---

[4]This claim is based on a work-in-progress database of Netflix Originals (distinguishing between different types of "originals") compiled by Chris Meir (as of July 2019), whom we thank for his help.

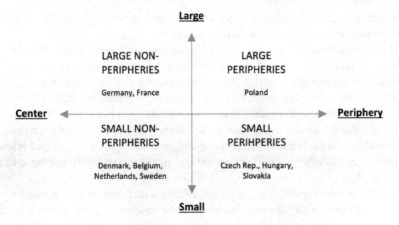

Fig. 1.3 Basic two-dimensional classification of audiovisual markets

The transnational dynamics of audiovisual markets in the age of global online services and platforms analyzed in this book imply that such a typology should take into account more than just the size and the position of media markets in the global media world-system and its center-periphery hierarchy. It should also acknowledge how globalization impacts small media markets differently due to their structural peculiarities. More specifically, it should look at how multinational media corporations approach and affect small markets, changing their media ecosystems from outside as well as from within.

The aforementioned characteristics of small and peripheral media markets indicate that one-dimensional classifications based on binaries of small-large or periphery-center are not sufficient for constructing a suitable model of these markets. However, these two binaries are obviously not mutually exclusive—on the contrary, in our proposed model they comprehensively establish two basic axes setting up a two-dimensional space acknowledging both market size and position on the center/periphery scale (Fig. 1.3).

The *size of a market* can be assessed by diverse indicators (that might be, eventually, combined into a single index). On the one hand, the term obviously refers to the size of an audience (country population serves well here) and/or the audience's purchasing power (measured, e.g., by average income or average individual expenditures on cultural consumption, both combined with population size). On the other hand, production volume can be used—though it may refer also to the center-periphery position of a market since it indirectly indicates relative export strength (obviously, there are large markets with a relatively low production volume and low export performance that can be classified as *large peripheries*, and vice versa).

The *center-periphery position* of a market can then be judged through an export/import ratio or "export efficiency" (Grece 2017: 91–98)—in both cases, the center-periphery designation refers to a market's position relative to other markets in terms of receiving and selling content. Simply said, central markets are hegemonic producers successfully shaping other markets with their goods, while peripheral markets are receiving content more than selling it.

This proposed two-dimensional model helps to classify markets into four distinct classes, but it still does not offer tools for a more nuanced classification of markets identified as small or peripheral. If the model is supposed to show the mutual distinctions, positions and specific trajectories of small and peripheral markets, it has to take into consideration characteristics that go beyond the two basic axes. The concrete choice of these additional characteristics will always be driven by particular research needs and questions, but here we propose one particular set which we find relevant for the current European small and peripheral markets, especially for those in the CEE region.

Firstly, national regulations and public subsidies and their roles in domestic production and cross-border distribution need to be considered. In this respect, we find that the interior terrain of a small market is usually specifically shaped and co-constructed by the state and its politically (or ideologically, if you want) driven relationship to the audiovisual sector. In small CEE markets, the existence and scale of state subsidies and their role in domestic production are typically legitimized by an economic narrative (the national market needs to be protected or supported) and a cultural narrative (the national culture needs to be protected and supported). What vary are the particular policies and institutional tools for collecting and allocating subsidies, as well as their amounts. For example, some EU countries have been introducing incentives to attract foreign investors (calculated as a percentage of their local spending) or what is being referred to as the "Netflix tax," i.e., financial obligations imposed on non-domestic VOD services, with the fee calculated as a percentage of the streamer's national revenues (Donders et al. 2018). Thus, the level of specific taxes and subsidies or the proportion of public funding in the total costs of domestic production can be used as a measure of state intervention in the market, while the (in)dependence of funding institutions from the direct decisions of political actors can be helpful in understanding and comparing the influence of partisan politics on particular markets.

Secondly, the structure and the broader socioeconomic context of national media ecosystems—ownership and concentration, horizontal and vertical integration, the role and strength of public service media—deserve to be assessed. The Czech Republic, if observed from a diachronic perspective, makes an illustrative case: Already since the 1990s, the Czech market was, on the one hand, marked by the strong presence of public service broadcasting, a relatively high level of concentration in the distribution sector (currently dominated by several local partners of Hollywood majors), and, on the other, by a high fragmentation of the private production sector consisting mostly of dozens of small and micro companies. While public service television has been one of the dominant content producers in the Czech audiovisual market since it was established in 1992, the two major commercial broadcasters focused in the 1990s mainly on importing content. In the 2000s, with strong foreign owners, even they started to invest more extensively in original content development, cooperating with the small production companies and targeting both TV and theatrical audiences. After 2010, the production environment changed again—with the introduction of film rebates and a minority co-production scheme attracting more international production, the renaissance of the Czech public service serial production, the launch of HBO Europe's original production, followed since 2014 by a boom in local Web TV production (Web series), all addressing Czech audiences with original domestic content. In each of these periods, the market was structured distinctly, marked by the changing ratio of content produced or co-produced by public service television, as well as by changes in market fragmentation (measured by the number of new titles per active production company).

Thirdly, the level of national or regional/international orientation of a market should also be a focus as it allows the distinguishing of specific variations and combinations of the characteristics of small and/or peripheral markets. This can be defined by the share of domestic production or services in the national market, measured for instance by the ratio of fully national, internationally co-produced, and imported titles in distribution, by the degree of presence of transnational broadcasting and VOD services (indicated, e.g., by the share Netflix has in the on-demand market), or by the intensity of inward and outward content flows. The volume, directions, diversity and cultural or commercial performance of the audiovisual export in individual distribution channels (theatrical, television, VOD) would be an especially suitable variable to distinguish different groupings of small and/or peripheral markets.

All of these three supplemental dimensions are described here without more thorough specification of particular indicators or measures. Nevertheless, as an example of a more detailed (and yet reasonably simple) tool assessing some of the aforementioned market parameters, we can use what we call "Netflaxis" (or rather "Netflaxes," because there are two axes in the proposed model). This tool draws on data derived from Netflix by third parties, describing the share of localization and local content in territorial Netflix catalogs. As such, the "Netflaxis" is inevitably limited since it includes data from just one particular VOD service, but with Netflix a worldwide strategic actor and present in almost every market, the "Neflaxis" still can be seen as an acceptably valid means for analysis well suited to the current situation.

The following figure employs Netflix data from a group of arbitrarily selected EU markets; the x-axis comprises the number of localized titles (i.e., dubbed or subtitled in the national language of each market), and the y-axis includes values summarizing the number of acquisitions of local titles and original local Netflix titles (in the latter case, the number is multiplied by 500 to reflect the estimated relationship between the cost of buying rights for one title and producing one original title) (Fig. 1.4).

When compared with the initial two-dimensional graph depicting small and/or peripheral markets, it is obvious that Netflix differentiates some of the positions and creates new clusters. For example, the practices of the global giant align the small non-peripheral Netherlands and Sweden with the large peripheral Poland, while leaving the small and peripheral Slovakia far away from the Czech Republic and Hungary, which are not much larger and less peripheral markets and yet enjoy significantly higher Netflix investments in localization. Unlike the previous set of characteristics that shape and differentiate the positions of media markets by their internal features, "Netflaxis" is an externally imposed parameter, whereby the positions of the markets in the global network of flows are (re)defined by a non-state, multinational entity.

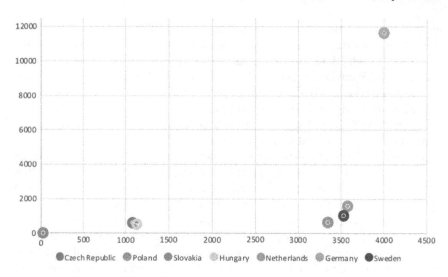

Fig. 1.4 Positions of individual EU national markets as defined by the number of Netflix's localizations (horizontal *X*-axis) and the number of acquisitions of local films and TV series plus original local content productions multiplied by 500 (*Y*-axis). *Sources* uNoGs database as of December 23, 2019; Ampere Analysis (2019) for the number of original local titles—produced and in production

As such, this tool is a useful example of a measurement index balancing nationally bound definitions of media markets with private transnational forces. It is also a simple example of the "alternative scaling models" Ira Wagman is calling for in his theoretical intervention included in this volume: a model that helps us see how "digital platforms fold and integrate different markets in new and powerful ways."

Another kind of a dynamic, "external" measure of uneven relationships between national media markets might be derived from comparing their positions as agents and objects of supranational regulation as exemplified in this book by the European Commission's Digital Single Market strategy. This policy debate about removing obstacles to cross-border trade and integration of the European digital market shows how important the scale of a media market together with its geo-political and cultural context is from a regulatory perspective (Ibrus 2016a).

1.5 Crossing Boundaries: The Impact of EU Media Policy at the Periphery

European media policy has been formed by two interconnected objectives, both aiming at European integration and creating a counterbalance to US media influence: establishing a single television (and later digital) market without national borders as a part of the "negative integration" of removing barriers to allow free movement of goods and services, and protecting European cultural identity as a part of "positive

integration" based on interventionist cultural policies balancing the side effects of
the free market (Nowak 2014). Audiovisual industries became a focus of European
policymaking relatively late, in the late 1980s, after the liberalization and privatization of broadcasting, which brought an end to the monopolistic position of European
public service media. The new private broadcasters mushrooming in many countries
across the continent had to feed their program schedules and Hollywood emerged as
the most attractive and relatively cheap source: The major US studios were able to
reduce prices after recouping their costs of production in their large domestic market.
The European Communities therefore faced the problem of how to protect European
media markets and cultures against the massive influx of US programming, which
was further extended with the spread of satellite and cable networks allowing for
easier cross-border transmissions.

Since the late 1980s, the main imperative for European policymakers has been to
unify the territorially fragmented European TV market and thus increase the competitiveness and cross-border accessibility of European audiovisual content, which has
been notorious for traveling far less than US programming. The idea of a single television market, articulated for the first time in the so-called Television Without Frontiers
directive (TWF 1989), was based on "negative" economic integration removing market barriers and simplifying rules for cross-border broadcasting, which was further
developed by the Satellite and Cable Directive (1993)[5] and the Audiovisual Media
Services Directive (AVMSD 2007).[6]

Although predominantly neoliberal and market-oriented, European policymakers balanced these economic measures with protectionist instruments of "positive"
integration aimed at supporting European audiovisual industries and cultures: quotas for European television programs (in TWF and AVMSD) and funding schemes
for the European audiovisual industry (Michalis 2014). The European Commission's MEDIA program was launched in 1991 to fund training, development and
cross-border distribution, leaving the support of European film co-production to the
Council of Europe's Eurimages program (1989), which is regulated by the European
Co-production Convention (1992). Hitherto strictly governed by national regulators,
film ultimately began to be understood as not just an economic force, but also a key
cultural tool to promote Europeanness as well as intercultural understanding, and
thus to assist in the process of European integration. This intervention of European
policymaking into the audiovisual sector was further grounded in Article 128 of the
Maastricht Treaty (1992) stipulating that the newly established European Union was

---

[5]Council Directive 93/83/EEC of September 27, 1993, on the coordination of certain rules concerning copyright and rights related to copyright applicable to satellite broadcasting and cable
retransmission.
[6]Council Directive 89/552/EEC of October 3, 1989, on the coordination of certain provisions
laid down by law, regulation or administrative action in Member States concerning the pursuit of
television broadcasting activities (the so-called Television without Frontiers Directive); Directive
2007/65/EC of the European Parliament and of the Council of December 11, 2007, amending
Council Directive 89/552/EEC on the coordination of certain provisions laid down by law, regulation
or administrative action in Member States concerning the pursuit of television broadcasting activities
(the so-called AVMS Directive).

to carefully balance respect for Member States' "national and regional diversity" with "bringing the common cultural heritage to the fore," while specifically mentioning audiovisual creation (Kolokytha and Sarikakis 2018). Both economic and cultural, the policies of negative and positive integration aimed at creating a counterbalance to the US media influence.

This has not changed much to the present day, except that the goal of shaping a common European identity was replaced after the 1990s with the objective of protecting the cultural diversity of Europe. Both economic and cultural media policies were recently reformulated in the strategy for the Digital Single Market (presented in 2015) and in the revised AVMSD (2018).[7] This regulatory initiative is in part a reaction to the growing importance of VOD services for the distribution of cultural content and to the unprecedented dominance of US-based technology companies known as FAANG (Facebook, Amazon, Apple, Netflix and Google). The development of the Internet-based communication and services exposed larger European states and markets to challenges and structural disadvantages—such as a decrease in national control over market developments due to competition from multinational corporations such as the FAANG group, which draw advertising and subscription revenues from local markets—known until recently only to smaller states. On the other hand, it is creators, producers and consumers (especially ethnic minorities and long-term migrants) in small states who can potentially profit the most from the transnational flow of audiovisual content across national borders and free themselves from the limits of a small market (see Trappel 2014: 251 and Kim's chapter in this book).

However, EU media governance has not as of yet achieved any of its key objectives. Despite the simplification of the cross-border clearance of copyrights introduced by EU regulation,[8] the European audiovisual market remains fragmented due to the licensing and business practices of legacy media players. Local producers, distributors and broadcasters strategically prefer exclusive territory-by-territory licensing in order to retain control over the sequence of distribution windows in individual

---

[7]Regulation (EU) 2017/1128 of the European Parliament and of the Council of June 14, 2017, on cross-border portability of online content services in the internal market (the so-called Portability Regulation); Directive (EU) 2018/1808 of the European Parliament and of the Council of November 14, 2018, amending Directive 2010/13/EU on the coordination of certain provisions laid down by law, regulation or administrative action in Member States concerning the provision of audiovisual media services (Audiovisual Media Services Directive) in view of changing market realities; Directive (EU) 2019/789 of the European Parliament and of the Council of April 17, 2019, laying down rules on the exercise of copyright and related rights applicable to certain online transmissions of broadcasting organizations and retransmissions of television and radio programs, and amending Council Directive 93/83/EEC; Directive (EU) 2019/790 of the European Parliament and of the Council of April 17, 2019, on copyright and related rights in the Digital Single Market and amending Directives 96/9/EC and 2001/29/EC (the so-called Copyright Directive).

[8]See the application of the country-of-origin principle to the clearance of rights for satellite broadcasting and the system of compulsory collective management of cable retransmission rights in the Council Directive 93/83/EEC of September 27, 1993, on the coordination of certain rules concerning copyright and rights related to copyright applicable to satellite broadcasting and cable retransmission (Satellite and Cable Directive).

national markets as well as over their marketing and localization investment that they want to protect from cross-border cannibalization by competitors. They claim that guarding territorial barriers is a way to protect European media industries and cultural diversity against the massification (Americanization) of cultural production, distribution and consumption. At the same time, territorial licensing practically traps cultural content within the constraints of national borders and inhibits wider cross-border accessibility, thus hindering the development of pan-European cultural exchange and diversity, which is the objective of the above-mentioned support programs and content quotas. Recent industry studies show that although the volume of European film production is relatively high (more than 2,000 feature films annually) and its share in theatrical as well as in TV and VOD distribution is higher than that of US content in terms of total supply (65% of theatrical distribution in the EU between 2005 and 2015), the ability of European films to travel across national borders and generate revenues in foreign markets is much lower (33% of all admissions, 12% generated by non-national EU films). And, importantly, all these limitations apply to the small and peripheral markets of the CEE significantly more than to the large EU countries (Higson 2018; Grece 2017). Although VOD distribution provides broader access to non-national EU films than cinemas and TV, its efficiency depends on investment in targeted marketing campaigns and on the selective approach of transnational online services (i.e., on their acquisition strategy and recommendation algorithms), which again disadvantages content coming from small peripheral markets (see Szczepanik's chapter in this book).

The EU cultural and media policymakers therefore face several challenges: How to stimulate interest in non-national European production and thus increase its cross-border circulation? How to overcome cultural and language barriers dividing the European national audiences? How to design support programs so that they fund not just development and production, but also efficient cross-border distribution and promotion over the Internet? And more generally: How to balance national and European regulation so they would face more effectively the global competition of FAANG while also making use of the US-based services as (currently) the most efficient vehicles for cross-border online distribution of European content? The question remains whether today's territorial fragmentation and practice of territory-by-territory licensing actually help to sustain the fragile audiovisual ecosystem and cultural diversity, or if they rather hinder access to European content. And whether the policy of negative integration potentially increases or weakens the global competitiveness of European audiovisual industries.

So far, it seems that the EU policymakers are inclined to economically motivated regulations (integration of the market, barrier-free access to products and services, European works defined by investment share) and tend to downplay or leave to national regulators the cultural and social aspects of market integration that are crucial for developing democracy and citizen participation (free movement of ideas, access to cultural heritage, support for creativity through contact with foreign cultures, etc.). Existing regulations also raise doubts whether they sufficiently take into account differences between large and small countries. The pursued cultural-political objectives and adopted regulatory measures apply to all countries, regardless of their size and the specificities of their media systems. However, apparently not all cultural-political goals—such as cultural diversity—can be achieved the same way regardless of the size and specificities of the media markets in question. As the existing literature suggests, the bigger states prefer a market approach endorsing freedom of choice and at most economic interventions to prevent market failure, while the small states lean more toward interventionist regulatory policies protecting the domestic media system against competition from abroad.

The European Commission's Digital Single Market strategy is a key example of such an economically motivated policy that does not take different sizes and positions of markets into account. It attempts to unify the European digital market by removing the territorial parceling of the digital market by banning geoblocking measures. It also aims at simplifying rights clearance through a legal fiction according to which the use of the work on the Internet takes place where the user (broadcaster, VOD service provider) has its principal establishment. This means that all an audiovisual online service provider needs for pan-European distribution is to buy a license for a country where the service is established (European Commission 2015, 2016).

According to the prevailing opinion of representatives of the European audiovisual industries,[9] these legislative proposals threaten not only local producers and distributors, but also consumers, especially those tied to small markets. The arguments can be summarized as follows: Producers will tend to create mainstream content in a widespread language that will have greater commercial potential within the single market than local content in the language of a small country. At the same time, local platforms will not have enough funding to purchase premium content (such as sports events) with pan-European availability and will only offer a limited amount of cheaper content. Local platforms will be gradually pushed out of the market, resulting in the unification of supply due to the dominance of transnational platforms and limited supply of content with international (cross-border) audience appeal. The homogenization of content and the dominance of transnational online services in a pan-European audiovisual space will therefore harm Europe's cultural diversity. Moreover, consumer welfare will also be adversely affected, as local distributors play an important role as cultural mediators who market, promote, localize and culturally mediate foreign audiovisual productions. Consumer outflows to global or pan-European services from local services will mean a decline in subscription and advertising revenue. The drop in revenue will reduce investment in content production by local distributors. Furthermore, the unified market will lead to an increase in the cost of services for residents of EU Member States with lower incomes (in CEE) as a result of the price alignment of services offered across the Member States. Also, the quality of services will worsen for consumers in small and peripheral markets: Despite the fact that the content on a pan-European service will be available to consumers earlier than on the local platform, and the pan-European catalog will

---

[9]We base the following account of reservations voiced by the representatives of European industry representatives and organizations on our own research on Czech distributors (Zahrádka and Szczepanik 2019) and on the most widely discussed industry report that focused specifically on threats of the Digital Single Market strategy for small CEE countries (Oxera 2016, 2017).

be more extensive, the content offered will not be sufficiently localized and contextualized (Oxera 2016, 2017). In this book, we attempt to engage and challenge the above arguments and consider the implications of such catastrophic scenarios for the development of the audiovisual market within the Digital Single Market in Europe, based not only on findings on the functioning of small audiovisual markets and arguments voiced by consumer rights advocates, but also through critical reflection on the relationship between the territoriality of copyright and territorial fragmentation of the European audiovisual landscape.

This does not deny the importance of scale for understanding the objectives and uneven impacts of EU regulation. The recent debate about the implementation of the Article 13 of the revised Audiovisual Media Services Directive, for example, illustrates how crucial differences in scale are with regard to regulating transnational VOD services and platforms. Small countries' public funds and producers' associations are worried that if the low-turnover and low-audience thresholds for exempting VOD services from financial obligations (levies payable to the national audiovisual funds and the direct investment in the production and acquisition of European works) will reflect the reality in large markets, the revised directive will not achieve its goals and will have a negative impact on the regulatory power of small countries and on their public audiovisual funds. In other words, if the thresholds are too high, even some of the biggest VOD players in smaller markets (especially those in the CEE region with a lower VOD penetration) will qualify for the mandatory exemptions in the targeted smaller Member States, whose public funds will not gain anything, but may lose some existing sources of income.[10] The example of AVMSD illustrates that EU media regulation is slowly adopting the scale-sensitive principle that the larger the service and the larger its impact on public opinion, the stricter should be its regulation and the more accountable it should be to the public interest (Ibrus 2016b).

This volume was born out of a need for theorization of media globalization "from the periphery" and should be approached as an experiment in its attempt to do so. It does not pretend to follow a consistent theoretical approach, but rather brings together four different frameworks of studying smallness and peripherality in media markets and media regulation. Individual sections and chapters have their inspiration in diverse disciplinary backgrounds ranging from media industry studies to media policy, cultural economy and audience studies, and can be read separately as individual contributions. But they can also be followed as a cross-disciplinary dialogue about the emerging field of global audiovisual flows that will continue to evolve with the changing relationships between transnational platforms, local industries, regulators and the public.

---

[10]The debate about the low-turnover and low-audience thresholds is ongoing as of December 2019 and relates to the preparation of the AVMSD guidelines to be issued by the European Commission.

1.5.1   An Overview of the Book Sections

All the chapters in this volume are framed by two interrelated steering questions: How are small and/or peripheral media markets affected by, and how do they respond to, the increasing digitalization and globalization of audiovisual distribution? What challenges and opportunities does the European Commission's Digital Single Market strategy bring to those markets?

Not all of the chapters look at small European countries and not all the markets discussed in the volume can be labeled peripheral. To provide a more sophisticated portrait of the relationships between the small and the big, or the core and the periphery, the editors decided to include one non-EU example, Canada, which is positioned as a smaller and peripheral market to that of the neighboring USA. The case studies from Belgium showcase how industry players in a small country can develop successful competitive strategies vis-à-vis global platforms, while the example of the Polish market illustrates how a country which is big in terms of population and whose production is very successful domestically still occupies a peripheral position in the EU market.

I. On Boundaries and Scales: Reconceptualizing Digital Markets

The first two chapters are theoretical, setting the stage for the following case studies and reflecting on some central concepts in the debate about small and/or peripheral digital markets and their regulation. Ira Wagman chooses the example of Netflix's disruptive presence in the highly regulated Canadian broadcasting market to provoke critical thinking about the vocabulary of *scale* in studies of media markets, tracing the conceptual consequences that "scaling" Canada as a "small" market has had for the understanding and governing of its media industries. He then proceeds to explore the possibilities of developing a subtler, more dynamic vocabulary that would better fit the relational and changing position of the national market in global cultural flows. He shows how Canada moved, partly due to its protectionist media policies, into a position of a "middle market" (both in the sense of being middle-sized and its intermediary position among various media flows), and how it has been used as a "test market" for new American services including Netflix and CBS's streaming platform—precisely because of its "middle" position characterized by high acceptance of foreign products. Wagman's conceptual experiment thus demonstrates how "rescaling" small and peripheral markets with a more nuanced terminology helps in understanding how they are shaped by both national regulators and transnational services.

In his chapter, Ramon Lobato considers the boundaries of digital markets from a social-constructivist point of view and draws attention to their cultural, socioeconomic, geographic and political dimensions, taking as an example the controversy about removing digital barriers to free trade in Europe and creating a pan-European audiovisual market. Lobato highlights the need to think of markets as social spaces constituted by their history, politics and culture rather than to reduce them to abstract spaces constituted by exchange. The chapter serves as a theoretical introduction to the following section which focuses on the digital audiovisual market in Europe from the legal perspective and from the viewpoints of its various stakeholders.

II. Regulating Online Boundaries: Territoriality Versus Digital Single Market

The main concern among small media market players regarding the European Commission's strategy for a Digital Single Market is territoriality. Advocates of territoriality or territory-by-territory licensing claim that it protects and promotes the local distribution of films on national markets, but critics point out that it hinders the development of European cultural diversity, as territorial licensing makes many films unavailable to national audiences across Europe. European cultural policy therefore faces the challenge of efficiently regulating the business models of the audiovisual industry in order to make European audiovisual production more accessible and competitive without disturbing the film production and distribution ecosystems in Europe. The second section of the book is devoted initially to a critical reflection on the relationship between the territoriality of copyright and the territorial fragmentation of the audiovisual online market in Europe. The subsequent chapters serve to explain and defend the reasons for and against the removal of obstacles to the free movement of audiovisual online services. The Commission's Digital Single Market strategy is analyzed both from the perspective of consumers—whose access to cultural content is blocked by virtual barriers separating not only national markets but also authors from their audiences—and from the point of view of industry actors (film distributors and producers) operating in a small market.

In his analysis, Radim Polčák considers the legal implications of EU copyright territoriality in terms of the cross-border online distribution of copyrighted works via video on demand services. Polčák points out that copyright does not protect the work as such, but rather certain forms of use, and these do not include consuming the work by the end customer. Thus, copyright cannot regulate the time and place where the consumer uses the work. Polčák further argues that the use of the work—namely its communication to the public—via streaming occurs either in a market that is actively targeted by the service provider or in the location where the on-demand video service provider is established, not the place where the consumer is located and begins his "travels on the Internet" by sending a request to the provider of the information society service to view the work. This interpretation of the right to communicate work to the public via the Internet has implications for the use of technical tools to prevent access to the service based on the location of the user. According to Polčák's interpretation, geoblocking does not protect copyright but rather the outdated business models of the audiovisual industry, which are based on the territorial fragmentation of the market.

Drawing from her experience as a Member of the European Parliament involved with legislative initiatives to address geoblocking from 2014 to 2019, Julia Reda explores the effects of geoblocking on consumers, as well as the friction between this practice and the idea of European integration. Reda discusses the proposals of the European Commission to eliminate or weaken geoblocking, which, as a result of resistance from the audiovisual industry, have been altered in the course of negotiations between the Commission, the European Parliament and the EU Council to the extent that they are not actually able to improve the availability of online audiovisual content across the borders separating EU Member States. However, according to Reda, the current territorial fragmentation of the audiovisual market strengthens the market dominance of a few transnational online streaming services. These companies were able to grow only thanks to the large single market in the USA where they got their start and have since been able to establish themselves in the EU, due to their substantial resources when entering the EU market. They have sufficient funds for their own in-house production and for the acquisition of worldwide distribution rights and are able to offer the same content in all EU Member States. According to the author, this threatens smaller production companies and Europe's cultural diversity. The independent audiovisual production from a small national market disseminated via local on-demand video services will continue to be bound by national borders due to geoblocking. The author concludes that abolishing geoblocking is in the interest of both consumers and a diverse film production market.

Pavel Zahrádka in his chapter reconstructs and compares the attitudes of Czech distributors of premium audiovisual content (films, television and Web series) toward reform measures proposed by the European Commission for the introduction of a Digital Single Market in Europe, and explains the basic operating mechanisms of the business model for audiovisual content in small markets. He shows that the greatest threat to Czech audiovisual industry stakeholders in the hypothetical scenario of a pan-European audiovisual market is not cross-border cannibalization of the local distributors' offerings, which is hindered by the language barrier, or the preference for localized content by domestic audiences or by the synchronized distribution of co-produced films in a culturally and linguistically affiliated territory (namely Slovakia) by the same distributor, but the expensive premium content which will become unaffordable for locally operating Czech distributors. Based on the lessons learned, the chapter offers a reflection on the sustainability of the present-day online business model of the film industry in the EU with respect to consumer demand and European Union competition law.

III. A New Game with Old Players: Distribution Practices in Small and/or Peripheral Markets

This section concerns the ways traditional distributors' business models and practices have changed with the advent of online distribution and new transnational competitors, and how the small size and/or peripheral position of media markets shape the role of distributors as cultural intermediaries. Adopting the perspective of critical media industry studies, the chapters in this section analyze old and new practices in their mutual interrelationships, dependencies, collaborations and new forms of competition with a balanced focus on the elements of continuity, disruption and innovation as perceived by key industry players. The players are contextualized by identifying their places in the respective local industry ecosystems and divided into categories based on their business models and content types, which allows for distinguishing between traditional or "legacy media" players (exhibitors, distributors, broadcasters, sales agents), non-media players assuming new roles in audiovisual media distribution (telecommunication companies, Internet platforms), new stand-alone audiovisual media services (VOD portals, Internet TV portals) and informal players (file-sharing platforms and communities). By discerning the distinctions and interactions between different kinds of players, each of the chapters provides a contextually specific picture of globalizing small and/or peripheral media industries, opening a space for drawing scenarios of their future development in the framework of technological change, increasing global competition and EU regulation.

Karen Donders and Tim Raats focus on legacy media managers' strategic responses to disruptions in the television distribution ecosystem in Flanders. Based on interviews with broadcasters, producers and telecom/cable distributors, they identify three core distribution strategies—scale, collaboration within domestic ecosystems, and diversification of offerings and valorization. By considering how the market's "smallness" enables or impedes these strategies, they provide a new vocabulary for discussing changes in business models in small media markets due to the boom of transnational over-the-top (OTT) distribution, nonlinear viewing, platformization, and the consequent loss in advertising revenue for Flemish broadcasters. By highlighting the fundamental uncertainty of media managers involved in the "war for control over the newly emerging value networks," they contribute to distribution studies' current interest in socioeconomic and cultural aspects of distribution decision making (Perren 2013). At the same time, they provide a critical perspective on what protectionist policies of small countries are actually achieving at the level of distribution practice.

While the responses of Flemish producers and broadcasters to digital disruptions include closer collaboration between different types of domestic players and attempts to develop more internationally competitive programs and formats, markets in the eastern and southern periphery of the EU remain more defensive and bound by their national borders. Poland is not a small market by the measure of population, but its media industries operate as a periphery in terms of delayed adoption of OTT technologies and reliance on old audiovisual business models with cinema exhibition and broadcasting at the center. Unlike Flanders, Polish producers and distributors do not see their future in the growing VOD market and concentrate their strategies on traditional theatrical distribution. After the recent demise of several independent VOD services, online distribution in Poland became tightly concentrated around a few dominant players (Internet portals, broadcasters and transnational giants), which, as Marcin Adamczak claims, are not willing to share the revenues or collaborate with domestic distributors, keeping the entry barriers into the field relatively high. At the same time, Poland is currently perceived as the most promising growth market in CEE by Netflix and other transnational OTT players such as HBO and Canal+ , which are ramping up their investment in local content. The chapter shows that the domestic success of national productions does not necessarily stimulate technological and business innovation—it can even hinder it—as Adamczak (himself a film distributor) documents with the help of interviews with key Polish distributors, who are currently content with the growing domestic box office revenues and consider VOD as a relatively unimportant additional window.

If the Polish case study focuses on the separation between traditional cinema distribution and VOD, Petr Szczepanik's chapter looks deeper into the interactions and intermediaries between the two sectors in the field of export, proposing a typology of key players and practices. The Czech Republic seems to be a strong exporter among other CEE countries at first glance when considering the absolute numbers of titles leaving the country. However, the export performance of Czech films and TV series appears much less impressive without the neighboring Slovakian market, with which the Czech Republic forms a tight cultural-geographic cluster. By critically inquiring into the actual practices and results of Czech online export to a selection of key foreign markets (based on interviews and catalog analyses), the chapter highlights striking gaps between the main circulation types: original productions and acquisitions of transnational SVODs that travel most widely and that enjoy the best marketing support, art house international co-productions with West European sales agents attached, that are sold via a variety of transnational and local SVOD and TVOD services, and the vast majority of titles that are offered mostly or exclusively on the TVOD platforms of iTunes and Amazon, either in packages compiled by local distributors or self-distributed by producers themselves, and whose low cultural prestige and the lack of a foreign sales agent and distributor contributes to their virtual invisibility in the VOD market. By pointing to these differences in export business models, the chapter provides a critical response to the existing literature on cross-border VOD distribution that is mostly limited to general catalog statistics.

Greece is another example of a peripheral market with little domestic innovation and no outward cross-border activity in the VOD sector. Unlike Poland, however, it remains deeply affected by the post-2008 economic crisis and subsequent drastic austerity measures in the field of public funding and public service television. In her chapter, Lydia Papadimitriou draws a complex picture of the local media industry ecosystem in the process of digital transition, marked by deep uncertainties about the actual economic potential of the OTT business model. She shows how socioeconomic developments, government digitization initiatives, as well as longer-term historical circumstances—especially in the field of Pay TV and terrestrial television (the latter partly unregulated until recently)—shape the adoption of online distribution in the country. Among the case studies assembled in this section, Greece serves as an extreme example of the limitations and barriers imposed by the small size and peripheral position of such domestic markets.

IV. The Other Audiences: Convergent Viewership in Small and Peripheral Markets

The fourth section discusses "the other" current convergent audiences that, in some crucial respects, differ from the usually studied audiences inhabiting the dominant, large audiovisual markets. The primary ambition is to illustrate the multiplicity of topics and problems linked with research on peripheral, small or otherwise atypical audiences. To this end, the section presents three methodologically and topically diverse empirical studies and, in turn, one theoretical text.

The first chapter of the section, "Finding Larger Transnational Media Markets: Media Practices of the Vietnamese Diasporic Community" authored by Tae-Sik Kim, offers unique insights into media-related practices of members of the Vietnamese diaspora. Tae-Sik Kim, a Korean scholar living and working for years in the Czech Republic, draws upon data from his longitudinal grounded research within the Vietnamese community in Central Europe and outlines a picture of an audience that is "different" from multiple angles. Kim's communication partners are members of an ethnic minority group in the Czech environment who live in diasporic conditions, and their community is split into several generational segments that differ in their identity, experience and lifestyle. And all this is strongly reflected in their media practices that feature content sources from far beyond the Czech media market.

Aram Sinnreich in his chapter entitled "Configurable Culture in Wealthy and Developing Markets: A Comparative Cross-National Perspective" argues that there are crucial binaries other than those linked with market size. Sinnreich focuses on the active use of audiovisual content and on the basis of his theory of "configurable culture" offers a large-scale quantitative study comparing multiple English-speaking countries. As the title of the chapter suggests, his main interest is in the differences between the advanced, economically strong audiovisual markets on the one hand (the USA, Canada, Australia, UK) and developing markets (the Philippines, South Africa) on the other.

In the third chapter, Aleit Veenstra and her co-authors Philippe Meers and Daniel Biltereyst address a specific segment of a typical small-market audience—Flemish youth film viewers. Their study "Structured Film Viewing Preferences and Practices: A Quantitative Analysis of Hierarchies in Screen and Content Selection among Young People in Flanders" deals with one of the symptomatic problems of the era of convergent audiences, the multiplication of screens used for domestic consumption of audiovisual content. Building an intriguing empirical design, Veenstra and her colleagues aim to identify patterns of screen selection and their relation to the perceived value of Hollywood, European and domestic Flemish films. Their conclusion is that there are well-articulated hierarchies applied by the audience members in the selection of both film titles and reception screens and that, to put it simply, in the case of screens, size matters.

The fourth and final chapter of the section differs from the other three in that it elaborates a theoretical argument. Jakub Macek's study "Uses Genres and Media Ensembles: A Conceptual Roadmap for Research of Convergent Audiences" draws on his team's research on Czech convergent audiences, but his main goal is to propose a theoretical and conceptual framework that enables one to assess satisfyingly the specifics of both current convergent and small-market audiences. For this purpose, Macek appropriates the concept of "uses genres" formulated by Maria Bakardjieva and amends it with his own concept of "media ensembles." The main argument focuses on current audiences' viewership, suggesting that it should be analyzed as typified and situated practices that are, at the individual level, reflexively organized into temporarily stable sets and cannot be studied as isolated phenomena. The chapter demonstrates the research application of the two concepts and their usefulness in finding the specifics of small-market media audiences.

V. Audiovisual Policy and the Future of the Copyright Economy

The last section tackles the economic, legal and political frameworks for audiovisual distribution in small European countries. Special attention is given to the challenges faced by regulators, national funding bodies and audiovisual industry actors in a small market with respect to the following questions: How to effectively compensate creators for using their works online? How to reduce the high transaction costs connected with licensing rights for film music in the case of cross-border online film distribution? How to set up a national film policy that can respond to the cultural and economic problems and opportunities of a small market in the twenty-first century?

In his chapter "Compensation Systems for Online Use", Christian Handke discusses an alternative model for compensating creators for using their works on the Internet. In the last two decades, it has been difficult to enforce exclusive rights in the digital economy. Handke's alternative model of compensating creators for their creative work is based on collecting and redistributing revenues from surcharges on more excludable goods such as Internet access. According to Handke, this model provides end users with greater legal certainty when using online sources with creative content, leads to better availability of online content, has the potential to increase creators' earnings and brings a number of benefits to "digital peripheries" such as enhancing cultural diversity and the competition between online platforms offering copyrighted content that is no longer based on exclusive license agreements with the rightsholders, but on the user-friendliness of the services offered.

In the chapter "Sync that Tune! The Role of Collective Management of Rights in Film Production and Distribution", Rudolf Leška deals with the transaction costs associated with the licensing of film music in the case of the cross-border online distribution of films. Whenever a film is produced and distributed, a license to use the music and sound recording may be needed. While the film producer usually owns the copyright in the film and underlying works or actors' performances, responsibility for the clearance of rights in music and sound recordings remains largely on the shoulders of users (broadcasters, cinema operators, VOD platforms). They usually need to get a license through a collective management organization or directly from the rightsholder. In the case of musical works, the procedures are largely standardized, mainly in offline use. When it comes to licensing the rights for cross-border online use or when phonogram producers and performers are involved, the licensing situation becomes messy, which introduces significant uncertainty into the market. Instead of advocating state regulation, the author pleads for the development of cross-border industry standards and procedures, good practices and reciprocal agreements between CMOs in collaboration with global organizations representing rightsholders.

In his chapter "Small Country, Complex Film Policy: The Case of the Czech Film Funding System", Petr Bilík describes the circumstances of national film policymaking in the Czech Republic after 1989, especially regarding the conflicted political and cultural interests connected with the establishment and development of the Czech Film Fund. The chapter is a case study mapping the transformations of the fund and its structure of grant and incentive schemes. In conclusion, Bilík reflects on the problems and opportunities that the Czech Film Fund currently faces. The main opportunities include strengthening the domestic economy and local production culture through co-production support, as well as incentives for international productions. The main problems of national film policy include the low international competitiveness of Czech films, their low cross-border availability and the rigidity of the established subsidy schemes, which are slow in responding to changes in the production and distribution of audiovisual content.

Acknowledgements This book was created as part of a project devoted to the development of the research-oriented study program "Research in Arts and Cultural Industries" (no. CZ.02.2.69/0.0/0.0/16_018/0002319) running from 2017 to 2022 and focused on building a doctoral program dedicated to critical research of the media industries in Central and Eastern Europe at Palacký University in Olomouc in cooperation with Charles University in Prague and Masaryk University in Brno. The book reflects on some of the key topics that dissertation projects in this program will focus on in the future, such as industrial and consumer practices, the legal regulation of cultural industries and cultural policy. Most of the authors presented preliminary versions of their chapters at the Screen Industries in East-Central Europe Conference VII, which was held as an International Communications Association (ICA) preconference in Prague (22–23 May 2018), devoted to industry developments and policies in the field of online distribution and Internet TV. The conference and research behind several of the chapters were supported by the European Regional Development Fund project "Creativity and Adaptability as Conditions of the Success of Europe in an Interrelated World," Charles University in Prague (reg. no.: CZ.02.1.01/0.0/0.0/16_019/0000734).

The editors would like to thank Benjamin Vail for his efficient and flexible copy editing and proofreading of individual chapters. The initial ideas for this book project emerged when some of us were working on industry reports on the impacts of the Digital Single Market strategy for the Czech Film Fund in Prague—special thanks go to the Fund's head Helena Fraňková for her interest and continuing support, as well as to those research team members who are not part of this book, namely Johana Kotišová, Ivan David and Petar Mitrić. There were many colleagues who helped us by discussing specific issues and preliminary versions of individual chapters, among them Catherine Johnson, Chris Meir, Massimo Scaglioni and Patrick Vonderau. More thanks go to our colleagues and friends who have supported us along the long way as we prepared the book: Jakub Korda, the Head of the Department of Theatre and Film Studies at Palacký University in Olomouc, for creating a supportive working environment, and Zuzana Pejpková from the same department for her administrative help. We would also like to thank the two expert reviewers who provided useful advice on the manuscript.

References

Alaveras, G., Gomez-Herrera, E., & Martens, B. (2018). Cross-border circulation of films and cultural diversity in the EU. *Journal of Cultural Economics, 42*(4), 645–676.

Ampere Analysis. (2019). Streaming TV: The quiet before the storm. A presentation by Guy Bisson at the VideoWars by ScreenLovers 4 conference. Warsaw, November 20, 2019.

Andrew, D. (2006). An atlas of world cinema. In S. Dennison, & S. H. Lim (Eds.), *Remapping world cinema: Identity, culture and politics in film* (pp. 19–29). London and New York: Wallflower Press.

Bohle, D., & Greskovits, B. (2012). *Capitalist diversity on Europe's periphery*. Ithaca and London: Cornell University Press.

Bondebjerg, I. B., & Redvall, E. N. (2015). Breaking borders: The international success of Danish television Drama. In I. B. Bondebjerg, E. N. Redvall, & A. Higson (Eds.), *European cinema and television: Cultural policy and everyday life* (pp. 214–238). Basingstoke: Palgrave Macmillan.

Buchholz, L. (2018). Rethinking the center-periphery model: Dimensions and temporalities of macro-structure in a global field of cultural production. *Poetics, 71*, 18–32.

European Commission. (2015). Communication to the European Parliament, the council, the European Economic and Social Committee and the Committee of the Regions—A Digital Single Market strategy for Europe, COM(2015) 100 final. https://eur-lex.europa.eu/legal-content/CS/TXT/?uri=celex%3A52015DC0192. Accessed May 6, 2019.

European Commission. (2016). Impact assessment on the modernisation of EU copyright rules—Part 1. Commission Staff Working Document. https://eur-lex.europa.eu/legal-content/EN/TXT/?uri=celex:52016SC0301. Accessed 20 September 2019.

Crane, D. (2014). Cultural globalization and the dominance of the American film industry: Cultural policies, national film industries, and transnational film. *International Journal of Cultural Policy, 20*(4), 365–382.

Curtin, M. (2009). Thinking globally: From media Imperialism to media capital. In J. Holt & A. Perren (Eds.), *Media industries: History, theory, and method* (pp. 108–119). Boston: Wiley-Blackwell.

Dobek-Ostrowska, B. (2019). How the media systems work in Central and Eastern Europe. In E. Połońska & C. Beckett (Eds.), *Public service broadcasting and media systems in troubled European democracies* (pp. 259–278). Cham: Springer International Publishing; Palgrave Macmillan.

Donders, K., et al. (2018). *Obligations on on-demand audiovisual media services providers to financially contribute to the production of European works*. Brussels: Vrije Universiteit Brussel and Research group imec-SMIT.

Donders, K. (2019). Public service media beyond the digital hype: Distribution strategies in a platform era. *Media, Culture & Society, 41*(7), 1011–1028.

Flew, T. (2018). Post-globalisation. *Javnost-The Public, 25*(1–2), 102–109.

Flew, T., Iosifidis, P., & Steemers, J. (2016). Global media and national policies: The return of the state. In T. Flew, P. Iosifidis, & J. Steemers (Eds.), *Global media and national policies: The return of the state* (pp. 1–15). Basingstoke: Palgrave Macmillan.

Fontaine, G. (Eds.). (2019). *Yearbook 2018/2019: Key trends*. Strasbourg: European Audiovisual Observatory.

Grece, C. (2017). *The circulation of EU non-national films*. Strasbourg: European Audiovisual Observatory.

Grece, C. (2019). *Films in VOD catalogues: Origin, circulation and age—Edition 2018*. Strasbourg: European Audiovisual Observatory.

Greskovits, B. (2008). Leading sectors and the variety of capitalism in Eastern Europe. In J. Pickles (Ed.), *State and society in post-socialist economies* (pp. 19–46). Basingstoke: Palgrave Macmillan.

Greskovits, B. (2015). Capitalist diversity and the media. In J. Zielonka (Ed.), *Media and politics in new democracies: Europe in a comparative perspective* (pp. 58–72). Oxford: Oxford University Press.

Guback, T. H. (1969). *The international film industry: Western Europe and America since 1945*. Bloomington: Indiana University Press.

Hallin, D. C., & Mancini, P. (2004). *Comparing media systems: Three models of media and politics*. Cambridge: Cambridge University Press.

Herrero, L. C., Humprecht, E., Engesser, S., Brüggemann, M., & Büchel, F. (2017). Rethinking Hallin and Mancini beyond the West: An analysis of media systems in Central and Eastern Europe. *International Journal of Communication, 11*, 4797–4823.

Higson, A. (2018). The circulation of European Films within Europe. *Comunicazioni sociali, 3*, 306–323.

Hjört, M., & Petrie, D. (2007). *The cinema of small nations*. Edinburgh: Edinburgh University Press.

Holdaway, D., & Scaglioni, M. (2018). From distribution to circulation studies: Mapping Italian films Abroad. *Comunicazioni Sociali, 3*, 341–355.

Houpt, S., & Robertson, S. K. (2019). CBC head under fire after comparing Netflix to the British Raj, warns of "cultural imperialism". *Globe and Mail*, 31 January, www.theglobeandmail.com/arts/article-cbc-head-warns-netflix-poses-cultural-threat-to-canada. Accessed December 20, 2019.

Ibrus, I. (2016a). The EU digital single market as a mission impossible: Audio-visual policy conflicts for Estonia. *International Journal of Digital Television, 7*(1):23–38.

Ibrus, I. (2016b). Serving small markets: Modelling the application of AVMSD on graduated, size-based regulation. Policy Papers: The future of audiovisual media services in Europe. www.etis.ee/Portal/Publications/Display/32a2cc3c-351f-4f2b-a875-da8f55671098. Accessed January 13, 2020.

Imre, A. (2019). Streaming freedom in illiberal Eastern Europe. *Critical Studies in Television, 14*(2), 170–186.

Iordache, C., Van Audenhove, L., & Loisen, J. (2018). Global media flows: A qualitative review of research methods in audio-visual flow studies. *Communication Gazette, 81*(7), 1–20.

Iordanova, D., Martin-Jones, D., & Vidal, B. (Eds.). (2010). *Cinema at the periphery*. Detroit: Wayne State University Press.

Iosifidis, P. (2007). Public television in small European countries: challenges and strategies. *International Journal of Media and Cultural Politics, 3*(1), 65–87.

Ji.hlava IDFF. (2019). East west index. https://www.ji-hlava.com/eastwestindex. Accessed January 22, 2020.

Jones, H. D. (2014). Introduction: The media in Europe's small nations. In H. D. Jones (Ed.), *The media in Europe's small nations* (pp. 1–18). Newcastle upon Tyne: Cambridge Scholars Publishing.

Kanzler, M., & Simone, P. (2019). *Focus 2019: World film market trends*. Strasbourg: European Audiovisual Observatory.

Kolokytha, O., & Katharine, S. (2018). Film Governance in the EU: Caught in a loop? In P. C. Murschetz, R. Teichmann, & M. Karmasin (Eds.), *Handbook of state aid for film* (pp. 67–82). Cham: Springer.

Lobato, R. (2018). *Netflix nations: The geography of digital distribution*. New York: New York University Press.

Lowe, G. F., & Nissen, C. S. (Eds.). (2011). *Small among giants: Television broadcasting in smaller countries*. Göteborg: Nordicom.

McElroy, R., & Noonan, C. (2018). Public service media and digital innovation: The small nation experience. In G. F. Lowe, H. van Den Bulk, & K. Donders (Eds.), *Public service media in the networked society* (pp. 159–174). Göteborg: Nordicom.

McElroy, R., Nielsen, J. I., & Noonan, C. (2018). Small is beautiful? The salience of scale and power to three European cultures of TV production. *Critical Studies in Television, 13*(2), 169–187.

Michalis, M. (2014). Focal points of European media policy from inception till present: Plus ça change? In K. Donders, C. Pauwels, & J. Loisen (Eds.), *The Palgrave handbook on European media policy* (pp. 128–142). Basingstoke: Palgrave Macmillan.

Michalis, M. (2016). Global communications and national policies: The view from the EU. In T. Flew, P. Iosifidis, & J. Steemers (Eds.), *Global media and national policies: The return of the state* (pp. 122–138). Basingstoke: Palgrave Macmillan.

Miller, T., Govil, N., McMurria, J., Maxwell, R., & Wang, T. (2005). *Global Hollywood 2*. London: British Film Institute.

Moretti, F. (1998). *Atlas of the European novel 1800–1900*. London and New York: Verso.

Müller, M. (2019). Goodbye, postsocialism! *Europe-Asia Studies, 71*(4), 533–550.

Nagib, L. (2006). Towards a positive definition of world cinema. In S. Dennison & S. H. Lim (Eds.), *Remapping world cinema: Identity, culture and politics in film* (pp. 30–37). London and New York: Wallflower Press.

Nagib, L., Perriam, C., & Dudrah, R. (2012). Introduction. In L. Nagib, C. Perriam, & R. Dudrah (Eds.), *Theorizing world cinema* (pp. xvii–xxxii). London and New York: I.B. Tauris.

Nowak, E. (2014). Between economic objectives and public remit: Positive and negative integration in European media policy. In K. Donders, C. Pauwels, & J. Loisen (Eds.), *The Palgrave handbook of European media policy* (pp. 96–109). New York: Palgrave Macmillan.

Oxera. (2016). The impact of cross-border access to audiovisual content on EU consumers. www.oxera.com/getmedia/dfe44fac-c028-4eb3-bb56-71bdfa79b2f9/2016-05-13-Cross-border-report-(final).pdf. Accessed December 20, 2019.

Oxera. (2017). Paying more for less: The impact of cross-border access initiatives on consumers in Eastern European and baltic countries. www.oxera.com/getmedia/4482cd7c-7c0c-4dc3-87c4-3c4f88981e30/Oxera-report-Paying-more-for-less_rev7.pdf.aspx?ext=.pdf. Accessed December 20, 2019.

Perren, A. (2013). Rethinking distribution for the future of media industry studies. *Cinema Journal, 52*(3), 165–171.

Poort, J., Hugenholtz, P. B., Lindhout, P., & Van Til, G. (2019). *Research for CULT committee—Film financing and the digital single market—its future, the role of territoriality and new models of financing*. Brussels: European Parliament, Policy Department for Structural and Cohesion Policies.

Puppis, M., d'Haenens, L., Steinmaurer, T., & Künzler, M. (2009). The European and global dimension: Taking small media systems research to the next level. *The International Communication Gazette, 71*(1–2), 105–112.

Raats, T., Evens, T., & Ruelens, S. (2016). Challenges for sustaining local audiovisual ecosystems: Analysis of financing and production of domestic TV fiction in small media markets. *Journal of Popular Television, 4*(1), 129–147.

Schneeberger, A. (2019). *The internationalisation of TV audience markets in Europe*. Strasbourg: European Audiovisual Observatory.

Scott, A. J. (2006). *Geography and economy: Three lectures*. Oxford: Oxford University Press.

Sinclair, J., Jacka, E., & Cunningham, S. (Eds.). (1996). *New Patterns in global television: Peripheral vision*. New York: Oxford University Press.

SPI Olsberg (2019). *Priority international markets for Czech producers*. Prague: APA.

Stachowiak, K., & Stryjakiewicz, T. (2018). The rise of film production locations and specialised film services in European semi-peripheries. *Hungarian Geographical Bulletin, 67*(3), 223–237.

Thompson, K. (1985). *Exporting entertainment: America in the world film market, 1907–1934*. London: BFI.

Trappel, J. (2014). Small states and European media policy. In K. Donders, C. Pauwels, & J. Loisen (Eds.), *The Palgrave handbook of European media policy* (pp. 239–253). Basingstoke: Palgrave Macmillan.

Tsing, A. L. (2005). *Friction: An ethnography of global connection*. Princeton, NJ: Princeton University Press.

Winseck, D. (2011). The political economies of media and the transformation of the global media industries. In D. Winseck, & D. Y. Jin (Eds.), *The political economies of media: The transformation of the global media industries* (pp. 3–48). London and New York: Bloomsbury.

Zahrádka, P., & Szczepanik, P. (2019). The white elephant in the room: Implications of the digital single market strategy for film and television distribution in the Czech Republic. In T. Mira, & S. Rajan (Eds.), *The Cambridge handbook of intellectual property in Central and Eastern Europe* (pp. 238–258). Cambridge: Cambridge University Press.

Petr Szczepanik is Associate Professor at Charles University, Prague. He has written books on the Czech media industries of the 1930s and on the state-socialist production mode. His current research focuses on (post-)socialist producer practices in Central and Eastern Europe. Some of his findings are published in *Behind the Screen: Inside European Production Culture* (Palgrave, co-edited with Patrick Vonderau, 2013). He led the EU-funded FIND project (2012–2014), which used student internships for a collective ethnography of production cultures. In 2015, he was the main author of an industry report on practices of screenplay development for the Czech Film Fund.

He is now working on a study of the digitalization of the Czech audiovisual industry and the impacts of the European Commission's Digital Single Market strategy.

Pavel Zahrádka is Associate Professor of aesthetics and cultural industries, Palacký University Olomouc. He specializes in the ethics of digital media and aesthetics. In 2015 and 2016, together with Reinold Schmücker (University of Münster) and Thomas Dreier (Karlsruhe Institute of Technology), he helmed the international research group "Ethics of Copying" at the Center for Interdisciplinary Research in Bielefeld. He is currently a principal investigator on a research project investigating the impact of the Digital Single Market strategy on the Czech audiovisual industry funded by the Technology Agency of the Czech Republic.

Jakub Macek is Associate Professor of media studies, Masaryk University, Brno, Czech Republic. His research interests include the roles of new media in the transformation of current audiences and in political and civic participation. He was previously a member of VITOVIN, an interdisciplinary research project on the Internet and new users (2012–2015). Recently, he led the postdoctoral research project "New and Old Media in Everyday Life: Media Audiences at the Time of Transforming Media Uses" (2013–2015) and worked as a researcher at CATCH-EyoU, a Horizon 2020 project (2015–2018).

Part I
On Boundaries and Scales: Reconceptualizing Digital Markets

Chapter 2
Small, Middle, Test: Rescaling Peripheral Media Markets

Ira Wagman

2.1 Introduction

This chapter considers how best to characterize the effect of the presence of global streaming video on demand (VOD) platforms within different national contexts. It contributes to recent work considering the impact of new screen technologies on what Amanda Lotz calls "the twenty-first century television distribution ecosystem" (Lotz 2018: 491). Of particular interest here is how these kinds of questions about the dynamics between the national and the global are understood within those nations that have historically been understood as "small" or "peripheral" markets for media-related products. Using Canada's historical experience with broadcasting and the relationship between successive governments and foreign-based SVOD services as a case study, I want to suggest that this exercise is helpful for thinking about the concepts we have used to study media industrial activity and the ways digital technologies have either altered those conceptions or forced researchers to consider the value of new, more appropriate terms.

A prominent figure in my discussion is Netflix, the global streaming platform. Canada was the first country chosen by Netflix to explore its international ambitions, in 2010, and it was the first in which consumers received content as a streaming service separate from the company's former status as a mail order DVD rental operation. Its arrival prompted a swift response; the company secured one million subscribers in the first six months, and it was claiming between 30 and 40% of downstream traffic in peak viewing hours. A recent study published by a group representing Canada's independent production sector claimed that Netflix accounted for 31% of all on-demand services (including SVOD, PPV and VOD) and 65% of SVOD services. Netflix revenue in Canada for 2016 was $709 million, which represented a 28% increase from $553 million the year before (Pinto 2018). These figures easily situate

I. Wagman (✉)
School of Journalism and Communication, Carleton University, 1125 Colonel By Drive, Ottawa, ON K1S 5B6, Canada
e-mail: ira.wagman@carleton.ca

© The Author(s) 2020
P. Szczepanik et al. (eds.), *Digital Peripheries*, Springer Series in Media Industries, https://doi.org/10.1007/978-3-030-44850-9_2

Netflix atop a group of over 20 different "over-the-top" streaming services that have largely saturated the Canadian market for streaming services.[1]

Netflix's penetration into the Canadian market was a powerful challenge to a highly concentrated media landscape that had been dominated by a handful of large vertically integrated firms that were subjected to extensive regulation, from content quotas and foreign ownership restrictions to direct contributions to funds supporting independent media production that had characterized the Canadian audiovisual sector for the better part of five decades. In spite of this, Netflix has received a very light regulatory touch to date, prompting some anxiety among industry players who feel that they are now operating on an uneven playing field.

To consider the situation with Netflix in the Canadian context, I begin with a brief methodological reflection. I suggest that while discussions of media-related markets are a way toward understanding cultural production within different contexts, but they are also an invitation to consider questions associated with scale and about the ways that scholars "size" the industrial objects under study. I do so to consider the relationship between the terms we use to characterize industrial activity and the language we use to explain that activity associated with value. From there, I illustrate some ways that Canada has been understood as a "small" market for media as part of a larger policy imagination that has seen Canada's cultural production as weak or at risk of extinction. Such characterizations have privileged particular measurements of media-related activity, and they have determined the shape of discursive frameworks around various cultural policy measures for nearly a hundred years. While the Canadian case has its own specificities, I want to suggest such that characterizations can be found more broadly in "small nation" media research in other countries as well, with similar effects.

As a counterweight to smallness, I wish to advance two other concepts that might be better both for conceptualizing the historical development of Canada's media marketplace and for appreciating how that marketplace has been transformed by the arrival of digital technologies. The first—a notion of "middle" markets—combines sociological work by Diana Crane with research drawn from cultural theory and cultural studies that encourages thinking of media production in terms of circulation and distribution. This allows for a subtler appreciation of certain characteristics of Canada's media sector—particularly television—that rhetorical language of "big" and "small" fails to take into account. The notion of the "test market" will be the second concept under analysis here. With test markets, one can see how nations— or regions or cities within nations—serve different purposes within global media systems. If thinking of media markets as big or small encourages relational and defensive thinking and leads toward questions of sovereignty and protection, and if

---

[1] These statistics and other information are derived from a research dossier on streaming television services written with Charles Acland for the Global Internet TV Consortium, a network of media study scholars contributing country-based dossiers on the effect of SVOD services on local, regional and national markets. See Acland and Wagman (2019). Special thanks to Smriti Bansal for research assistance.

considering media markets as "middles" encourages ideas of circulation and broker-age, then understanding media markets as testing grounds can encourage ideas of experimentation and adaptation.

In advocating a number of alternative terms for appreciating media industrial activity, I do not wish to dispose with characterizations such as "small" and "periph-eral" to talk about media activity within different contexts, and this chapter is far from a considered attempt to engage more seriously with the conceptualizations of markets within political economic treatments of media.[2] Instead, it aims to encour-age the elaboration of a more refined set of methodological terms to more effectively analyze the positioning of media-related markets in digital environments. I conclude by arguing for a turn away from "scalar narratives," in Swyngedouw's (1997: 140) terms that emphasize size and a turn toward those narratives that characterize media markets in more structural terms to better describe media environments that are sub-jected to global flows of culture and which are shuffled and repositioned by different digital actors and then served to users through algorithmically determined delivery of media texts.

2.2 Scale, Markets and Value

An important theme in this chapter is a methodological concern with the role played by *scale* in our study of media industries. In one sense, we can say that scale is a useful point of emphasis because it draws attention to the interaction between peo-ple, media technologies and place, raising questions about how academics draw the boundaries around the concepts that they use (McCarthy 2006: 25). In addition to this conceptual component, we can also say that such terminological determinations have a powerful *narrative* effect, something that Swyngedouw (1997: 139) characterizes as "providing the metaphors for the construction of 'explanatory discourses'." This points us to the question of the stakes involved in naming. Do we say that a media market is small to draw attention to issues having to do with threats, with concerns about influence from outside forces, or to advocate for increased state involvement? Or do we focus on the ways that people build alliances or work with larger forces to ensure survival? From the same label, we can see very different sets of meanings.

Scholars interested in the study of media industries are no doubt familiar with the impact of these terms on the way their work is framed and on the stories they tell about the subjects they are discussing. They are also familiar with the ways ideas of scale—economies of scale or the "scaling up" of digital media operations—point us to questions about the effects of mass production, the conditions under which things like films and television show are produced and the issues of the expansion of media companies beyond national or regional boundaries. Such notions of scale

---

[2]This is to say nothing of the work outlining the characteristics of cultural commodities as forms, as products from specific types of labor employing a number of different approaches. For example, see Miège and Garnham (1979, 1997), Lash and Lury (2007), Banks (2007) and Cohen (2016).

are essential to the study of media industries more broadly, and they sit underneath our consideration of how digital technologies reshape the ways those media products circulate across both physical and virtual spaces. More broadly, they also contribute to theories of world systems, of the relations between centers and peripheries that are common in geopolitical discussions and, more recently, within the recent literature accounting for processes of economic and cultural globalization (cf. Hannerz 1991). They are, in that sense, a window into accounting for media power in Freedman's (2014: 3) sense, as "a relationship between different interests engaged in struggles for a range of objectives that include legitimation, influence, control, status, and increasingly, profit."

An ideal place to appreciate the complexities and consequences of scale in media industry research would be to consider the ways we study and describe systems of exchange for media-related products and services, and the rules that govern them, the most obvious of which is that of the "market." As Kari Karppinen and Hallvard Moe point out, while used in a number of different contexts, scholars spend little time characterizing the scale or dimensions of the markets they study. Two common conceptions that frequently are used are an *empirical* understanding that equates the market as a concrete, observable institution and a *normative* orientation that considers the market as a "logic" for comprehending different social phenomena (Karppinen and Moe 2014: 328).

We might combine this consideration of "the market" with our earlier discussion of narrative to conclude that either of these two connotations is linked inextricably to conceptions of value; the way they are used is often connected to how we understand the relationship between forms of cultural production and larger economic frameworks. If value is constructed relationally, between an object and aspects of the production process, as Bolin (2011, 2012) has suggested, then we might say that normative understandings of markets for media usually come in different forms. While one of the more common is by thinking of markets as existing within the boundaries of nation states, we often adopt a normative view of markets whereby they are understood in relation to publicly funded or state-funded media organizations or regulatory systems. Such conceptions largely determine how we understand a market's analytical function in the study of media industries.

It is because of the tremendous ontological and narrative power of those conceptualizations that we must be attentive to the various attempts—and narrative techniques—that have been used to construct media markets. Those techniques often emerge when specific *data about markets* come to be understood against the backdrop of broader *ideas about markets*. Such issues are particularly important when studying markets within media industries that have typically been considered "small" or "peripheral," as each of these terms carries important connotations of how markets should be understood within global economic systems and within media-related systems of exchange. To illustrate the conceptual and narrative consequences of scaling media markets, the remainder of this chapter considers a few characterizations of media markets in Canada to show how those characterizations have determined both the ways the industries have been structured and the analytical tendencies that have emerged through those characterizations.

2.3 (Relatively) Small Media Markets

One place to consider the methodological issues associated with "sizing up" media markets is to turn to the literature that is concerned with media-related activity in small nations. Such work has been valuable for understanding the specific challenges that forms of media and cultural production take in settings with populations or media sectors which pale in comparison with larger states, and the power relations between different states in spheres of global media production. For our purposes, however, the literature is also instructive as representing attempts at differentiation and measurement, when it comes to media industries, and about the choices that people make to differentiate one country from another as a way to understand the media activity taking place within their borders.

In some cases, the characteristics are implied; in a recent article, McIlroy et al. (2018) review the production environments in three contexts (Denmark, Ireland and Wales), noting the importance of relationship-building—especially among public service broadcasters, with larger nations and broadcasters, and assertive policymaking, as essential components of the nations under their review. However, that characterization encourages us to consider what levels of activity distinguish small nations from big ones. Others perform more active definitional work. Drawing on distinctions derived from political science and international relations, Manuel Puppis placed countries with a minimum population of 100,000 and a maximum of 18 million people (ranging from the Netherlands to Mali) into the "small state" category (Puppis 2009). In Mette Hjort's analysis of cinema in small states (Hjort 2011), gross domestic product is one of the key determinative measures, along with population size and a history of rule by non-co-nationals. Other descriptions of small media markets refer to their organizational and bureaucratic characteristics, such as the presence of smaller groups of social elites, whose primary role is to facilitate forms of consensus or collaboration among different stakeholders to bring about specific results (Jones 2004; Boucher and Watson 2017).

While such measures are not intended to advance objective measurements of smallness, they serve as invitations to reflect on methodologies of measurement and their relation to different media forms. Outside of filmic activity, it may also be the case that thinking in terms of GDP is based on assumptions about media as commodity forms that may not be viable in all cases, whether it is appropriate for accounting for the presence of "free culture" that exists online (Watanabe et al. 2018). It also invites us to consider a range of other possible choices we could make in generating a series of claims about media markets that equates size with value. For example, we could follow Keane's (2006) perceptive observation about how such characterizations failed to grant agency to those "peripheral" nations, and are unable to account for the varying levels in which their participation in global media markets was more active and cooperative than originally understood, or failed to account for the power of diasporic communities operating within those marketplaces. We could continue down this road of pointing to the ways that nations that might be "small" in some senses are "big" in others, just as we do when we look with amazement at the success at "tiny" countries like Norway in the biathlon during the Winter Olympics. In that sense, we could point to cases like Luxembourg or Monaco in the fields of broadcasting, as countries whose proximity to larger nations and high concentrations of wealth afford them a level of power among nations and a level of strength within their own borders in ways that "small" seems unable to account for.

Moreover, we could take note of the more positive associations with smallness—like that offered by Newbigin (2014) that small nations are actually ideal for contributing to new media economies through the lowered barriers to entry offered by online forms of communication and participation—as reflections of a more assertive attempt to think about the relationships among different nations in global media systems. Finally, a turn to the small is also useful for showing mixed populations within national contexts, such as the Flemish in Belgium or Catalonians in Spain, and the presence of diasporic communities located in a number of different locales. In any of these cases, one can see what happens when the analyst compares nations to each other and signals what kinds of size matter more than others.

Canada is a particularly interesting country for thinking about how markets for media products can have "sizable" characteristics and how notions of smallness are understood in relative terms. This is because a country that occupies one of the world's largest landmasses has historically suffered from anxieties associated with the size of its population and its proximity to the USA. Those anxieties have routinely been expressed in the rationales for government cultural policy measures from the early 1920s until well into the 1980s. Central to those discourses were powerful themes of protection on the grounds of cultural nationalism; Canada's proximity to the USA and its comparatively small and dispersed population were reasons for ambitious attempts at state involvement in cultural production to ensure sovereignty over communication in the national interest and to resist forces of imperialism from the south. This sentiment has been fueled in large part by situations where US media industries have considered Canada to be an extension of their territorial market in calculating revenues or in negotiating distribution rights.[3]

With smallness understood in relative terms and seen through a lens associated with cultural sovereignty, a series of policies were implemented across Canada's cultural sector. These included the nationalization of radio broadcasting from the 1930s to the 1960s and a broadcasting system featuring private and public entities working together to support production, distribution and exhibition of films, television programs and music. This was achieved through a range of policy instruments that were deployed starting in the 1970s and include: direct subsidies to funds supporting film and television production, content quotas on radio and television to ensure "Canadian content" on programming schedules, restrictions on the foreign ownership of television broadcasters and rules allowing Canadian broadcasters the rights

[3]Canada is certainly not alone with this development. Ramon Lobato recently observed that the incredibly large catalogues of Netflix offerings in "small" countries such as Guadeloupe and Martinique likely result from the fact that many Caribbean countries were lumped together with the USA when rights deals were negotiated (Lobato 2017: 246). Such tendencies are also present in other media sectors, such as those which lump together Europe, the Middle East and Africa for video game coding (Kerr 2014).

to simulcast television programs airing on US networks while substituting Canadian commercials. A recognition that competing with American film companies and television networks was a useless enterprise encouraged policymakers to develop policies that encouraged participation in what were once peripheral areas of cultural production, such as documentaries, animation, sports coverage and art house films. Policies to protect French language cultural production and measures to encourage the development of media outlets reflecting Canada's ethnic and cultural diversity and to serve Canada's indigenous communities were also undertaken (Roth 2005; Hayward 2019). These moves offered up a vision of "Canadian broadcasting" that was more reflective of different communities within the country, and further elaborated the contours of Canada's marketplace for media and cultural products under regimes of relative smallness on the one hand and cultural diversity on the other.

Over the last two decades, the overall orientation toward cultural production has articulated a different position, one that sees Canadian media production as a significant player in global systems of exchange. As Zoe Druick maintains, these moves are part of an attempt to situate Canadian cultural production more firmly under the rubric of creative and cultural industry logics (Druick 2012). The content regulations that were established for television and radio stimulated the development of an independent production sector which produced some highly marketable talent across genres, most notably in music, as well as encouraging active participation in different market sectors, such as the international television format trade and the global location market. Prior supports for the protection of territorial rights and intellectual property regimes, and restrictions on foreign ownership encouraged the development of powerful media corporations, companies whose holdings now extend across media platforms and from telecommunications into broadcasting, radio and television programs, and online presences. While by no means addressing all of the concerns justifying the existence of aggressive policy intervention in the cultural field, such measures, along with the development of the lucrative market for cellular phones and online communication, have had the effect of making Canada's media marketplace far less "small" than it may have once appeared in its rhetorical constructions. In fact, as Dwayne Winseck has pointed out, Canada's media economy now ranks eighth in the world overall. This places it within an ecosystem similar to that of countries like South Korea, Italy and Spain rather than where it is occasionally placed, such as with Belgium (Winseck 2012: 153).

It is into this context that Netflix and other "digital intermediaries," in Nielsen and Ganter's (2018) terms, enter the scene. Unlike many foreign media companies who have attempted to break into Canada's media marketplace over the course of the last 100 years, the presence of the big online platforms has been largely obstacle-free. To date, virtually none of the rules that apply to Canada's domestic media industries have been extended to Netflix. In part, this is a self-inflicted wound; Canada's broadcasting regulator determined many years ago that it would not regulate the Internet in the same way it had more traditional broadcasting technologies. Under what is known as the Digital Media Exemption Order, Internet-based video services (including SVODs like Netflix; AVODs like YouTube; and TVODs like iTunes) are not required to contribute a portion of their revenues to the creation of Canadian content. This has had the effect of such platforms being considered as complementary pieces to Canada's media environment at the time when they consolidated their business positions within that environment. As a result, there are no formal requirements that force Netflix to submit audience or subscriber data, or to appear before Canada's public broadcaster for questioning, and there are no content quotas on Netflix's service. Until recently, the company was under no obligation to contribute to funds supporting Canadian television and film production—a condition for receiving a broadcasting license in Canada. While there are occasional threats that the digital platforms will be brought into line, in reality there has been a surprising absence of political will from both of Canada's main political parties to upset the company or its subscribers through the application of regulations.

Some recent developments point to further changes coming in relations between Canada and global streaming platforms like Netflix. In one development, two Canadian provinces—Quebec and Saskatchewan—forced the company to charge goods and services taxes to subscribers based in the province, in the interest of leveling the field versus competing services (Curry 2019). In another, the company pledged to invest $500 million over the next five years on production in Canada. However, the announcement was met with considerable resistance, as there were virtually no reporting or oversight conditions attached to this commitment. Shortly after announcing that investment in the Canadian media industries as part of a deal with the federal government, the company hired an official from the organization traditionally tasked with sponsoring film and television production with funds derived from traditional broadcasters to serve as its director of public policy. Unions representing Canada's actors and media industries have called for content quotas to be applied to the service as are now in place in the European Union to increase the prominence of Canadian-based works on the platform.

Starting from this last point and moving backward, there are a few conclusions we could draw by considering these developments through the lens of Canada's relative smallness. The obvious one is that discourses of smallness lend themselves to discourses of cultural imperialism and highlight long-standing concerns about Canada's annexation from below that have featured in Canadian discussions about broadcasting for nearly a century. Second, we can see the re-emergence of the key actors from previous regimes of content regulations—namely creative unions and film and television production bodies operating on the grounds that platforms should be modeled roughly around systems we have associated with broadcasting. Finally, we can see that it is an even smaller jurisdiction with its own perception of relative size where the themes of protectionism and fair competition have resulted in policies aimed at curbing Netflix's capabilities. From this, one can easily see the analytical benefits of appreciating notions of smallness to account for media markets. At the same time, however, the cases above indicate the need for better concepts to account for relations between different media markets that are more fluid and dynamic than ideas of small and big can encompass.

2.4 Middle Media Markets

What would happen if we were unable to describe media markets as small or big, but rather as operating within a very large section in the middle, between *very small* markets and those that are considerably bigger? If we could do such a thing, the effects would be very significant. This is because this kind of rescaling—even into the broader territory of the middle—would have the effect of drawing our attention away from the questions of *whether* those nations protect their markets and ensure industrial success to questions of *how* nations negotiate the circulation of media texts—domestic and foreign—within and *between* different markets.

In a suggestive article, sociologist Diana Crane characterized a group of film-producing countries, including Brazil, Switzerland, Taiwan and Canada, as "medium producer nations." This category applies when nations adopt cultural policies that "contribute to the maintenance and even growth of national film industries but do not increase their capacity to challenge the domination of the American film industry in the global film market" (Crane 2014). Using a sample of films from 2009, Crane detailed a range of different metrics, from market share to number of films produced, to "number of films in the national top 10" as factors in her middle market definition. In a large-scale comparison of a hundred different countries, Bustamente (2015) situated Canada alongside countries like Egypt, Chile and Germany when measured according to levels of state support for cultural policies and balances between private funding and public funding.[4]

Even if we want to quibble with the fact that Crane's model deals exclusively with film and that neither she nor Bustamente offers much in the way of a discussion of the transformations of creative economies due to the Internet, there is still considerable value in seeing Canada and these other nations as "middles." First, we are able to temporarily step away from discourses of defensiveness and toward a subtler more media-related understanding of proportionality outside of geopolitical terms. A language of balance is complemented with a consideration of flows and of the interaction between media texts from "here" and those from "elsewhere." This shift in orientation can inspire questions about how individuals and institutions negotiate policy measures meant to ensure national participation in cultural spheres with content imported from other places. This "middle management" work affects the velocity at which media moves within markets, as diverse figures like film distributors, television networks, retail operations, fan-focused events like comics conventions, and even filmmakers and other local influencers try to anticipate what aspects of global culture will appeal to local audiences, thereby affecting both its monetary value and its cultural legitimacy (Jenkins 2006: 152–172; Meissner 2014; Woo 2018: 207–208). Thinking in terms of middle markets draws our attention to discourses associated with brokerage and various kinds of cultural intermediaries (cf. Negus 2002) and continues to challenge the power relationships between nations that notions of small and big often perpetuate.

---

[4]This is something I discuss in more detail in Wagman (2019: 4–5).

In media market terms, we can then think about national participation in global markets through the lens of units within market sectors (such as format television production) or within generic forms (such as documentary or animation) or by paying attention to various aspects of the production system, such as location production. Measures such as content regulations for radio and television broadcasting—an important fixture in Canadian media regulation—can then be seen as an attempt to ensure a Canadian presence within media flows that feature music or television programs that come from elsewhere. Other figures and factors include local production companies that license global formats, companies who negotiate territorial rights to distribute international films, specialty channels that offer "Canadian editions" of global channels like HGTV, programs like *Deal or No Deal* and networks like Discovery or the Food Network, along with co-production agreements with other countries (Baltruschat 2009; Wagman 2013; Quail 2015).

An interesting place to think about "middle-ing" in media terms would be to consider Crave, Netflix's largest Canadian competitor in the SVOD market. Crave is a subscription video on demand service that is owned by Bell Media, a company that has holdings that include telecommunication systems, radio and television broadcasting networks, newspapers and Internet portals. The service's ability to compete with much more powerful platforms like Netflix and Amazon Prime comes through access gained through national licensing agreements that allow Bell to air programs on the cable and satellite networks it owns. Most notable are Bell Media's licensing agreements with HBO and Showtime which allow it to offer programs such as *True Detective* and *Veep*, along with popular content either made specifically for domestic audiences or produced with a mix of Canadian and foreign talent that satisfies domestic content quotas but are able to be sold internationally (such as *Cardinal*, which was produced in Canada but is now available on services like BBC Four in the UK and Calle 13 in Spain). Finally, Crave users can select a more expensive option that allows them to watch programs on US cable networks HBO and Starz at the same time that they air in the USA, an offering that gained particular significance recently with the weekly release of episodes of *Game of Thrones* on the Crave service.

In the Crave example, it is clear how companies like Bell benefit from the regulatory protections in small markets, whose existence depends to some degree upon foreign ownership restrictions that prevented companies like HBO from establishing a Canadian version of the service. This means that Bell could purchase the license to distribute HBO's programs on its own HBO Canada channel and then add that content to its Crave catalogue. What is also clear is that Bell is able to work in areas that Netflix has yet to explore—live broadcasting—through its ability to offer more domestic distribution windows to production partners than a SVOD service is able to offer.

From this discussion, we can see the benefits to media industry analysis of an emphasis on middle states. In one sense, it allows us to appreciate the ways that a country such as Canada developed a set of institutions and policy instruments over time to provide a range of mediated forms of expression for a country operating in proximity to a powerful neighbor. In another sense, those same characteristics had the effect of situating Canadian producers within broader global media networks according to more horizontal and lateral terms that are present within media industry business dynamics than in hierarchical terms drawn from world system theories or with a language associated with nationalism.

2.5 Test Markets

It is in the concept of the "test market" that the lateral relations between media markets can be further appreciated. It is drawn from the worlds of advertising and marketing, in which a group of people or a geographic locality is selected to try out new products and provide feedback before they are launched to wider audiences. Ideal test markets typically offer companies a representative mix of people, behavior and infrastructure most likely to mimic a "real" market where the product or service will be available. Test markets are often conceived in the context of research and experimentation and within a rubric of risk management; performance in the test market can often determine the pathways by which a given product will travel in different settings. With origins in the social sciences, test markets also remind us of the link between various forms of market research and the development of communication and media studies as academic disciplines.[5]

Test markets are useful for our discussion for a number of reasons. First, they draw specific attention to matters having to do with the relationship between media and audiences. They are reminders of the power of various kinds of "testing" that goes into the production of a range of technological forms, from focus groups and audience measurement techniques to present-day "beta testing." In other words, it is in the test market where we can appreciate the various components that comprise market research. Second, they draw attention to the role played by particular locations within more traditionally understood national markets. Third, they help us to think about the geography of innovation by recalling the cities where early media technologies were developed and refined. This turns markets into sites of experimentation and adaptation.

While we could certainly consider focus groups or broadcasting ratings or efforts of beta testing as illustrative of the relationship between media industries and marketing research, test markets draw particular attention to the role of cities as ideal simulations of larger populations of potential consumers. In his recent history of interactive television in the USA, Noah Arceneaux focuses on the role of Columbus, Ohio, as an ideal test market, a medium-sized city with the technological infrastructure to support experiments in television (Arceneaux 2018). The city of Brussels is identified on a Belgian economic development Web site as an ideal test market, characterized as an "international and cosmopolitan city where different cultures and nationalities meet, mingle and do business." The city's multicultural population and

---

[5]For an overview of the history of marketing research, see Marchand (1985) and Schwarzkopf (2016).

what it calls its population's "high acceptance of foreign products" are seen as a perfect setting for companies to test marketability before launching something into the European marketplace (HSBC 2019). The same characteristics have been attributed to the Canadian city of Montreal, as an ideal place where entrepreneurs can develop products for local testing before exporting to foreign markets (Stolarick and Florida 2006: 1811–1812). The city of London, Ontario, with a population of just under 500,000 and located halfway between Toronto and Detroit, has been the setting for the evaluation of many consumer products, from debit cards to McDonald's Chicken McNuggets (Vermond 2015).

In the context of our discussion here, it is when these contexts are seen as media test markets that they also are often cited for exhibiting high degrees of media literacy or possessing high levels of quality media infrastructure. As mentioned before, Canada was the first country to get Netflix outside of the USA, both as a nationally available service and as a stand-alone streaming service, and it is serving a similar role as the test case for the export of CBS's streaming video platform, CBS All Access. It is not just SVOD services where Canada (either nationally or regionally) is being used as a test market for digital services. Facebook has used Canada as the test market to experiment with free phone calls (Hamburger 2013), and it tested out its election advertising transparency efforts in Canada in order to refine its systems before the 2018 US midterm elections (Lagaya 2017).

Here we can see how test markets bring together many of the positive things we associate with small media markets with the more flexible, dynamic characteristics we can use to talk about "middle" markets for media. Furthermore, if we were to think retrospectively we could consider the ways specific market segments—like independent music or film companies—function within what Lobato (2017: 7) calls the "distribution ecology" for digital media services. This would encourage us to think about where the industry tests out new content or modes of delivery or how large digital platforms use certain users on their sites or sub-brands to test out ideas that will later be implemented on the main stage.[6] Moreover, we might consider the way that smaller locales serve as "test" markets for the regulation of those same digital platforms. Authorities in cities like Brussels have played a role in banning the ride-sharing service Uber through regional administrative tribunals; a temporary injunction was issued against the company by a regional court in the Czech city of Brno in 2017 before the company negotiated a settlement with the government. Finally, a regional court found that Facebook's data collection was in violation of German consumer law. While it may be multinational regulations like the EU's "Right to be Forgotten" that gathers most of the attention, it may also be that it is in these really small jurisdictions where regulatory models for the taming of these platforms are being tested out by local authorities for application on a wider scale.

---

[6]Examples such as Amazon's use of Twitch to test new television shows (AdAge 2016), or the ways that Google's Sidewalk Labs is using the Canadian city of Toronto's waterfront district to test out its new "smart city" initiative, serve as illustrative cases.

2.6   Conclusion

In this chapter, I have argued for the development of a more subtle set of terms to understand the impact of digital platforms on screen and media industries within markets we have tended to see as small or peripheral. The suggestion here is that the characterization of markets as "small" carries with it a powerful narrative force that is tied up with a set of value propositions that characterize that market in cultural terms as much as it does in the economic sense. As a complement to notions of smallness, I have suggested that Canada's experience to date with Netflix serves as a reminder that of the role of "middle" market countries like Canada, including its position within a geography of test markets that come to be used by media companies operating both nationally and internationally.

The concepts outlined very briefly here point us in a more productive direction toward thinking more closely about how digital media technologies and platforms rescale marketplaces for media products by drawing attention to processes of convergence and ordering. Moreover, they also allow us to consider more profitably the role played by digital intermediaries that serve us media content according to their own international market logics, dictated by the predictive capacities of algorithmic communication (see Kennedy 2016; Napoli 2014). They also allow for a consideration of various ways different national contexts—both "big" and "small"—contend with the various platforms through their interrelationship to different institutional and infrastructural dynamics and call for a consideration of how those relations can be shaped and reshaped over time. Such a move may not result in us relegating these terms to the side, but rather to think of better ways to situate them within alternative scaling models for a more effective characterization of their effects within those markets themselves. If digital platforms fold and integrate different markets in new and powerful ways, it pays to think a little more about how we have understood those different markets to better appreciate the character of the new folded, hybrid forms these platforms produce.

One way to continue this conversation would be to think about alternative scalar narratives to discuss media markets that continue to encourage a move away from a language associated with size to terms and concepts more associated with structures. For example, Winseck (2012) suggests that we think of media economies through a language of *scaffolding* to best appreciate the arrangements within markets of more traditional media sectors, like broadcasting and film, but also to better capture the roles played by search engines and social networking platforms within the context of a networked media economy. In his analysis on Spotify's business models, Patrick Vonderau suggests that the music service demonstrates the capacity to "fold markets into each other" by hiding their aggressive growth strategies behind a rhetoric of public benefits (2017: 3–4). Finally, in another productive characterization, Bratton (2016) uses the concept of *stacks* to talk about the ways that computer platforms link information and actors across space and time through layers of software applications.

As the discussion of Netflix has shown, the characterization of media markets through the use of terms beyond those associated with size can be useful for thinking more broadly about matters of sovereignty, the circulation of media products and the role of audiences operating in different localities, but each one of them also communicates important ideas about the value of those media products or services in those different settings. Our ability to continue to understand media markets in different contexts—and the scalar narratives we write about them—will rely on these structural metaphors going forward, a development which will place different nations in new kinds of relations and interrelations which can change with a keystroke or click of a mouse.

References

Acland, C., & Wagman, I. (2019). Canada—Update 2019. *Global Internet TV Consortium*. https://global-internet-tv.com/canada-update-march-2019/#_edn1. Accessed May 7, 2019.

AdAge. (2016). Amazon using twitch audience as focus group for new TV shows. *AdAge*, September 2. https://adage.com/article/media/amazon-twitch-audience-focus-group-tv-shows/305696. Accessed May 8, 2019.

Arceneaux, N. (2018). The many sides of QUBE: Interactive television and innovation in electronic media, 1977–1983. *Journal of Broadcasting and Electronic Media, 62*(3), 531–546.

Baltruschat, D. (2009). Reality TV formats: The case of Canadian Idol. *Canadian Journal of Communication, 34*(1), 41–59.

Banks, M. (2007). *The politics of cultural work*. London: Palgrave Macmillan.

Bolin, G. (2011). *Value and the media: Cultural production and consumption in digital markets*. Farnham: Ashgate.

Bolin, G. (2012). The forms of value: Problems of convertability in field theory. *Triple C: Communication, Capitalism, & Critique, 10*(1), 33–41.

Boucher, G., & Watson, I. (2017). Introduction to a visual sociology of smaller nations in Europe. *Visual Studies, 32*(3), 205–211.

Bratton, B. (2016). *The stack: On software and sovereignty*. Cambridge: MIT Press.

Bustamente, M. (2015). Les politiques culturelles dans le monde. *Actes de la recherche en sciences sociales, 206–207*, 156–173.

Cohen, N. (2016). *Writer's rights: Freelance journalism in a digital age*. Montreal: McGill-Queen's University Press.

Crane, D. (2014). Cultural globalization and the dominance of the American film industry: Cultural policies, national film industries, and transnational film. *International Journal of Cultural Policy, 20*(4), 365–382.

Curry, B. (2019). Saskatchewan joins Quebec in requiring Netflix to pay sales tax. *Globe and Mail*, January 22. https://www.theglobeandmail.com/politics/article-saskatchewan-joins-quebec-in-requiring-netflix-to-collect-sales-tax/. Accessed May 1, 2019.

Druick, Z. (2012). Continuity and change in the discourse of Canada's cultural industries. In I. Wagman & P. Urquhart (Eds.), *Cultural Industries.ca: Making Sense of Canadian Media in the Digital Age* (pp. 131–146). Toronto: James Lorimer and Company.

Freedman, D. (2014). *The contradictions of media power*. London: Bloomsbury.

Hamburger, E. (2013). Facebook tests free voice calling in messenger app. *The Verge*, January 3. https://www.theverge.com/2013/1/3/3832250/facebook-messenger-voip-calling. Accessed November 9, 2019.

Hannerz, U. (1991). Scenarios for peripheral cultures. In A. King (Ed.), *Culture, globalization and the world system* (pp. 107–128). Minneapolis: University of Minnesota Press.

Hayward, M. (2019). *Identity and industry: Making media multicultural in Canada*. Montreal: McGill-Queen's University Press.

Hjort, M. (2011). Small cinemas: How they thrive and why they matter. *Mediascape*. https://www. tft.ucla.edu/mediascape/Winter2011_SmallCinemas.pdf. Accessed May 7, 2019.

HSBC. (2019). *International business guides: Belgium*. https://www.business.hsbc.com/business-guides/belgium. Accessed May 1, 2019.

Jenkins, H. (2006). *Fans, Bloggers And Gamers: Exploring participatory culture*. New York: New York University Press.

Jones, H. D. (2004). Introduction: The media in Europe's small nations. In H. D. Jones (Ed.),*The media in Europe's small nations* (pp. 1–15). Cambridge: Cambridge Scholars Publishing.

Karppinen, K., & Moe, H. (2014). What we talk about when we talk about 'The Market': Conceptual contestation in contemporary media policy research. *Journal of Information Policy, 4*, 327–341.

Keane, M. (2006). Once were peripheral: Creating media capacity in East Asia. *Media, Culture, and Society, 28*(6), 835–855.

Kennedy, H. (2016). *Post, mine, repeat: Social media data mining becomes ordinary*. Basingstoke: Palgrave McMillan.

Kerr, A. (2014). Placing international media production. *Media Industries, 1*(1), 27–32.

Lagaya, A. (2017). Facebook to use Canada as testing ground for new ad transparency features. *Financial Post,* October 27. https://business.financialpost.com/pmn/business-pmn/facebook-to-test-ad-transparency-features-in-canada. Accessed November 9, 2019.

Lash, S., & Lury, K. (2007). *Global cultural industry: The mediation of things*. Malden: Polity.

Lobato, R. (2017). Rethinking international TV flows research in the age of Netflix. *Television and New Media, 19*(3), 241–256.

Lotz, A. (2018). Evolution or revolution? Television in transformation. *Critical Studies in Television, 13*(4), 491–494.

McCarthy, A. (2006). From the ordinary to the concrete: Cultural studies and the politics of scale. In M. White & J. Schwoch (Eds.), *Questions of method in cultural studies* (pp. 21–53). London: Blackwell Publishing.

McIlroy, R., Nielsen, J. I., & Noonan, C. (2018). Small is beautiful? The salience of scale and power to three small European cultures of TV production. *Critical Studies in Television, 13*(2), 169–187.

Marchand, R. (1985). *Advertising the American dream: Making way for modernity, 1920–1940*. Berkeley: University of California Press.

Meissner, N. (2014). Opinion leaders as intermediaries in audience building for independent films in the digital age. *Convergence, 21*(4), 450–473.

Miège, B. (1979). The cultural commodity. *Media, Culture and Society, 1*, 297–311.

Miège, B. (1997). *The capitalization of cultural production*. New York: International General.

Napoli, P. (2014). On automation in media industries: Integrating algorithmic media production into media industries scholarship. *Media Industries, 1*(1), 33–38.

Nielsen, R. K., & Ganter, S. A. (2018). Dealing with digital intermediaries: A case study of the relations between publishers and platforms. *New Media and Society, 20*(4), 1600–1617.

Negus, K. (2002). The work of cultural intermediaries and the enduring distance between production and consumption. *Cultural Studies, 16*(4), 501–515.

Newbigin, J. (2014). Will small nations be winners in the twenty-first century? In H. D. Jones (Ed.),*The media in Europe's small nations* (pp. 19–30). Cambridge: Cambridge Scholars Publishing.

Pinto, J. (2018). Production spending surged in 2016/2017: CMPA Report. *Playback*, February 2.

Puppis, M. (2009). Introduction: Media regulation in small states. *International Communications Gazette, 7*(1), 7–17.

Quail, C. (2015). Anatomy of a format: So you think you can dance Canada and discourses of Canadian nationalism. *Television and New Media, 16*(5), 472–489.

Roth, L. (2005). *Something new in the air: The story of first peoples television broadcasting in Canada*. Montreal: McGill-Queen's University Press.

Schwarzkopf, S. (2016). In search of the consumer: The history of market research from 1890 to 1960. In B. Jones & M. Tadajewski (Eds.), *The Routledge companion to marketing history* (pp. 61–84). London: Routledge.

Stolarick, K., & Florida, R. (2006). Creativity, connections, and innovation: A study of linkages in the Montreal region. *Environment and Planning A, 38*(10), 1799–1817.

Swyngedouw, E. (1997). Neither global not local: Glocalization and the politics of scale. In K. Cox (Ed.), *Spaces of globalization: Reasserting the power of the local* (pp. 137–161). New York: The Guilford Press.

Vermond, K. (2015). Why London, Ontario is the perfect test market. *The Globe and Mail.* October 19. https://www.theglobeandmail.com/report-on-business/small-business/sb-managing/london-test-market/article26846284/. Accessed February 4, 2019.

Vonderau, P. (2017). The spotify effect: Digital distribution and financial growth. *Television and New Media, 20*(1), 3–19.

Wagman, I. (2013). Global formats and Canadian television: The case of deal or no deal. *Canadian Journal of Communication, 38*(4), 611–627.

Wagman, I. (2019). Three Canadian film policy frameworks. In W. Straw & J. Marchessault (Eds.), *Oxford handbook of Canadian cinema* (pp. 3–20). Oxford: Oxford University Press.

Watanable, C., Tou, Y., & Neittaanmaki, P. (2018). A new paradox of the digital economy: Structural sources of the limitations of GDP statistics. *Technology in Society, 55*, 9–23.

Winseck, D. (2012). Critical media research methods: Media ownership and concentration. In I. Wagman & P. Urquhart (Eds.), *Cultural industries.ca: Making sense of Canadian media in the digital age* (pp. 147–165). Toronto: James Lorimer and Company.

Woo, B. (2018). *Getting a life: The social worlds of Geek culture.* Montreal: McGill-Queen's University Press.

Ira Wagman is Associate Professor of Communication and Media Studies, Carleton University, Ottawa, Canada. He researches and teaches in the areas of television history, media policy and the study of media industries in North America and Europe. He is the co-editor of two books, including Cultural Industries.ca: Making Sense of Canadian Media in the Digital Age (2012). He is currently working on a research project considering the circulation of Canadian audiovisual works on different VOD services.

Chapter 3
On the Boundaries of Digital Markets

Ramon Lobato

3.1 Introduction

The purpose of this chapter is to investigate a fundamental, but highly opaque, concept that is integral to current policy debates about European audiovisual industries. The concept in question is the "digital market." This chapter asks: What exactly is a digital market? Just as importantly, *where* is a digital market? How are digital markets defined and bounded? What does it mean to describe a market as digital, as European, or as both? Can a digital market have a defined geography?

I have written this chapter with a specific policy context in mind—namely, the European Union's Digital Single Market (DSM) strategy. The DSM is a major policy intervention that raises fascinating questions for consumers, audiences, cultural producers, technology companies and regulators inside and outside Europe. The issues in play within the DSM are enormously varied, ranging from telecommunications standards to geoblocking. However, it is worth stressing that virtually all the issues being debated relate in some way to a central problematic: the boundaries of digital markets. Hence, it is an appropriate time to critically reflect on these three concepts (boundaries, the digital and markets) and the relations between them.

Most of the literature on market boundaries is produced by economists and lawyers for the purposes of regulatory analysis. In the context of antitrust and competition law, market definition is a technical exercise to delineate what regulators call the "relevant market" and then to assess market shares, power and competition within that market (Evans 2012). A vast law and economics literature attends to the nuances of this topic, with the effect that market definition techniques have acquired a quasi-scientific character through the use of formalist quantitative methods. However, the

R. Lobato (✉)
School of Media and Communication, Digital Ethnography Research Centre,
RMIT University, 124 La Trobe Street, Melbourne, VIC 3000, Australia
e-mail: ramon.lobato@rmit.edu.au

© The Author(s) 2020
P. Szczepanik et al. (eds.), *Digital Peripheries*, Springer Series in Media Industries,
https://doi.org/10.1007/978-3-030-44850-9_3

act of defining markets is always partly discursive. Market boundaries are inevitably malleable and open to contestation, because "the rigid and linear market boundaries envisioned by the law simply do not have parallels in the real world: border zones are invariably wide, and blurry" (Christophers 2013: 129).

Fortunately, there are other ways to approach this problem. Scholars in the social sciences have been thinking about, and around, the general problem of market boundaries for some time. Recent work in sociology, geography and political theory provides useful concepts for understanding how market boundaries are drawn—politically, discursively and institutionally (Aspers 2011; Christophers 2013; Keat 1999). There is also a tradition of critical inquiry into the geography of markets within various strands of communication research (de Sola Pool 1990; Morley and Robins 1995; Berland 2009). Drawing on the analytical frameworks established in these fields can deepen our understanding of media policy debates, providing new ways to think about old problems.

This chapter offers a selective summary of relevant ideas from these fields. By putting these ideas into dialogue with more familiar ways of thinking about markets, such as those inherited from economic and legal analysis, I hope to provide a conceptual frame through which we can see the DSM differently. My intended audience here is media and culture scholars and other readers who are interested not only in the DSM itself but also in what it might mean for debates about the geography of cultural markets. It should be emphasized that my aim is not to get into the weeds of policy detail but rather to interrogate some of the metaphors and concepts used *within* policy.

3.2   What Is a Market?

The market is a spatial metaphor, in the sense that it evokes a space of exchange whose boundaries are defined in such a way as to produce an inside and an outside. Hence, the question of market boundaries becomes essential. "To distinguish between markets, we must look at the boundaries of markets", writes the economic sociologist Patrik Aspers. "When does a market begin, and when does it end?" (Aspers 2011: 100).

Defining markets is always a discursive exercise, because it involves asking questions about demand, value, comparability and commensurability. In other words, it involves asking questions about culture. Legal and statistical techniques for defining markets are still, by and large, based on an assumption of substitution (i.e., that a consumer will switch from one brand of sugar to another brand if the price rises beyond a certain amount). If substitution occurs, then it is assumed that a market of some kind exists, and the boundary is drawn accordingly. While this principle may work well enough for raw commodities, cultural goods—including audiovisual content—are not straightforwardly substitutable because they are subject to the vagaries of individual and collective taste, language, identity and comprehensibility. Their value is always uncertain. From the perspective of economics, this is "imperfect substitution"; for those in the arts and humanities, it is more likely to be understood as the fundamental irreducibility of human creativity.

Audiovisual markets are paradigmatic cultural markets in the sense that they involve trade in images, affects and ideas, as well as physical products. It is often unclear where the audiovisual market begins; what dynamics of competition and substitution are at play within its boundaries; and how it interfaces with other kinds of markets, including leisure, entertainment and information markets. Is the consumer lining up at the cinema box office "in the market for" a movie only, or would they be just as happy watching something on television, going to a restaurant or reading a book? How substitutable are these experiences?

Economic sociology provides some useful tools for thinking through these problems (Aspers 2011; Callon 1998). To summarize one strand of a complex literature, we can simply say that markets are a way of seeing and structuring economic activity. Markets exist to the extent that they are rendered visible through discourse and measurement, or formalized through regulation. However, transactions that occur within and define a given market are not always understood through the market frame. Many filmmakers simply do not accept the argument that they are operating within a market, preferring instead to see themselves as driven by creative, social and critical motivations. Even though markets become a necessary consideration at the point of distribution, the language of "the market" is not part of their professional identity, or exists as something that they define their work *against*. This is similar to what the political theorist Keat (2000) writes about in his work on market boundaries, which is concerned with delineating what he describes as the "limits of the market." For Keat, the critical study of market boundaries is a philosophical project addressing the following question: "where, and on what grounds, are the lines to be drawn between those social practices that properly belong to the market domain, and those that do not?" (Keat 2000: 70).

This point about the limited acceptance of market discourse within audiovisual industry practice applies even to professions that are explicitly commercial. For example, many YouTube influencers would struggle to respond if asked about the boundaries of their market. However, they would certainly have a clear idea of who their audience is, what those individuals are looking for, how much they will pay, what forms such payment might take (attention, subscription, advertising, direct purchase) and where else they may go for similar content. In other words, "market" is a way of narrating a network of socioeconomic relations, rather than a thing that exists in its own right. Once defined or enumerated, markets also create their own social realities, hence the emphasis on the performativity of markets in recent economic sociology (Callon 1998).

3.3   Market Space and Social Space

A vital insight from the social science of markets is to always consider the messiness and friction built into markets. In other words, we must think of markets as social spaces constituted by history, politics and culture rather than abstract spaces constituted by exchange (Lefebvre 2000; Shields 2013: 74). This involves, among other things, paying attention to how official market boundaries come into contact with—and inevitably conflict with—consumer preferences, practices, activities and institutions that may or may not respect those boundaries. The effect of this thought experiment is to pluralize the idea of "the market" by acknowledging that there are, in fact, many different kinds of markets. More to the point, each market comprises a palimpsest of layers that interact in complex ways.

In the case of audiovisual markets, these layers include:

- The boundaries of territorial markets in copyright licensing, which usually but do not always align with the borders of nation states[1];
- The preferred market boundaries of local distributors as expressed through their established sales practices (i.e., territorially anchored industry practice);
- The geography of taste and demand (what people want to watch and where), which never aligns neatly with national borders or territorial market boundaries;
- The linguistic geography of language competency and preference, and the availability of subtitles and dubbing;
- The socioeconomic geography of consumers' ability and willingness to pay for such content;
- The differential pricing and availability of that content in both formal and informal markets, and so on.

In other words, the market as a regulatory construct is only one layer in the larger assemblage of preferences, transactions and dispositions that comprise this market. The official market, then, is one layer in a stack.

The next logical step in this line of analysis is to consider the relations *between* layers. The most appropriate way to understand these relations, in my view, would be to describe them as disjunctive, following Arjun Appadurai's use of the term. Appadurai, in his canonical essay "Disjuncture and Difference in the Global Cultural Economy" (Appadurai 1996), famously envisaged the cultural economy as a series of "scapes" encompassing flows of finance, technology, media, migration and ideology.[2] Appadurai's basic point—often overlooked in subsequent commentary—is that the relations between these scapes are disjunctive: Flows in each "scape" are connected but not determinant. Each domain "is subject to its own constraints and incentives […] at the same time as each acts as a constraint and a parameter for movements

---

[1] For example, distribution contracts used in audiovisual licensing may refer to Benelux (Belgium, The Netherlands, Luxembourg), North America (USA plus Canada) or the Caribbean region.

[2] Appadurai's essay was first published in *Theory, Culture & Society* (Appadurai 1990). The extended and better-known version of this essay appeared several years later as a chapter in his book *Globalization at Large* (Appadurai 1996).

in the others" (Appadurai 1996: 35). Hence, there is a degree of autonomy between ideas and technology, for example, or between human migration and technological development. Of course, there are also structural connections.

This notion of disjuncture is a useful starting point for understanding the relations between audiovisual market layers. Extending this idea, we could say two things. First, relations between market layers are neither aligned nor coordinated, and often function out of kilter with one another. The geography of European languages, for example, often bears little resemblance to the territorial market boundaries established in copyright law, because linguistic communities are often spread across multiple national borders, and because many European nations contain multiple linguistic communities within their borders. Hence, the "language" layer and the "copyright territory" layer are not always aligned. Language is shaped by the contingency of history rather than the formal geometry of market boundaries.

A second observation about market layers is that conflict tends to arise where there is an obvious disparity between two or more layers. This is the case, for example, when there is pent-up demand for a particular work but no formal availability to satisfy that demand (i.e., when the consumer demand layer is out of sync with the copyright licensing and/or availability layers and/or the socioeconomic layer). The result in this case would be market failure or piracy. Too much demand and too little formal availability means that activity tends to spill over into informal markets (Lobato and Thomas 2015).

The analytical approach I have suggested allows us to see official market boundaries as one layer in a larger structure. This, I would argue, is an appropriate starting point for thinking about audiovisual markets. It is especially helpful for understanding controversies surrounding the DSM—a grand policy exercise that brings into focus the tension between market layers.

3.4   The Digital Single Market and Its Discontents

Let us now consider what this multi-layered approach to markets can reveal about the DSM. For those unfamiliar with the DSM, I begin with a summary of its key components and some well-known areas of controversy relating specifically to the audiovisual sector. By necessity, this is a brief overview of a complex topic. More detailed analysis can be found in subsequent chapters in this book and in other expert studies (Bondebjerg et al. 2015; Gomez Herrera and Martens 2018; Ibrus 2016; Trimble 2019).

The DSM is a set of interlocked EU reforms designed to reduce barriers to trade in digital services and goods within the EU. It involves a raft of changes to EU law, standards and regulations across several policy areas, including copyright, consumer protection, telecommunications, e-commerce, media regulation and data policy. Many of the measures have already been passed by the European Parliament, though others, at the time of writing, are yet to be legislated. A key objective of the overall DSM package is to create seamless access to European digital services across the continent by reducing "unjustified" geoblocking and eliminating other technological barriers. A discussion of EU-wide copyright licensing was also part of the initial DSM agenda, but this was scaled back in the face of strong objections from filmmakers, producers and audiovisual distributors.

The elements of the DSM that are most relevant for our analysis include new rules mandating the portability of digital media content for users moving between EU countries (so that Europeans can take their online subscription services with them when they travel within Europe) and measures designed to reduce geoblocking in e-commerce. Another important change is the 2018 revision of the Audiovisual Media Services Directive (AVMSD), which introduces a 30% European content quota and rules about the promotion and recommendation of this content within video streaming services.

The DSM has been highly controversial, and it is helpful to reflect on why this is so. One reason is that the DSM embodies a number of connected, but philosophically incompatible, principles. These principles can be summarized as follows:

- A rights-based principle of free movement and access to European culture, transposed into the realm of digital goods and services;
- A vision of economic liberalization, competition and innovation;
- A contemporary discourse of Internet freedom and a "borderless Internet" (especially evident in the comments of Andrus Ansip, EU Commissioner for the DSM);
- An efficiency argument about solving market failures and blockages and improving consumer welfare;
- A protectionist policy agenda (visible especially within the revised AVMSD) focused on supporting European producers through legislated protections and quotas;
- A commitment to cultural diversity in line with EU principles.

Clearly, these goals exist in a somewhat tense relationship. For example, the protectionism of content quotas pulls, ideologically, in a different direction from the DSM initiatives that prioritize liberalization.

A second reason why the DSM has been divisive, especially among European filmmakers, is because the DSM is not strictly audiovisual policy. Instead, it is economic policy that encompasses audiovisual markets alongside other kinds of markets—including telecommunications and e-commerce. In this sense, the DSM's controversial nature can be partly attributed to the fact that it appears, at least discursively, as an attempt to redraw market boundaries around film and television and to reframe these media as part of a larger, non-medium-specific "digital" market. This was more a rhetorical move than a substantive policy shift. Despite the rhetoric of a single digital market, the DSM is really a collection of distinct initiatives designed to boost pan-EU trade *within* existing markets. Nonetheless, the rhetorical force of DSM—as a catchphrase—has been powerful, and somewhat counterproductive in terms of managing expectations for industry-specific solutions.

Part of the problem here is the term "digital," itself a highly contentious category. Trade in digital goods frequently expands the geographic boundaries of the market, because it lowers transaction costs (Elzinga 1981). To add further complexity, digital markets also blur boundaries between formally distinct media such as cinema and television (media convergence), which means that product categories *within* a market may shift. In other words, the digital both pushes the geographic boundaries of the market outward while redrawing boundaries on the inside of the market. However, the digital is always bounded and territorialized through social practice, language and taste. It can only exist on the rough terrain of culture. Hence, we return, once more, to the disjuncture between market boundaries and social space.

3.5 The Geoblocking Problem

Let us turn to a specific issue within the DSM—geoblocking—that neatly illustrates this problem of disjuncture. Notwithstanding the many inherent tensions within the DSM project, it was the European Commission's proposals on geoblocking that generated the strongest opposition on the part of AV industry stakeholders and their representatives. Geoblocking is a technique of digital rights management in which IP geolocation is used as the basis for granting or restricting access to digital content, in order to conform to licensing agreements organized on a territorial/national basis. In this sense, geoblocking is the technical solution for extending the principle of territoriality online.

Many consumers, of course, see geoblocking as a cause of great frustration. The European Commission's stated objective with the DSM was to reduce unjustified geoblocking, and by extension, to reduce digital market segmentation, geographic price differentiation and uneven availability of services within the EU. However, the implications of an end to geoblocking for long-established business models within the EU audiovisual sector were underestimated by EU policymakers. Anna Herold of the European Commission, writing in a personal capacity, has described this tension over geoblocking as "a fundamental controversy" that the DSM "stumbled upon" (Herold 2018: 255).

Zahrádka (2018) has studied in detail how geoblocking became such a controversy within the DSM discussions, dividing stakeholders along different lines. On the one hand, consumer groups and Internet advocates strongly supported the aspects of the DSM that promoted cross-border access. On the other hand, European filmmakers, producers and distributors saw in the DSM's anti-geoblocking agenda a weakening of territorial copyright and pointed to unforeseen consequences. A key concern of these objectors was the destabilization of the presale financing model, which is premised on territorial exclusivity and market segmentation. For example, John McVay of the Producers Alliance for Cinema and Television (UK) warned that "Any intervention that undermines the ability to license on an exclusive territorial basis will lead to less investment in new productions and reduce the quality and range of content available to consumers" (Roxborough 2015).

Other objectors were concerned that the DSM might reorganize the market around the needs of Netflix, Amazon, Google and Apple, who were arguably in the best position to benefit from the increased efficiencies of a single market. Indeed, several Silicon Valley companies expressed strong approval of the DSM. Google's Chairman Eric Schmidt stated that "To succeed globally, Europe needs a single digital market" (Mizroch and Jervell 2015), while Netflix CEO Reed Hastings went further, noting that "We really want the world to be a single market" (Stupp 2015). Comments such as these did not allay suspicions among smaller European players that they may have little to gain from redrawing market boundaries.

Critics of the DSM also warned of harmful knock-on effects that would result from any weakening of territoriality. These included everything from the crippling of the theatrical exhibition sector and the financial ruin of smaller distributors who could not afford to license films on an EU-wide basis to the equalization of pricing across the EU (so that Romanians would have to pay the same as Germans for their digital movie rentals) and even the rise of dubbing in subtitle nations (because dubbing could be used as a de facto market separation measure) (Trimble 2019).

As an example, consider the following remarks from Jelmer Hofkamp, secretary of the International Federation of Film Distributors' Associations (FIAD), offered in 2015 when the DSM territoriality debate was at its peak:

> If we look at the kind of tools they [the European Commission] want to use to create this DSM with a strong focus on availability, that is where they [the EC] go wrong because availability is not the same thing as building bigger audiences or having better circulation of European works. [...] Is it the principle of availability of the single market they want, or is it actually a flourishing European production market and more circulation within the EU of European product? (Macnab 2015)

Hofkamp's point here is that the stated aims of the DSM—including pan-European availability and circulation of EU works, and a flourishing European screen production culture—may be incompatible. In other words, the dream of unfettered digital availability cannot always be reconciled with the political economy of film and television production. This was not a consensus position, as those on the other side hotly disputed the claim. Pirate Party MEP Julia Reda argued that "Europe's 'natural' cultural and linguistic barriers are much more effective and unintrusive in achieving some market segmentation than discriminating viewers based on the country they are currently in." Reda added that "Nobody's going to stop going to the cinema in Portugal because a film is already viewable online on an Estonian website" (Reda 2016).

As we can see from these various interventions, the key issue here for both sides was the relationship between the ideal boundaries of the market and the actual functioning of those markets in practice. Rightsholders, producers, audiovisual industry associations and some filmmakers argued that the dream of a pan-European audiovisual space was blind to the *realpolitik* of production, including the complex relationship between distribution guarantees and production financing. Meanwhile, consumer and Internet advocates argued that the existing system of territoriality simply could not be reconciled with the everyday practices of consumers, nor with the circulatory logics of data in the Internet age.

3.6 Boundary Trouble

How do we make sense of all this complex position-taking? One analytical possibility is to see the whole DSM/geoblocking affair as symptomatic of a wider conflict between the regulatory, industrial, social and cultural layers of the market, as defined earlier.

For European filmmakers, producers and distributors, the vision of borderless consumption within the EU was problematic because it clashed with the existing institutional arrangements in the audiovisual sector. In other words, it was a conflict between the existing social space of the market and its new (proposed) abstract form. Internet and consumer advocates saw the situation through a different lens, but using similar categories. They argued that the artificial constraints of an outdated copyright system were being imposed on the "natural" geography of consumer demand. In both cases, the core conflict involved a perceived clash between real-world markets and official market boundaries.

A second vector of conflict was whether market boundaries in the DSM would reflect consumers' needs or rightsholders' needs. Markets designed for rightsholders will logically have different boundaries from markets designed for consumers. Copyright is a system designed for rightsholders, in the sense that its incentives rely on protections and rights granted on a territorial basis, following the publishing industries' historical business model. In the DSM debate, the most vocal industry stakeholders—many of whom felt they had little to gain from an EU-wide market, because demand for their work was concentrated in a handful of key territories—wanted to retain the licensing cost structures that come with territory-by-territory licensing. In other words, they wanted *small markets* with tightly defined, enforceable boundaries.[3]

On the other hand, consumers—to the extent that they care about market boundaries at all—are likely to prefer larger markets (for increased choice and to avoid the hassle of geoblocking) with permeable boundaries and no enforcement, except in those instances when drawing the boundary in such a way results in price differences.

In other words, there is a clash not only between the material interests of producers and consumers, but also in how these interests map onto the abstract form of the market. The idea of a single audiovisual market, as articulated in the DSM discussions, proved to be divisive rather than unifying, because it brought into focus the many conflicts that arise when a boundary is moved.

---

[3] The interests of rightsholders and creators are not necessarily aligned, as many creators seek the widest possible circulation of their work. The different interests of rightsholders and creators are often grouped together under the category of "producer," but these need to be carefully disentangled.

3.7 Conclusion

In this chapter, I have argued that the Digital Single Market controversy is emblematic of a wider set of tensions about market boundaries, which are reconfigured but also reinforced by digitization. In this sense, the DSM draws our attention to the contradictions between the spatial free flow and spatial restriction that characterize digital media. Far from creating a flat space of friction-free commerce, the DSM reminds us that digital distribution has the potential to create new kinds of borders, new enclosures and new territorialities, as well as new mobilities.

Scholarship and policy in this area need to retain a spatialized understanding of markets that sees them not as flat spaces of flow and exchange but as social spaces of friction. The coming years are likely to be marked by further disjuncture between the market layers I described earlier. While these problems are not unique to Europe, they will play out in an intensified form in Europe—because of its dense patchwork of media markets, institutions, languages and histories.

The DSM is the most developed policy response to the problem of geoblocking that has been tried anywhere in the world. As such, it represents a major intervention into a hitherto unregulated aspect of everyday media usage affecting millions of users. Any scholar interested in questions of distribution, copyright, piracy and so on should be paying attention to the DSM, and especially to its evolution over time as the early proposals hit the hard ground of stakeholder self-interest.

However, a key lesson from the DSM case is that territoriality in copyright cannot be reduced to a Manichean conflict between two sides, such as corporations versus the consumer, capital versus creativity or the powerful versus the powerless. The DSM has shown us, among other things, that moving a market boundary can have many unforeseen effects. As I have argued throughout this chapter, each stakeholder's position in the DSM debate has relied on a particular set of claims about the proper boundaries of the market. None of these claims are pure in their own right, but all of them reveal something about the disjuncture that characterizes cultural markets.

Acknowledgements This research was partly funded by the Australian Government through the Australian Research Council (projects DP190100978 and DE150100288). The views expressed herein are those of the author and are not necessarily those of the Australian Government or the Australian Research Council. Thank you to Tessa Dwyer for invaluable research assistance, to the editors for their careful reading and to Patrick Vonderau, Jennifer Holt, Amanda Lotz and participants at the Defining Digital Markets symposium at Stockholm University (2017) for stimulating conversations on this theme.

References

Appadurai, A. (1990). Disjuncture and difference in the global cultural economy. *Theory, Culture & Society, 7*, 295–310.

Appadurai, A. (1996). *Modernity at large: Cultural dimensions of globalization*. Minneapolis: University of Minnesota Press.

Aspers, P. (2011). *Markets*. Cambridge: Polity.

Berland, J. (2009). *North of empire: Essays on the cultural technologies of space*. Durham and London: Duke University Press.

Bondebjerg, I., Redvall, E. N., & Higson, A. (2015). *European cinema and television: Cultural policy and everyday life*. London: Palgrave Macmillan.

Callon, M. (Ed.). (1998). *The laws of the markets*. Malden, MA: Blackwell.

Christophers, B. (2013). The law's markets: Envisioning and effecting the boundaries of competition. *Journal of Cultural Economy, 8*(2), 125–143.

de Sola Pool, I. (1990). *Technologies without boundaries: On telecommunications in a global age*. Cambridge: Harvard University Press.

Elzinga, K. G. (1981). Defining geographic market boundaries. *The Antitrust Bulletin, 1981*, 739–752.

Evans, D. (2012). Lightening up on market definition. In E. R. Elhauge (Ed.), *Research handbook on the economics of antitrust law* (pp. 53–89). Cheltenham: Edward Elgar.

Gomez Herrera, E., & Martens, B. (2018). Language, copyright and geographic segmentation in the EU digital single market for music and film. *Review of Economic Research on Copyright Issues, 15*(1), 20–37.

Herold, A. (2018). Digital single market for audiovisual content: Utopia or win-win for all? In J. Hammett-Jamart, P. Mitric, & E. N. Redvall (Eds.), *European film and television co-production: Policy and practice* (pp. 255–263). Basingstoke: Palgrave.

Ibrus, I. (2016). The EU digital single market as a mission impossible: Audio-visual policy conflicts for Estonia. *International Journal of Digital Television, 7*(1), 23–38.

Keat, R. (1999). Market boundaries and the commodification of culture. In L. Ray & A. Sayers (Eds.), *Culture and economy: After the cultural turn* (pp. 92–111). London: Sage.

Keat, R. (2000). *Cultural goods and the limits of the market*. Basingstoke: Palgrave.

Lefebvre, H. (2000). *The production of space*. Oxford: Blackwell.

Lobato, R., & Thomas, J. (2015). *The informal media economy*. Cambridge: Polity.

Macnab, G. (2015). European digital single market: Winds of change. *Screen Daily*, November 2. https://www.screendaily.com/features/digital-single-market-winds-of-change/5096211.article.

Mizroch, A., & Jervell, E. E. (2015). Google is ready to support European digital innovation. *Wall Street Journal*, June 12. https://www.wsj.com/articles/google-ready-to-support-european-digital-innovation-says-eric-schmidt-1433946280.

Morley, D., & Robins, K. (1995). *Spaces of identity: Global media, electronic landscapes, and cultural boundaries*. London: Routledge.

Reda, J. (2016). Post on Juliareda.eu website. https://juliareda.eu. Accessed March 10, 2016.

Roxborough, S. (2015). European film industry reacts to digital single market proposals. *Hollywood Reporter*, December 9. https://www.hollywoodreporter.com/news/european-film-industry-reacts-digital-847175.

Shields, R. (2013). *Spatial questions: Cultural topologies and social spatialisation*. London: Sage.

Stupp, C. (2015). Netflix CEO: Europe needs strong net neutrality rules. *EurActiv*, May 6. https://www.euractiv.com/section/digital/news/netflix-ceo-europe-needs-strong-net-neutrality-rules.

Trimble, M. (2019). Copyright and geoblocking: The consequences of eliminating geoblocking. *Boston University Journal of Science and Technology Law, 25*. https://ssrn.com/abstract=3330876.

Zahrádka, P. (2018). Geo-blocking: Protection of author's rights, of cultural diversity, or of an outdated business model? *Jahrbuch für Recht und Ethik, 26*, 191–208.

Ramon Lobato is Senior Research Fellow at the School of Media and Communication, RMIT University, Melbourne. A screen industry scholar, he is known for his work on informal distribution, streaming and piracy. He is the author of *Shadow Economies of Cinema: Mapping Informal Film Distribution* (2012), *The Informal Media Economy* (2015) and *Netflix Nations: The Geography of Digital Distribution* (2019). He is a member of the editorial collective for the journal *Media Industries*.

Part II
Regulating Online Boundaries: Territoriality Versus Digital Single Market

Chapter 4
Territoriality of Copyright Law

Radim Polčák

4.1 Territoriality and Sovereignty

Territoriality represents one of the key ontological features of the continental legal culture. It has developed throughout the centuries and its recent shape was laid down at the dawn of the law of nations in the late medieval period.

Territoriality of law is conceptually linked with sovereignty. Before Grotius (1901) and de Vattel (1797), sovereignty was mostly a factual concept, whereby a sovereign had jurisdiction only if she was able to constitute and maintain factual control over people residing in a certain territory. Consequently, the traditional concept of sovereignty consisted of territory, population and effective power over these two. The fact-based establishment of international order led to permanent violent conflict because armed action represented a regular tool in political competition between various nations.

Overall exhaustion of nations from permanent wars, expressed in the Peace of Westphalia, led to the establishment of recognition as an additional criterion of sovereignty (Beaulac 2004). Unlike the first three factual elements, i.e., people, territory and power, recognition was of a normative nature. It meant that sovereignty was no longer only a matter of factual effective control, but rather of normative (legal) recognition by the international community. Consequently, it was no longer possible to claim sovereignty based on military control, but rather on legal compliance under the established rules and principles of the newly founded complex international legal order. The shift of sovereignty from a factual to a normative concept also meant that all sovereigns were considered equal, regardless of their powers or the size of their sovereign domains.

R. Polčák (✉)
Faculty of Law, Institute of Law and Technology, Masaryk University, Veveří 70, 602 00 Brno, Czech Republic
e-mail: radim.polcak@law.muni.cz

© The Author(s) 2020
P. Szczepanik et al. (eds.), *Digital Peripheries*, Springer Series in Media Industries,
https://doi.org/10.1007/978-3-030-44850-9_4

65

In Europe, sovereignty is deemed to be naturally linked with territoriality. This is primarily because Europe was and is relatively densely populated and thus the afore-mentioned permanent wars were fought mostly over territories. Even the term "West-phalian sovereignty" or "Westphalian order" is mostly interpreted as the principle that each nation (state) has exclusive sovereign rule over its territory.

Territoriality is not as relevant in all legal cultures around the world. For example, legal cultures based on religious belief, such as Islamic or Hindu laws, are typically based on personality (Glenn 2014). In these legal cultures, the physical location where respective persons reside is not of primary importance for the rule of law, but rather their confession. Even Roman law, which is believed to be the basis for the current continental European legal culture, used the personality principle rather than territoriality (Duff 1938)—the distinctive element was citizenship rather than confession (Rieder and Pappas 1998).

The traditional territoriality of the law came under strong pragmatic pressure in Europe and the USA with the introduction of the Internet, precisely because of the almost total deconstruction [or virtualization (Lévy 1998)] of the notion of matter or space as such. In his Declaration of Independence of Cyberspace, Barlow (1996) points to virtualized matter and territory in a strong anarchic statement as follows:

> Cyberspace consists of transactions, relationships, and thought itself, arrayed like a stand-ing wave in the web of our communications. Ours is a world that is both everywhere and nowhere, but it is not where bodies live.[...] Your legal concepts of property, expression, identity, movement, and context do not apply to us. They are all based on matter, and there is no matter here.[...] Our identities have no bodies, so, unlike you, we cannot obtain order by physical coercion. We believe that from ethics, enlightened self-interest, and the common-weal, our governance will emerge. Our identities may be distributed across many of your jurisdictions.[...] These increasingly hostile and colonial measures place us in the same position as those previous lovers of freedom and self-determination who had to reject the authorities of distant, uninformed powers. We must declare our virtual selves immune to your sovereignty, even as we continue to consent to your rule over our bodies. We will spread ourselves across the Planet so that no one can arrest our thoughts.

The question of territoriality was also at the core of the famous debate between Goldsmith (1998) and Post (2002) about whether private international law should specifically acknowledge the cross-border nature of the Internet. Goldsmith (1998: 1250) argued against treating cross-border Internet transactions differently from their offline counterparts by saying that they:

> are no different from "real-space" transnational transactions. They involve people in real space in one jurisdiction communicating with people in real space in other jurisdictions in a way that often does good but sometimes causes harm. There is no general normative argument that supports the immunization of cyberspace activities from territorial regulation. And there is every reason to believe that nations can exercise territorial authority to achieve significant regulatory control over cyberspace transactions.

Post (2002: 1383), labeled an "exceptionalist," did not even look for any "norma-tive" counterarguments, but argued pragmatically by pointing to the nature and scale of legally relevant cross-border acting on the Internet saying that

[a] world in which virtually all events and transactions have bordercrossing effects is surely not "functionally identical" to a world in which most do not, at least not with respect to the application of a principle that necessarily requires consideration of the distribution of those effects. A world in which the Effects Principle returns the result "No Substantial Effects Outside the Borders" when applied to the vast majority of events and transactions is not "functionally identical" to a world in which application of the same principle to the vast majority of events and transactions returns the opposite result. A world in which, on occasion, bullets are fired from one jurisdiction into another is not "functionally identical" to a world in which all jurisdictions are constantly subjected to shrapnel from a thousand different directions.

Nearly two decades later, it is now obvious that acknowledging the pragmatic aspects of jurisdiction over the Internet, as argued by Post, is inevitable. The scale and societal relevance of various Internet-based cross-border transactions, many of which are utterly impossible to physically localize, force us to develop new ways to deal with this jurisdictional (and even ontological) dilemma. Consequently, specific methods have arisen for resolving the "Internet jurisdictional puzzles" (Svantesson 2017) in various areas, from consumer contracting to personal data to intellectual property (Reindenberg 2005).

In addition to the aforementioned challenges to the traditional territorial understanding of sovereignty, there has arisen the phenomenon of extraterritorial application of the law on the Internet. The term "extraterritoriality" in this sense refers to regulatory actions that are, thanks to the cross-border nature of the information network, effective far beyond the territory of the respective sovereign (Svantesson 2015). Typical recent examples include cross-border forensic activities and global delisting orders.

Surely there is, as noted above by John Post, nothing entirely new about situations in which some sovereign action might affect the regulatory domains of other sovereigns. However, the scale, frequency and relevance of such extraterritorial exercises of jurisdiction make it necessary to tackle this specific issue in order to prevent positive conflicts between sovereign powers.

This does not mean that the Westphalian territorial concept of sovereignty is dead for the Internet. It is still valid in that every sovereign has the ultimate jurisdiction over her territory (meaning the physical area within its respective state borders). However, ultimately territorially based sovereign rule must be supplemented, with growing relevance, with various balancing mechanisms[1] in order for individuals and states to truly benefit from all the advantages of an internationally networked information society (Svantesson 2016) and for international law as such to prevail (Kohler 1917).

---

[1]One example is the Zippo Sliding Scale that was established for trademark disputes between US states (Aiken 1997).

4.2 Territoriality in Copyrights

The relationship between copyrights and territorial jurisdiction is quite complex (Trimble 2015). One reason is that the object of copyrights, i.e., the work, does not need to have a material form and thus can appear in objectively viewable form in multiple physical locations at once. Or, it might objectively exist, while not being physically present at any particular location. A second, and even more problematic, a factor of complexity in the relationship between territory and copyrights is that copyrights, although considered a kind of "property," do not provide for true appropriation of respective works.

Lawrence Lessig quotes in his book *Free Culture* the following statement made by recording industry lobbyist Jack Valenti during his testimony to the US Congress in 1982 (2004: 117):

> No matter the lengthy arguments made, no matter the charges and the countercharges, no matter the tumult and the shouting, reasonable men and women will keep returning to the fundamental issue, the central theme which animates this entire debate: Creative property owners must be accorded the same rights and protection resident in all other property owners in the nation. That is the issue. That is the question. And that is the rostrum on which this entire hearing and the debates to follow must rest.

Following this quotation, Lessig (2004: 118) elaborately argues why property and intellectual property do not represent the same concept. He notes that

> [w]hile "creative property" is certainly "property" in a nerdy and precise sense that lawyers are trained to understand, it has never been the case, nor should it be, that "creative property owners" have been "accorded the same rights and protection resident in all other property owners." Indeed, if creative property owners were given the same rights as all other property owners, that would effect a radical, and radically undesirable, change in our tradition.

As to the territoriality of copyrights, what is most important is what Lessig points out as property in the "precise sense that lawyers are trained to understand." In such a "precise sense," we first must distinguish what is the true object of intellectual property, or even more precisely, copyrights. In the case of the property of tangible assets, the object of exclusive property rights is exactly those tangible assets. However, with intellectual property, the object that is appropriated by the owner is not the copyrighted work as such, but only certain precisely specified rights (Dillenz 1987–1988). While the proprietor of a tangible thing owns the thing as such, the intellectual proprietor does not own the intellectual creation as such but only particular rights (copyrights). Thus, one cannot legally own a movie, but it is legally possible to own copyrights to a movie (Zemer 2006).

The idea of owning rights corresponds to the nature of inventions and intellectual creations. It was originally adopted by the Paris Convention and the Berne Convention, both of which laid down the basic structure of rights to inventions or creations that the signatories promised to protect.

Although there are conceptual differences between the Common Law concept of copyright and the continental concept of *droit d'auteur*, their common denominator is, besides the definition of the work as such, the notion of the use of protected work.

The particular proprietary rights to use the work cover practically all economically relevant forms of utilization of copyrighted works such as reproduction, distribution and broadcasting and form the core economic mechanism of copyrights (Zemer 2006).

The legal definition of use is not general, but it always covers only a specifically defined form of economically relevant utilization of copyrighted work. Consequently, there is relatively precise definition in statutory law as to the use by making copies or by making the work available to the public.

This means that forms of possible factual "use" of copyrighted works that are not listed in statutes are not covered by copyrights. A typical example is screening a movie or playing a music record at home—such forms of "use" of copyrighted works do not constitute a use in terms of copyright law and so the holder of copyrights has no claims against those who do so. This specification of particular rights that are owned by copyright holders differentiates copyrights from (standard) property rights. Ownership of tangible assets is universal and the law only defines particular exemptions, while, on the contrary, ownership of copyrights is always particular and any non-specific forms of "use" of copyrighted works are thus permitted.

The Berne Convention does not even explicitly mention the use of copyrighted works for the personal purposes of individuals. It implies that the signatories have no obligation to care about such form of "use" (or rather non-use) of copyrighted works.

In addition, the Berne Convention names certain cases of free use of copyrighted works. This means forms of use that would normally be covered by copyrights, but are for some reason exempted. These exemptions include using citations that would normally qualify as making a copy of a cited work or its part.

To sum up, the Berne Convention distinguishes between, firstly, particular forms of use of copyrighted works that are covered by specifically defined appropriative copyrights; secondly, "non-use" which is not covered by any rights; and thirdly, free use which is specifically permitted by the Convention or by the laws of its Member States. It is not compulsory for Member States to maintain these indications or structures of rights as long as the normative content of the Convention is preserved. The copyright laws of continental European members, then, mostly distinguish between (1) use in the sense of the Convention, (2) free use, which they mostly regard as making copies for personal purposes,[2] and (3) implied or statutory licenses that are regarded as specifically permitted forms of free use within the domain of copyrighted use.

Thus, only two forms of use of copyrighted works are relevant for the territorial scope of sovereign powers and subsequent applicability of copyright law—use and free use—according to the Berne Convention. Use is important because respective property rights are protected if the use takes place within a certain territory.

Free use is relevant depending on whether local laws provide for the exemption from copyright protection. For everything else, namely for the "use" of copyrighted

---

[2]Other forms of use of works for personal purposes, such as viewing, listening, reading, are not regarded as free use, because they do not constitute a "use" at all.

works for personal purposes, territorial jurisdiction is irrelevant, as no legal limitations for such "use" apply. Consequently, those who "use" copyrighted works for personal purposes (e.g., those who screen movies at home), do not have to be legally concerned about the place where they do so.

4.3 Geoblocking and Technical Measures

What this implies is that, contrary to general public belief, geoblocking or other forms of limiting access to copyrighted works based on geographic location have very little to do with copyrights. Geoblocking measures, if applied, are in many cases not deemed to serve the purpose of protecting copyrights, simply because there are no rights to decide with regard to the form or place of "use" of copyrighted works for personal purposes.

One intersection between copyright law and geoblocking measures can be argued by the possible classification of geoblocking measures as de iure "technological measures," in the meaning e.g., of Art. 6(3) of Directive No. 2001/29/EC[3] or 17 USC § 1201(a)(3)(A) (Ginsburg 2000). These "technological measures" are regarded as a special object of legal protection and their circumvention is specifically sanctioned. If geoblocking tools were disabled or circumvented by individual users in order to view or in any other way consume copyrighted content, and if these geoblocking tools are legally regarded as "technological measures," such circumvention would per se constitute violation of law even if the user does not violate any copyrights related to the content as such (Kra-Oz 2017).

The possibility of classifying geoblocking tools as "technological measures" mostly depends on their specific definition in applicable statutes. Art. 6(3) of Directive 2001/29/EC defines technological measures as "any technology, device or component that, in the normal course of its operation, is designed to prevent or restrict acts, in respect of works or other subject-matter, which are not authorised by the rightsholder".

This definition of technological measures, and especially its caveat "as provided for by law," can be interpreted in two ways. The first is that a "technological measure" consists of any kind of technology that protects the copyrighted work as such. Another possible interpretation is that a "technological measure" can be regarded as only a tool that protects certain actual copyrights.

EU Member States differ as to how this interpretative dilemma is resolved in their statutory laws. Some Member States specifically legally protect all technological measures, while others regard as "technological measures" only those that technically back some actual rights.[4]

---

[3]See Directive 2001/29/EC on the harmonization of certain aspects of copyright and related rights in the information society.

[4]For instance, the Czech Copyright Act speaks in Art. 43(1) only about "technological measures that protect rights implied by this statute."

The latter approach, i.e., limiting the scope of protection using technological measures to only those measures whose purpose is to protect some actual (existing) copyrights, was adopted by the European Court of Justice in the Nintendo case.[5] The reference for the preliminary ruling involved a question as to whether the Directive is meant to protect against circumvention of a technological measure that prohibits the use of any software on a gaming console other than original products authorized by the manufacturer. The official reasoning for such a measure was the prevention of unauthorized copying of games. However, the same measure prevented the console from running software offered by independent developers. Consequently, a dispute arose as to whether a hack that would allow independently developed software to run on a Nintendo console is to be regarded as circumventing technological measures pursuant to Art. 6(1) and 6(2) of Directive 2001/29/EC. The Court concluded that "with a view to examining the purpose of those devices, products or components, the evidence of actual use which is made of them by third parties will, in the light of the circumstances at issue, be particularly relevant. The referring court may, in particular, examine how often PC Box's devices are in fact used in order to allow unauthorized copies of Nintendo and Nintendo-licensed games to be used on Nintendo consoles and how often that equipment is used for purposes which do not infringe copyright in Nintendo and Nintendo-licensed games."[6]

It is clear from the judgment that the scope of protection of technological measures is to be interpreted in light of their main teleology, i.e., to protect copyrights. Geoblocking measures that do not protect any copyrights but only prevent copyrighted works from being accessed by consumers from a certain location shall thus not be, following this interpretive approach, regarded as legally immune from circumvention.

While copyright law is relatively indifferent toward geoblocking, other areas of law might, depending on the circumstances, even outlaw these measures. Although there is no case law to date, doctrinal publications from different jurisdictions have already provided for solid arguments, particularly with respect to antitrust law, consumer protection law and antidiscrimination law (cf. Earle 2016; Zareh 2018).

It is, then, a bit paradoxical that the only sign of the explicit legality of geoblocking is found in a statute that was originally meant to ban it. Regulation (EU) 2018/302[7] should have helped establish the common digital single market by banning discriminatory geoblocking in cases where users from one Member State are willing to access content provided through an information society service from another Member State

[5]See Case C-355/12, *Nintendo Co. Ltd, Nintendo of America Inc., Nintendo of Europe GmbH v. PC Box Srl, 9Net Srl.* It is to be noted that the case involved software of a specific legal nature. Unlike other copyrighted works, software cannot be freely used by individuals for personal purposes (a license is required for any use of software).

[6]See Case C-355/12, para. 34–36.

[7]See Regulation (EU) 2018/302 on addressing unjustified geoblocking and other forms of discrimination based on customers' nationality, place of residence or place of establishment within the internal market, and amending Regulations (EC) No. 2006/2004 and (EU) 2017/2394, and Directive 2009/22/EC.

(Hoffman 2016). However, as explained in recital 8, "[a]udiovisual services, including services the principle purpose of which is the provision of access to broadcasts of sports events and which are provided on the basis of exclusive territorial licenses, are excluded from the scope of this Regulation".

Besides the paradox that the Regulation does not cover services of utmost practical importance for European consumers, it may even give the impression that all those geoblocking tools applied by audiovisual services, which are excluded from the scope of the Regulation, are actually legal.

4.4   Place of Availability of Works

Another intersection between geoblocking and copyrights may derive from an interpretive claim that is being heard mostly from lobbyists from the recording industries and that is based on the assumption that a work is used in a legal sense in all places where it can be accessed. In this interpretation, the work is used by the provider (or a distributor) in a country where a consumer can access it, which means that the work is considered, legally, to be distributed or broadcasted (depending on the technology) in that country. If the interpretation of the place of consumption as a place of use of copyrighted work prevails, geoblocking could be considered a tool to protect copyrights because it would limit not the users but the providers in using (distributing, broadcasting) copyrighted works in different jurisdictions.

The idea that a copyrighted work that is accessible online is being used simultaneously in all jurisdictions where it can be accessed by users is attractive for rightsholders, but it is problematic from both a normative and a pragmatic perspective. It would mean that making a copyrighted work available on the Internet automatically means the active use of it in all jurisdictions in the world (perhaps excluding North Korea). If such publication of a work is not lawful, there would be instant simultaneous establishment of separate causes of action in nearly 200 countries worldwide (or at least in the 176 Member States of the Berne Convention).

The general question of the place of something happening, legally speaking, on the Internet and consequent jurisdictional dilemmas will, in any case, keep lawyers occupied for decades. The essence of the problem goes back to the core of the Post-Goldsmith debate and the "puzzle" that is composed of the growing number of issues, from defamation to gambling to cybercrime, that is far from being truly resolved (Trimble 2016).

The basic ontological question with regard to the territorial application of copyright law relates to the choice of criterion according to which it is possible to determine the applicable law and the court that is entitled to decide about the use of copyrighted work. The options include the country of origin, meaning the country from which the provider operates, and the country of damage, i.e., the country where the damage occurred. The country of damage can, depending on circumstances and interpretation (see below), be the same as the country origin or it can also theoretically be regarded as another place including the country of consumption.

The country of origin was established as the lead principal for a number of Internet-related legal agendas such as liability of information society services and protection of personal data. However, the country of damage still exists as a subsequent subsidiary jurisdictional criterion that makes it possible to claim damages in the place where it occurred (Hellner 2004). In practice, the question is then reduced to the relation between the damage and respective territory.

Courts around the world have relatively broad experience dealing with that question, especially in cases of defamation (Svantesson 2003). In a landmark case, *Gutnick v. Dow Jones*, Australian courts asserted their jurisdiction over a defamatory article published in the USA by an American publisher based on the physical availability of that article in Australia (because it was available on the Internet), combined with the fact that the affected person resided in Australia and had nearly all his personal interests there. The ECJ (CJEU respectively) adopted a similar approach through the doctrine of "center of interests" when it ruled in Joined Cases C-509/09 and C-161/10[8] that "in the event of an alleged infringement of personality rights by means of content placed online on an Internet website, the person who considers that his rights have been infringed has the option of bringing an action for liability, in respect of all the damage caused, either before the courts of the Member State in which the publisher of that content is established or before the courts of the Member State in which the centre of his interests is based."

The Court, however, also noted that the plaintiff: "may also, instead of an action for liability in respect of all the damage caused, bring his action before the courts of each Member State in the territory of which content placed online is or has been accessible. Those courts have jurisdiction only in respect of the damage caused in the territory of the Member State of the court seized."

In Case C-194/16, the Court limited the jurisdictional reach of all Member States on whose territory the defamatory content was accessible only to damages related to that respective territory, and established the "center of interests" as the sole jurisdiction that is entitled to decide on removal or rectification of defamatory data. The court argued that:

> in the light of the ubiquitous nature of the information and content placed online on a website and the fact that the scope of their distribution is, in principle, universal (...), an application for the rectification of the former and the removal of the latter is a single and indivisible application and can, consequently, only be made before a court with jurisdiction to rule on the entirety of an application for compensation for damage (...) and not before a court that does not have jurisdiction to do so. (...) [A] person who alleges that his personality rights have been infringed by the publication of incorrect information concerning him on the internet and by the failure to remove comments relating to him cannot bring an action for rectification of that information and removal of those comments before the courts of each Member State in which the information published on the internet is or was accessible.

In C-194/16, Advocate General (AG) Bobek went even further in his written opinion and suggested establishing a simple dichotomy between country of origin/country of center of interests for all possible claims. The AG asked "if it were established

---

[8]See Joined Cases C-509/09 and C-161/10 *eDate Advertising GmbH v. X and Olivier Martinez, Robert Martinez v. MGN Limited*.

that the Appellant may bring its claim before the Estonian courts with regard to the damage that has occurred in Estonia, the question would become: would and could the partial competence of these courts also be reflected at the level of partial competence to issue an injunction? Could the Respondent reasonably be asked to correct a proportional part of the allegedly harmful information and comments? If yes, how would that part be determined? Would the respondent be asked to delete only a proportionate segment of the information? Or just a portion of the comments?"

Consequently, the AG ambitiously recommended "to limit the international jurisdiction over Internet-related tortious claims to two heads of special jurisdiction [meaning country of origin and country of the center of interest]. The national courts competent under those two heads of jurisdiction would then have full jurisdiction for both determination and award of damages as well as any other remedies available to it under national law, including injunctions." The Court, despite consenting to the main idea of the priority of the center of interest, did not go further and maintained the possibility of courts in all Member States to individually decide about damages that physically occur in their respective jurisdictions.

That conclusion corresponds to the only relevant case of cross-border copyright infringement where the Internet played some role—case C-170/12.[9] The case involved copyrights to a music record that was unlawfully (without a valid license) pressed onto CDs in Austria, then marketed through an e-shop located in the UK and at least one copy was, upon an order made through that e-shop, delivered by post to France. The preliminary question was whether this cross-border situation allowed French courts to exercise their jurisdiction over the case.

The CJEU ruled that French courts do have jurisdiction based on the fact that the CDs were physically distributed in France and that French courts can decide only about damages that arose in France. In particular, the Court held,

> in the event of alleged infringement of copyrights protected by the Member State of the court seized, the latter has jurisdiction to hear an action to establish liability brought by the author of a work against a company established in another Member State and which has, in the latter State, reproduced that work on a material support which is subsequently sold by companies established in a third Member State through an internet site also accessible with the jurisdiction of the court seized. That court has jurisdiction only to determine the damage caused in the Member State within which it is situated.

In its decision, the Court also noted that "[i]n circumstances such as those at issue in the main proceedings that likelihood arises, in particular, from the possibility of obtaining a reproduction of the work to which the rights relied on by the defendant pertain from an Internet site accessible within the jurisdiction of the court seized."

C-170/12, however, does not help much in resolving the question as to the place of damage in the case of publication of a copyrighted work on the Internet. What makes C-170/12 inapplicable here is that the "circumstances such as those at issue" involved a physical copy of a record that was only marketed through an e-shop, while the actual legally relevant distribution took place physically by post. The seller thus had to actively send a physical copy of a CD to a known address in France. If the

---

[9]See Case C-170/12 *Peter Pinckney v. KDG Mediatech AG.*

work was distributed only online, there would be no particular targeted activity of the "seller" required for a work to end up at a certain location (which could literally be anywhere). In addition, the music CDs in question were sold to end users, so it was possible to relatively easily calculate actual local damage caused in France to the rightsholder by simply summing up the sales in the respective territory.

Hypothetically, it would be possible to combine the conclusions of C-170/12 with those from C-128/11,[10] in which the Court ruled that "from an economic point of view, the sale of a computer program on CD-ROM or DVD and the sale of a program by downloading from the Internet are similar. The on-line transmission method is the functional equivalent of the supply of a material medium." That would lead to the conclusion that in a case of illegal online distribution of digital copies of copyrighted works, damages could be sought separately in every jurisdiction from which copies could have been obtained. It would then be possible to argue that a geoblocking measure that prevents copies from being distributed to a certain territory is to be regarded as a technological measure in terms of Directive 2001/29.

4.5 Place of Communicating Works to the Public

One problem with the chain of arguments above is that, despite being normatively valid, they are pragmatically very problematic for a number of reasons that have been forcefully articulated not only by AG Bobek, but also in European and US copyright doctrine (Trimble 2019; Torremans 2016). It might, then, simply be a matter of time before the jurisdictional uncertainty, generated by the possibility of cause of action for damages in every EU Member State (not to mention the other approximately 150 Member States of the Berne Convention), is limited legislatively or judicially and the whole chain of arguments leading to the conclusion above regarding the link between copyrights and geoblocking is broken.

Even more problematic is the fact that many online distribution platforms for copyrighted content do not operate on the basis of distributing copies (files) but instead use various streaming technologies. In that case, there are no copies being de iure distributed[11] between various jurisdictions and thus no distribution rights can be protected here by the use of geoblocking tools according to the aforementioned interpretation of the existing case law of the CJEU.

Copyrighted works, in this instance, are without doubt made available to the public in terms of Art. 3 of Directive 2001/29/EC, but the question is whether "the act of communication to the public of their works, by wire or wireless means, including the making available to the public of their works in such a way that members of the public may access them from a place and at a time individually chosen by them" physically takes place simultaneously in all Member States (and ultimately in all

---

[10] See Case C-128/11, *UsedSoft GmbH v. Oracle International Corp.*, para. 61.

[11] See Art. 4 of Directive 2001/29/EC.

states where the Internet is accessible), or only in the country of origin (i.e., in the Member State from which the work is being made available).

The answer to that question is relatively simple to find in the wording of Art. 3 of Directive 2001/29/EC. This question is also answered by the definition of the term "information society service" as provided in Directive (EU) 2015/1535.[12]

It is a definitional element of "communication to the public" that "the public" decides the place and time that copyrighted works are accessed and viewed or in any other way used for personal purposes (i.e., "non-used" in terms of the Berne treaty). The fact that place and time of access is by definition out of the control of the provider directly implies that the provider cannot be seen as using the work within a territory which is arbitrarily chosen by the consumer as a matter of legally irrelevant "non-using" of that work.

Recently, the CJEU considered multiple cases in which "communication to the public" was at stake, namely with regard to indirect forms of communication of copyrighted works such as linking (Savola 2017). Although these cases do not give an explicit answer as to possible fora where such a use of copyrighted work can be claimed, the actions were always determined to be in the country of origin of the provider (i.e., never in any other jurisdiction where such "communication to the public" was merely available).

The only remaining possibility for arguing that the copyrighted work, when it is available through the Internet, is legally used by the provider simultaneously in all jurisdictions is if the provider legally engages in broadcasting such work in all the jurisdictions at the same time. This would mean that by making the work available on the Internet, the provider legally broadcasts that work in every jurisdiction where the work is accessible.

Besides the problem in such circumstances of finding the particular places of broadcasting within every single jurisdiction (e.g., for the purpose of determining which particular court in that jurisdiction would be entitled to hear the case), it is not even possible to consider the communication to the public in this way as a form of broadcasting. The reason is that copyrighted works are made available on the Internet through services that are provided, in legal terms, upon the individual request of a user.

Broadcasting typically consists of coverage of a certain target group with a signal that can be refined by specific technologies (receivers) into particular casts. In contrast, transmitting content over the Internet always technically requires an individual request from a user. The ECJ (CJEU) acknowledged this in case C-607/11, which considered the webcast of TV programs, by noting that "[t]he software on the edge server creates a separate stream for each user who requests a channel through it. An

---

[12] See Directive (EU) 2015/1535, which lays down a procedure for the provision of information in the field of technical regulations and of rules on information society services.

individual packet of data leaving the edge server is thus addressed to an individual user, not to a class of users."[13]

The key element of a webcast, i.e., the provision of the service in response to an individual request by a user, means that any distribution of content via the Internet is not a broadcast service but rather an information society service, according to the meaning of Art. 1(b) of Directive (EU) 2015/1535.

While the user of a broadcasting service only waits for the signal to arrive at her doorstep, the user of an information society service always individually requests service at the place from which it is provided. Upon such a request, an individual connection is always established. This individually established connection normally involves not only transmitting the requested content, but also mutual communication with the client device such as the processing of cookies. But in broadcasting, all communication goes only one way from the broadcaster to the (deemed) user.

The nature of the communication, unidirectional versus bidirectional, makes an important distinction between broadcasting and information society service. It is not only a technicality that information society service is based on direct communication between the provider and a user. Besides the provider knowing about each request and eventually even knowing in detail about the individual behavior of each user (which might have massive economic meaning), it is also significant that an information society service must be dimensioned in order to individually cater to its users. In broadcasting, there is no concern about too many viewers, for example, while too many requests for an information society service leads to a technical denial of that service.

Thus, in broadcasting, the signal is transmitted solely at the will of the provider, while in information society service, the user "travels" with her request to the place of origin. This, then, clearly implies that an information society service that consists of making content available for viewing is both technically and legally provided from the country of origin. This has been the conclusion of the ECJ (CJEU) in similar cases outside the copyright domain, such as sui generis rights[14] and personal data protection.[15]

---

[13] See Case C-607/11 *ITV Broadcasting Ltd, ITV 2 Ltd, ITV Digital Channels Ltd, Channel 4 Television Corporation, 4 Ventures Ltd, Channel 5 Broadcasting Ltd, ITV Studios Ltd v. TVCatchup Ltd.*

[14] See Case C-173/11 *Football Dataco Ltd, Scottish Premier League Ltd, Scottish Football League, PA Sport UK Ltd v. Sportradar GmbH, Sportradar AG*, where the ECJ held that "the mere fact that the website containing the data in question is accessible in a particular national territory is not a sufficient basis for concluding that the operator of the website is performing an act of re-utilization caught by the national law applicable in that territory".

[15] See Case C-101/01 *Bodil Lindqvist*, where the ECJ ruled that "[t]here is no 'transfer [of data] to a third country' (...) where an individual in a Member State loads personal data onto an internet page".

4.6 Concluding Remarks

In this chapter, we focused on territoriality in the online distribution of copyrighted works. We concluded that geoblocking tools have de iure only very limited links to copyrights. We also noted that any criteria other than country of origin are quite problematic, both pragmatically and normatively, for determining the legally applicable and appropriate forum for protecting copyrights on the Internet.

We mostly focused on the EU in our discussion of particular legal issues. However, the problem of territorial aspects of copyright enforcement on the Internet is the same, or even worse, worldwide. When speaking about practices in the EU, where it is legally possible to independently litigate (only for damages, however) in all jurisdictions where an Internet-based publication is available, one should not forget that such a practice may be important for countries outside the EU, as well.

In cases when jurisdictional or other rules are open to interpretation, as in the question of place of damage on the Internet, copyright enforcement is often factually dependent on reciprocity. Courts often look at interpretive practices in other jurisdictions and apply analogous principles. If courts in the EU allow claims for damages against a provider in one Member State to be placed independently and simultaneously in all jurisdictions within the EU, it is quite likely that such a provider will be similarly treated offshore—which means being potentially targeted for litigation in 150+ more or less exotic jurisdictions.

In any case, both the issues of geoblocking and the jurisdictional criteria of copyright infringement are only symptoms of two diseases that are much more general and much more important for the future of the information society. The first relates to the issue of the territoriality of law on the Internet as such. While territory was crucial when the Westphalian concept of sovereignty was established, it is of less or even no importance when it now comes to various online societal relations and business transactions. Retaining normative links between the territory of states and the applicability of law when such links have no societal, economic or other actual raison d'être, is at least highly inefficient.

The second general disease, whose symptoms we briefly discussed, relates to the fundamental teleology of copyrights. Throughout the last half century, the function of copyrights (or rather of *droit d'auteur*) has transformed from that of an economic incentive for creative productivity into a tool for restricting access to creative and inventive content. While the original purpose of copyrights was to help generate material value from the quality and popularity of creative works, the theory behind more recent copyright laws tends in many respects only to mimic the logic of property rights by attempting to generate value by making creative works (the copyrighted work) scarce. As a result, some areas of creative production, such as music, videogames and software, already depend economically on legal mechanisms that use copyright tools only minimally or even not at all.[16]

---

[16]Typical examples include music streaming services like Spotify, Tidal and Apple Music that use economic models based on a purely contractual quasi-collective administration of profit generated through access subscriptions; gaming platforms such as Steam that instead of particularized statutory

All this means that even if we get the issue of geoblocking and territorial delimitation of jurisdictions in copyright matters in Europe right, the law as such may or may not work well to promote creativity. Fortunately, creative industries are still relatively capable of finding innovative ways to get the business cycle going even without much help from the law. The only question is, how long can this system continue to work and reproduce the existing creative potential in Europe and the US?[17]

References

Aiken, J. H. (1997). The jurisdiction of trademark and copyright infringement on the internet. *Mercer Law Review, 48*, 1331–1350.

Barlow, J. P. (1996). *A declaration of the independence of cyberspace*. Electronic Frontier Foundation. https://www.eff.org/cyberspace-independence. Accessed April 4, 2019.

Beaulac, S. (2004). The Westphalian model in defining international law: Challenging the myth. *Australian Journal of Legal History, 8*(2), 181–213.

de Vattel, E. (1797). *The law of nations: Or, principles of the law of nature applied to the conduct and affairs of nations and sovereigns*. London: G. G. and J. Robinson.

Dillenz, W. 1987–1988. What is and to which end do we engage in copyright. *Columbia-VLA Journal of Law & the Arts, 12*(1), 1–30.

Duff, P. W. (1938). *Personality in Roman private law*. Cambridge: Cambridge University Press.

Earle, S. (2016). The battle against geo-blocking: The consumer strikes back. *Richmond Journal of Global Law and Business, 15*(1), 1–20.

Ginsburg, J. C. (2000). Copyright use and excuse on the internet. *Columbia-VLA Journal of Law & the Arts, 24*(1), 1–46.

Glenn, P. (2014). *Legal traditions of the world*. Oxford: Oxford University Press.

Goldsmith, J. L. (1998). Against cyberanarchy. *University of Chicago Law Review, 65*(4), 1199–1250.

Grotius, H. (1901). *The rights of war and peace*. New York: M. Walter Dunne.

Hellner, M. (2004). The country of origin principle in the E-commerce directive—A conflict with conflict of laws? *European Review of Private Law, 12*(2), 193–213.

Hoffman, J. (2016). Crossing borders in the digital market: A proposal to end copyright territoriality and geo-blocking in the European Union. *George Washington International Law Review, 49*(1), 143–173.

Kohler, J. (1917). The new law of nations. *Michigan Law Review, 15*(8), 634–638.

Kra-Oz, T. (2017). Geoblocking and the legality of circumvention. *IDEA: The IP Law Review, 57*(3), 385–430.

Lessig, L. (2004). *Free culture: How big media uses technology and the law to lock down culture and control creativity*. New York: Penguin Press.

Lévy, P. (1998). *Becoming virtual: Reality in the digital age*. New York: Plenum Trade.

---

legal tools (that differ from one jurisdiction to another) rely on uniform proprietary soft law combined with technical measures; or the booming market of SaaS (software as a service) where the legal meaning of "use of software" has been rendered practically irrelevant due to the fact that software is no longer licensed but rather directly provided to users.

[17]This study was supported by the Technology Agency of the Czech Republic project "Research on the Impact of Current Legislation and the European Commission's Strategy for Digital Single Market on Czech Audiovisual Industry: Evaluation of the Copyright System and Preparation of Cultural Politics within the DSM" (No. TL01000306).

Post, D. G. (2002). Against "Against Cyberanarchy." *Berkeley Technology Law Journal, 17*, 1365–1387.

Reindenberg, J. R. (2005). Technology and internet jurisdiction. *University of Pennsylvania Law Review, 153*, 1951–1974.

Rieder, C. M., & Pappas, S. P. (1998). Personal jurisdiction for copyright infringement on the internet. *Santa Clara Law Review, 38*(2), 367–417.

Savola, P. (2017). EU copyright liability for internet linking. *Journal of Intellectual Property, Information Technology and Electronic Commerce Law, 8*(2), 139–150.

Svantesson, D. J. B. (2003). The place of action defence: A model for cross-border internet defamation. *Australian International Law Journal, 2003*, 172–198.

Svantesson, D. J. B. (2015). A jurisprudential justification for extraterritoriality in (private) international law. *Santa Clara Journal of International Law, 13*(1), 517–571.

Svantesson, D. J. B. (2016). Nostradamus light—Selected speculations as to the future of internet jurisdiction. *Masaryk University Journal of Law and Technology, 10*, 47–72.

Svantesson, D. J. B. (2017). *Solving the jurisdictional puzzle*. Oxford: Oxford University Press.

Torremans, P. (2016). Jurisdiction for cross-border intellectual property infringement cases in Europe. *Common Market Law Review, 53*(6), 1625–1645.

Trimble, M. (2015). The multiplicity of copyright laws on the internet. *Fordham Intellectual Property, Media & Entertainment Law Journal, 25*, 339–405.

Trimble, M. (2016). Undetected conflict-of-laws problems in cross-border online copyright infringement cases. *North Carolina Journal of Law & Technology, 18*(1), 119–159.

Trimble, M. (2019). The territorial discrepancy between intellectual property rights infringement claims and remedies. *Lewis & Clark Law Review, 23*(2), 501–552.

Zareh, B. M. (2018). Dr. Strange geo-blocking love. Or: How the E.U. learned to stop worrying about cultural integration and love the TV trade barrier. *Columbia Journal of Law & the Arts, 41*(2), 225–288.

Zemer, L. (2006). What copyright is: Time to remember the basics. *Buffalo Intellectual Property Law Journal, 4*(2), 54–83.

Radim Polčák is the head of the Institute of Law and Technology, the Law Faculty of Masaryk University, Brno, Czech Republic. His research interests include cyberlaw and legal philosophy.

Chapter 5
Geoblocking: At Odds with the EU Single Market and Consumer Expectations

Julia Reda

5.1 Introduction

"This video is not available in your country" is a message that has for many years been a common grievance for Internet users trying to legally access audiovisual content online. This chapter takes a consumer perspective on geoblocking, explaining how this practice is detrimental to the consumer experience, disproportionately affects those consumers who are prepared to pay for copyrighted online content and ultimately constitutes a form of discrimination based on national and language barriers. The article draws from the author's experience as a Member of the European Parliament who has served as her political group's shadow rapporteur on the European Commission's major legislative initiatives to address geoblocking during the legislative period of 2014–2019. The European Parliament's politicians and staff form one of the groups highly affected by geoblocking, since they spend extended time in a European country other than their home country and typically consume media in a number of different languages to follow public debate in different European countries. I draw on my experience as a lawmaker tasked with addressing the issue of geoblocking, as well as my firsthand experience as a particularly privileged consumer of international media as part of the Brussels expatriate community, to describe and analyze the EU response to geoblocking as well as the political controversy around these measures. This unique perspective necessitates a more personal approach than a typical academic article based mainly on the academic literature; this chapter relies mainly on official European Union documents in the context of the policymaking process to address the geoblocking phenomenon.

We begin in Sect. 5.2 with an overview of the general effects of geoblocking on consumers, while the third section explores geoblocking as a form of discrimination, particularly affecting consumers at the periphery, such as linguistic minorities,

J. Reda (✉)
Berkman Klein Center for Internet & Society, Harvard University, 23 Everett Street, Cambridge, MA 02138, USA
e-mail: jreda@cyber.harvard.edu

© The Author(s) 2020
P. Szczepanik et al. (eds.), *Digital Peripheries*, Springer Series in Media Industries,
https://doi.org/10.1007/978-3-030-44850-9_5

residents of small Member States and long-term migrants. Section 5.4 briefly examines possible negative effects of geoblocking on artists, who are often presumed to benefit from the practice. Section 5.5 examines possible economic consequences of unmet consumer demand for non-geoblocked audiovisual offers. Furthermore, Sect. 5.6 puts particular focus on the friction between the practice of geoblocking and the concept of a European Single Market, as well as the nascent European public sphere. Section 5.7 briefly presents three recent legislative attempts at the European Union level to abolish or reduce geoblocking as part of the EU's Digital Single Market strategy. Last but not least, Sect. 5.8 attempts to present a prognosis of future developments in the audiovisual market online in the absence of adequate legislative interventions to abolish geoblocking.

5.2   Geoblocking Locks Out Audiences

From the perspective of a consumer trying to legally access cultural material online, the practice of geoblocking appears as a form of "discrimination of content" based on criteria of location. This means that content is blocked based on the user's actual or presumed geographic location. Geoblocking can be the consequence of explicitly blocking audiences from a particular location, or it can be due to the unavailability of global licenses, where content is only made available to specific audiences in countries or regions where a license has been obtained, while all other regions are blocked by default. However, geoblocking does not refer solely to the "blocking" of copyrighted content, such as audiovisual works, although this form of geoblocking is the primary focus of this article. Geoblocking also refers to acts of refusing to sell a specific product when a consumer makes an order online from a different country, rerouting the users to a Web site different from the one they chose or even offering different products or the same products but with a differentiated price depending on the place of order. To do so, content providers verify the IP address of the users and identify the geographic location of their devices. These acts are particularly harmful to certain marginalized groups of consumers and negatively impact their fundamental rights by failing to respond to the fundamental principles of the European Single Market. In other words, the EU promises freedom of movement within its physical borders, but blocks the free movement of services online by allowing digital borders to persist.

The EU promises freedom of expression and access to information for its citizens and residents. However, geoblocking undermines these rights by enforcing geographic boundaries on the free flow of information, especially in the form of cultural and educational material. Geoblocking practices will continue to exist as long as laws, but also business models that incentivize geoblocking fail to modernize. Instances of such sectors and services are online providers of goods and services most notably in the retail, tourism and leisure services sectors (European Commission 2016b), but also broadcasting and streaming services, such as TV and radio programs, broadcasting of sports events, and the video games (European Commission 2019), music and film sectors. This article focuses on geoblocking in the audiovisual sector, but will also briefly describe policy initiatives to address geoblocking in other sectors.

As a result of geoblocking, citizens traveling, working or studying within Europe cannot access content that they could access from their home countries, or they find themselves permanently on the wrong side of a national border and are thereby deprived of access to cultural, educational or other content that is available in other parts of the EU. While recent EU initiatives to address geoblocking have promised to solve this issue at least with regard to temporary travelers trying to access content from their country of residence, as described in Sect. 5.7 below, enforcement of these rules is still far from complete. As a result, consumers are less likely to get to know new content originating from a different Member State, as it may not be financially attractive to the service providers to purchase geographic licenses for content that is not (yet) popular in a given region. This illustrates that there is not always an economic interest in restricting access to content in order to provide exclusivity: Geoblocking can also apply to older, economically less relevant content such as historical TV shows or outdated news programs. This surprising phenomenon could often be observed by Brussels-based expatriates trying to catch up on online free-to-air TV news programs from their home country, which they may find subjected to geoblocking or removed from the Internet entirely after a certain period of time, despite the questionable economical need to protect the investment in past news programs. Cultural programs with limited geographic significance would also be subjected to geoblocking. Occasionally, outraged consumers would air their frustration on social media, sharing screenshots of blocked news programs (e.g., see Twitter 2019a, b). European film productions are also particularly affected: 63% of European films are only released on video on demand (VOD) in a single national market, neglecting the cross-border demand for cultural works and limiting the potential commercial success of European films (Grece 2016). In the absence of global licenses, geoblocking of audiovisual content in particular is the norm rather than the exception and it requires conscious effort and financial resources by service providers to make audiovisual material available globally, which is rarely in the business interest of such providers.

Some consumers react to the geoblocking of content that they feel they have the right to access by using alternative methods to gain access to content, such as the purchase of a VPN service that changes their IP address to one that is associated with a different geographic location or illegal methods. The strategies of EU policymakers and administrators for circumventing geoblocking, most of whom had moved to Brussels from another EU country, were often a topic of discussion at the fringes of shadow meetings or trilogue negotiations on the very legislative proposals intended to address geoblocking in the EU. The use of VPN services as a means of circumventing geoblocking, particularly popular among Brussels expats, has even led some media companies to voice demands during closed-door lobby meetings that policymakers outlaw or technologically restrict the use of VPNs, which is worrying from a cybersecurity perspective, as VPN services are an essential element of IT security strategies, facilitating for example the secure connection to company or government intranets for traveling employees. In policy discussions, the use of

VPNs is often conflated with illegal means of accessing content online, although VPNs are perfectly legal and consumers who use VPNs still have to pay for access to the subscription services they access via VPN, in addition to eventual charges for the VPN service as well.

Last but not least, consumers confronted with geoblocking may avoid conducting cross-border purchases or other transactions altogether and may show lack of trust in small and medium-sized enterprises based in other European countries as a consequence of the large number of unsuccessful purchase attempts due to geoblocking. A mystery shopping survey conducted by the European Commission in 2015 aimed at quantifying the problem found that "only 37% of Web sites actually allowed cross-border EU visitors to reach the stage of successfully entering payment card details, i.e., the final step before completing the purchase" (European Commission 2016b). When considering what consequences this frequent frustration may have on consumer behavior, it is likely that consumers would prefer larger platforms with a uniform presence in most European countries that have managed to concentrate the necessary human and economic resources to offer a solution closer to their demands. Geoblocking thus not only contributes to locking in audiences to geographically segmented programs, but may drive consumers toward a smaller number of multinational service providers.

5.3   Geoblocking Is Discrimination

It is self-evident that geoblocking constitutes a form of discrimination of content, differentiating the offer based on geographic boundaries. Proponents of geoblocking may argue that the practice is not discriminatory, as it is not strictly based on nationality, but on temporary geographic location, which the consumer can influence. This view does not take into account the very real financial, educational and cultural restrictions on freedom of movement within the EU. New policy interventions like the Portability Regulation particularly help affluent consumers who can afford to travel frequently between EU countries, all the while ignoring that geoblocking frequently results in discrimination against marginalized groups of consumers, whose cultural consumption needs are different from those of the general population. It is hardly a solution for members of a linguistic minority to give up their cultural traditions and move to another country where their language is the majority language, simply to be able to access cultural content in their mother tongue online. Nor is it helpful to tell low-income migrants that limiting their access to news programs from their home country is not discrimination, because they can always travel back. Discrimination based on geographic location, while not identical with discrimination based on nationality in the sense that geographic location can more easily change over time, disproportionately affects those parts of the population that are less mobile, less affluent and culturally marginalized because they speak a language that is not the majority language in their country of residence. Consumer groups particularly negatively affected by geographic discrimination in the form of geoblocking include travelers, exchange students and commuters, who may temporarily lose access to the content they are used to, as well as linguistic minorities, language learners or long-term migrants, who find themselves permanently on the wrong side of a national border separating them from the majority of consumers wishing to access content in a particular language. Furthermore, professionals who regularly rely on accessing a broad range of cultural, educational and news material from different countries, such as academics or journalists, are also disproportionately affected by geoblocking. Generally speaking, geoblocking most strongly affects consumers who have a particular interest in cultural, social, political or other content most frequently consumed in another country, an interest that the EU has long been trying to cultivate through exchange programs and attempts to foster the development of a European public sphere. News and other relevant information about another European country may also to a large degree be hidden from interested parties. Reducing geographic discrimination in the form of geoblocking should therefore be high on the EU policy agenda.

Despite the fact that geographic discrimination is strictly prohibited in the EU, reports by consumer associations (Reyna and Silva 2017), occasional court cases[1] as well as the European Commission's own investigations into the subject (European Commission 2016a) show that geographic discrimination in the form of geoblocking continues to be a significant problem in the EU. More specifically, consumers have long been "geoblocked" due to their nationality, place of residence, place of establishment or, more generally, the location from which they access content online.

Finally, geoblocking reproduces existing inequalities between large EU economies and smaller countries at the periphery. Due to economic inefficiencies caused by geoblocking, the online streaming market favors large multinational streaming companies, as is explained in Sect. 5.5 below. Those multinationals have less incentive to invest in licenses for globally successful audiovisual content that cover small European countries, as the smaller number of potential customers makes it more difficult to recoup the investment. For instance, bias in favor of consumers in large, economically significant countries can be demonstrated on Netflix, where the country-by-country repertoire of films varies substantially (Kidman 2016). While the German Netflix library is 28% the size of the US library, this number is 18% for Slovakia and 15% for Estonia, respectively. As cultural proximity and shared language seem to be the main drivers of cross-border availability on Netflix (Batikas et al. 2015), this also means that countries with less common languages are at a disadvantage. To illustrate this phenomenon, Slovak Netflix users were recently successful in gaining access to a much wider range of regionally suitable content by petitioning Netflix to make the much larger catalogue of Czech language dubbing and subtitles available to Slovak users, as the two languages are very similar and mutually understandable (Kafkadesk 2019). The fact that consumers had to organize and petition Netflix to enact this change also illustrates the limits of multinationals' ability and willingness to study the needs of smaller, peripheral language communities.

---

[1] See Joined Cases C-403/08 and C-429/08, *Football Association Premier League Ltd and Others v QC Leisure and Others*.

Language minorities find themselves in a particularly difficult situation when they try to access online content in their native language: National language minorities may speak a language the majority of whose speakers live in another country. One example is the island of Åland, a Swedish-speaking language community in the Baltic Sea that belongs to Finland. Such linguistic minorities often find themselves geoblocked from TV or radio content online that they have no trouble accessing via traditional broadcasting. Many language minorities speak a language that is not the majority language in any country, a situation which makes language discrimination through geoblocking particularly rampant when members of that language community travel abroad or permanently move to another country. One example is the availability of Scottish Gaelic television (Hicks 2016). Under the BBC rights system, it is problematic to rebroadcast programs outside of the UK. This results in a situation where Gaelic speakers, members of the language community and language learners are not able to access such programs if they are outside the UK. It is obvious that this form of geoblocking does not protect an investment by the BBC, as the economic value of streaming rights for minority language programs outside the country in which that linguistic minority is primarily located can be expected to be very low. Yet native speakers and learners of minority languages face discrimination as a form of collateral damage caused by rights management systems that are designed to protect the economic investments in globally successful, often English language programs. As many minority or small national languages are threatened by extinction, the unavailability of cultural content in those languages in most of the world is an additional contributing factor to the shrinking of those language communities that goes against the EU's goal of cultural diversity.

Some progress has recently been made in the passing of legislation aimed at addressing the demand for cross-border accessibility of content by the—overall more privileged—consumer groups of professional travelers, tourists, commuters and exchange students. The Portability Regulation, which will be presented in Sect. 5.7 below, is designed to extend the accessibility of content for consumers who have their principal place of establishment in the "right" country, while traveling temporarily abroad within the EU. Remarkably, this legislative intervention does nothing to address the concerns of those often less privileged groups of European consumers who find themselves permanently on the wrong side of the border, such as long-term migrants or language learners who lack the financial resources to travel in order to further their education. Geoblocking thus contributes to social inequality in the EU, and the policy initiatives to counter it are criticized that they may do more to make the problem invisible to the political elites such as Members of the European Parliament and other Brussels officials, who can often afford to maintain a place of residence in their home country, than to actually end the practice of geoblocking to the benefit of all Europeans, including those who cannot afford to travel.

All in all, geoblocking is causing and strengthening discrimination in the EU. The differentiated treatment of consumers based on their nationality or place of residence, place of establishment, native language or other factors is increasingly acknowledged by the European institutions, and an effort was made to tackle the issue during the European legislative period of 2009–2014. As Sect. 5.7 will explore in greater detail, these efforts have largely excluded the most relevant area of audiovisual cultural content and have been more focused on cross-border e-commerce. However, discrimination is not only a question of the cross-border availability of goods and the feasibility of cross-border payments, but also a question of equal and fair access to cultural and educational content from anywhere in the EU.

5.4 Geoblocking Locks in Creators

Advocates of geoblocking may claim that practices that lead to geoblocking serve the interests of rightsholders. Rightsholders' organizations in the audiovisual sector (with the notable exception of some public service broadcasters) have consistently responded negatively to European Commission initiatives to abolish or reduce geoblocking, including legislation to improve portability, arguing that market-led solutions are sufficient to meet consumer demand, and where cross-border audiovisual services are not available, this is due to lack of consumer demand. Film producers in particular held that territorial restrictions were beneficial to their business model, improving the possibility to secure financing for future productions through exclusive contracts with different regional distributors, as evidenced by the stakeholder consultation conducted by the European Commission in preparation for the portability proposal (European Commission 2015a).

However, a more thorough look into the dynamics of cultural production calls that claim into question. Geoblocking has two directions. The first is, as previously explored, the blocking, or in any other way hindering, of access to content. The second is the blocking, or in any other way hindering, of dissemination of such content. The former affects the potential consumers of cultural content, while the latter affects artists, creators, rightsholders and service providers. In fact, geoblocking is rarely in the interest of all parties on the supply side of content. For example, in response to a public questionnaire conducted by the European Commission, of the 68% of providers who geoblocked users located in other EU Member States, 59% reported that they were doing so based on a contractual obligation, for example based on licensing restrictions imposed by the rightsholder (European Commission 2016c).

One of the differences between the analog and digital environments is that the latter offers faster, easier and wider access to content. This is also one of the most significant advantages of the Internet for creators, not just for consumers. Nowadays, people have a tool which allows them to access information from anywhere at an instant. At the same time, they have the ability to express themselves and disseminate their own content, whether this is a product, service or free content, more widely than ever before and without having to rely on intermediaries. That being said, it is evident that geoblocking is largely affecting the visibility of content, which ultimately affects original creators and the business of online enterprises.

When content is blocked, the providers of content, products or services are deprived of a wider audience and lose on visibility, "visitibility" and ultimately revenue. Fewer consumers become aware of their work or products and services, while those who are aware and who would like to make a purchase are blocked. Geoblocking may lead consumers to look for illegal sources of online content (Australian Government Productivity Commission 2016), which do not generate revenue streams for the rightsholders or original creators at all, or divert parts of the consumers' budgets for cultural content to third parties, such as the providers of VPN services, also leading to less money available for paying creators. Based on the assumption that consumers have a limited budget for cultural content, the incurring of additional costs such as paying for VPN services, in order to be able to access legal cultural content of their choice, is likely to reduce the budget available to spend on streaming subscriptions or downloads of cultural content as such, which is supposed to financially benefit the creators of the cultural content in question. Especially considering the advertising market online, where platforms earn more with every "click," it is evident that the blocking of access directly affects their economic well-being.

However, the above logic is not the same for large platforms that tend to monopolize the digital market. These platforms have the necessary economic and human resources to respond to contemporary practices and obsolete laws. As they earn more and more market share, not being represented on these platforms becomes more and more costly for artists, creators and other rightsholders, since this is where consumers will likely discover new content. By becoming dependent on large online platforms, creators cede some of the independence that the Internet has promised them to the gatekeepers. Therefore, similar to the position of large retailers of physical goods that have dominated the analog world of commerce, dominant digital platforms such as Amazon and Netflix concentrate market resources and end up being the sole sources for access to digital goods and services.

In contrast to the film sector, where the platform either produces the content itself or has purchased a geographically limited license that is often exclusive in nature, the music sector relies more heavily on the global licensing of repertoire, which seems to be more closely aligned to user expectations (European Commission 2015a). Since exclusive licenses are less common in the music sector, it follows that there is a better possibility for more streaming services to offer the same music catalogues. Nevertheless, fringe artists that are not associated with a traditional music label may have difficulty being included in the repertoire of those streaming platforms and therefore find it difficult to gain visibility with their potential audiences (Farrand 2014). This problem may be exacerbated by a crackdown on user-generated music platforms such as SoundCloud or Bandcamp, which are increasingly forced into a licensing-based business model and negotiations with traditional collecting societies through recent changes in liability rules for copyrighted content uploaded by users (Reda 2019). While geoblocking may continue to be a lesser concern for independent music creators, they may still face greater restrictions on dissemination of their material online through consolidation of the online platform economy.

5.5 Geoblocking Harms the Economy

Contrary to claims made by representatives of certain media companies in the European policy debate (European Commission 2015a), abolishing geoblocking does not mean harming rightsholders. In many respects, geoblocking is harmful to the economy at large and constitutes a market consolidation practice employed by already large players in the market to the detriment of smaller players. Additionally, the issue of geoblocking is largely unrelated to controversies around the fair remuneration of original creators, who, as discussed above, do not necessarily benefit from geoblocking.

The potential economic impact of geoblocking can be estimated by examining a number of different indicators, such as the figures regarding the total European consumer spending on paid subscriptions to online content services. Technological development and the spread of portable devices have improved access to online content services. The purchase or rental of films and TV series delivered over the open Internet or on a subscription basis keeps growing every year (International Video Federation 2017). The total spending on digital video in 2017 was €5.7083 billion, a 32% increase compared to the previous year (ibid.).

Another important indicator is the potential demand for cross-border services. Free movement of people in the internal market, availability of portable devices, increasing broadband speed and decreasing roaming charges have contributed to the increased demand for the cross-border availability of online content services. As a result, according to recent estimates, up to €1.6 billion worth of cross-border demand is kept from EU VOD platforms, EU start-ups and artists (Plum Consulting 2012). Willingness to pay for content by frequent travelers was estimated to be around €90 million annually (ibid.).

The European Parliament's own research service also concluded that many millions of Euros in sales are lost annually due to this unmet demand. The amount that consumers are willing to spend is estimated at a lower bound of €189 million and an upper bound of €945 million per annum (European Parliament 2017a).

Increasingly, some of the biggest traditional media companies are acknowledging the growing demand for subscription-based services and launching their own streaming services (Anderton 2019). Due to their economic resources and the size of their license portfolios, they can provide European consumers with interesting offers; however, their repertoire remains limited compared to US catalogues. The most attractive audiovisual streaming services in the European market combine internationally successful US content with European productions. The multinational streaming platforms of US technology companies, although they do not allow access to the entirety of content available, are often in the best position to offer a diversity of content by combining the purchase of licenses for third-party content with an increasing number of their own productions, TV shows and even feature-length films that are entirely financed, produced and distributed by the streaming service provider itself. Increasingly, these in-house productions include big-budget European TV series, partially to increase the attractiveness of their services in the most important EU markets such as Germany, Spain and France, but also to address regulatory demands for European content in the repertoires of streaming services.[2]

In the case of their own productions, the streaming service provider holds the worldwide rights to the online exploitation of the content, enabling it to offer the same content on its service worldwide without any geoblocking imposed by third-party rightsholders. The most well-known examples of such streaming service providers in the audiovisual sector are Netflix and Amazon Prime. Both companies were able to grow their business in the USA with a large single market available to them and later branched out into global audiovisual streaming only after they had already built considerable revenue streams in the USA. Their substantial financial means put them in a position to gradually buy up geographic licenses for popular audiovisual content in different EU countries, rolling out their services country by country over a number of years. Eventually, their profit margins allowed them to build up their own production capacities, with in-house productions making up an ever-increasing share of their streaming catalogues and functioning as a means of differentiating their offer by providing their own productions exclusively.

In-house productions have become an attractive business model for established streaming companies not least as a reaction to a regulatory environment that may have been intended to prop up traditional European media companies. The proposed ban on geoblocking, initially championed by European Commission Vice-President for the Digital Single Market Andrus Ansip (Reda 2015), has largely failed to materialize due to opposition from the European cultural sector, as shall be explored in the next section. Similarly, a policy to increase obligations for investment in European productions was also championed by European TV, film and cinema companies (European Commission 2015b) during the review of the Audiovisual Media Services Directive. For technology companies with successful streaming services, both legislative developments have increased the attractiveness of investing in their own productions, thereby becoming competitors against the very media companies lobbying to maintain geoblocking. Consequently, a small number of large enterprises with origins in the technology sector rather than the cultural sector have started a trend toward "oligopolizing" the audiovisual streaming market, which could end up having detrimental effects on the established European media production companies as well as on consumers, who may once again see themselves confronted with a lack of choice between streaming services offering a wide repertoire.

It would be difficult to imagine a European streaming start-up growing to the scale of Netflix or Amazon Prime, considering that such a company would not have a single market of hundreds of millions of potential customers to rely on, despite the EU's ambitions to build a Digital Single Market. Rather, such a company would have to start out in a relatively small national market and could not grow without making an early investment by the purchase of additional national streaming licenses, which would enable it to offer services across national borders within the EU. Without a

---

[2]The recent legislative overhaul of the Audiovisual Media Services Directive requires on-demand audiovisual services to devote 30% of their repertoires to European productions, as well as contributing to the financing and visibility of European works (European Union 2018b).

change in legislation and licensing practices, EU-based market entrants are unlikely to be able to compete with the likes of Netflix or Amazon, and further consolidation of the streaming market seems likely.

This threat of further consolidation of the streaming market must be viewed against the backdrop of mounting concerns about competition related to geoblocking. There is ample evidence that geographic discrimination may violate competition law. One of the earliest cases pointing in this direction is European Court of Justice case C-403/08—*Football Association Premier League and Others*, which found that: "The clauses of an exclusive licence agreement concluded between a holder of intellectual property rights and a broadcaster constitute a restriction on competition prohibited by Article 101 TFEU where they oblige the broadcaster not to supply decoding devices enabling access to that rightsholder's protected subject-matter with a view to their use outside the territory covered by that licence agreement."[3] The European Commission subsequently launched a sector inquiry into geoblocking in the e-commerce sector between 2015 and 2017 (European Commission 2017a), and opened several investigations into specific geoblocking practices, including the question of online content in the video games sector (European Commission 2017b). It is notable that despite these concerns about a fundamental lack of compatibility of geoblocking with EU market principles, legislative action to ban geoblocking has remained rather timid. The interaction of geoblocking with EU principles and the most recent legislative reactions will be the subject of the two following sections.

5.6 Geoblocking Betrays EU Principles

On a global level, the Universal Declaration of Human Rights (United Nations 1948) states in Article 19 that "everyone has the right to freedom of opinion and expression." Similarly, Article 11 of the Charter of Fundamental Rights of the European Union (European Union 2000), hereafter Charter, states that "everyone has the right to freedom of expression. This right shall include freedom to hold opinions and to receive and impart information and ideas without interference by public authority and regardless of frontiers." It is therefore enshrined in the core principles of the European Union that its citizens enjoy freedom of speech, but also freedom to access information, without any hindrance by any physical or digital borders.

Furthermore, Article 21 of the Charter prohibits any acts of discrimination, whether based on race, language, religion or other beliefs and opinions, while Article 22 more specifically states that "the Union shall respect cultural, religious and linguistic diversity." Last but not least, Article 38 of the Charter requires the European Union to "ensure a high level of consumer protection."

In accordance with the above, the European Commission has identified as its core principles for the single market in the EU the four freedoms—namely the freedom

---

[3] See Joined Cases C-403/08 and C-429/08. *Football Association Premier League Ltd and Others v QC Leisure and Others*, paragraph 5.

of movement of goods, capital, services and labor. The same applies—or should apply—for the Digital Single Market of the EU. In other words, access to digital goods and services should be enhanced under the principles of proportionality and equality, taking into account the fundamental freedoms of EU citizens. Remarkably, the European institutions have recently started promoting the free flow of data as a "fifth freedom" (European Parliament 2018), calling into question why cultural content online should be an exception to this principle.

Also, the Council has adopted the EU Human Rights Guidelines on Freedom of Expression Online and Offline (Council of the European Union 2014), which advocates among other things to promote and respect human rights, including freedom of expression, in cyberspace and in the use of other information and communication technologies.

The European institutions have long been aware of barriers to the free flow of information caused by copyright law, an area of law that remains fragmented and outdated, failing to respond to the demands of the digital era. For this reason, the European Commission pursued the modernization of the law in line with the Digital Single Market via a series of legislative proposals, which lightly touched upon the issues of copyright reform in particular and geoblocking more generally, but eventually brought no sustainable solutions for consumers. These initiatives shall be examined in the next section.

5.7 European Commission Initiatives to Abolish Geoblocking, 2014–2019

During the period of 2014–2019, the European Commission launched several initiatives that had the goal of addressing the issue of geoblocking. However, these proposals, already lacking ambition from the start, were substantially watered down during the legislative process due to lobbying, particularly from the entertainment industry (Society of Audiovisual Authors 2018; Association of Commercial Television in Europe et al. 2017).

In 2015, the European Commission presented the proposal for a regulation on ensuring the cross-border portability of online content services in the internal market (European Commission 2015c). The proposal aimed at ensuring that consumers subscribed to portable online services in their Member State of residence would also be able to use these services when temporarily present in another EU Member State. The proposal, however, was an unambitious attempt to address geographic limitations. It was limited to a restricted amount of time (temporarily), to those services that were already available in the consumers' Member State of residence, and subjected to verification of residence by the service provider. However, those citizens who never had legal access to certain content in their own Member State in the first place were largely ignored. The European Parliament and Council approved the Portability Regulation without substantial amendments, although they did clarify that the new legal mechanism does not prevent a service provider from enabling the subscriber to additionally access and use the content lawfully offered by the provider in the Member State where the subscriber is temporarily present. The co-legislators maintained a relatively onerous system of verification of a user's country of residence, which appears disproportionate considering that the most negative outcome of a consumer "cheating" by falsifying his or her country of residence is that he or she would be able to pay to subscribe to a legal online content offer that was not intended for their geographic location.

Certain statements by commission representatives[4] substantiate the suspicion that the Portability Regulation may have done more to assuage the concerns of European Union officials working temporarily abroad in Brussels about still being able to access the content they were used to from back home, than to take steps toward abolishing geoblocking more generally. While constituting a significant step forward for the relatively privileged minority of Europeans who spend a substantial amount of time in a European country other than their country of residence, the regulation's benefits are limited to that group and do not extend to the European population at large. Furthermore, as a survey by the German consumer organization in the state of Rhineland-Palatinate illustrated, by the end of 2018, several months after the entry into force of the Portability Regulation, half of the surveyed consumers who had used paid streaming services abroad still faced problems in practice when trying to access content under the Portability Regulation.[5] By addressing the most pressing concerns of Brussels-based expats in charge of shaping European legislation, the Portability Regulation may have lessened EU lawmakers' appetite for more far-reaching reforms to abolish geoblocking altogether rather than bringing tangible improvement.

The Portability Regulation was followed in 2016 by the proposal for a regulation on addressing geoblocking and other forms of discrimination based on customers' nationality, place of residence or place of establishment within the internal market (European Commission 2016d). This was meant to address situations when service providers put in place a technological restriction or otherwise make it impossible for consumers in one Member State to access their Web site or application, or apply different conditions for the purchasing of goods or services. According to the original plans of the commission, this would have covered digital content services, such as streaming services, music, computer games, software and e-books, at least where the geoblocking was not the consequence of licensing restrictions under copyright law (Plucinska 2016; TorrentFreak 2016). However, due to a political compromise made internally in the commission cabinet (undoubtedly following interventions by the entertainment industry), this part disappeared from the version of the proposal that was officially released. Following its own assessment of the problem (European

---

[4]"The reform is a hobbyhorse of Commission Vice-President for the Digital Single Market Andrus Ansip, an Estonian unhappy that he is unable to stream Estonian football matches when away from his home country" (Sayer 2015).

[5]Survey conducted by the consumer protection authority of the German state of Rhineland-Palatinate of 2590 consumers of paid streaming services based on an online representative sample, 500 of which reported having used those streaming services in EU countries other than their country of residency since entry into force of the portability regulation in April 2018 (Marktwächter 2018).

Parliament 2016), the European Parliament attempted to reintroduce such services into the scope of the regulation (European Parliament 2017b), but eventually gave up its ambition to tackle the geoblocking of copyrighted content during trilogue negotiations among the three European Institutions (European Union 2018a). The final regulation merely contains a review clause which states that the first evaluation carried out by the European Commission shall examine the scope of the regulation and in particular whether the prohibition clause introduced in the regulation should be extended to cover copyrighted content (ibid.). Finally, the commission also issued a statement to affirm its commitment to the review.

In an effort to modernize and harmonize EU copyright law and increase the availability of EU broadcasting content online, the European Commission announced a plan to review the Satellite and Cable Directive, which resulted in the proposal for a new regulation to apply the country of origin principle to the online offers of broadcasters, just as it is to satellite broadcasts (European Commission 2016e). Despite the evaluation (European Commission 2016f), study (European Commission 2016g) and public consultation[6] that were conducted for that purpose, the European Parliament met the proposal with hostility. In November 2018, the European Parliament adopted its report, which significantly watered down the original proposal by limiting it to news and current affairs programs. A compromise was eventually found in trilogue negotiations, which applies the country of origin principle to broadcasters' ancillary online services, which are radio or TV programs that are news and current affairs programs or their own fully financed productions. At the same time, the report clearly excludes other types of content, such as audiovisual sports content (European Union 2019).

In summary, the legislative proposals adopted by the European institutions in the legislative period of 2009–2014 lacked the ambition to abolish geoblocking in the EU and complete the Digital Single Market. In one instance, the European Commission and the Council of Ministers opposed a more ambitious approach by blocking the inclusion of licensed copyrighted content in the geoblocking regulation; in another, the European Parliament echoed the entertainment industry's opposition to extending the country of origin principle to all broadcasters' online services, in analogy to the EU satellite broadcasting rules. As a consequence, consumers affected by geoblocking may find a wider variety of legal content on legacy technologies such as satellite broadcasting than they can find online.

5.8   Conclusions—Solutions

As this chapter has demonstrated, geoblocking remains a problem of the digital era, perpetuated by a persistent failure of laws and commercial practices to modernize and respond to the demands of the digital environment. The European Union's attempts

---

[6]For a summary of the responses, see European Commission (2016f) Annex 2C—Synopsis report on the responses to the public consultation on the review of the satellite and cable directive.

to ban geoblocking have failed to meet consumer expectations thus far, though review clauses and continuing attention paid to the issue by the EU's competition authorities may still bear fruit in the coming years. The realization that geoblocking undermines the European Union's principles of the single market, freedom of information and cultural diversity is a first step toward addressing the problem more effectively. Both lawmakers and the commercial actors should boost cross-border access to content and consider and accommodate the needs of contemporary and future consumers in a true Digital Single Market.

As regards future legislative solutions, the EU institutions should support laws that respond to consumer demand for cross-border access to content and stand firm against the lobbying efforts of the legacy entertainment industry. In other words, laws should promote competition among a wide variety of market players, in line with the principle of non-discrimination and the fundamental rights of Europeans, both at the center and at the periphery. Access to European cultural diversity must no longer be dependent on belonging to a majority linguistic group and having the means to travel frequently. Online goods and service providers should be obliged to offer the same goods and services across the EU and should refrain from any "geodiscrimination."

However, their work should not finish there. The abolishment of geoblocking should follow not only the legal route via the adoption of new laws or the amendment of old ones. The EU institutions should require ongoing informed and regular impact assessments, in order to recognize contemporary issues and find ways to solve them, without harming the consumer or the economy. Also, consumers should have the necessary tools to identify and report unfair practices easily and swiftly.

Only the abolishment of geoblocking practices promises an attractive alternative to illegal access to cultural content by giving consumers the possibility to pay for the works they want to see. If the legislature fails to respond, consumer preferences will further gravitate toward the increasing number of in-house productions presented by a very small number of multinational technology companies, thereby undermining the sustainability of the very European entertainment companies that have been lobbying against the abolishment of geoblocking. By the time these companies realize that lobbying-induced legislative apathy does not protect a legacy business model from going with the times and satisfying consumer demand for real-time access to content, it may be too late for them to change their business model and break the emerging duopoly of online streaming services that threatens European cultural diversity and the fundamental rights of European consumers.

References

Anderton, E. (2019). NBCUniversal planning a streaming subscription service, may take back 'The Office' from Netflix. *Slashfilm*, January 15. https://www.slashfilm.com/nbcuniversal-streaming-service. Accessed August 11, 2019.

Association of Commercial Television in Europe, et al. (2017). Comments on geo-blocking trialogue negotiations. https://www.europa-distribution.org/assets/Comments-from-av-stakeholders-on-geo-blocking-re-Presidency-compromise-proposal_FINAL.pdf. Accessed May, 28 2019.

Australian Government Productivity Commission. (2016). Inquiry Report No. 78: Intellectual property arrangements. https://www.pc.gov.au/inquiries/completed/intellectual-property/report. Accessed August 11, 2019.

Batikas, M., Gomez-Herrera, E., & Martens, B. (2015). Film availability in Netflix country stores in the EU: Institute for prospective technological studies digital economy working paper 2015/11. European Commission Joint Research Centre (JRC) Technical Reports. https://ec.europa.eu/jrc/sites/jrcsh/files/JRC98020.pdf. Accessed May 28, 2019.

Council of the European Union. (2014). EU human rights guidelines on freedom of expression online and offline. Foreign Affairs Council meeting Brussels, 12 May 2014. https://eeas.europa.eu/sites/eeas/files/eu_human_rights_guidelines_on_freedom_of_expression_online_and_offline_en.pdf. Accessed August 11, 2019.

European Commission. (2015a). Impact assessment accompanying the document "Proposal for a regulation of the European Parliament and of the council to ensure the cross-border portability of online content services in the internal market. (COM(2015) 627 final). Commission Staff Working Document. https://ec.europa.eu/transparency/regdoc/rep/10102/2015/EN/SWD-2015-270-F1-EN-MAIN-PART-1.PDF. Accessed August 11, 2019.

European Commission. (2015b). Synopsis report of the public consultation on Directive 2010/13/EU on Audiovisual Media Services (AVMSD): A media framework for the 21st century, 6 July–30 September 2015. https://ec.europa.eu/digital-single-market/en/news/report-public-consultation-review-audiovisual-media-services-directive-avmsd. Accessed August 11, 2019.

European Commission. (2015c). Proposal for a regulation of the European Parliament and of the council on ensuring the cross-BORDER portability of online content services in the internal market. COM(2015) 627 final. https://eur-lex.europa.eu/legal-content/EN/TXT/?uri=COM%3A2015%3A0627%3AFIN. Accessed August 11, 2019.

European Commission. (2016a). Mystery shopping survey on territorial restrictions and geoblocking in the European digital single market: Final report. https://ec.europa.eu/info/sites/info/files/geoblocking-final-report_en.pdf. Accessed August 11, 2019.

European Commission. (2016b). Impact assessment accompanying the document "Proposal for a regulation of the European Parliament and of the council on addressing geo-blocking and other forms of discrimination based on place of residence or establishment or nationality within the single market. (COM(2016) 289 final) (SWD(2016) 174 final). Commission Staff Working Document. https://ec.europa.eu/digital-single-market/en/news/impact-assessment-accompanying-proposed-regulation-geo-blocking. Accessed August 11, 2019.

European Commission. (2016c). Commission publishes initial findings on geo-blocking from e-commerce sector inquiry—Factsheet. Press release: Antitrust. https://europa.eu/rapid/press-release_MEMO-16-882_en.htm. Accessed May 28, 2019.

European Commission. (2016d). Proposal for a regulation of the European Parliament and of the council on addressing geo-blocking and other forms of discrimination based on customers' nationality, place of residence or place of establishment within the internal market and amending Regulation (EC) No. 2006/2004 and Directive 2009/22/EC. COM(2016) 289 final. https://eur-lex.europa.eu/legal-content/EN/TXT/?uri=COM:2016:0289:FIN. Accessed August 11, 2019.

European Commission. (2016e). Proposal for a regulation of the European Parliament and of the council laying down rules on the exercise of copyright and related rights applicable to certain online transmissions of broadcasting organisations and retransmissions of television and radio programmes. COM/2016/0594 final—2016/0284 (COD). https://eur-lex.europa.eu/legal-content/EN/TXT/?uri=CELEX%3A52016PC0594. Accessed May 28, 2019.

European Commission. (2016f). Impact assessment on the modernisation of EU copyright rules accompanying the document "Proposal for a directive of the European Parliament and of the council on copyright in the digital single market" and "Proposal for a regulation of the European Parliament and of the council laying down Rules on the exercise of copyright and related rights applicable to certain online transmissions of broadcasting organisations and retransmissions of television and radio programmes". (COM(2016) 593) (COM(2016) 594) (SWD(2016) 302). Commission Staff Working Document. https://ec.europa.eu/digital-single-market/en/news/proposal-regulation-laying-down-rules-exercise-copyright-and-related-rights-applicable-certain. Accessed August 11, 2019.

European Commission. (2016g). Survey and data gathering to support the evaluation of the satellite and Cable Directive 93/83/EEC and assessment of its possible extension. The Centre for Strategy & Evaluation Services LLP and Ecorys UK. https://ec.europa.eu/newsroom/dae/document.cfm?doc_id=17713. Accessed August 11, 2019.

European Commission. (2017a). Antitrust: Sector inquiry into e-commerce. https://ec.europa.eu/competition/antitrust/sector_inquiries_e_commerce.html. Accessed May 28, 2019.

European Commission. (2017b). Commission opens three investigations into suspected anticompetitive practices in e-commerce. Press release: Antitrust. https://europa.eu/rapid/press-release_IP-17-201_en.htm. Accessed May 28, 2019.

European Commission. (2019). Commission sends statements of objections to valve and five videogame publishers on "geo-blocking" of PC video games. Press release: Antitrust. https://europa.eu/rapid/press-release_IP-19-2010_en.htm. Accessed May28 May 2019.

European Parliament. (2016). Combating consumer discrimination in the digital single market: Preventing geo-blocking and other forms of geo-discrimination. Directorate General for Internal Policies, Policy Department A: Economic and Scientific Policy. https://www.europarl.europa.eu/RegData/etudes/STUD/2016/587315/IPOL_STU(2016)587315_EN.pdf. Accessed May 28, 2019.

European Parliament. (2017a). Extending the Scope of the geo-blocking prohibition: An economic assessment. Directorate General for Internal Policies, Policy Department A: Economic and Scientific Policy. https://www.europarl.europa.eu/RegData/etudes/IDAN/2017/595364/IPOL_IDA(2017)595364_EN.pdf. Accessed May 28, 2019.

European Parliament. (2017b). Report on the proposal for a regulation of the European Parliament and of the council on addressing geo-blocking and other forms of discrimination based on customers' nationality, place of residence or place of establishment within the internal market and amending Regulation (EC) No 2006/2004 and Directive 2009/22/EC. https://www.europarl.europa.eu/doceo/document/A-8-2017-0172_EN.pdf. Accessed May 28, 2019.

European Parliament. (2018). Free flow of non-personal data: Parliament approves EU's fifth freedom. Press release. https://www.europarl.europa.eu/news/en/press-room/20180926IPR14403/free-flow-of-non-personal-data-parliament-approves-eu-s-fifth-freedom. Accessed May 28, 2019.

European Union. (2000). Charter of fundamental rights in the European Union. (2000/C 364/01). https://www.europarl.europa.eu/charter/pdf/text_en.pdf. Accessed August 11, 2019.

European Union. (2018a). Regulation (EU) 2018/302 of the European Parliament and of the council of 28 February 2018 on addressing unjustified geo-blocking and other forms of discrimination based on customers' nationality, place of residence or place of establishment within the internal market and amending Regulations (EC) No. 2006/2004 and (EU) 2017/2394 and Directive 2009/22/EC. https://eur-lex.europa.eu/legal-content/EN/TXT/?uri=uriserv:OJ.LI.2018.060.01.0001.01.ENG&toc=OJ:L:2018:060I:TOC. Accessed May 28, 2019.

European Union. (2018b). Directive (EU) 2018/1808 of the European Parliament and of the council of 14 November 2018 amending Directive 2010/13/EU on the coordination of certain provisions laid down by law, regulation or administrative action in Member States concerning the provision of audiovisual media services (Audiovisual Media Services Directive) in view of changing market realities. https://eur-lex.europa.eu/legal-content/EN/TXT/HTML/?uri=CELEX:32018L1808&from=EN. Accessed May 28, 2019.

European Union. (2019). Directive (EU) 2019/789 of the European Parliament and of the council of 17 April 2019 laying down rules on the exercise of copyright and related rights applicable to certain online transmissions of broadcasting organisations and retransmissions of television and radio programmes, and amending council Directive 93/83/EEC. https://eur-lex.europa.eu/legal-content/EN/TXT/?uri=uriserv%3AOJ.L_.2019.130.01.0082.01.ENG. Accessed August 11, 2019.

Farrand, B. (2014). The role of industry representatives in framing policies regarding cross-border licensing. In *Networks of power in digital copyright law and policy* (pp. 136–160). New York, NY: Routledge.

Grece, C. (2016). *How do films circulate on VOD services and in cinemas in the European Union? A comparative analysis.* Strasbourg: European Audiovisual Observatory. https://rm.coe.int/16807835be.

Hicks, D. (2016). Presentation at the JURI working group on IPR and copyright reform. European Language Equality Network (ELEN). https://www.europarl.europa.eu/cmsdata/97245/HICKSv02.pdf. Accessed May 28, 2019.

International Video Federation. (2017). Online and physical video market figures. https://www.ivf-video.org/new/public/media/2018_IVF_Industry_report_Total_Europe.pdf. Accessed May 28, 2019.

Kafkadesk. (2019). Slovakia's Netflix users gain access to Czech Content. https://kafkadesk.org/2019/02/07/slovakias-netflix-users-gain-access-to-czech-content/. Accessed August 11, 2019.

Kidman, A. (2016). Netflix USA vs the world: Content libraries compared. *Finder*, February 27. https://www.finder.com/netflix-usa-vs-world-content. Accessed May 28, 2019.

Marktwächter. (2018). Geoblocking: Weiterhin probleme beim Streaming im EU-Ausland. https://www.marktwaechter.de/pressemeldung/geoblocking-weiterhin-probleme-beim-streaming-im-eu-ausland. Accessed August 11, 2019.

Plucinska, J. (2016). Leak: The commission's latest geo-blocking plans. *Politico Europe*, September 5. https://www.politico.eu/pro/geoblocking-ecommerce-european-commission-leak-eu/. Accessed May 28, 2019.

Plum Consulting. (2012). The economic potential of cross-border pay-to-view and listen Audiovisual Media Services: Final report for the European Commission. https://publications.europa.eu/en/publication-detail/-/publication/a1fa4b64-242d-44a1-ba9f-4110ebdc8c6a. Accessed May 28, 2019.

Reda, J. (2015). European Commission reveals first details of copyright reform. https://juliareda.eu/2015/03/i-hate-geoblocking/. Accessed May 28, 2019.

Reda, J. (2019). Upload filters. https://juliareda.eu/eu-copyright-reform/censorship-machines/. Accessed August 11, 2019.

Reyna, A., & Silva, F. (2017). Proposal for a regulation on online broadcasting. Position Paper. BEUC: The European Consumer Organisation. https://www.beuc.eu/publications/beuc-x-2017-032_are_beuc_position_paper_regulation_on_online_broadcasting.pdf. Accessed August 11, 2019.

Sayer, P. (2015). EU aims to give streaming content same freedom of movement as people. *PCWorld*, December 9. https://www.pcworld.com/article/3013503/eu-aims-to-give-streaming-content-same-freedom-of-movement-as-people.html. Accessed August 11, 2019.

Society of Audiovisual Authors. (2018). Joint call of European creators and producers to the negotiators of the broadcasting legislation. https://www.saa-authors.eu/en/news/553-joint-call-of-european-creators-and-producers-to-the-negotiators-of-the-broadcasting-legislation#.XLXXZaRS858. Accessed May 28, 2019.

TorrentFreak. (2016). Leaked EU draft reveals geo-blocking can stay for video. https://torrentfreak.com/leaked-eu-draft-reveals-geo-blocking-can-stay-for-video-160513/. Accessed August 11, 2019.

Twitter. (2019a). Tweet by user @h4uk3. 26 Jan 2019, 14:08. https://twitter.com/h4uk3/status/1089284026383429632. Accessed August 18, 2019.

Twitter. (2019b). Tweet by user @Luisabal_. 02 Jun 2019, 07:12. https://twitter.com/Luisabal_/status/1135187315830247424. Accessed August 11, 2019.

United Nations. (1948). Universal declaration of human rights. https://www.ohchr.org/EN/UDHR/Documents/UDHR_Translations/eng.pdf. Accessed August 11, 2019.

Julia Reda was Member of the European Parliament for the German Pirate Party from 2014 to 2019. She was vice-chair of the Greens/EFA group and a co-founder of the Parliament's Digital Agenda Intergroup. As rapporteur for the review of the 2001 copyright directive, she advocated for a European copyright regime that is adapted to the digital era that is easy to understand and enables the free exchange of culture and knowledge across borders. Since 2019, Julia has been a research fellow at the Berkman Klein Center for Internet & Society at Harvard University. She holds an M.A. in political science and communications science from Johannes Gutenberg University in Mainz, Germany.

Chapter 6
The Czech and Slovak Audiovisual Market as a Laboratory Experiment for the Digital Single Market in Europe

Pavel Zahrádka

6.1 What's Wrong with the Audiovisual Industries in Europe?

In mid-2015, the European Commission introduced the Digital Single Market (DSM) strategy, the principal goal of which was to remove obstacles to the free movement of digital products and services within the EU. One of the areas targeted by the strategy was to improve the cross-border availability of cultural content, which is often inhibited by geoblocking (the restriction of access to Internet content based upon the user's geographic location). Customers from Member States other than the Member State of the content provider are, for example, unable to purchase access to audiovisual digital libraries. Until recently, consumers were also denied access to prepaid online video libraries if they crossed the borders of the country where the purchase was made. While for the most part the internal market for the free movement of goods in the EU is working, the development of a Digital Single Market—which would provide a wider and barrier-free supply of digital goods and services to EU citizens, regardless of their nationality or place of residence—remains an unrealized economic and political goal of the European Union.

The Commission hopes that a Digital Single Market will, among other things, improve access to European audiovisual works offered by online audiovisual services in the EU Member States. European audiovisual works do not travel easily beyond the country of origin, not only in the context of classical film distribution and television broadcasting, but also in the context of on-demand audiovisual media services. The European Audiovisual Observatory found that in 2015, European films were available on TVOD platforms in 2.8 EU countries on average (and coproduced films in 3.6 Member States on average), while US films were available on TVOD platforms

P. Zahrádka (✉)
Faculty of Arts, Department of Theater and Film Studies, Palacký University, Křížkovského 10, 771 47 Olomouc, Czech Republic
e-mail: pavel.zahradka@upmedia.cz

© The Author(s) 2020
P. Szczepanik et al. (eds.), *Digital Peripheries*, Springer Series in Media Industries,
https://doi.org/10.1007/978-3-030-44850-9_6

in 6.8 EU countries on average (Grece 2016: 12). The limited export of European audiovisual works concerns mainly smaller countries (Grece 2017: 15).[1]

The Commission considers geoblocking one of the main causes of the fragmentation of the European digital market for cultural content, as it divides national markets with virtual barriers (European Commission 2015a). Cultural content includes copyrighted works of authorship. Copyright is, nonetheless, territorial in the EU, and every Member State has its own copyright law applicable to its territory. Works of authorship are consequently protected in the EU by 28 national copyright laws. The territorial fragmentation of copyright is reflected in the territorial fragmentation of the licensing and business practices of the audiovisual industry. Producers sell the rights to audiovisual works, in most cases, in the form of monoterritorial licenses to local distributors operating in each State. Geoblocking is a technical means employed to ensure the owner of a territorial license makes the work available only to consumers within the licensed territory.

Another reason why there is no pan-European digital audiovisual market is, the Commission holds, the complicated rights clearance process. Films are distributed within a territory mostly on a sequential basis. This means that a film reaches the audience through gradually opening release windows (theaters, Pay TV, DVD, VOD and FTA TV). The order of the channels of distribution is determined by the highest marginal income generated in the shortest possible time.[2] Providers of on-demand video services (VOD) wishing to deliver a film to a larger number of EU countries, therefore, mostly have to clear digital distribution rights for each country separately, i.e., they need to purchase territorial licenses from local distributors. The Commission warns that this increases both the information costs of identifying the relevant transactional actor and the transaction costs related to the high number of transactions and transactional actors (European Commission 2016: 52–55).

The territorial fragmentation of the audiovisual market is also criticized by consumer protection advocates. While the European Commission is concerned about violations of free market principles, consumer rights organizations are concerned about discrimination against consumers in their access to European cultural wealth.[3] Monoterritorial licensing of audiovisual works is the cause of cross-border unavailability and (until recently) the limited cross-border portability of online audiovisual services in the EU. In other words, the blocking of access to content or an audiovisual service based on the location where the consumer connects to the Internet occurs when the service provider lacks the license needed for the territory from which the consumer wants to use the service. Enclosing content within the borders of nation states is discriminatory against language minorities, foreign students, short-term and

---

[1] See also Petr Szczepanik's chapter "Channels and Barriers of Cross-Border Online Circulation" in this book.

[2] In some European countries, such as France, the chronology of media distribution is even determined by law.

[3] According to the founding documents, the European Single Market is an area with no internal borders, an area of free movement of goods, people, services and capital. Cf. Article 26 of the Treaty on the Functioning of the European Union.

long-term migrants, and those interested in foreign language and culture. The borders of national states in many cases do not respect cultural and linguistic borders.

The argument gains momentum if the share that European financial grants (Eurimages, MEDIA) play in the funding and distribution of audiovisual production is considered. The fact is that the citizens of countries contributing to the production of audiovisual works are then denied access. In addition, blocking access to culture not only confines audiovisual work within the borders of nation states, but it also deprives authors of a potential source of income or a new audience that is willing to pay for the content but that lacks legal access to it, which can lead to the use of illegal content sources (Macek and Zahrádka 2016; Dootson and Suzor 2015).[4]

6.2 Don't Panic? The Digital Single Market and the Concerns of the Audiovisual Industry in the EU

The Commission, therefore, proposed a series of legislative measures in 2015 and 2016 aimed at eliminating the unjustified geoblocking of consumers within the European market and facilitating the clearance of rights to online services of broadcasters which are ancillary to linear broadcasting (simulcasting and catch-up TV). The legislative reforms were strongly opposed by representatives of the audiovisual industry, despite the fact that the proposed measures did not promote any pan-European audiovisual digital market. Audiovisual services were explicitly excluded from the scope of the Geoblocking Regulation.[5] The proposal for a regulation on online transmissions—aimed at simplifying the clearance of rights for broadcasters' ancillary online services with the help of the country of origin principle[6]—was limited by amendments either to content fully funded by the broadcasting organization or to news and current affairs content. Moreover, the application of the country of origin principle to the clearance of rights for online services ancillary to broadcast was accompanied in the Regulation by contractual freedom, namely the option of a contractual (e.g., territorial) limitation on the exercise of the right.[7]

---

[4] See Kim Tae-Sik's chapter "Finding Larger Transnational Media Markets: Media Practices of the Vietnamese Diasporic Community" in this book.

[5] See Recital 8 of the European Union Regulation 2018/302 of February 28, 2018 on addressing unjustified geoblocking and other forms of discrimination based on customer nationality, place of residence or place of establishment within the internal market and amending Regulations (EC) No 2006/2004 and (EU) 2017/2394 and Directive 2009/22/EC.

[6] Based on the country of origin principle, a broadcaster providing content via its ancillary online services throughout the EU is not obligated to clear the broadcasting rights for each Member State separately; the broadcaster only needs to clear rights for the Member State in which it has its principal establishment.

[7] However, this contractual freedom is limited by the fact that the restriction on the exercise of the rights agreed upon by the contractual partners must be in accordance with EU law. See Recital 11 of the Proposal for a Regulation laying down rules on the exercise of copyright and related

What is interesting about the political debate over the DSM is the clash between the idea of a free digital market and the reasons why this concept raises strong opposition from audiovisual industry stakeholders.[8] The discussion reveals the basic principles of the audiovisual business models and their limits. This provokes the question of the sustainability of the fundamental mechanisms of the audiovisual market in connection with globalization and digitalization, which result in the increasingly frequent crossing of physical territorial borders and hinder the control of nation states' virtual borders.

In this chapter, I first describe and analyze the attitudes of distributors and providers of online audiovisual services in the Czech Republic (a particular category of stakeholders in a small audiovisual market) toward the DSM concept. Are their attitudes any different from those held by the European audiovisual industry? Are small-market players threatened by the DSM more or less than those operating in the big market? Does the DSM offer any opportunities and advantages? For whom? In the second part, I reflect on the sustainability of online audiovisual business models in the EU with respect to the industry's operating principles, consumers' expectations and European law.

The Czech audiovisual market is a small national market in the EU, limited by the national language. The main language, Czech, is not much used or understood outside the Czech Republic, except for Slovakia where, to a large extent, Czech audiovisual works can be distributed without localization, i.e., without subtitles or dubbing in Slovak. The Czech Republic and Slovakia form a culturally intertwined region. This is strongly felt in cross-border distribution in particular. Distributors often buy licenses for both the Czech and Slovak markets, and the highest share of exported audiovisual works produced in the Czech Republic goes to Slovakia and vice versa. The degree of mutual export dependence is the highest of all the culturally connected regions in the EU. My analysis of the attitudes of audiovisual players in the Czech market, therefore, serves as a model for the functioning of the single digital (audiovisual) market in two linguistically (and culturally) affiliated and separate territories, namely the Czech–Slovak market versus the other EU Member States.

6.3   Who Was Interviewed and What About?

The attitudes were reconstructed based on an analysis of qualitative data collected between 2016 and 2018 through a series of semi-structured interviews with selected audiovisual distributors and providers of audiovisual online services in the Czech

---

rights applicable to certain online transmissions of broadcasting organisations and retransmissions of television and radio programmes, COM (2016) 594 final.

[8] Audiovisual industry representatives were some of the loudest critics of the DSM, among other cultural industries.

Republic.[9] The sample includes the most influential representatives of the various types of distribution practices on the opposite poles of the audiovisual field, namely representatives of commercial and art house audiovisual distribution.

The research sample included four types of respondents participating in the digital distribution of audiovisual works: (1) video on demand providers[10]; (2) distributors who, in addition to other channels (theater, TV, DVD), distribute content as video on demand (VOD) using a business model based on one-time payment for content (TVOD), subscription (SVOD) or advertising (AVOD)[11]; (3) television broadcasters[12]; and (4) providers of satellite and cable retransmissions who also offer VOD as part of their services.[13]

The respondents were questioned about their views on the cross-border portability of online audiovisual services and the cross-border availability of audiovisual works, the importance of territorial licenses and geoblocking for audiovisual industry business models, obstacles to the international circulation of European (Czech) audiovisual works and their attitudes toward proposed legislation. An audiovisual work, in the scope of this project, includes feature films and television and Web series which meet the definition of authored work and have the status of premium content in official distribution channels.

The following three scenarios for the development of a Digital Single Market were discussed with the respondents in relation to the cross-border accessibility of audiovisual content: (1) permission of passive sales for online audiovisual service providers; (2) extension of the country of origin principle to the ancillary online services of television providers; and (3) extension of the country of origin principle to all online audiovisual services. According to the passive sales model, providers of online audiovisual services would be obligated to clear rights only for the territories in which they actively promote and offer the content. However, they could not deny access to their service to a consumer from an unlicensed territory where they do not actively offer their services. In other words, the current practice of selling audiovisual works on the basis of territorial licenses would be accompanied by a ban on blocking access to content from a territory where the service provider does not have the rights cleared. The model-based scenario of applying the country of origin principle to clear the rights to distribute works through on-demand audiovisual media services would allow service providers wishing to offer their content to consumers in other Member States or throughout the EU to do so by purchasing a single license for the Member State where the provider has its principal establishment. If combined with a ban on contractual territorial limitation of rights, this scenario would create

---

[9]The descriptive part of the chapter is based on the findings of a study published by Zahrádka and Szczepanik (2019).

[10]Banaxi, O2 Czech Republic, Seznam, Google.

[11]Bontonfilm, CinemArt, Aerofilms, Doc Alliance Films, Film Europe, Bioscop, Association of Czech Film Clubs (AČFK), Artcam Films.

[12]Prima, Czech Television.

[13]Skylink, UPC, DIGI CZ.

a pan-European space for the provision of online audiovisual services and eliminate the fragmentation of the audiovisual market based on national borders.

6.4 Digital Single Market as a Threat or Opportunity for Small-Market Players?

6.4.1 Cross-Border Portability of Online Audiovisual Services

The Online Portability Regulation has been effective since March 20, 2018, improving the user-friendliness of paid audiovisual online services in the sense that subscribers are able to use the services even if temporarily abroad, away from the territory in which the provider is licensed to provide the content.[14] The regulation, based on a legal fiction, rules that the access to and use of such an online content service is deemed to occur only in the subscriber's Member State of residence. This means that the temporary use of the online service in another Member State is, in accordance with the Regulation, considered as use in a Member State for which the content distributor has purchased the license. Freed from the fear of infringing copyright or license agreements, the content distributor no longer needs to block service access to subscribers who travel outside the licensed territory.

Our respondents considered the Regulation to be an acceptable concession to the Commission's demand for the DSM. The Regulation respects established business practices and the territorial fragmentation of the market; it does not violate the territorial monopoly of the exclusive territorial license holder (content distributor). The only point of dispute was the verification mechanisms for the place of residence of the service user.

Service providers operating in only one Member State, without the possibility of price discrimination across EU Member States, were more benevolent when discussing various possible verification mechanisms (e.g., ownership of a bank account or real estate, or payment of a license fee for another type of service such as rent or a monthly phone plan) to ensure the portability of the service for customers such as long-term migrants or subscribers who own an account or property in the given Member State. Their attitude was driven by a desire to minimize the costs of verification of the place of residence of the service user, as they did not expect the cross-border portability of the service to generate an increase in new subscribers. Nor did they expect consumers from other countries to circumvent the verification mechanisms to use the service abroad on a permanent basis, given the fact that their catalogues target local audiences (Czech or dubbed content).

Providers of online audiovisual services in multiple territories, in contrast, preferred more stringent verification mechanisms (e.g., limitation of the duration of

---

[14]Regulation (EU) 2017/1128 of 14 June 2017 on cross-border portability of online content services in the internal market.

"temporary residence in a Member State other than the Member State of permanent residence," registration in local electoral registers, etc.). The Regulation would, according to this scenario, only allow the cross-border portability of audiovisual online services for tourists and short-term migrants. The rationale behind the promotion of stricter verification tools was the fear that consumers from countries with a more expensive service could—if they circumvented weak verification mechanisms—start using a cheaper service offered in another Member State. Opening an account with a streaming service provided in another Member State and using it in one's home territory in accordance with the Cross-Border Portability Regulation would violate the principle of territoriality, namely territorial barriers between national markets, which are crucial to the functioning of the audiovisual industry.

6.4.2 Cross-Border Availability of Audiovisual Content and the Importance of Geoblocking

The discussion on improving cross-border content availability proved a controversial topic in the interviews with distributors. Although distributors recognize that each new service customer from the territory of another Member State generates economic benefit, breaking the exclusive territorial monopoly over content distribution would, in their view, entail a series of negative consequences for the audiovisual industry, which would eliminate this hypothetical benefit: (1) the loss of territorial monopoly would lead to the cross-border cannibalization of revenues generated by the differently timed release windows and make premium content unaffordable for local providers of online audiovisual services; (2) the disruption of territoriality threatens the funding of audiovisual works through presales, particularly for international coproductions; (3) facilitated rights clearance would not improve the international circulation of European works, and the DSM threatens local distributors, who play an important role in the promotion and localization of an audiovisual work in the national market; and (4) reduction of transaction costs related to contracts between licensing stakeholders in connection with the introduction of the DSM is unnecessary; it would reinforce the market dominance of multinational VOD providers over small markets and weaken the position of small local VOD providers. Despite widespread reservations about the DSM, my data analysis also revealed that some of the stakeholders welcomed the DSM or questioned the worst-case scenarios predicting devastating impacts from the DSM on the Czech audiovisual market.

6.4.2.1 Loss of Territorial Monopoly and Unaffordable Premium Content

Territorial limitation of licenses is important for European distributors who purchase foreign audiovisual content and make it accessible to local audiences. They view geoblocking as a tool that protects their business model as it secures, with an exclusive territorial license, a distribution monopoly in the licensed territory. License providers (producers or sales agents) are, in return, guaranteed that their audiovisual work will be used in the licensed territory only and retain the option to sell an exclusive license for another territory to another local distributor at an advantageous price.

Unlike the European associations of film industry stakeholders, local distributors do not fear losing territorial monopoly due to cross-border content availability, since the Czech market has a high demand for localized, preferably dubbed content. They are of the opinion that the majority of Czech consumers would be discouraged from accessing streaming services offered in other Member States due to the lack of Czech content localization, payment in foreign currency and communication in a foreign language. The respondents were therefore not concerned about losing Czech audiences to foreign services with a wider or cheaper range of content. Cross-border services, in their view, would be used primarily by consumers who already use illegal sources to gain access to content. In the majority of cases, these are movie geeks and active viewers dissatisfied with the range provided by local film distribution. The respondents maintained that such a change in consumer behavior would not have a significant impact on the existing domestic market.

Local distributors were concerned about the loss of territorial monopoly, specifically in connection with the availability of services on the Czech and Slovak audiovisual markets due to the linguistic and cultural affiliation of the two countries. This concern, however, was mitigated by the fact that most of our respondents treated the Czech and Slovak markets as a single market, purchasing licenses for both countries. This meant that the local distributors controlled the distribution of content in both territories. The Digital Single Market would not threaten content distributors in the Czech Republic who buy licenses for both markets and are able to synchronize the distribution of content so as to avoid the overlapping of different types of release windows within the DSM, for example, to prevent having content available in Slovakia as VOD when it is just entering theaters in the Czech Republic.

The separation of both markets was, on the other hand, vital for respondents who did not have licenses to distribute content in both territories and yet offered their services there, or who distributed content within only one national market and yet were damaged by the cross-border availability of the same content from a linguistically affiliated territory. Such respondents included commercial free-to-air TV providers (TV Prima and TV Nova), who did not have licenses to distribute content in both the Czech Republic and Slovakia and yet offered their services through sister TV stations in both territories. Recent disputes between commercial broadcasters and cable/satellite TV providers (Skylink, DIGI CZ and UPC) demonstrate that blocking the satellite reception of Czech TV stations in Slovakia and vice versa is important for the protection of broadcasters' business models. Satellite transmission brought Czech TV stations, which are popular in Slovakia, into competition with Slovak stations, depriving them of ratings and advertizing revenue. Another reason is the fact that commercial broadcasters were concerned about cross-border revenue cannibalization in the case of broadcasting an acquisition program (e.g., a foreign film) which was already available to viewers in Slovakia via cable or satellite service, since it had been broadcast by a Czech broadcaster. In addition, broadcasters did not have the rights to distribute foreign films in Slovakia, and the satellite transmission of full-format television stations (i.e., without switching off selected TV shows) to Slovakia infringed the copyright of producers.

Distributors also agreed that cross-border cannibalization of revenues mainly threatened the distribution of content in widely spoken languages and of sports broadcasts, where the language component is not particularly important. The possibility of cross-border access to content, therefore, primarily threatens the economic interests of sports broadcast rightsholders, US film studios, European producers of audiovisual works in English, and content distributors on linguistically affiliated, but territorially separate, markets where two mutually independent local distributors operate.

Local distributors with a business strategy based on purchasing distribution rights for foreign films said they were threatened by an increase in the price of premium content licenses more than by the loss of territorial monopoly. They were concerned that many of them would not be able to afford premium audiovisual content within the Digital Single Market. In addition, pan-European licenses were irrelevant to them because their business activities were solely targeted at the domestic market. They were not interested in distributing content to markets in other Member States apart from Slovakia. Nor did they expect there to be economically relevant demand for their online services among short-term or long-term migrants in other Member States or parties interested in Czech culture and language. They maintained that the unified market would generate a poorer or extremely delayed supply (compared with the film premiere abroad), or that foreign content would need to be dubbed due to pressure from producers, which is much more costly than subtitling. This would reduce the appeal and competitiveness of local online audiovisual services in relation to global or foreign competition. Worse, foreign producers could demand that online distribution rights be excluded from licensing rights packages. In other words, release windows compromising the value of the license to distribute content in other Member States could be excluded.

Respondents with a positive or neutral attitude toward a Digital Single Market in Europe included (a) a multinational provider of an online audiovisual service whose ambition was to serve a higher number of territories than the Czech–Slovak market only (Google Play); (b) local AVOD services with original online content, such as the Czech Internet company Seznam, which runs the online Stream portal providing professional short video content based on the AVOD business model and product placement; (c) niche distributors with a specific business model sustainable within the DSM; and (d) retransmission service providers such as satellite TV providers.

(a)   Google, as a multinational online audiovisual service provider (Google Play), had a positive view of the DSM free of geoblocking barriers. The goal of the company was to make use of current technology which allows the transfer of digital content at extremely low logistical costs across many territories and to provide it to the widest possible range of consumers around the world. Simplification of legal operations was therefore in line with the company's business objectives.

Although Google faced high transaction costs associated with the purchase of licenses for content distribution in Member States, its business model had managed to adapt to the rules of the audiovisual market and, moreover, turned them into a competitive edge over local content distributors. Although a facilitated rights' clearance for the online distribution of audiovisual works would, in the opinion of local distributors, mainly assist the providers of US-based transnational online audiovisual services (e.g., Google Play, iTunes, Netflix and Amazon), the high transaction costs associated with clearing online rights for each territory separately also helped to strengthen the global providers' dominant position in the European market. Global online portals have access to extensive legal services, which helps them deal with the fragmented market and the territorial fragmentation of copyright law in the EU. The European providers of online audiovisual services, on the other hand, may be discouraged by this fact from their plans to become pan-European distributors. The dominance of global US platforms in the European market is therefore not dependent on the size of transaction costs of copyright clearance but rather on the uniqueness of their business model, broad consumer base, the high economic capital invested by some content providers in global licenses and in the development of their own premium content (such as Netflix and HBO GO). Additionally, the transaction costs associated with the purchase of licenses are reduced by rights aggregators who specialize in buying online rights to large libraries of digital content, which they then offer to transnational VOD portals.

(b)   Most producers and distributors of original content developed for local audiences were indifferent to the reform proposals since they were already able to distribute their content globally or multi-territorially, without facing any transaction costs incurred when concluding license agreements.

(c)   Although the majority of local distributors were concerned about the introduction of the DSM, those whose business model was largely independent of online distribution took a neutral stance toward DSM. An example is Film Europe, a rights aggregator and film festival distributor, who has been expanding its festival films into European markets (Belgium, the Netherlands and Luxembourg) through partnerships with local VOD providers and satellite operators. Film Europe's business model involves the monetization of curator-selected collections of films through themed festivals held in Czech and Slovak theaters, television broadcasting and VOD portals.[15] Even if the introduction of a single digital market were to enhance the dominant position of global online audiovisual service providers, Film Europe would not lose its position in the market, according to its director. He was convinced that FE would play an important curatorial role for global streaming portals in terms of selecting and promoting collections of art house films and actively generating a digital audience for them. The indispensable curatorial role of Film Europe derived from its strong

---

[15]B2Can, the best-known label of Film Europe, offers a selection of competition titles (often winners) from the Berlin, Cannes and Venice festivals.

position at content purchase, thanks to its ability to recognize and purchase the rights to winners before the films were awarded by festival juries.

(d) Satellite operators providing retransmission services were against geoblocking consumers. Their reasoning, as providers of technology infrastructure for transmissions of audiovisual works, was similar to the reasoning of Google, which offers audiovisual works through Internet technology. As the satellite signal covers the whole of Europe, it is in the commercial interest of operators to have the service available for subscription by the maximum number of customers. The only requirement for consumers to receive satellite TV services is to purchase a decoder card. According to Skylink, customers interested in purchasing the decoder could not be discriminated against based on their nationality or place of residence: "The free movement of goods and services has a higher priority than copyright restrictions."[16] Consumers should be able to use a prepaid service regardless of their physical location (provided the territory is covered by a satellite or Internet network), which is technically impossible to check in the case of satellite reception—unlike Internet transmission. Furthermore, the providers of cable and satellite retransmission services operate in a different legal framework compared with the other licensing chain stakeholders.[17] The retransmission operators need to clear the necessary rights with the broadcasters whose channels they retransmit and with collective management organizations (i.e., with organizations that represent a multitude of rightsholders and not with individual rightsholders) in the territory where they retransmit the content under the regime of mandatory collective administration of rights. The operator seeking to use audiovisual work therefore does not need to ask for the rightsholder's consent, but must pay for the license fee to the respective collective management organization. In short, their business strategy is not based on the territorial exclusivity of content, but on the widest and most attractive possible range of content.[18]

6.4.2.2 The Importance of Territorial Exclusivity for Film Coproduction

The cross-border accessibility of content would, in the opinion of distributors involved in the production of audiovisual works, jeopardize their production, which largely relies on the presales of exclusive territorial rights. The inability to provide

---

[16]Interview with Jaromír Glisnik, Ostrava, Czech Republic, November 27, 2018.

[17]See the amendment to the Czech Copyright Act (Act No. 102/2017 Coll.) or the Proposal for a Regulation laying down rules on the exercise of copyright and related rights applicable to certain online transmissions of broadcasting organisations and retransmissions of television and radio programmes, COM(2016) 594 final.

[18]An exception to this is the rights exercised by a broadcasting organization with respect to their own transmission ("signal"), which satellite and cable operators are obligated to contractually secure from broadcasters.

investors or future distributors with exclusive rights to distribute content in a specific territory would reduce their willingness to invest and thus reduce the number of audiovisual works produced, international coproductions in particular. Given the similarity of the national languages, this problem is most striking in joint Czech–Slovak productions, which are the most common type of coproduction in the Czech audiovisual landscape. The threat to international coproduction—the risk of cannibalization of revenues generated by the release window, which the cross-border availability of content could hypothetically cause—is mitigated in the Czech–Slovak context by the possibility of amending coproduction contracts. The coproducers could commit themselves to holdbacks or synchronization of release windows in the respective Member States. This option—possible in the Czech–Slovak market thanks to the fact that many distributors operate in both markets and buy distribution rights for both territories at the same time, which means they are able to synchronize parallel distribution of content in both markets—is not possible to the same extent in all the EU market clusters of linguistically and culturally affiliated countries (such as France and Belgium or Germany and Austria).

6.4.2.3   The Cross-Border Circulation of (Czech) Audiovisual Works

The respondents maintained that copyright territoriality did not prevent the international distribution of European films, nor did it cause territorial fragmentation of supply. Facilitating the clearance of rights would therefore not increase the international circulation of European films. Provided it is in their economic interests, producers can sell a multi-territory license to a distributor for the whole of Europe (some independent producers do so in a minority of cases). Entry into foreign markets is not hindered by territorial differences in copyright, given the high degree of harmonization of property rights: it is the costs incurred in localizing content in the relevant national language and marketing the content with regard to local audience preferences. Business practices in most cases diverge, however, from selling a multi-territorial license. The reasons are economic: (1) Low demand for content within a territory, caused by cultural and linguistic differences and different consumer preferences, does not exceed the transaction costs the online audiovisual service provider would have to expend on the license and content localization. (2) Selling a monoterritorial license to local distributors who are familiar with the local market and are best able to prepare a promotional campaign and distribute the content is advantageous in terms of maximizing profits and reduces the business uncertainty of producers associated with poor knowledge of the market. (3) The business strategy of premium content producers involves retaining the commercial value of a license for additional territories, namely the option to sell it to a local distributor in another territory. To avoid damaging the commercial potential of the license for use of the work in additional territories, distributors signing the license agreements commit themselves not to offer the licensed work to consumers in other Member States for which they do not have the relevant licenses. (4) According to some of the local distributors, the public support for film production fails to motivate producers, whose business model is based on obtaining subsidies for film making, to invest greater efforts in the international distribution of the title. Instead, they tend to seek support for another project.

6.4.2.4   The Dangers of Multinational VOD Providers Dominating a Small Market

The majority of our respondents—local distributors—dealt with audiovisual content mainly in the Czech and Slovak territories, purchasing the relevant territorial licenses directly from producers or rights aggregators. They thereby avoided the high number of transactions necessary to clear copyright for each territory and the information costs associated with the identification of the contracting party. Reduction of transaction costs associated with rights clearance—through the application of the country of origin principle to online audiovisual services—therefore has no benefit for local distributors. On the contrary, most of the respondents were of the opinion that it could strengthen the major global players (Netflix, Amazon, Apple and Google) as they are the only ones who want to deliver content to all territories and have sufficient funds for expensive titles. The purchase of a single EU-wide license would reduce their transaction costs of rights clearance. This argument is reinforced by the fact that the only VOD services operating on the Slovak VOD market are Czech, as there is almost no original Slovak VOD service.[19]

In addition, global online portals serving the pan-European digital market would become the most attractive contracting partners for producers and sales agents, since they can afford to invest in a pan-European license as they have the necessary capital and are able to valorize the license to use a work across EU Member States. The Czech distributors were of the opinion that territorial fragmentation of the audiovisual market thereby protects local audiovisual services from the competitive pressure of Netflix, which—if the company wants to offer the same content in all EU Member States, and unless it has purchased a Europe-wide license directly from the producer—has to buy online rights from local distributors in individual territories. This protects the traditional model of sequential distribution respected by local distributors.

Local distributors pointed out that competition with global players over content purchase was already in progress—regardless of the DSM implementation. However, significant differences between transnational online audiovisual services were noted in the ways the purchased licenses are used. For example, Amazon respects the traditional model of audiovisual content distribution through gradually opening windows when it distributes its own and acquired films. The first release window is theatrical, which helps, in combination with a marketing campaign, create awareness of the title and thereby a digital audience for the subsequent monetization of the title listed in the catalogue of an online audiovisual service. This distribution practice respects the

---

[19] In mid-2018, the telecommunication company Slovak Telekom launched its VOD service, Magio Kino.

importance of local distributors and the traditional sequential distribution model in terms of the title promotion on the local market. Collaboration between global and local players suggests that large global video libraries need to win local audiences for their titles. Local distributors are those who know the specifics of local markets and have a curatorial role and therefore are able—before the film is released on the VOD platform—to create a (digital) audience through a targeted and dramaturgically sophisticated distribution of the film in theaters and festivals. Netflix, on the other hand, deliberately disrupts the traditional distribution chain, offering purchased titles globally through its online service, regardless of their theatrical distribution.

Some of the local distributors were therefore not concerned about the danger posed by American giants like Netflix, Amazon and Google securing a distribution monopoly or oligopoly. They believed that the specificities of local markets are so different that content distribution will always require knowledge of the market (e.g., the network of cinema operators, consumer habits, culture and calendar year) possessed by local distributors or local representatives of film studios. Furthermore, services offering a large amount of content are grappling with insufficient content localization, curation and promotion. Film producers, therefore, according to the local distributors, face a dilemma whether to sell content to a global distribution portal (Netflix) and risk that their film becomes lost among the great number of other titles, or whether to offer the content to distributors in several selected territories who follow the traditional sequential model of distribution and will duly localize and promote the film. Producers who sell a license to a global VOD portal which will make their film globally available, risk not being able to sell the film to any local distributor due to the missing guarantee of investment appreciation.

The entry of global portals purchasing territorially exclusive rights (Netflix, Amazon and HBO GO) into the Czech market is threatening mainstream local VOD portals. Respondents said they did not feel threatened in the case of services (a) with distinctive repertory and strong branding (such as Aerofilms or Doc Alliance) focused on specific minority content; (b) with a fixed base of subscribers, such as the video libraries of FTA broadcasters (Voyo, Czech Television online) or Pay TV channels (HBO GO) providing its own exclusive content. Nor is any service under threat that is (c) an add-on bonus in relation to other commercial services (e.g., MALL.TV Internet television, which experiments with the acquisition of feature films) or (d) an Internet television organization producing its own short format content exclusively for online consumption (Stream, Obbod and Playtvak). The best defenses against global competitors, respondents said, are highly specific dramaturgy, close contact with a clearly defined user base or links to other commercial services, and original short content developed for online consumption.

6.5   Sustainable Business Models?

The respondents' attitudes revealed the basic mechanisms of audiovisual business models in a small market. The production and distribution of audiovisual works in the Czech Republic (and throughout Europe) is dependent, in addition to public support, on the sale and purchase of exclusive territorial licenses. An exclusive territorial license is a tool used by the value chain stakeholders to eliminate market risks associated with the monetization of audiovisual works whose production requires large financial investments.

The territorial exclusivity of a license encourages a prospective distributor to duly promote and localize films (subtitles, dubbing, etc.) within the licensed territory and in the relevant national language. In addition, it is a tool which helps a producer generate funds needed to produce a costly audiovisual work in exchange for the territorially exclusive license the producer grants to the investor or future distributor of the work (presale of rights). In return, the investor is assured the same work will not be offered by another audiovisual service provider within the given territory. If the distributor could not be certain about this, other market entities could take advantage of the distributor's investments in the production of the work.

Geoblocking is a technical measure serving to protect the value of an exclusive territorial license online. The reason for territorial exclusivity, which is absolute in the case of geoblocking, is the protection of an investment in the production, distribution and promotion of audiovisual works.[20] Without geoblocking, Czech consumers could, for example, buy access to a work from a foreign online audiovisual service provider who does not have a license to distribute the work in the Czech Republic. Therefore, the territorial license for the Czech Republic would lose its exclusivity.

In addition to the business considerations, there are also legal reasons for geoblocking. For example, if a Czech viewer could subscribe to a VOD service provided in Poland, the service provider would violate copyright law since the work would be used (communicated to the public) in unlicensed territory. The fact is that the rightsholder controls territorial use of the work concerning its communication to the public.[21] This means that the rightsholder may prevent unauthorized entities from using the work within a particular territory and the licensee from offering the

---

[20] Absolute territorial exclusivity refers to an agreement in which the parties eliminate third-party competition; for example, the parallel import of a product from another territory. This type of agreement is problematic in terms of European Union competition law as it may breach free competition. The European Commission, for example, opened an investigation into contractual arrangements between Sky UK, a Pay TV provider and six Hollywood film studios in 2014. In the agreement, Sky UK committed not to provide its Pay TV services available in the UK and Ireland to consumers outside the licensed territories, while the Hollywood studios agreed to put in place contractual restrictions that prevent audiovisual service providers in other Member States from making their Pay TV services available in the UK and Ireland. For more details, see European Commission (2015b).

[21] On the contrary, under the exhaustion principle, the copyright holder has no control over the territorial circulation of copyrighted works on physical carriers from the moment the holder, or an entity authorized by the holder, offers the carriers for sale on any national market in the European Economic Area. The holder of the rights to use the work, specifically to distribute the copies of the work, is therefore unable, following its first sale (on a physical carrier) to prevent, for example, the parallel import of the work from another EEA territory, where it may be sold at a lower price. See Article 4 of Directive 2001/29/EC of May 22, 2001 on the harmonization of certain aspects of copyright and related rights in the information society.

work outside the licensed territory. According to the prevalent statutory interpretation, the right to communicate a work to the public, which includes streaming films and television shows as part of an on-demand video service, is subject to the country of destination principle. The service provider is obligated to clear the rights to use the work with the rightsholder for each territory where the work is used (communicated to the public).[22] For example, Czech Television is the holder of the rights to the *Svět pod hlavou* [*World under your Head*] mystery television series. Anyone who wants to make *Svět pod hlavou* available in Poland needs to purchase a license from Czech Television for this territory. Holding a license for Slovakia, for example, is not enough. Therefore, there is no competition between the Slovak and the Polish providers of the content.

From the nature of copyright territoriality and the possibility of exclusive territorial restrictions with regard to the exercise of the rights, it follows that competition among audiovisual distributors takes place mostly for national markets and not within a national market. Distributors do not compete over who will offer the same content but cheaper within a given territory, but who will offer more attractive content at a better price within the given territory. Geoblocking therefore restricts competition among distributors selling the same content from the same producer (intra-brand competition) and not competition among distributors selling the same type of content from different producers (interbrand competition).[23] Rather than being a cause, geoblocking is a consequence of this business practice since the possibility of selling exclusive territorial licenses restricts free competition. Even if geoblocking barriers were removed, content providers would not be allowed to offer their services to customers in a territory where they do not have a license.

Nevertheless, the territory-based structure of audiovisual business models is limited in relation to the cross-border mobility of consumers, the demand for content offered in other Member States and the global availability of digital technologies. A secondary negative consequence of the audiovisual business models is content piracy or VPN piracy, a practice of some consumers who are willing to pay for desired content that is available only from a foreign on-demand video service provider, but who lack access due to limited territorial supply and geoblocking barriers.

The size of this consumer group can only be indirectly inferred from the statistics. A poll conducted by the European Commission in 2015 revealed that very few Europeans (5%, compared to 7% in the Czech Republic) have tried to access audiovisual content (films, series, video clips and all TV content excluding sports) through online services intended for users in other Member States. The reasons why most

---

[22] Although the Information Society Directive (2001/29/EC) regarding copyright clearance does not address whether the right of communication to the public is governed by the country of origin principle or the country of destination principle, the introduction of the country of origin principle for the clearance of rights to satellite broadcasting in the Satellite and Cable Directive (93/83/EEC) is understood to be an exception to the rule, and therefore the prevailing opinion is that copyright territoriality means that the rights need to be cleared for each country where the work is exploited [c.f. Doukas (2012); Batchelor and Montani (2015); Ibáñez Colomo (2017)]. Radim Polčák voices a different view in chapter "Territoriality of Copyright Law" in this book.

[23] For more on the distinction between intra-brand and interbrand competition, see Gundem (2016).

consumers have not attempted cross-border access to digital content on the Internet include lack of interest in this type of content (56% in the CR); sufficient supply of content in the domestic territory (64% in the CR); not knowing how to access the content technically (18% in the CR); content incomprehensibility due to foreign language (26% in the CR); distrust of services offered abroad (13% in the CR); and conviction that cross-border access to content is impossible (6% in the CR). The findings need to be interpreted in a wider context, however. Firstly, the multiple choice survey method does not take into account Internet piracy, particularly the fact that the lack of interest in content from foreign services may be due to the availability of such content, distributed illegally. Responses to other questions likewise indicate that 30% of Czech respondents (29% of Europeans on average) who have not attempted to access online services offered in another Member State would be interested to do so in order to access films, series, video clips and TV content excluding sports. In the case of sports broadcasts, 18% of respondents express interest in cross-border access (TNS Political and Social 2015). A survey requested by the Federation of German Consumer Organizations (VZBV) in February 2016, carried out by TNS with German consumers (N = 1032), indicated that 73% of respondents would welcome legal access to paid audiovisual services (sports broadcasts, films and series) from other Member States (VZBV 2017). The current business model of the audiovisual industry is unable to satisfy this demand.

A change in the business model may, in principle, arise from either a change in the business strategy (in response to consumer demand and technological developments) or a change in law (reflecting political, legal and ethical debates). Three options are available in relation to a change in the business strategy.[24] The first is represented by Netflix, which overcomes territorial barriers to pan-European distribution of content by producing its own content (Netflix originals) and by purchasing rights for the particular territories, or a multi-territory license, and by offering 28 national versions of its VOD service in the 28 Member States. The second option involves a change in the licensing strategy and segmentation of the market based on national languages. Licenses for the distribution of content would no longer be limited by territory but only by language version, and the cost would depend on the size of potential audiences speaking the language. The problem with this scenario is the territorial limitations of a number of local distributors or providers of national VOD services. Another drawback is the risk of cross-border cannibalization of revenues generated during a particular release window in the case of content produced in widely spoken languages (predominantly English) or sports broadcasts. The third option is to base the licensing agreement not on the territory where the content is to be viewed but on the quantity of content that is viewed, i.e., on the number of subscribers with the SVOD model, the number of transactions with the TVOD model and the number of views with the AVOD service.[25] The disadvantage of this solution is the lack of motivation for the

---

[24]This is not an exhaustive list of all possible scenarios of the transformation of the audiovisual industry business model.

[25]This solution is advocated by Erle (2016), for example.

distributor to invest in production and promotion, as the competitive advantage over other distributors, provided by absolute territorial exclusivity, will be lost.

The application of the country of origin principle to the online communication of audiovisual works to the public and the passive sales scenario are changes currently being discussed in the context of the transformation of the legal framework under which on-demand video service providers operate. In the first option, instead of the country of destination principle, the right to communicate the work to the public would be subject to the country of origin principle. Property rights would no longer need to be cleared for each country separately; content distributors (users of the work) would only need to clear the rights for the country of their principal establishment. Geoblocking would no longer be backed by copyright and it is uncertain whether it could be applied without violating free market principles, namely that of competition law.[26]

Article 101(3) of the Treaty on the Functioning of the European Union contains exceptions to the prohibition on agreements restricting competition within the internal market. The exceptions concern any agreement between undertakings, "which contributes to improving the production or distribution of goods or to promoting technical or economic progress, while allowing consumers a fair share of the resulting benefit." However, the agreements must not impose restrictions which are not indispensable, nor may they eliminate competition with respect to a substantial part of the products in question. Application of these requirements to the geoblocking of audiovisual content reveals that while geoblocking eliminates intra-brand competition, it does not remove interbrand competition. The interbrand competition would therefore not be eliminated, even if absolute territorial exclusivity was granted. In addition, representatives of the audiovisual industry argue that geoblocking is necessary for the production and localization of audiovisual content, which is advantageous for consumers.

If geoblocking continues to be allowed, in all probability, the current functioning of the audiovisual market will not change much. At most, geoblocking barriers would be canceled for audiovisual content for which there is no business reason to geoblock, i.e., content which cannot find a foreign distributor. However, if geoblocking is prohibited, the impossibility of territorial protection could disturb the audiovisual

---

[26]The rulings of the European Court of Justice on the dispute between pub landlady Karen Murphy and FA Premier League, C-403/08 and C-429/08, are relevant in this context. The owner of a UK pub was brought to court for using cheaper decoding cards purchased in Greece for satellite broadcasting of soccer matches. The Court concluded that the prohibition on the import, sale or use of foreign decoder cards restricts the free movement of services. The judgment is relevant because the clearance of rights to satellite broadcasting is subject to the country of origin principle and because geoblocking (restricting the online availability of content) is a technical means similar to the prohibition on the use of cards decoding satellite signals outside the licensed territory. According to the Satellite and Cable Directive (93/83/EEC), content may only be communicated by satellite broadcasting where the satellite transmission is initiated. The satellite broadcaster is obligated to clear the rights only for the country in which the broadcaster resides. If a card subscriber receives a satellite television signal in a Member State other than the one in which the subscriber purchased the decoder card, the satellite broadcaster is not infringing the copyright and cannot justify refusing to sell the card to a customer from another Member State by referring to copyright protection.

industry ecosystem. The Czech audiovisual market would be hit by some of the negative impacts of this radical scenario (notably, unaffordable premium content in the main languages for providers of local audiovisual online services) despite the fact that it is protected by language barriers, consumer preference for content localized in the Czech language, and the fairly synchronized distribution of content within the combined Czech-Slovak market, where natural language barriers do not apply.

An alternative scenario of legislative reform therefore comprises explicit recognition of consumer rights (e.g., the right not to be discriminated against in the access to the cultural life of the community based on place of residence or nationality) in copyright legislation and the application of the country of origin principle only in cases where a consumer from an unlicensed territory is interested in subscribing to a service or purchasing content ("unsolicited request") and the service provider does not target consumers in the unlicensed territory.[27] This scenario combines the licensing practice of territorially exclusive licenses and the prohibition of geoblocking and thereby eliminates absolute territorial exclusivity. This may produce unintended negative consequences for the industry due to intra-brand competition wherever there are no natural language barriers. Fearing cross-border competition, investors—potential distributors—will not be willing to invest in the purchase of an exclusive territorial license and in content localization and promotion. This may lead to a drop in the number of films made or lower rates of promotion and localization of audiovisual works in Europe, which would, however, be offset by their cross-border availability to all EU citizens on non-discriminatory terms. The question, therefore, is whether a compromise solution for a sustainable audiovisual business model could be a combination of the passive sales scenario and a list of permitted territorial restrictions (e.g., of limited duration) grounded in the protection of investment in the development, promotion and localization of audiovisual works.[28]

References

Batchelor, B., & Montani, L. (2015). Exhaustion, essential subject matter and other CJEU judicial tools to update copyright for an online economy. *Journal of Intellectual Property Law & Practice, 10*(8), 591–600.

Doukas, D. (2012). The sky is not the (only) limit: Sports broadcasting without frontiers and the court of justice: Comment on Murphy. *European Law Review, 37*(5), 605–626.

Dootson, P., & Suzor, N. (2015). The game of clones and the Australia tax: Divergent views about copyright business models and the willingness of Australian consumers to infringe. *University of New South Wales Law Journal, 38*(1), 206–239.

---

[27]Copyright law has, to date, reflected consumer rights only in the form of exemptions from and limitations on copyright protection, and not through an explicit definition of a consumer right to access cultural wealth.

[28]This study was supported by the European Regional Development Fund-Project "Creativity and Adaptability as Conditions of the Success of Europe in an Interrelated World" (No. CZ.02.1.01/0.0/0.0/16_019/0000734) and and by the Internal Grant Agency of the Palacký University Olomouc in 2020 (No. IGA_FF_2020_007).

European Commission. (2015a). Communication to the European Parliament, the Council, the European Economic and Social Committee and the Committee of the Regions—A Digital Single Market Strategy for Europe, COM(2015) 100 final. https://eur-lex.europa.eu/legal-content/CS/TXT/?uri=celex%3A52015DC0192. Accessed May 6, 2018.

European Commission. (2015b). Antitrust: Commission sends Statement of Objections on cross-border provision of pay-TV services available in UK and Ireland. https://europa.eu/rapid/press-release_IP-15-5432_en.htm. Accessed July 23, 2018.

European Commission. (2016). Impact Assessment on the Modernisation of EU Copyright Rules—Part 1. Commission Staff Working Document. https://eur-lex.europa.eu/legal-content/EN/TXT/?uri=celex:52016SC0301. Accessed September 14, 2019.

Erle, S. (2016). The battle against geo-blocking: The consumer strikes back. *Richmond Journal of Global Law & Business, 15*(1), 1–20.

Grece, C. (2016). *How do films circulate on VOD services and in cinemas in the European Union?* Strasbourg: European Audiovisual Observatory.

Grece, C. (2017). *The circulation of EU non-national films.* Strasbourg: European Audiovisual Observatory.

Gundem, I. M. (2016). Geo-blocking in Licence Agreements: Whether Agreements to Block Access to Digital Content Infringe EU Competition Rules. University of Oslo. https://www.duo.uio.no/bitstream/handle/10852/50979/592.pdf?sequence=1&isAllowed=y. Accessed October 15, 2019.

Ibáñez Colomo, P. (2017). Copyright licensing and the EU digital single market strategy. In R. D. Blair & D. D. Sokol (Eds.), *The cambridge handbook of antitrust, intellectual property and high tech* (pp. 339–357). New York: Cambridge University Press.

Macek, J., & Zahrádka, P. (2016). Online piracy and the transformation of the audiences' practices: The case of the Czech Republic. In D. H. Hick & R. Schmücker (Eds.), *The aesthetics and ethics of copying* (pp. 335–358). London: Bloomsbury.

TNS Political and Social. (2015). Flash Eurobarometer 411: Cross-border Access to Online Content. https://data.europa.eu/euodp/en/data/dataset/S2059_411_ENG. Accessed April 1, 2018.

VZBV. (2017). Geo-blocking: Tearing Down Borders for Digital Content. https://www.vzbv.de/sites/default/files/2017_vzbv_factsheet_geo-blocking_digital_content_1.pdf. Accessed April 1, 2018.

Zahrádka, P., & Szczepanik, P. (2019). The white elephant in the room: Implications of the digital single market strategy for film and television distribution in the Czech Republic. In M. T. S. Rajan (Ed.), *The Cambridge handbook of intellectual property in Central and Eastern Europe* (pp. 238–258). Cambridge: Cambridge University Press.

Pavel Zahrádka is Associate Professor of aesthetics and cultural industries, Palacký University Olomouc. He specializes in the ethics of digital media and aesthetics. In 2015 and 2016, together with Reinold Schmücker (University of Münster) and Thomas Dreier (Karlsruhe Institute of Technology), he helmed the international research group "Ethics of Copying" at the Center for Interdisciplinary Research in Bielefeld. He is currently a principal investigator on a research project investigating the impact of the Digital Single Market strategy on the Czech audiovisual industry funded by the Technology Agency of the Czech Republic.

**Part III
A New Game with Old Players:
Distribution Practices in Small
and Peripheral Markets**

Chapter 7
Television Distribution in Flanders: Who Takes the Lead and Is Content Always King?

Tim Raats and Karen Donders

7.1 Introduction

Media scholars have focused extensively on the consequences of the digitization, internationalization and convergence of legacy media (Küng 2013; Picha Edwardsson and Pargman 2014; Collins 2011; Barwise and Picard 2012). Scholars have observed increasing merger and acquisition activities (Evens and Donders 2016), a further commodification of media products [visible, for example, in the mounting relevance of formats (Esser 2013; Bielby and Harrington 2008)], and pressure on existing revenues in this regard. All of these changes have increased the pressure on the financing of original, quality domestic content (Raats et al. 2016; Picard et al. 2016). The increasing dominance of multi-layered platforms (Hoelck and Ballon 2015), especially, has been considered central to the disruption of existing legacy players' business models across the globe. Video on demand (VOD) services and platforms such as Netflix, Amazon, Google, YouTube and Facebook challenge existing media players with a business model that is driven by scale and network advantages (in other words, the value of the platform increases as the number of viewers or subscribers increases)—a user-driven approach boosted by investments in data collection, algorithms and strategies to keep users "glued" to the screens (Lobato 2019; Tandoc 2014). Moreover, these players are willing and able to invest significant sums of money on an international scale, regardless of the accumulation of debt. As a result, the existing production and distribution models of legacy players and their economic profitability are not the only things challenged by the new business model, as this platform strategy also puts pressure on original content production, and the contribution legacy players make to society in terms of cultural diversity, pluralism

T. Raats (✉) · K. Donders
Imec-SMIT, Vrije Universiteit Brussel, Pleinlaan 2, 1050 Brussel, Belgium
e-mail: Tim.Raats@vub.be

K. Donders
e-mail: Karen.Donders@vub.be

© The Author(s) 2020
P. Szczepanik et al. (eds.), *Digital Peripheries*, Springer Series in Media Industries,
https://doi.org/10.1007/978-3-030-44850-9_7

and providing quality local content (Evens and Donders 2016; Davis and Zboralska 2017). The advent of innovative platforms and shifting business models has not only instigated new forms of competition, but it has also forced media players to explore different forms of collaboration and co-option (Evens and Donders 2018).

Most of the academic literature at this point has discussed the challenges media players face on a more generic level by looking at the nature of disruptions and their consequences, focusing mostly on the effects of either large markets or the media market in general. In this chapter, we discuss disruptions and consequences for legacy media players by centering our attention on the different answers given by media managers regarding the strategic distribution of audiovisual content in small markets (for an elaboration on small markets, see Puppis 2009; Syvertsen et al. 2014; Lowe et al. 2011a, b). We thereby focus on three core strategies: scale, collaboration within domestic ecosystems and diversification of offerings and valorization.

Although the chapter presents evidence from Flanders, it also provides a broader view by discussing shifts on the level of small markets in Europe and by addressing the challenges and concerns in other small media markets. The questions addressed are firstly, what strategic options are put forward by media managers themselves in small markets? Secondly, how valuable are these (especially short-term) strategies and how have they thus far been rolled out in practice? Thirdly, to what extent does market context and "smallness" enable or impede these strategies? In this chapter, we investigate media companies' strategic responses to specific challenges from 2016 to 2019. Evidence derives from three sources: firstly, observations—as both authors were involved in studies commissioned either by governments or media managers in response to disruptive trends; secondly, interviews with the media managers of private media players in Flanders (e.g., broadcasters, independent producers and telecom/cable distributors); and thirdly, insights from recent research looking into the sustainability of content production and delivery in Flanders, commissioned by the minister of media and conducted in collaboration with the research institute Econopolis (from June to October 2018). Our analysis focuses mainly on television distribution, but has wider relevance due to clear parallels that can be drawn with strategic responses in other areas, such as news provision and the publishing industry.

In the next section, we briefly address ongoing shifts in television distribution and their implications for media sustainability. "Distribution" is mainly understood as the combination of means to deliver audiovisual content to audiences, be it in the form of digital or pay television services (e.g., cable and telecom distributors), or in the form of online delivery (e.g., broadcasters' online catch-up and VOD services and subscription-based portals such as Netflix). In the third section, the structural fragility of small television markets and what it means for television production and distribution, and how trends of platformization and digitization add to that fragility, are thoroughly discussed. The fourth part presents the case of Flanders as an example of a typical, yet unique, small European television ecosystem. Part five presents the different managerial strategies taken in Flanders concerning television distribution in response to these trends and how effective they are. The chapter ends with a number of conclusions and critical observations for further research.

7.2 Television Distribution: From Cable to Over-the-Top Delivery

Television distribution was a fairly simple thing in the past, where analog transmission occurred via terrestrial technology or cable only. The transition to digital has affected these technologies, as well as their underlying economic infrastructures. The evolution from analog to digital terrestrial television (DTT) was far from a smooth process and was heavily subsidized by all EU Member States, bound to deliver on goals set at the European level (Brown and Picard 2005). Notably, in Southern and Eastern Europe, the timetable of the digital transition has proved to be highly challenging. In other countries such as the Netherlands and Belgium, the density of cable made DTT less of a priority (Evens 2013). Cable itself also changed: Whereas analog cable was largely a matter for local communes and considered a public utility, digitization also came with the privatization of many cable networks (Brown and Picard 2005). This in turn resulted in consolidation, a trend that has impacted different European markets in various ways (Evens 2014). Highly cabled countries such as Belgium and the Netherlands have evolved into cable monopolies in which, currently, American multinational Liberty Global plays an important role (Evens 2013). In other countries such as Spain, numerous regionally active cable operators still exist. This means that cable at the European level is still a highly fragmented market. However, digitization not only affected existing technologies, but it also enabled the rise of the satellite (rather early on) and new forms of television distribution, notably Internet Protocol Television (IPTV). This was embraced by the preexisting telecommunications incumbents and became a very popular distribution model in some of the Baltic states. Moreover, over-the-top (OTT) television distribution can nowadays be added to the list of distribution models. Over-the-top does not require the use of a physical network for content distribution, even though over-the-top players are bound to make use of the network of Internet Service Providers (Evens and Donders 2018; Thompson and Chen 2009).

In the pre-OTT world, both analog and digital television distribution were part of fairly neat value chain. Consumers paid a company in charge of distributing television signals for access to these signals and in many cases for access to premium content such as sports, film and drama. In combination with telephony or Internet subscription, so-called bundles or packages were born. This resulted in a fairly stable market environment where broadcasters reached consumers via intermediary companies. All of the involved actors had clearly defined roles in the value chain, and the consumer was the seemingly natural end point of the value chain (Evens 2013, 2014).

Together, the decline of linear television (even if still popular, certainly with older segments of the population) and the birth of over-the-top television have put pressure on this well-established system. While most companies active in the audiovisual market would argue that they embrace the anytime, anywhere, anyhow consumer logic, it is specifically this logic that has destabilized their industry enormously.

Broadcasters are challenged for obvious reasons. They have more difficulties in attracting viewers and securing advertising and yet, in the case of public broadcasters, insist on their relevance in the digital age. Traditional distributors of television signals (analog and digital), often divisions of more wealthy cable and telecommunications enterprises, face major challenges: the need to make massive investments in network capacity, meet the demands of broadcasters to compensate them for the transmission of their signal—even as linear television declines, and they struggle to keep consumers locked in via all kinds of packages (Evens and Donders 2018; Haucup and Heimeshoff 2014). Over-the-top players seem to be winners in this story, although they also face uncertainty. Netflix, for example, sees itself confronted with Disney and Apple going rogue. The acquisition of Time Warner by AT&T might also put pressure on the success of Netflix. Yet, it is relatively uncertain how these changes will affect European markets. In these markets, several broadcasters in Norway, France and the UK are experimenting with their own over-the-top offers, but so far without much success. Practices such as zero-rating, meaning that infrastructure players do not charge for data streaming or downloading of content, add to the uncertainty of where the market will take companies next. While for some Netflix seems to be invincible, the practice of cable operators of zero-rating their own premium bundles might provide an incentive for consumers to opt for that content instead of the services of Netflix or other market entrants, as the subscription prices are more attractive.

The everyday reality of the audiovisual industry is thus one of uncertainty. There is an ongoing war for control over the newly emerging value networks, without a clear indication of who is coming out on top. Evens and Donders (2018) have argued that content, connectivity, consumer data and capital are the ingredients for platform power. Nevertheless, how companies can be successful in mastering these elements has not yet fully crystallized. Distribution is, in such a volatile context, not something of the past, but an essential step to connect with viewers. A battle for control over user interfaces, i.e., the places where content is aggregated and distributed to consumers, is raging between rightsholders, Pay TV operators, telecommunications companies, broadcasters, OTT players and also relatively new entrants such as social media companies.

7.3 Why Small Media Markets Should Care About Pressure on Broadcasting

7.3.1 The Structural Fragility of Small Television Markets

There are several factors following the dynamics described above that affect small media markets. Firstly, small media markets are characterized by a limited number of players. In most of these markets, the public service broadcasters still play the most important role in terms of content production (Raats et al. 2018). Independent producers are dependent on a smaller number of "commissioners" to secure deals, which puts significant pressure on them. Secondly, these markets are characterized by less available funding. Public broadcasters have less funding than media companies in large markets, and their advertising revenues are considerably lower compared to those in larger markets. Advertising revenue, income from video on demand and subscription payments are lower given the limited size of the domestic market. As a consequence, in terms of production, overall budgets are lower and the budget per production is generally less. For Flanders, Econopolis (2017) calculated that purchasing a foreign drama is eleven times cheaper than investing in a domestic TV drama.[1] At the same time, the production budgets of foreign series are up to nine times the size of the budgets of the Flemish series. So, for most broadcasters, especially in small television markets, investing in foreign dramas is more attractive (Picard 2011). Media markets in small countries are therefore often characterized by higher levels of purchased content (Lowe et al. 2011b). From a distribution point of view, the development of online services to recoup investments is precarious given the significant investment, marketing costs and the limited scale. In contrast to the French-speaking Wallonian part of Belgium, where audiences clearly have an appetite for television content produced in the French market or the preferences of Irish audiences for UK content, Flemish audiences rarely turn to programming from the Netherlands (and vice versa). This limits the potential both of cross-border circulation of Flemish content in the Netherlands and for developing budgetary scale through co-productions, for example (Dhoest 2004).

Given the limited domestic audience, distributors usually lack the scale to compete for head-on with low fare subscriptions and usually take little interest in original production themselves, as the footprint of their subscriptions (and thus available resources) is lacking. Furthermore, issues concerning market size limit, theoretically, the export potential and thus recoupment through international distribution. Additionally, cultural specificity and language form an important barrier for content export. The popularity of Scandi-noir is based in part on the fact that series in the Nordic countries can secure higher budgets due to the Scandinavian geocultural market, which results from a traditionally higher cultural proximity between these countries, which has as an outcome a higher chance of a Swedish series, for example, to be picked up by Norwegian and Danish viewers (Jensen et al. 2016). However, small countries sharing a language with a large neighboring market (e.g., the French-speaking part of Belgium and France and Ireland and the UK) show great dependence on those larger markets. In this case, local broadcasters must compete with the public and private offerings of the neighboring country (examples include the BBC's popularity in Ireland and TF1 and RTL's popularity in Wallonia) and are by nature characterized by a limited production and distribution capacity. From a distribution point of view, there is also substantial potential when these structural barriers can be bypassed. One of the most promising developments over the past

---

[1]In Flanders, TV dramas are mostly produced by independent producers and broadcasters are thus given a limited license period, which limits the number of reruns and cost-efficiency for broadcasters.

year in the French-speaking part of Belgium was the launch of a joint public broad-caster and government fund (Fonds RTBF-FWB) which set out to only produce a 100% domestic Belgian 10-h drama series with particular reference to Belgian cul-ture and identity. The subsidies ensured the financial support for the series to be produced and was—given language proximity—picked up immediately in France and later on by streaming services such as Netflix, as was the case with the Belgian public broadcaster RTBF's hits *Ennemi Public* (*Public Enemy*) and *La Trêve* (*The Break*). The fact that no French co-producer was involved (which usually pushes French-speaking Belgian producers into the role of minority co-producers) meant that all profits flow back to the Wallonia region. The result is a significant uptake in the export of Wallonian drama and a significant recovery of costs due to local production, yet with international distribution at the core of its strategy.

A number of important lessons can be gleaned about small markets: They lack scale to develop volume, which impedes levels of domestic programming; it is dif-ficult to develop new large-scale distribution VOD services in these markets; they show a particular dependence on public funding (Milla et al. 2017; Raats et al. 2018), either directly from subsidies or from investments made by the public service broad-caster; and finally, they show the likely continued importance of broadcasters for the production of domestic content. It is precisely these players that seem to be confronted the hardest by the consequences of digitization and media convergence (cf. Berg 2011).

7.3.2   When Small Television Markets Are Hit, They Are Hit Hard

In the past decade, a combination of shifts has significantly affected the distribution of television content in Europe. Nonlinear viewing and ad-skipping have increasingly put pressure on the viewer ratings and advertising income of broadcasters, forcing them to expand existing activities online and develop 360° distribution strategies (Doyle 2016; Lobato 2019; Lotz 2007). Ironically, the most expensive genre (drama) also shows the highest rate of ad-skipping.

Aside from ad-skipping and delayed viewing, over-the-top players have entered the European market and have presented manifold challenges for traditional players. Firstly, media use has shifted toward video on demand (VOD), mainly subscription-based services (SVOD), provided by national distributors, broadcasters and telecoms or by international over-the-top streaming services such as Netflix, Hulu and Ama-zon, whose quality offerings for a monthly subscription compete directly with the offerings of traditional broadcasters. Not only do these new players compete for subscriptions and viewing time, but their entire business model, based on innova-tive forms of content consumption including binge-viewing and algorithm-based personalization of offerings, has significantly challenged traditional broadcasters' production and distribution strategies. Scale advantages allow these new players to compete with relatively cheap subscription fees. The recent addition and direct competitor of Netflix and Amazon Prime and Disney+, expected to be launched at the end of 2019, has already announced its monthly subscription fee of $6.99 (Spangler 2019). For broadcasters, this has proven to be highly challenging as they are limited to existing programming schedules, channels and brands, and a significant increase in their on-demand catalogs is not expected to secure sufficient returns on investment. Broadcasters have stretched their services to online, allowing different forms of catch-up, VOD and live-streaming services and allowing short form or web-only content to attract viewers. For larger markets, such as Poland and Germany, these services might be a relevant source of revenue due to the scale of the market, yet in smaller markets such as Flanders, the return on investment generally remains limited at this point, due to the relatively low number of viewers (interview Medialaan, June 2017; interview SBS, June 2017).

Secondly, scale advantages also allow these players to invest significant sums of money in original content and acquisition of licensed content. Legacy broadcasters and domestic telecom incumbents directly compete with OTT players like Amazon and HBO Go for rights acquisition of high-end content. Broadcasters, traditionally sharing rights only with independent producers or no players at all, are now forced to share exclusivity with players like Netflix, Pay TV operators or telecom companies. Moreover, domestic offerings directly compete with high-quality original content from Netflix, Amazon and others. For content producers, the advent of these non-domestic and domestic distribution services theoretically provides an additional outlet for expanding budgets, and valorizing return on investment (Raats and Jensen forthcoming). Yet, in practice, various media professionals and policymakers fear an increasing fragmentation of financing and a return that does not compensate for losses incurred due to direct competition with platforms.

Thirdly, platforms like Google and Facebook are also competing with domestic players for advertisement revenue. A recent study found that more than half of all online advertisement in Europe flows to Google and Facebook, revenue that is not re-invested in the production and distribution of original European content (such as quality journalism, local fiction or children's television) (Fontaine et al. 2018).

The fragmentation of the European market, being characterized by significant differences between large and small Member States and diversity of cultural preferences and languages, has resulted—notwithstanding exceptions such as the UK—in a clear focus by European players on domestic markets only within territorial boundaries. The focus on domestic audiences has in turn hampered European-wide releases of television content and reinforced the existing fragmentation in audiovisual markets within the VOD offerings in European markets (Bignell and Fickers 2008; Fontaine et al. 2018).

7.4   Flanders: A Fragile, yet Vibrant Market

The Flemish market can be considered an example of a small media market. Aside from the public broadcaster VRT, two private broadcasters (Medialaan and SBS) operate in the market, each of which is comprised of a generalist channel and thematic smaller channels. Cable distributor Telenet and telecom incumbent Proximus both offer digital television and a number of Pay TV services (transactional VOD as well as subscription-based services) to their audiences. The independent production industry is scattered across more than 60 companies, which have seen an increasing consolidation over the past decade, characterized by increasing foreign ownership. In 2019, for example, one of the largest production companies, "De Mensen," was taken over by the TF1-owned French "Newen" (De Tijd 2019). Flanders demonstrates the limits of a small television market (Raats et al. 2016; Puppis 2009): limited audiences and thus limited potential for return on investment, limitations on export due to language and lack of scale and a limited number of players. Yet, the Flemish television market is a highly vibrant market characterized by a significant proportion of domestically produced television content due to its enormous popularity. This is clearly illustrated in an example from 2012, when private broadcaster SBS's ownership changed from ProsiebenSat.1 to a consortium including one of the most successful Flemish production companies, Woestijnvis. The takeover resulted in an increased volume of domestic original production and thus increased competition in an already fragile market. Pressure on existing financing of television production and limited return on investment should thus be considered side by side with an already highly competitive market where competition seems to be driven by the media companies' credo that maximizing local content is the best strategy for outperforming competitors (see several interviews with independent producers, broadcasters and cable/telecom distributors).

Even more important for understanding the increasing pressure on the financing of television content is the increased popularity of nonlinear and time-shifted viewing. In Flanders, a subscription for digital television comes not only with the option to watch different linear channels, but also to record multiple programs at the same time on the set-top box. This allows viewers to record multiple programs at once, or rewatch content and skip ads and is considered an acquired right by the customer (interview with television distributor, July 2018). Research from Econopolis and the Free University of Brussels indicated that 17.5% of viewing in general is now time-shifted, going up to 32.7% for the age group of 18–54 for commercial broadcasters, the primary target group for advertisers. The high levels of time-shifted viewing are comparable with the proportions of time-shifted viewing in Switzerland (16.7%), but are significantly higher than other European markets—for instance, the Netherlands (9.4%), Sweden (7.5%), Germany (2.8%) and Spain (2.2%) (Econopolis 2018: 9).

The popularity of locally produced Flemish content also explains the slower uptake of domestic subscription services from cable and telecom providers, and of foreign subscription-based services such as Amazon and Netflix. Despite having no official insights into the number of subscriptions on Netflix, recent audience research from Digimeter showed that 21% of the Flemish population has Netflix, and within the age groups of 16- to 24-year-olds and 25- to 34-year-olds, respectively, 55% and 59% had access to Netflix (Digimeter 2019).

Partly mitigating the pressure on domestic production are the various policy support mechanisms for the television industry. In addition to media fund financing, which supports television drama, documentary and animation series, a tax shelter measure has proven to be incredibly important to sustain and develop television production volume (a recent study estimated more than €80 million in indirect government support flows back annually into audiovisual production in this way) (Econopolis 2018). Additionally, domestic distributors of television signals must contribute an annual fee based on their number of subscriptions to the domestic original production. Since 2019, under the new Audiovisual Media Services Directive provisions, the government has also obliged players not based in Flanders but targeting the Flemish market (like Netflix) to contribute a percentage of their turnover in Flanders to audiovisual production (Donders et al. 2018a, b, c).

7.5   How Media Managers Act Upon This: A Case Study of Flanders

7.5.1   A (One-Sided) Ecosystem Approach

A strategic goal that is often repeated in Flanders is the need to collaborate more. Over the past five years, private media players' rhetoric has repeatedly emphasized the idea of collaboration in order to protect the domestic "media ecosystem." Small media markets such as Flanders were quite stable in the face of foreign takeovers and market entrants during the 1990s and 2000s, but much has changed with the introduction of social network platforms, over-the-top streaming players and aggregators. In our interviews with Flemish media players (private broadcasters, distributors and producers), three concerns were repeatedly voiced with regard to these new market entrants. Firstly, players like Facebook and Google have become competitors in the advertising market. Advertising spending that used to go to domestic players now migrates to platforms operating outside the nation's borders. The business models of the new players rely much more on acquiring user data, which enables targeted advertising on a large scale. Finally, players like Netflix and Google operate on a scale that grants them the opportunity for significant investment in platforms, standards and services and to enjoy brand marketing on a global scale. In essence, the logic for these proposed collaborations for local production is the same: By doing things together, Flemish media players can build the scale required to compete with larger market entrants. The "smallness" of the Flemish market is put forward by the interviewees as the key to legitimizing domestic collaborations. For example, they consistently use the terms "ecosystem" and "sustainability" and refer to the importance of "Flemish quality content" as opposed to mainly US-originated content, to highlight the importance of balance between international and domestic offerings. The need for collaboration among "Flemish" domestic players is emphasized especially in the rhetoric of a "shared fate" and having a common adversary in the form of on-demand streaming services such as Netflix or video-sharing platforms such as Google. Policymakers themselves have adopted and propagated discourse on partnerships and pushed collaboration in several domains, not least by proclaiming partnerships and "market strengthening" as key roles for the public broadcaster VRT (Raats and Donders 2017).

However, it is problematic that thus far, this partnership rhetoric has not resulted in many actual partnerships, and the rhetoric of collaboration has proven especially painful since interests within the ecosystem itself have been opposed to one another. The push for collaboration in various domains has often led to some sort of standstill (Donders et al. 2018c). Collaboration proved especially difficult in discussions on finding a solution for the increase in time-shifted viewing, where the opinions and interests of distributors, who wanted to offer delayed viewing to their clients, were diametrically opposed to the views of broadcasters, who called for some sort of limit to ad-skipping. In three parliamentary hearings (in 2016, 2017 and 2018), often held on occasions when new data on ad-skipping or increased advertisement revenue loss were presented by researchers (see Econopolis 2017, 2018), the broadcasters SBS and Medialaan urged a "common solution." The Minister of Media Sven Gatz, for his part, has on various occasions acknowledged the need to find a common solution and urged broadcasters to collaborate with distributors to find a way forward. A first attempt resulted in an "ultimatum" according to which the minister of media would intervene if the players did not come to a solution themselves. A second attempt resulted in the media cabinet launching a backdoor consultation in which the different stakeholders could propose their own views. However, in the meantime a common solution seems even further away as Medialaan recently launched its new streaming service "VTM GO" (see below), directly aimed at competing with Telenet (the owner of broadcaster SBS), which launched its own Pay TV service only a few weeks prior to the launch of "VTM GO."

The "common adversary" approach taken by domestic players did prove successful in securing more financial support for Flemish television productions and raised the budget of the Flemish media fund to its level before cutbacks were imposed in Flanders in 2018. It also motivated the government to oblige domestic television distributors to invest in domestic production. Interestingly, in recent years these distributors have positioned themselves more clearly as supporters of local content (which led to an increase in license and co-production deals) to differentiate themselves from Netflix.

7.5.2   Increasing Scale, or the Continuing Struggle for a Joint VOD Portal

One strategic goal of these initiatives was to grow in scale in order to develop new distribution services. One of the ideas resulting from the "shared fate" and "common adversary" rhetoric was the idea to launch a Flemish Netflix: by collaborating, overcoming barriers of scale, sharing investment, development and marketing costs, and pooling limited volumes of content into one large service. This idea is neither new, nor restricted to the Flemish market. In Denmark, discussions are taking place regarding the launch of a VOD service proverbially called "Danflix." Moreover, in the UK, France and the Netherlands, similar services have already been set up.[2] What the already existing similar streaming services have in common is that they have all been developed in large media markets where investment and marketing costs are likely to be more easily recouped due to a larger number of subscriptions. The portals have also highlighted the importance of significant catalog volume, as well as the importance of having exclusive content in the form of previews, first-look deals or real "originals."

In Flanders, ideas for a joint Flemish VOD streaming service for television content date back to 2010, when plans by VRT for a Flemish online platform resulted in a policy push to include private players as well (Van den Bulck and Donders 2014). Different interests and opposing business models caused these plans to stall, only to be picked up in a second attempt in the form of "Rumble" (later "Stievie"). It was presented as a monthly subscription-based service combining content from the public broadcasters as well as the two private broadcasters. Again, a lack of subscriptions necessitated a different strategy, whereby Stievie was provided in both free (advertisement) and subscription-based forms. The difficult history of developing joint distribution services in Flanders shows the limited potential of a domestic so-called Flemish Netflix today, because of a combination of factors: (i) the difficult position of the public service broadcaster, which, as part of the fulfilling of its public remit, must reach as many Flemish viewers as possible, irrespective of the type of service (linear, mobile, online, etc.) with its programming; (ii) the lack of scale and potential number of subscribers, which puts heavy pressure on catalog, licenses and marketing costs (cf. Green 2018); and (iii) the different interests of the players involved, which is especially difficult due to private broadcaster SBS being owned by a distributor, as both do not always have the same interests (a local Netflix could prove harmful for the business model of television distributors' VOD streaming and linear streaming offerings).

---

[2]Namely "Salto" (France), "Nederland Ziet" (Netherlands) and "Britbox" (UK).

7.5.3 Increased Valorization: The Many Attempts to Compensate for TV Advertisement

It is clear that a one-size-fits-all approach to compensate for the decrease in an advertisement on linear television is not sufficient. Instead, and in line with various other small television markets in Europe, media managers in Flanders have focused on a combination of strategies to increase revenue through distribution.

One way of doing this is by expanding the available slots for television advertisement. This has partly motivated Medialaan's decision to acquire thematic channels "Vitaya" and "Acht" (now "Caz") and motivated SBS's decision to launch "Zes" alongside its other two channels. The strategy allows broadcasters to program more advertisement and thus partly compensates for the loss of Gross Rating Points (GRP) due to delayed viewing (interview with broadcaster, June 2018). Advertisements that are skipped are thus not valorized. But these can now be valorized through the programming of more slots, hence the need for increased broadcast volume. As a consequence, the number of broadcast hours of the two main commercial broadcasters increased by 39% between 2008 and 2018 (age category 18–54) (Econopolis 2018: 33). Note that the increase in output does not necessarily mean an increase in Flemish content. On the contrary, the content is often part of a package deal acquisition which does not have a place in the regular programming of the generalist commercial channels, mostly due to the concentration of local content (interview with broadcaster, June 2018). SBS's channel Zes, for example, was explicitly launched in the market with the tagline "USA. All Day." Aside from advertisement inventory, audiences are also increasingly guided toward the online portals of these channels. As illustrated by a Flemish broadcaster:

> The viewing of short form videos from *The Voice* has tripled over the last five years. From 300,000 clips to 900,000 per episode… We have 150,000 additional registered viewers of *The Voice* on our online platform, a lot of whom are new viewers that we did not reach before (Flemish broadcaster, June 2016).

In our earlier interviews from 2016, user data was seen as giving more control. Media managers often referred to the importance of reaching younger audiences and the fact that large platforms like Google and Facebook had an enormous advantage in terms of scale in developing ways of measuring audience preferences, commercializing audience data and building platforms that integrated existing services. However, whereas until 2017 Web sites mainly served as an additional promotional tool, now more and more online-only content is being produced, especially around commercial hits such as *The Voice*, *Love Island* and *My Restaurant Rules*. Medialaan explicitly invested in promoting its "app," because not only is direct views of advertisements important (in the form of pre-, mid- or end-rolls), but also is the collection of user data. In 2019, Medialaan launched its VTM GO app that not only provides the possibility of rewatching or live-streaming television content, but also includes a back catalog of old Medialaan programs, films and international drama through a partnership with the UK service "Walter Presents."

Another means to intensify ad revenue is the introduction of targeted advertisement on linear television. As ad revenues are said to be much higher when explicitly targeting audience preferences and demographics, media managers expect a lot from this new form of advertisement. Experiments in 2017 received some public concern related to privacy, but in their defense, media managers have highlighted the importance of sustaining domestic content production. Whether these ads will be more interesting for audiences because they promote more "relevant" products that are less likely to be skipped is yet to be seen (an often-heard prediction by media managers). However, the strategy might at least partly compensate for current losses. Additionally, media managers emphasize that not all advertisers want to participate in targeted campaigns, since many players still prefer large, nation-wide campaigns (interview with distributor, July 2018).

7.5.4 Valorization Through International Content Distribution

In addition to increased valorization through online services taken up by legacy players in order to remain sustainable, we also find increased valorization through expanding exports. This strategy is mainly driven by Flemish independent production companies, which in recent years have become much more active in selling television content overseas. One way of doing this is by increasing production budgets by involving foreign broadcasters or distributors as investors in content production, in the form of co-production or a presale deal (in which financing is provided in the form of a minimum guarantee, as an advance for sales in specific territories). Recent examples of Flemish TV dramas, such as *Hotel Beau Sejour* (2016) (co-production with ARTE and sold to Netflix), *Tabula Rasa* (2017) (co-production with ZDFe and ZDFNeo and sold to Netflix) and *Over Water* (2018) (co-production with ZDFe), have shown that increased budget and production quality can result in broader international sales and wider acclaim (Raats 2018). The increased potential of return on investment has also made broadcasters, especially the public broadcaster, more interested in attracting co-financing and co-production on the international market. In that regard, interestingly, Netflix, although perceived as an adversary on many levels, has seemingly become part of the solution, in the form of return on investment. In 2019, the strategy resulted in the first Flemish "Netflix original" (*Undercover*), in which Netflix co-invested with VRT and the Dutch public broadcaster and local distributor (Raats and Jensen forthcoming).

On the other hand, however, there are some risks. Firstly, investments made by these players are, especially given the size of the territories they are obtaining a license for, quite limited at this point, as are the direct investments in production financing (interview with independent producers, January 2019; interview with broadcaster, May 2017). Secondly, it may be difficult for domestic players to maintain brand distinctiveness, which could be especially problematic for public broadcasters. Thirdly, it increases the volume of domestic content in the catalogs of portals that were hitherto associated with international content. This reduces the current competitive advantage of domestic distributors and broadcasters vis-à-vis these international portals. And finally, it increases pressure on private broadcasters to invest bigger sums in more "risky" high-end content that does not always appeal to the tastes of domestic audiences. In the past two years, this resulted in VRT securing bigger-budget quality drama deals with producers and especially broadcaster Medialaan losing out on interesting content deals due to lack of funds (interview with broadcaster, June 2016).

It is clear that generating some increased return on investment is only limited to specific genres (mainly television drama) and has not reduced the pressure on various other forms of domestic television content that are still expensive to produce and yet whose costs are very difficult to recoup (e.g., reality TV, live entertainment, etc.). Flemish producers and broadcasters have therefore increased their efforts (albeit modestly) to develop program formats, primarily to boost creativity within their local market, but also to increase the potential for international returns on investment. The Flemish production company Shelter, for example, fully owned by DPG Media, managed to develop hit after hit in terms of international acclaim (*Benidorm Bastards*, *What If?*, *Did You Get the Message?*) that also resulted in worldwide remake deals (interview with broadcaster, May 2017). Other Flemish production companies opened offices in the Netherlands or have pooled resources on international television markets.

7.6   Discussion and Conclusions

This chapter provided a case study of current strategic responses from media managers in small markets to changing production and distribution patterns. With particular attention to the future of domestic broadcasting, we focused on the one hand on the combination of production and distribution of content, as shifts in both are continuously interrelated, and on the other hand on discussions about future distribution in Flanders, which are always presented with a focus on "domestic Flemish production." Firstly, we acknowledged how these strategies are clearly affected by (i) shifting user behavior, (ii) internationalization and market concentration trends and (iii) the penetration of new global platforms into small domestic markets. Our research clearly confirmed existing literature that mainly focuses on large markets. However, Flanders differs from large markets with regard to the spectacular increase in delayed viewing, which has put significant pressure on the ad revenue of commercial broadcasters, and can be considered an even more pressing problem than the competition with new VOD streaming services. The situation has become more precarious since Telenet acquired a broadcaster, which has offered more leeway for SBS, yet has put even more pressure on the largest commercial (and still Flemish-owned) company, Medialaan. In 2019, Medialaan announced the full integration of its newspaper division and broadcasting company in an attempt to exploit user data and valorize revenue on a number of services, under the heading "DPG Media" (De Morgen 2019).

In addition to increased consolidation of brands and companies, we have discussed a combination of strategic responses: a focus on collaboration and a common adversary in policy and industry discourse; strategies to develop joint VOD services; increasing valorization of revenue through increased ad inventory on linear television; increasing investments in online services; international export (remakes and license deals); investments in targeted or "addressable" advertisement; and increased collaboration between domestic media players. Clearly, a combination of strategies is preferred to compensate for the loss in advertising revenue seen by linear broadcasters.

Interestingly, many of the strategies are based on the advantages of scale and thus difficult to operationalize in a small market. A service that pools resources and aims to compete with relatively cheap and ever-growing catalogs of international offerings, such as the aforementioned "Flemish Netflix," is at present not very likely to stand a chance, at least as long as delayed viewing is allowed. In a similar vein, the strategies of broadcasters to increase investment in domestic content, in order to differentiate themselves from foreign players, puts even more pressure on domestic markets, as the scale is lacking to valorize the high costs of these programs. While domestic volume still attracts significant audiences, the problem is that the programs are mainly meant for traditional broadcasting viewing and yet are unlikely to keep viewers glued to traditional broadcasting, especially younger generations. What is more, the continuous rat race of programming more local content might encourage more delayed viewing as broadcasters compete with one another in the same programming slots. More Flemish content also implies higher costs (compared to foreign acquisitions) and thus increases pressure on existing business models. As a response, the pressure on governments to ensure sustainability is rising even more. However, support policies in the form of fiscal advantages and subsidies only partially remedy the current difficulties of content production in small markets. They do not provide a fundamentally new model of arranging investment and revenue in audiovisual ecosystems. And governments in small markets have themselves proven to be inconsistent on the matter. In Flanders, the government has attempted to sustain production by several measures (including a Netflix tax, investment obligations for distributors, and a Flemish media fund). But, at the same time, they insufficiently anticipated the likely impact of concentration in the market and have significantly cut back on public broadcasting budgets.

Thus, we find that the different strategies are mostly driven by short-term considerations to increase valorization rather than lay the groundwork for long-term sustainability. The fact that to date no agreement between distributors and broadcasters has been reached is a testament to the problematic situation. Similarly, although launching more channels might generate more return in the short run, it also increases the fragmentation of existing broadcasting channels and contributes to a faster uptake in nonlinear viewing.

It is clear that the current trends are likely to result in significant consolidation in the next decade. Levels of domestic content production are likely to decrease at some point, as private broadcasters will not be able to maintain high spending levels on original programming. It is reasonable to predict that players like Netflix will step in and, in the next decade, significantly invest in content deals and Flemish (co-)productions, as will legacy distributors. However, it is unlikely that current levels of production will be sustained without the backbone of traditional broadcasters. [3]

References

Barwise, P., & Picard, R. (2012). *The economics of television in a digital world: What economics tells us for future policy debates.* Oxford: Oxford University Reuters Institute for Journalism.

Berg, C. E. (2011). Sizing up size on TV markets: Why David would lose to Goliath. In G. F. Lowe & C. S. Nissen (Eds.), *Small among giants: Television broadcasting in smaller countries* (pp. 57–89). Göteborg: Nordicom.

Bielby, D. D., & Harrington, L. (2008). *Global TV: Exporting television and culture in the world market.* New York, NY: NYU Press.

Bignell, J., & Fickers, A. (Eds.). (2008). *A European television history.* London: Wiley-Blackwell.

Brown, A., & Picard, R. G. (Eds.). (2005). *Digital terrestrial television in Europe.* New York NY: Routledge.

Collins, R. (2011). Content online and the end of public media? The UK, a canary in the coal mine? *Media, Culture & Society, 33*(8), 1202–1219.

Davis, C., & Zboralska, E. (2017). Transnational over-the-top media distribution as a business and policy disruptor: The case of Netflix in Canada. *Journal of Media Innovations, 4*(1), 4–25.

De Morgen. (2019). Mediabedrijf Persgroep wordt DPG Media. *De Morgen,* 23 May 2019. www.demorgen.be/nieuws/mediabedrijf-de-persgroep-wordt-dpg-media~ba4df333. Accessed June 4, 2019.

Donders, K., Enli, G., Raats, T., & Syvertsen, T. (2018a). Digitisation, internationalisation, and changing business models in local media markets: An analysis of commercial media's perceptions on challenges ahead. *Journal of Media Business Studies, 15*(2), 89–107.

Donders, K., Raats, T., Komorowski, M., Kostovska, I., Tintel, S., & Iordache, C. (2018b). *Obligations on on-demand audiovisual media services providers to financially contribute to the production of European works: An analysis of European member states' practices.* Brussels: imec-SMIT-VUB.

Donders, K., Raats, T., & Van den Bulck, H. (2018c). The politics of pleasing: A critical analysis of multistakeholderism in Public Service Media policies in Flanders. *Media, Culture and Society, 41*(3), 347–366.

Doyle, G. (2016). Digitization and changing windowing strategies in the television industry: Negotiating new windows on the world. *Television and New Media, 17*(7), 629–645.

De Tijd. (2019). Fransen kopen productiehuis achter Reizen Waes. *De Tijd,* 19 February. www.tijd.be/tech-media/media-marketing/fransen-kopen-productiehuis-achter-reizen-waes/10103012.html. Accessed June 4, 2019.

Dhoest, A. (2004). Negotiating images of the nation: The production of Flemish TV drama, 1953–89. *Media, Culture and Society, 26*(3), 393–408.

Digimeter. (2019). *imec.digimeter 2018.* Louvain: imec.

Econopolis. (2017). *Doorlichting Vlaams audiovisueel beleid. [Evaluation of the Flemish audiovisual policy]* Wilrijk: Econopolis/imec-SMIT-VUB.

Econopolis. (2018). *Leefbaarheid van productie, aggregatie en distributie van audiovisuele content in Vlaanderen.* Wilrijk: Econopolis/imec-SMIT, VUB.

---

[3]Disclosure statement: No potential conflict of interest was reported by the authors.

Esser, A. (2013). Format is king: Television formats and commercialisation. In K. Donders, C. Pauwels, & J. Loisen (Eds.), *Private television in Western Europe: Content, markets and policies* (pp. 151–168). Basingstoke: Palgrave Macmillan.

European Audiovisual Observatory. (2018). *Online video sharing: offerings, audiences, economic aspects*. Strassbourg: EAO.

Evens, T. (2013). The political economy of retransmission payments and cable rights: Implications for private television companies. In K. Donders, C. Pauwels, & J. Loisen (Eds.), *Private television in Western Europe: Content, markets and policies* (pp. 182–196). Basingstoke: Palgrave Macmillan.

Evens, T. (2014). If you won't pay them, buy them! Merger Mania in distribution and content markets. *International Journal of Digital Television, 5*(3), 261–265.

Evens, T., & Donders, K. (2016). Mergers and acquisitions in TV broadcasting and distribution: Challenges for competition, industrial and media policy. *Telematics and Informatics, 33*(2), 674–682.

Evens, T., & Donders, K. (2018). *Platform power and policy in transforming television markets*. Basingstoke: Palgrave.

Fontaine, G., Grece, C., & Pumares, M. J. (2018). *Online video sharing: Offerings, audiences, economic aspects*. Strassbourg: European Audiovisual Observatory.

Green, T. (2018). Netflix's 8.3 million new subscribers didn't come cheap. *The Motley Fool*, January 23. https://www.fool.com/investing/2018/01/23/netflixs-83-million-new-subscribers-didnt-come-che.aspx. Accessed June 4, 2019.

Haucup, J., & Heimeshoff, U. (2014). Google, Facebook, Amazon, eBay: Is the Internet driving competition or market monopolisation? *International Economics and Economic Policy, 11*(1–2), 49–61.

Hoelck, K., & Ballon, P. (2015). Competitive dynamics in the ICT sector: Strategic decisions in platform ecosystems. *Communication & Strategies, 99*, 51–71.

Jensen, P. M., Nielsen, J. I., & Waade, A. M. (2016). When public service drama travels: The internationalization of Danish television drama and the associated production models. *Journal of Popular Television, 4*(1), 91–108.

Küng, L. (2013). Innovation, technology and organisational change: Legacy media's big challenges. In T. Storsul & A. H. Krumswik (Eds.), *Media innovations: A multidisciplinary study of change* (pp. 9–12). Göteborg: Nordicom.

Lobato, R. (2019). *Netflix nations: The geography of digital distribution*. New York NY: NYU Press.

Lowe, G. F., Berg, C. E., & Nissen, C. S. (2011a). Size matters for TV broadcasting policy. In G. F. Lowe & C. S. Nissen (Eds.), *Small among giants: Television broadcasting in smaller countries* (pp. 21–41). Göteborg: Nordicom.

Lowe, G. F., Berg, C. E., & Nissen, C. S. (2011b). *Small among giants: Television broadcasting in smaller countries*. Gothenborg: Nordicom.

Lotz, A. D. (2007). *The television will be revolutionized*. New York NY: NYU Press.

Milla, T., Julio, G. F., & Kanzler, M. (2017). *Public financing for film and television content: The state of soft money in Europe*. Strassbourg: European Audiovisual Observatory.

Picard, R. G., Charles, H., Davis, F. P., & Park, S. (2016). Platform proliferation and its implications for domestic content policies. *Telematics and Informatics, 33*(2), 683–692.

Picard, R. G. (2011). Broadcast economics, challenges of scale, and country Size. In G. F. Lowe & C. S. Nissen (Eds.), *Small among giants: Television broadcasting in smaller countries* (pp. 43–56). Göteborg: Nordicom.

Picha Edwardsson, M., & Pargman, D. (2014). Explorative scenarios of emerging media trends. *Journal of Print and Media Technology Research, 3*(3), 195–206.

Puppis, M. (2009). Media regulation in small states. *International Communications Gazette, 71*(1–2), 7–17.

Raats, T. (2018). The Flemish TV market: Crime drama as a driver for small market sustainability? In S. Turnbull, S. Peacock, & K. T. Hansen (Eds.), *European television crime drama and beyond* (pp. 233–251). Basingstoke: Palgrave.

Raats, T., Evens, T., & Ruelens, S. (2016). Challenges for sustaining local audiovisual ecosystems: Analysis of financing and production of domestic TV fiction in small media markets. *Journal of Popular Television, 4*(1), 129–147.

Raats, T., & Jensen, P. M. (forthcoming). The role of public service media in sustaining TV drama. *Television and New Media* (accepted for publication).

Raats, T & Donders, K. (2017). Public service media and partnerships: Analysis of policies and strategies in Flanders. In M. Glowacki, B. Ostrowska (Eds.), *Public service media renewal: Adaptation to digital network challenges* (pp. 39–60). Berlin: Peter Lang.

Raats, T., Schooneknaep, I., & Pauwels, C. (2018). National distribution support for film: An analysis of 20 years of distribution enhancing policies in Europe. In P. C. Murschetz, R. Teichmann, & M. Karmasin (Eds.), *Public funding for film—Challenges, purposes and international cases* (pp. 193–210). Berlin: Springer.

Spangler, T. (2019). Disney+ to launch in November, priced at $6.99 monthly. *Variety*, April 11. https://variety.com/2019/digital/news/disnesy-plus-streaming-launch-date-pricing-1203187007. Accessed June 4, 2019.

Syvertsen, T., Enli, G., Mjøs, O. J., & Moe, H. (2014). *The media welfare state: Nordic media in the digital era*. Ann Arbor MI: University of Michigan Press.

Tandoc, E. C. (2014). Journalism is twerking? How web analytics is changing the process of gatekeeping. *New Media & Society, 16*(4), 559–575.

Thompson, G., & Chen, Y. F. (2009). IPTV: Reinventing television in the Internet age. *IEEE Internet Computing, 13*(3), 11–14.

Van den Bulck, H., & Donders, K. (2014). Pitfalls and obstacles of media policy making in an age of digital convergence: The Flemish signal integrity case. *Journal of Information Policy, 4*, 444–462.

Tim Raats is Assistant Professor in the Communication Sciences Department, the Vrije Universiteit Brussel, where he lectures on domestic and European media policy. He heads the Media Economics and Policy Unit at SMIT, part of the Vrije Universiteit Brussel and IMEC. He specializes in policy and market research on production and distribution in small media markets. He coordinated several research projects for the Minister of Media, the Flemish Department of Culture, Youth and Media, the Sector Council for Media in Flanders and the Flemish producers' associations—VOFTP and VRT. Since 2018, he has served as a member of the board of governors of the Flanders Audiovisual Fund.

Karen Donders is Assistant Professor of Media Policy and European Media Markets, the Vrije Universiteit Brussel. She is senior researcher of the research group Studies on Media Innovation and Technology where she heads the Media and Society Research Program. She specializes in European media policy, competition policy and its impact on media sectors, public service media, valorization of media content, and the interplay between media policy and economics. She has published widely on these issues in international peer-reviewed journals such as *European Journal of Communication Media Culture & Society Journal of Media Law* and *Convergence*. She is the author of *Public Service Media and Policy in Europe* (2012) and co-author of *Platform Power and Policy in Transforming Television Markets* (with Tom Evens, 2012).

Chapter 8
Industry Divide: The Interdependence of Traditional Cinematic Distribution and VOD in Poland

Marcin Adamczak

8.1 Introduction

This chapter examines interrelations between traditional cinematic distribution and the relatively new field of video on demand (VOD) distribution in Poland. The market logic behind the approach of local cinema distributors to this new phenomenon requires some elaboration. Historically, new modes of movie distribution such as terrestrial, satellite, cable TV, VHS and DVD were sooner or later incorporated into the traditional business model of the film industry, concentrated around cinemas as the primary market and treated as additional sources of revenues. VOD seems to be a challenging technology to incorporate because of its distinct operational logic and a new set of corporate players that are no less powerful than traditional film market behemoths. The chapter is based on seven semi-structured interviews with Polish cinema distributors and managers of VOD services and on statistical market data. It outlines the structure of the VOD market and the differences between this new field and traditional cinematic distribution, interrelations between sectors, power plays between both sides and the impact of the VOD market—perceived by theatrical distributors as an opportunity for additional revenue and as a competitor at the same time. The influence of particular business actors in the VOD sector on traditional distribution will also be examined.

M. Adamczak (✉)
Department of Anthropology and Cultural Studies, Adam Mickiewicz University in Poznań, ul. Szamarzewskiego 89a, 60 568 Poznań, Poland
e-mail: m_adamczak80@wp.pl

© The Author(s) 2020
P. Szczepanik et al. (eds.), *Digital Peripheries*, Springer Series in Media Industries,
https://doi.org/10.1007/978-3-030-44850-9_8

8.2   Structure of the Polish Market and Interdependence of Industries

Polish cinema cannot be clearly defined as "small" or "big." The number of annual productions is relatively low, with just over 50 feature films made every year. However, from 2016 onward, the Polish cinema market has been among the top 20 world markets in terms of US dollar-denominated revenue and has been steadily on the rise for the past couple of years. The most accurate description of the Polish market would be to say that it is on the move, undergoing a transformation from a "small" to at least a middle-sized market (Table 8.1).

The market transition process is undoubtedly shaping the relationship between traditional cinematic distribution and the VOD sector in Poland. There are two factors at play—the development of Internet distribution and the VOD market as well as the dynamic development of the traditional cinematic distribution market, which is now the largest in history in terms of box office. Both are interconnected, and significantly growing box office revenues have an impact on the VOD market.

Cinematic distribution allows distributors to make profits or, in some less fortunate situations, at least to cover the print and advertising (P&A) costs and open up a further possibility of selling television rights, which is still a lucrative business, especially in Pay TV (Pay TV contracts are oftentimes higher than the distributor's net profit from cinematic distribution). In contrast, the once-profitable DVD/Blu-ray market

Table 8.1 Development of the Polish cinema market compared to the five biggest markets in Western Europe and the two biggest markets in Central and Eastern Europe (box office and tickets per capita sold, 2010–2017)

	France	Germany	UK	Italy	Spain	Czech Republic	Hungary	Poland
Box office, 2010 (admissions in millions)	206.3	126.6	169.2	123.4	101.6	13.5	11	37.5
Tickets per capita, 2010	3.28	1.55	2.72	2.05	2.21	1.3	1.1	0.98
Box office, 2017 (millions of admissions)	209.4	122.3	170.6	99.2	100.2	15.2	14.9	56.6
Tickets per capita, 2017	3.1	1.5	2.6	1.6	2.2	1.4	1.5	1.5
Growth in percent (%)	+1.5	−3.3	+0.8	−19	−1.3	+12	+35	+51

Source calculations based on Focus: World Film Market reports

has become so unappealing that in the case of many smaller titles, the distributors are not even particularly inclined to release their film on such media.

For big cinema distributors, the VOD market remains a fairly "technical" sphere treated as an additional source of income—not particularly profitable for now, although this could change in the future (that is why they secure long-term rights to this release window). However, no particular effort is directed in Poland at VOD in terms of intense or innovative promotion. For big distributors such as Kino Świat, Monolith or the subsidiaries of Hollywood studios, the real profit lies in the traditional market (cinema and subsequent television rights), while small- and middle-sized distributors such as Gutek Film carry out a sort of art house vertical and horizontal integration (cinematic distribution, controlling at least a few cinemas, organizing film festivals and controlling their budget for licenses, educational programs financed from public funds). Additionally, large stakeholders among distributors know not only that traditional cinematic distribution offers them the biggest and quickest profits, which is crucial for the company's cash flow, but also that success in this field is the basis for creating an attractive catalogue and gaining a good position in negotiations with VOD services (Table 8.2).

It is particularly telling that apart from Monolith (its Cineman service—www.cineman.pl—has a fairly marginal reach), no distributor has ever even tried to set up their own VOD portal, nor have there been any plans to create a joint platform for several distributors. Kino Świat previously had shares in Strefa VOD and Iplex and is currently distributing its films on YouTube in the AVOD mode. There are, however, a few cases of vertical integration by a distribution company and a large cinema network. Examples include the ITI Group (ITI Cinema—cinematic distribution, Multikino—network of cinemas, TVN and its theme channels—TV station),

Table 8.2 Market shares of Polish distributors, 2013–2017 (in percent)

Company	2013	2014	2015	2016	2017
UIP	16.98	12.11	24.11	18.19	25.84
Kino Świat	13.57	18.16	15.20	19.69	19.24
Disney	12.59	8.13	13.74	14.88	13.69
Forum Film	12.49	10.50	10.07	4.98	1.33
Monolith	11.04	14.49	8.55	11.03	10.68
Imperial Cinepix	8.41	10.01	10.38	12.41	6.56
Warner	7.75	6.91	5.57	8.25	9.28
Next Film	3.87	6.88	4.73	1.53	5.97
Vue Movie	8.35	6.88	1.45	3.02	–
Best Film	1.26	–	1.04	–	–
Gutek Film	1.1	1.72	1.63	1.12	1.25
Interfilm	–	2.09	1.68	2.17	–

Source calculations based on reports of the Polish Film Institute; the data includes all companies with more than one percent of market share

Agora (Next Film and its Helios network of cinemas) and an integration of the distribution company Forum Film with the Cinema City network. The VOD market comes across as a quite different and separate entity.

8.3   The VOD Market in Poland: Concentration Around the Powerful

The VOD market is characterized by high barriers to entry for new or smaller platforms. The most important is the amount of financial capital needed to acquire comprehensive, fresh and attractive content for the catalogue and to cover the advertising and technological requirements, in addition to the process of operating a portal. Even if smaller players find a niche (e.g., documentary films) or a specialization (e.g., older titles still in demand), they still have to prepare digital files—a costly endeavor, which is not eagerly subsidized by the Polish Film Institute, even though it does support promoting the Polish audiovisual culture abroad. Jan Mogilnicki from Torus Films, a company specializing in the VOD distribution of Polish documentaries, including older titles, points out:

> In 2014, we were close to introducing our films to big, global platforms, such as Hulu or iTunes. Then, to my surprise, it turned out that neither we, nor the producers had proper digital materials. Preparing subtitles and screening material for the whole bunch of films is a significant expense. I'm still working on it, step by step (interview, 3 August 2018).

The bankruptcy or closure of independent (Iplex) or smaller (Kinoplex) local companies, even if they were pioneers with initial advantages in the market, and the withdrawal of medium-sized international players (Showmax) indicates that the VOD market is becoming an increasingly concentrated sphere, controlled by global behemoths (Netflix and HBO GO) or local branches of media corporations (player.pl and ipla.tv). Traditional cinematic distribution, on the other hand, is a more open space due to digitalization, which decreased the cost of preparing screening copies. Distributors have a lot of freedom in their purchasing choices, allowing for the existence of smaller players and for the curatorial practices of intermediaries, such as special screenings and a fairly active network of art house cinemas.

The biggest entities of the Polish VOD market are currently: VoD.pl, player.pl, cda.pl, TVP VOD, ipla.tv and WP Pilot, as well as Netflix and HBO GO (Showmax left the market in 2018). A classification of the major VOD providers in terms of ownership shows the structure of the market and differences in comparison to traditional cinematic distribution players and their business roots. The major VOD providers are owned by four types of entities:

- Internet portals (parts of larger media corporations): VoD.pl and WP Pilot
- Powerful TV broadcasters: player.pl, ipla.tv and TVP VOD
- Big international companies with a global reach: Netflix, HBO GO and ncplusgo.com
- Former pirate site on the way toward legalization: cda.pl

Table 8.3 Leading VOD platforms in Poland (October 2017–October 2018)

Domain	October 2017		October 2018	
	Users	Range (%)	Users	Range (%)
vod.pl	4,066,682	14.81	3,791,192	13.64
player.pl	3,609,619	13.14	3,218,020	11.58
cda.pl-premium	2,931,623	10.67	3,107,222	11.18
vod.tvp.pl	2,560,870	9.32	2,606,523	9.38
netflix.com	1,208,480	4.40	1,986,895	7.15
ipla.tv	2,185,550	7.96	1,781,479	6.41
wp.pl-pilot	826,170	3.01	1,393,499	5.01
showmax.com	969,068	3.53	1,269,447	4.57
hbogo.com	522,294	1.90	739,336	2.66
ncplusgo.com	309,786	1.13	383,948	1.38

Source Gemius/PBI for wirtualnemedia.p)

Furthermore, TVOD services are also offered by mobile networks—T-Mobile, Orange, Plus and Play, the last being the most active player in the field. Its Play Now service aggregates content from different content providers, actively participates in television markets and buys content independently from the producers. Zuzanna Pawłowska, an expert from the VOD sector (currently working for TVP VOD, who previously collaborated with Iplex and VoD.pl), says: "It's hard to name a platform which would be completely independent. Iplex was one and we all know how it ended up" (interview, 19 November 2018) (Table 8.3).

The visibly strong position of VOD services connected with Polish television channels (Player.pl, Ipla.tv and TVP VOD) is the result of their successful strategy of combining Hollywood blockbusters with popular local television formats (series, talk shows, social and political commentary). As a result, their catalogue is diverse and attractive. Rather than focus on the domestic market, their strong position seems to stem mostly from the wide offer of television programs available on VOD. This gives the online services connected with large television broadcasters an advantage and sets the dichotomous structure of the market, dominated by two types of entities—services linked to the broadcasters and international corporate content providers with a large reach. The market position of the former is the result of the fact that a large portion of the content is produced beforehand by the TV station for its own channels, while VOD is only an extension of TV distribution for the previously created content. Onet and WP are also among the portals with their own VOD services producing original content. However, television stations have much larger content resources. Zuzanna Pawłowska observes that a large portion of her job at the public service broadcaster is convincing other departments that VOD is not cannibalizing television and that the VOD and terrestrial broadcasting are not taking away viewers from each other, but instead both gain by copromoting content on the two platforms simultaneously or by coordinating release times.

It could be argued that the attitude of the cinematic distributors toward VOD (the aforementioned mixture of disdain and fear) shows that they are mistaken in not paying enough attention to this prospective form of distribution, and therefore are not leveraging it to the fullest. Indeed, it would seem that one of the side effects of the dynamic development of cinema exhibition is a certain conservative attitude of the Polish distribution market. However, statistics concerning the traditional cinematic distribution market and VOD services reveal a more complex picture than it might be initially assumed.

First of all, the Polish VOD market is quite well developed. The 48% market growth observed in the 2015–2016 European Audiovisual Observatory report seems fairly unimpressive compared to the growth in other countries during the same time period—the Czech Republic (226%), Croatia (197%) or Bulgaria (137%) (Grece and Fontaine 2017: 14). However, the authors of the report point to the fact that the growth was much more intensive in countries where the market had previously been less saturated with VOD services. The Polish market, with its 11% penetration, was comparable to many western countries, such as Italy (9%), France (10%), Belgium (11%) and Spain (13%), and was far ahead of the growth leaders in the first comparison—the Czech Republic, Croatia and Bulgaria (each with 2% penetration) (Grece and Fontaine 2017: 13). It is also worth noticing that Poland's penetration was far lower than in European countries with the highest VOD penetration—Scandinavia and the UK (Norway 53%, Sweden 31%, Finland 28%, the UK 43%). Moreover, Poland was the country with Netflix's lowest market share in Europe (only 16%), which reflects the strength of the portal's local competition (Grece and Fontaine 2017: 24).

It should also be noted that due to the size of the population, the general number of subscribers is currently high. According to *Rzeczpospolita,* in October 2018, Netflix reached 760,000 individual subscribers. The VOD sector's revenue in Poland in 2016 was estimated at €56.2 million, which constituted 6.5% of the British market revenue (€804 million) and 10% of German market revenue (€540 million), while the cinema market in Poland at the same time was estimated at 14% of the British market volume and 21% of the German market volume. The full US dollar-denominated box office in Poland 2016 was $245 million, compared to British $1.66 billion and German $1.13 billion (Kanzler and Talavera 2017).

Therefore, the VOD market in Poland is less developed than the cinema market when comparing the gap between Polish markets and the most advanced Western markets. At the same time, SVOD revenue in Poland was ten times higher than in the Czech Republic and 25 times higher than in Hungary (while the potential consumer base in both countries is only four times smaller, and the per capita GDP is slightly higher in Hungary and much higher in the Czech Republic) (Grece and Fontaine 2017: 15–16). Thus, the Polish VOD market is quite well developed in the regional context of Central and Eastern Europe. It is very competitive, and it has recently been shaped by two major events—Showmax's withdrawal from the market and attempts by the previously pirate portal cda.pl to legalize its content and become a publicly traded entity.

Showmax, an international player controlled by Naspers, operating out of South Africa, entered the Polish market in February 2017. From the very beginning it stood out from the crowd with its showy promotional campaigns (widely commented upon promotional videos made by renowned filmmakers—Wojciech Smarzowski and Patryk Vega) and its focus on local content, including a satirical political Web series *Ucho prezesa*, the well-received series *Rojst* and the *SNL Polska* format. In December 2018, the platform announced its withdrawal from Poland. The failure of Showmax demonstrates that in such a dichotomous market, divided between VOD services linked to local TV stations, big Internet portals and global players, it is not enough to be a relatively strong international entity. You have to be a powerful global player with significant financial resources that can be invested in content production and marketing (e.g., companies like Netflix, HBO and Canal+). The VOD market seems particularly difficult for online services without the backing of TV stations or a global reach, even despite their dynamic promotion and the attractive, original content they produce.

The only entity breaking out of the dichotomous structure of the market is cda.pl. It is an interesting case of a pirate platform trying to legalize its operation in the hope of going public and raising capital for further expansion. CDA, which has existed for over a decade, introduced a paid premium SVOD service and shares a portion of its profits with distributors. CDA offers a sizable catalogue, whose volume can be appreciated through a comparison with Netflix's offer for Polish viewers. Netflix offers 2100 films and 800 series for the equivalent of €8.50 per month. CDA offers 4700 films (although the video quality of the files is usually lower) for the equivalent of €5 a month. The portal wants to be listed on NewConnect, a part of the Warsaw Stock Exchange, to raise capital for the expansion of its legal content (increasing the number of films with license fees and developing a SmartTV app). NewConnect is intended mostly for companies with a relatively low capitalization, operating in the sector of new technologies, and is less regulated than the standard stock exchange. To this end, CDA boasts about its good relationships with the distributors, not only due to the speed of their notice and takedown procedure (and emphasizing that the illegal content is uploaded by the users), but also thanks to a direct takedown tool available for distributors collaborating with the platform. CDA also reports that in 2018 it handed over PLN 6 million in license fees to the distributors it worked with and stresses the dynamic increase in the number of subscribers.

According to the platform, in November 2018, they had 155,000 active subscribers (compared to 100,000 in early 2018 and 47,000 in early 2017). CDA also reports that its profit for 2018 is the equivalent of US $1 million net. Yet at the same time, the portal was featured on the MPAA list of notorious pirate sites, and its mode of action is a source of controversy for the industry. One of the Polish VOD market players said anonymously:

> I've heard the distributors working with them are satisfied. They're getting some money out of it and they control whether their content is published – that's also crucial. But generally, the VOD market and foreign entities are distrustful of the platform. I think building your position on an illegal platform and entering the market saying: "We have this many viewers,

we can pay the distributors, and we have the people we can sell films to", seems rather unfair (interview, 6 August 2018).

The case of CDA is a clear-cut example of how the only way to survive in a difficult, competitive market for an entity which is not a part of the dichotomous system is capital accumulation (let us not forget about the downfall of the pioneering Iplex, the closing of Kinoplex and the retreat of Showmax), drawing on its initial position based on piracy and profiting from the distribution of content without paying the rightsholders. In other words, to base the development on unpaid, illegally obtained content. An anonymous market observer accurately noted that only the accumulation of financial capital in the gray zone of piracy and, first and foremost, the accumulation of the viewer base in the same way can lead to legalizing the operations of such a platform. Obtaining a wide base of free content seems to be the only development option other than gaining backing from a TV station or being a global player with a budget and potential customer base significantly bigger than that of the competition.

8.4   The Separation of Cinema Distribution and the VOD Market

The size of the SVOD market in Poland in 2016 was about 25% the size of the cinema market revenue (Grece and Fontaine 2017; Kanzler and Talavera 2017). The volume for 2016 was €56.2 million, while the combined revenue from cinemas was €217.5 million. It is a significant amount, especially if we treat is as a potential new source of revenue.

However, the interviews reveal that the VOD sector offers very low fees to cinema distributors, the rightsholders for online fields of exploitation. An anonymous distributor reveals: "Iplex paid 0.25 zloty per view and went bankrupt. Ipla pays 0.2–0.3 zloty per view, but initially it used to pay a little more. Kinoplex paid 0.5 zloty per view. And I need to further split this amount 50/50 with the producer" (interview, 6 August 2018).

It is a very low level of income for distributors compared to revenues from cinemas and television. Meanwhile, the net profit for the Polish distributors from one cinema ticket sold, after splitting the revenue with the cinema owner, is around 7–8 zloty, over 200 times more than from VOD proceeds. The profit is reduced due to the producer taking its share, which is usually 50–80% of the amount received after splitting the profits with the cinema, but first the distributor deducts its P&A costs from the revenue.

Moreover, the VOD market in Poland has shown a strong tendency to concentrate around the strongest players. Even though the traditional cinematic distribution market is also dominated by the biggest players, such as the distribution agencies of Hollywood studios, companies in business with the "Big Six" and other entities with access to the biggest local commercial hits, the market still leaves a lot of room for smaller distributors. Hollywood studios sell their films based on long-term general contracts, in TVOD and SVOD packages of films from the studio library as well as new, premiere titles. VOD services leave much less room for smaller entities and the degree of market concentration around the biggest players is significantly higher. There are no small VOD companies hiring a few employees and successfully distributing fewer mainstream titles.

The fees paid by VOD operators to outside rightsholders is an indicator that any future growth of the market and its revenue stream will most likely be consumed by entities other than cinema distributors—corporations owning TV stations and producing in-house content, further distributed via the VOD portals they control. The exception is the corporate Hollywood "Big Six" studios. However, they stopped using the local distributors as middlemen for the selling of VOD licenses, and therefore operate somehow beyond the local context through their European branches. Nowadays, Disney and Warner have their own Polish distribution agencies. United International Pictures is the sole rightsholder for the films of Universal, Paramount and Sony, and the fate of Imperial Cinepix (the Polish distributor of Twentieth Century Fox) is uncertain, as its content provider has been taken over by Disney.

The functioning of the VOD sector is connected to the advantage of scaling. According to Pawłowska, contracts for SVODs are usually signed for 100 titles or 50 h of programming delivered every quarter, for example for two years, not for a small selection of five titles. Smaller deals do happen, but the pragmatic factor of a similar amount of time devoted to a small contract (for a few titles) and a big contract (around 100 titles) usually rules in favor of the latter.

Furthermore, since 2018 there has been a noticeable change in the approach of cinema distributors to the VOD market. Thus far, one of the only conditions they insisted on was the sequential opening of distribution windows and a shortened, but nevertheless long, hold-back period for cinematic distribution—blocking the availability of the film in other distribution channels for four months after its premiere. Only the smaller distributors were open to negotiations in this matter, but these revolved around shortening the hold-back period, not its elimination. The question remained whether people would actually not go to see a film in the cinema if they had the alternative of watching it at the same time in the comfort of their home—on Pay TV or a VOD platform. This is a crucial issue for the future of the interdependence and relations between the traditional cinematic market and VOD and the whole system of hold-backs which was the cornerstone of the distribution market's structure. At least a partial answer could be obtained by experiments with suspending hold-backs.

The first two such experiments related to distributing content produced by Netflix were made on the Polish market recently. In the autumn of 2018, Monolith distributed Paul Greengrass' *22 July* at the time of its Netflix premiere. In December 2018, a similar move was made by Gutek Film distributing Netflix's famed production *Roma* by Alfonso Cuarón. In an interesting twist, the film was distributed by the very same company whose board member and main buyer, Jakub Duszyński, in an interview conducted just a year before had expressed the absolute importance of opening distribution windows sequentially. At the moment, a more flexible approach and attitude of openness on the part of at least some cinema distributors may be observed and they are partly testing out a suspension of window sequencing.

And yet, the circumstances surrounding the distribution of the two films, regardless of which company distributed them, were rather unusual and thought-provoking. A viewer not familiar with the film market could easily miss the seemingly unimportant detail that the distributors' logos did not appear before the screenings. Only Netflix's logo was displayed. It was also rather difficult to find information about the distributors of the films online. In the case of *22 July* and Monolith, it may even be that the earlier information about the theatrical distributor was, for some reason, removed, and—as nothing can be completely erased from the Internet—there were only some traces left: a trailer taken down from YouTube, a note in the repertoire of one of the cinemas, and a piece of information on the Twitter account of a film fan (Kozłowsky 2018; Twitter 2018).

What is more, we do not know the box office results of the films, since the distributors—two serious, seasoned companies—did not report them to boxoffice.pl, a members-only portal for film professionals, the main tool for any distributor and market analyst. As a result, only Netflix has the data necessary to analyze the impact of the lack of sequencing of distribution windows on the *box office* results of a given title. It seems reasonable to assume that the "hidden" details behind distribution of the films and the lack of box office data are the results of contracts signed between distributors and Netflix. We do not know the conditions under which Monolith and Gutek Films agreed to distribute the American portal's content (e.g., their share of the profits). Nevertheless, it may be supposed that the terms were not particularly favorable to the distributors, who were clearly the weaker partners in this relationship. Netflix's tactics of restricting the industry's access to distribution data seem to be part of an aggressive corporate strategy, an informal "war" the portal wields against other film market entities. The portal's possessiveness does not inspire confidence in the future of the relationship. Local distributors were treated as subcontractors of secondary importance who offered the service of contacting cinemas and convincing them to screen the film, and there appears to be a visible tendency by Netflix to push them into anonymity. In some way, the theatrical distribution was also part of a marketing campaign for a parallel release of these titles on VOD in a *day-to-date* model.

However, it should be noted here that Amazon Studios takes a different approach. It has worked with various distributors in the Polish market, including Kino Świat, Gutek Film and M2Films, with titles such as *Handmaiden* (2016, directed by Park Chan-wook), *Manchester by the Sea* (2017, directed by Kenneth Lonergan), *Paterson* (2017, directed by Jim Jarmusch), *Suspiria* (2018, directed by Luca Guadagnino) and *Beautiful Boy* (2019, directed by Felix Van Groeningen). At no time has Amazon "covered up" the local distributor, nor has it concealed the film's box office results.

Nevertheless, in the new power structure, especially if Netflix's approach prevails, the key powerful players of traditional cinema, such as the distributors, will likely become increasingly marginalized, pushed into the position of second-rate subcontractors, with their role limited to that of unnecessary middlemen or even eliminated. This sheds new light on the defensive approach of the distributors toward the new forms of distribution. The distributors are well aware of the importance of relationships with cinema owners and programmers, with journalists and the media, and of the value of knowledge about the preferences and habits of the audiences in the local context. These factors, at least to some extent, promote the national players, turning them into typical intermediaries, so crucial in the modern culture of content (over)abundance. The unique knowledge, contacts and the function of intermediaries allow even small local distributors to survive the confrontation with bigger international players although their budgets for licenses and promotion are minuscule compared to the global behemoths (obviously this means surviving in a market niche).

8.5 Conclusions

The traditional cinematic distribution and VOD markets in Poland are characterized by a much larger degree of separation and independence than one might suspect. The two markets are ruled by different logics and, most important, controlled by different entities with different revenue streams, which rarely overlap. The entities active in the cinema distribution sector and in the VOD sector almost never actively operate in the parallel market as players, not just as rights vendors or content providers. The VOD sector is much closer to the television sector than to traditional cinematic distribution. It is linked not only on the level of corporate management (those VOD services with the backing of powerful television broadcasters who control them), but also on the level of content, which is delivered by broadcasters. According to Pawłowska, TV formats such as series, talk shows and journalistic programs are the most popular formats among Polish VOD users. What can be seen here is the hybridization of content when an Internet platform produces content in TV formats or when TV content is a very popular part of its offer. In this way one can notice the "second life" of television on the Internet.

The revenue stream is more tightly controlled by the entities dominating the VOD market, acting mostly in the interest of their own and their superior corporate structures, unwilling to share it with outside content providers. Therefore, the traditional cinematic market players—distributors and, indirectly, producers—are largely cut off from the stream of VOD revenue and are looking for alternative development models. These include both traditional vertical integration and a modified approach: a distribution company with its own festival, which allows it to control the license budget of the festival (and practically sell its own films to itself), thus reducing the risk of buying expensive licenses. At the same time, traditional cinematic distribution in Poland has experienced constant and dynamic growth in recent years. Hence, one may expect that it will remain partially separated from the VOD market.

Furthermore, there were interesting experiments with simultaneous distribution of content on VOD portals and in cinemas without the hold-back periods (the examples of *22 July* and *Roma*). However, in those cases, cinema distributors were hired as subcontractors to perform the service of introducing the film to cinemas. The sub-contractor remained a mostly anonymous entity and was certainly not treated as an equal partner. It can be assumed that if such arrangements come to characterize the business, the position of the distributor will be much weaker, and if the experiments prove lucrative, the content provider could easily set up its own cinematic distribution department, supported by large advertising budgets. After a period of building up contacts and gathering experience, the need for an outside cinematic distribution provider would be eliminated. Establishing a direct line between consumer and filmmaker and the elimination or marginalization of intermediaries—independent distributors and producers—will clearly benefit VOD services.

The Polish VOD market is more concentrated around the most powerful players and has much higher barriers to entry than the traditional cinematic distribution market. The barriers are also much higher than is generally assumed based on the image of the Internet as a particularly open medium, stemming from the popular start-up mythology of the IT sector. In reality, it is the traditional cinematic market that turns out to be more freewheeling and open to smaller and new local players. It is less controlled by the biggest corporate players than the VOD services.

The distributors recognize the limitations of Polish cinema—the language barrier, a modest number of productions with fairly low budgets, and the export opportunities limited to the Polish diaspora abroad and the art house sector (after gaining the symbolic capital of awards at respected festivals). Localness—understood as the capital of relations and inside knowledge—is their best, if not only tool to compete successfully, or at least to survive the competition against huge international media conglomerates and their cinema distribution branches. At the same time, Polish distributors are aware that factors that help them in the local market (such as relationships with cinemas, media contacts, knowing the preferences of domestic audiences, expertise in creating promotional campaigns *and* familiarity with regulations) are also their weaknesses in foreign markets, as they are controlled by similar players there.

Traditional cinematic distributors and, indirectly, producers seem to be aware they exist in a comfortable *production–distribution niche*, based on the cofinancing of their projects from public funds, promotion in the international festival circuit, and the "reversed economy" of European cinema in recent decades, which is based on symbolic capital and prestige (English 2008), where symbolic values can be more important than simply the bottom line. They are even less inclined to think about exports and international expansion than some smaller VOD market entities. The cinematic distributors and the majority of the producers seem to assume, quite realistically, that the world beyond their niches is an immense ocean, and trying to cross it in their humble ships now and in the foreseeable future will lead to certain death by sinking or crashing upon the cliffs rather than the discovery of a bountiful New World.

The current growth of profits in Polish cinematic distribution is caused by the expanding traditional market. The cinematic distribution and VOD sectors in Poland will most likely be characterized by parallel development, with limited spheres of contact and overlap, aside from the selling of content to VOD services by cinematic distributors, while the VOD sector itself, both on the level of corporate management and content, will be characterized by an increasing level of convergence with television.[1]

References

English, J. (2008). *The economy of prestige: Prizes, awards, and the circulation of cultural value.* Cambridge: Harvard University Press.

Grece, C., & Fontaine, G. (2017). *Trends in the EU SVOD Market.* Strasbourg: European Audiovisual Observatory.

Kanzler, M., & Talavera, J. (2017). *Focus 2017: World film market.* Strasbourg: European Audiovisual Observatory.

Kozłowsky, K. (2018). Filmy Netflix w kinach w Polsce – są, będą, ale jakim cudem się tam znalazły? *Antyweb*, October 19.

Twitter. (2018). Tweet by user @Sfilmowani. 4 October 2018, 4:31. https://twitter.com/Sfilmowani/status/1047811558133391360. Accessed November 16, 2019.

Marcin Adamczak is Associate Professor at the Institute of Cultural Studies, Adam Mickiewicz University, Poznań and Visiting Professor at the Łódź Film School and University, Gdańsk. He specializes in contemporary film markets, distribution and European film industries. He also worked as Director of the Cinemaforum Short Film Festival in Warsaw (2016-2018) and is co-founder of the distribution company Velvet Spoon (since 2018).

---

[1]This work was supported by the European Regional Development Fund project "Creativity and Adaptability as Conditions of the Success of Europe in an Interrelated World" (reg. no. CZ.02.1.01/0.0/0.0/16_019/0000734). This work was also supported by Ministry of Science and Higher Education through the National Program for the Development of the Humanities, module Development 2b, 2016–2019 (0135/NPRH/H2b/83/2016) and the National Science Center, Poland (UMO-2017/27/Z/HS4/00039).

Chapter 9
Channels and Barriers of Cross-Border Online Circulation: Central and Eastern Europe as a Digital Periphery

Petr Szczepanik

9.1 Introduction

The European Commission's Digital Single Market (DSM) strategy is being presented, among other things, as an answer to the notoriously low levels of cross-border circulation of European audiovisual content, as well as to the threats of cultural and economic domination by the USA. In fact, the DSM is just a continuation of long-term policy concerns with barriers in the EU's audiovisual market and has been proposed in hopes that digital technologies will provide a means for improvement, namely for achieving the "objective of intensified and efficient cross-border online distribution of audiovisual works between Member States" (European Parliament 2012: 69). For example, MEDIA—as the European Commission's program supporting audiovisual industries—introduced a scheme focusing on video on demand (VOD) catalogues with a strong European dimension already in 2007, although without significant impact on actual online circulation (De Vinck and Pauwels 2015: 112–113). More generally, these proposals are also in many ways a continuation of the long-lasting debates reflecting concerns about one-way transnational flows and cultural imperialism that started in the 1970s with the boom in transnational satellite and cable broadcasting (Iordache et al. 2018). But within the DSM debate, American-based digital services do not stand entirely on the other side of a barricade from EU policymakers. Companies such as Netflix and Amazon can potentially benefit from some elements of the DSM, and they are also seen as key gatekeepers and vehicles for the circulation of European content within and beyond the continent.

The Netherlands EU Presidency Conference "Promoting Cross-Border Circulation of European Audiovisual Content" (March 3 and 4, 2016, Amsterdam) symptomatically started with a lengthy clip from Netflix's UK series *The Crown* and a keynote delivered by Netflix CEO and co-founder Reed Hastings. Hastings warned

P. Szczepanik (✉)
Filozofická fakulta Univerzity Karlovy, nám. Jana Palacha 1/2, 116 38 Prague, Czech Republic
e-mail: Petr.Szczepanik@ff.cuni.cz

© The Author(s) 2020
P. Szczepanik et al. (eds.), *Digital Peripheries*, Springer Series in Media Industries,
https://doi.org/10.1007/978-3-030-44850-9_9

against introducing new content quotas and claimed that Netflix does not present a threat but is rather contributing to national cultures by producing local shows and distributing them globally with multiple subtitles. The key condition for this "new global entertainment world," based on "sharing" national cultures across national borders, to flourish in Europe is, according to Hastings, "a lighter regulatory orientation" and policy based on the country of origin principle that allows for one set of regulatory rules to be applied to a company operating across the whole EU (Hastings 2016). The presumption of the European Commission that global digital services will help European films and television programs circulate between individual Member States' territories more widely and smoothly than cinemas and television seems natural, but there is very little empirical evidence of the actual impact VOD services have or are going to have on European distribution ecosystems.

The only EU-wide data on cross-border online circulation publicly available at the moment come from quantitative studies of VOD catalogues—often limited to transactional video on demand (TVOD) or covering subscription video on demand (SVOD) to a lesser extent than TVOD. Since transnational VOD services publish statistics neither on their actual revenues and consumption, nor on the composition of their catalogues in individual markets (and they sometimes make it hard to identify the nationality of individual titles), researchers need to adopt alternative analytical tools and methods to compile distribution and reception data, some of them resorting to unofficial third parties' databases such as uNoGS (cf. Lobato 2018; Aguiar and Waldfogel 2018). The most useful pan-EU studies so far have been produced by the European Audiovisual Observatory (EAO), although even they still provide only rough approximations due to the lack of data and skewed samples, especially for SVOD.[1] These reports typically ask about the share of national, EU28, or non-national EU28 (NNE) content in VOD catalogues, sometimes distinguishing between different types of services or between TV series and films. On the most general level, recent studies reflecting on developments in the period between 2016 and 2018 showed that SVOD catalogues are smaller, less diverse in terms of the country of origin, more recent and more TV-dominated and include less EU28 content than TVODs: on average 21% versus 29% of EU films and 25% versus 40% of EU TV fiction, respectively. There are significant differences between national and transnational services, though. National TVODs and even more so national SVODs are less diverse in terms of the number of producing countries but include a higher share of national and EU28 titles (45 and 48% for EU28 films and 19 and 20% for national films, respectively) and a lesser share of US titles than their multi-country competitors (23 and 18% for EU28 films and 6 and 3% for national films, respectively). For example, EU28 films comprised 48% of the catalogue of Czech SVOD Voyo (27% NNE and 21% national titles). This means that national services, although more "European," devote a large part of their catalogues' EU28 segments (42% in TVOD and 41% in SVOD) to national productions, thus limiting the circulation of NNE content. Significant differences occur not just between various VOD services (national and

---

[1] The following two paragraphs are based on Fontaine (2019a: 26–29, 2019b: 12–14), Grece (2017a: 90, b: 19, 2019).

global, niche and mainstream), but also between the different territorial catalogues of the same transnational service: The share of national content in the transnational services' catalogues is largest in the big film-producing countries (the so-called EU5: the UK, France, Germany, Italy and Spain) and is significantly smaller or close to zero in smaller countries. For example, it was just two films in the Czech Netflix catalogue as of July 2019, out of almost 5000 titles.

These data do not say much about the actual demand and revenues of the online distribution, they do not distinguish between different types of content (beyond national origin, the year of production and film vs. TV), nor do they indicate—most importantly for this chapter—why and how specific titles ended up in a specific VOD catalogue. They demonstrate only a general pattern of cross-border circulation. At the same time, the data have begun (after having been repeatedly updated and methodologically upgraded) hinting at specific regularities in and barriers to the cross-border circulation of EU28 content. The obvious barriers include overproduction (too many EU28 titles released every year if compared to the USA), linguistic and cultural distance, narrow theatrical releases, weak marketing campaigns and territory-by-territory licensing. The emerging regularities indicate that EU28 films travel more widely on TVOD, that TV series cross borders more often on SVOD and that there are persistent differences between the circulations of US and EU28 content. While in 2018 a single EU28 film was available on TVOD in 2.7 EU countries and on SVOD in 2.5 EU countries on average, a US film fared much better across borders, being available in 6 EU countries on TVOD and 4.8 on SVOD. There is also a significant level of concentration: The biggest production countries, especially the UK, are dominating both SVOD and TVOD catalogues' EU28 segments. The UK, France and Germany alone represent 60% of all EU films in TVOD and SVOD catalogues combined. In the case of smaller EU countries, cultural–geographic clusters (such as the Czech Republic and Slovakia) are the most significant and predictable drivers of cross-border circulation.

This chapter looks beneath the purely quantitative data on cross-border availability by investigating industry practices of online distribution from a peripheral, small-market perspective, using the example of export from the Czech Republic. The key research question is: How have transnational VODs integrated into the local industry ecosystem and to what extent have they changed the circulation trajectories of Czech films and TV series? First, it places online distribution within the local industry ecosystem and reveals the systemic barriers that discourage producers and distributors from strategically focusing on foreign markets. Second, it identifies the key intermediaries and practices of cross-border online distribution, focusing on the approach of global VOD services to distributing small nation content across borders. The chapter concludes with a typology of cross-border online distribution to distinguish different strategies and tactics employed by key players when approaching foreign markets. Thus, it calls for a more nuanced perspective on the position of "digital peripheries" in cross-border cultural networks and flows.

Methodologically, the research behind the chapter draws on the approaches of critical media industry studies, distribution studies, transnational media flow studies and the recent critical literature on Netflix. It is based, first, on a set of semi-structured in-depth interviews with producers, distributors, broadcasters, aggregators, sales agents and VOD portal operators[2]; second, an analysis of European and national policy documents; and third, on an original catalogue data analysis of the biggest transnational VOD services in four key export territories for Czech films: the USA, Germany, France and Poland.[3] It focuses on the circulation of Czech content as a case study and compares it with similar post-socialist markets in the region (the other so-called Visegrad countries: Slovakia, Poland and Hungary). The chapter avoids presumptions of one-directional domination; instead, it looks at business models and distribution practices of both global services and local producers and distributors, their mutual interrelationships, and how they are conditioned by national and EU policies. In doing so, it identifies inextricable links between traditional intermediaries and the new on-demand market on the one hand, while also pointing at disruptive, disintermediation practices on the other.

9.2   VOD in the Small Media Industry Ecosystem

Existing studies of cross-border circulation show that the small media markets of Central and Eastern Europe (CEE) are by far the least successful exporters of audiovisual content among EU Member States, including small West European countries such as Belgium and Denmark (Higson 2018). The reasons include the typical economic characteristics of small countries' media industries such as the shortage of financial resources, inability to benefit from economies of scale in the home market, a limited pool of internationally established talent and language barriers (see Alaveras and Martens 2018). My own research of producer practices indicates that there are also more specific, cultural–historical factors typical for post-socialist media systems: the lack of strong production houses and low levels of vertical and horizontal integration, the relatively late professionalization and internationalization of independent producers, high levels of dependence on public subsidies and, more generally, enduring structural elements of the former state-socialist media, mainly in the form of the local public service broadcaster (PSB) Česká televize (Czech Television), which is the major local producer and exporter of audiovisual content (Szczepanik 2018).

Although on paper the Czech Republic appears to be the strongest exporter of films among the CEE states,[4] a closer look reveals that most of its theatrically exported films travel only to neighboring Slovakia, a country of five million with which it

---

[2]The total of 16 interviews were conducted between 2016 and 2019: three producers, five distributors (two of them acting as aggregators, as well), two broadcasting executives, four local VOD operators and two international sales agents.

[3]Catalogue data were compiled from the EU-funded database JustWatch and selectively cross-checked with EAO's new database Lumiere VOD.

[4]According to Holdaway and Scaglioni (2018), the Czech Republic ranked sixth in terms of the total number of films exported in the EU's cinema market between 2007 and 2017 (after the big five countries France, UK, Germany, Italy and Spain).

shares a common state history, and forms a cultural–geographic cluster with the strongest bilateral dependence among all comparable clusters in the EU.[5] While Slovakia represented 64% of all Czech film exports in the cinema market, the Czech Republic was even more important export market for Slovakia, taking 71% of its theatrical film exports in 2015 and 2016 (Grece 2017a: 33). It is not surprising, then, that the average total foreign attendance per theatrical title (when it travelled abroad) was just 18 thousand viewers: far less than the biggest EU exporters such as the UK (627 thousand) and France (140 thousand), but also significantly less than smaller Western European markets such as Denmark (93 thousand) and Belgium (118 thousand) (Holdaway and Scaglioni 2018: 349).

In theatrical distribution, Czech films travel to other countries beyond Slovakia only if they are international co-productions: 95% of Czech cinematic exports beyond Slovakia between 2013 and 2017 were international co-productions, of which 77% were minority co-productions (SPI Olsberg 2019). The importance of international partnerships, foreign talent and sales agents (who are generally not interested in fully national Czech films) indicates that in theatrical distribution, there are strong industry regularities determining a film's export potential even before it is finished and before its quality can be judged by buyers and consumers. The typical Czech film that travelled beyond Slovakia (most frequently to Poland, less often to Germany or France, and occasionally to another CEE country) has been an art house international co-production with a French or German sales agent attached; fully national Czech films, on the other hand, have negligible theatrical distribution outside the Czech Republic and Slovakia (SPI Olsberg 2019). The problem is that the production and distribution ecosystem of art house films, as the main export commodity of the CEE screen industries, are not compatible enough with the system of transnational VOD distribution.

The vast majority of online distribution in the local Czech market is still controlled by the established legacy media players: cinema or home video distributors and broadcasters. While the local production sector is extremely disintegrated, consisting of approximately two hundred small companies without any organizational links to other stages in the value chain, the distribution field is quite concentrated with a handful of US studios' local partners (in theatrical and home video distribution) being the dominant players. Home video and cinema distributors are buying and reselling territorial VOD rights, too, but not from the US majors, whose online rights have been traded directly by the studio branches to the transnational and local VOD services. From the domestic market's perspective, online distribution is mostly an undisruptive addition to the well-established licensing practices in theatrical, TV and home video windows. The dominant legacy media players simply expanded their portfolios of rights, but—with the exception of broadcasters—have not invested in their own online portals, largely leaving the field to local telcos and transnational online services (similarly to Poland, as described in Marcin Adamczak's chapter of this book).

---

[5]That is why Slovakia is intentionally excluded from the selection of export territories in this study.

However, as the following sections of the chapter show, the cross-border online distribution of Czech films is changing this arrangement. The local home video distributors still sell a significant proportion of Czech films abroad, but they remain fully dominant only in Slovakia, which tends to be seen as a single market territory together with the Czech Republic. In the case of ambitious art house films and international co-productions, foreign online sales tend to be controlled either by the foreign co-producers and their partners, or by foreign sales agents. Foreign online sales of less internationally appealing, fully national films are relatively decentralized and partly conducted by the small local producers themselves, who are effectively becoming self-distributors by selling their films via TVOD catalogues. Original local productions and exclusive acquisitions of transnational SVODs (HBO and Netflix) are a separate category: Their cross-border circulation is the most selective, but also the most dynamic. A significant exception among the local legacy media players is the Czech PSB "Česká televize," which increasingly focuses on selling the foreign online rights of its vast original production and occasionally acts as a sales agent representing local film producers who have no capacity to handle cross-border distribution themselves. Overall, cross-border online distribution allows Czech films and TV series to reach foreign territories that would have been inaccessible to them in the traditional theatrical or broadcasting windows, especially the USA and Asia.

VOD can either disrupt or enhance the existing business models and practices. In most of the EU so far, VOD represents only a small fraction of the market, but it is growing fast, especially in the small CEE countries (the most rapid SVOD growth of 226% between 2015 and 2016 was recorded in the Czech Republic, which was also one of the fastest growing markets between 2016 and 2017 with 175%),[6] which were late adopters and still have a low level of penetration. It also seems that Netflix is currently on an especially steep rise in CEE. After subscription numbers stagnated in 2016 and 2017 (after Netflix's "global switch on") due to the weak localization of its CEE catalogues, it has become the largest paid streaming platform in the Czech Republic with approximately 100 thousand subscribers as of May 2019.[7] Netflix is the second-fastest growing paid SVOD in Poland (Netflix's top country in the CEE region), with an estimated 760 thousand subscribers as of 2018 (which could potentially translate to 1.9 million actual monthly viewers, according to the widely accepted estimate of an average of 2.5 viewers per account).[8] A business intelligence forecast by Digital TV Research estimated that Netflix will double its 2018 subscription base across Eastern Europe (including Russia) by 2024, reaching 8 million subscribers (two million in Poland alone), and control a 30% share of the regional market (Thomson 2019a). While we hear a lot about the expansion of Netflix and other transnational over-the-top (OTT) services, we still know very little about how cross-border VOD distribution from small EU countries is actually

[6]See Grece and Fontaine (2017: 14), OD-SERV (2018).
[7]See a May 2019 estimation by Tomáš Vyskočil, a well-informed owner of a VOD metadata aggregator (Vyskočil 2019).
[8]See Nowakowska (2019); see also Marcin Adamczak's chapter in this volume.

accomplished on the ground and how is it changing the established practices and business models.

The only study that has tried to systematically compare cross-border circulation of European films across different distribution windows is a recent report by the European Audiovisual Observatory called *The Circulation of EU Non-national Films* (Grece 2017a). Although it covered only TVOD (and not SVOD or AVOD— ad-supported video on demand) catalogues, it was able to identify a clear pattern indicating that online distribution brings a potential for wider circulation of films from small nations. While the big EU5 countries were hegemonic in the NNE film distribution in all the distribution windows, there were significant differences in the level of their domination. The average cross-border circulation of a single title fluctuated between 2.9 countries in cinemas, 1.8 in TV and 3.7 in TVOD, which means that online distribution facilitates the widest average reach. NNE in TVOD catalogues also showed the lowest dependency on international co-productions (41% as opposed to 55% in cinemas and 51% in TV), which implied that fully national films had a better chance of traveling online than offline (Grece 2017a: 82, 90).

When compared with the theatrical and television distribution of Czech content, TVOD services facilitated an even wider international reach than the EU average quoted above: When exported inside the EU, Czech films travelled to five countries on average (as opposed to 1.0 in theatrical and 1.6 in TV distribution). This trend was similar for other CEE countries: Polish films travelled to 3.8 countries in TVOD (cinema: 1.8; TV: 1.0), Hungarian films to 3.9 (cinema: 3.7; TV: 1.1) and Slovakian to 2.9 (cinema: 1.0; TV: 1.3). At the same time, the Czech dependency on the Slovak market shrunk to 12% (exactly the same number applies to Slovakia's exports to the Czech Republic) (Grece 2017a: 35, 52, 67). Speaking strictly in terms of supply, TVOD distribution might play a positive role in widening cross-border circulation of small CEE countries' content—in comparison with not only the larger EU markets, but also some smaller Western European ones. However, as noted above, this optimism should be tempered by the fact that the actual foreign consumption and revenues are still extremely low, discouraging local players from taking a more active approach.

9.3 Online Distribution Practices and Intermediaries

Extensive international marketing campaigns are rare for international co-productions and virtually nonexistent for fully national Czech films. This disinterest in international marketing partly results from the low foreign revenues that producers expect. Even more importantly, though, it is a consequence of a business model that is based on producing rather than on selling their product: A typical art house producer earns most of her income from the so-called production fee, which is up to seven percent of the production budget, while the majority of the average budget consists of public subsidies and PSB investment. This production-oriented, publicly funded business model makes the producers focus on speedy development, rushing all projects to the shooting stage without much consideration of international markets (Szczepanik 2018). Although distribution and promotion support schemes do exist on the national as well as EU level, they are disproportionately low if compared to the volume of production grants and incentives (there are currently no specialized schemes supporting international distribution in the Czech Republic).[9] For many industry insiders, this—and not the lack of potential demand—is the crucial reason for the low levels of cross-border circulation of European films.

The national orientation of film and TV production affects online distribution, too. The local distributors and producers are relatively active in getting Czech films released in the Czech VOD market, comfortably reaching the average presence of cinematic films in national VOD catalogues in the EU (62% of EU28 films present in a VOD catalogue in at least one EU country between 2011 and 2016).[10] The local leader among VOD services in terms of the volume of and revenues from recent Czech film output is Voyo, an SVOD owned by the biggest commercial broadcaster in the country. This focus on domestic VOD fits perfectly with the preexisting industry ecosystem dominated by a handful of cinema distributors, who rely on the relatively high and stable market share of Czech films in domestic theatrical distribution and who are relatively disinterested in cross-border circulation.

Indeed, interviews with industry insiders, be it producers, distributors, broadcasters, aggregators or sales agents, reveal prevailing skepticism with regard to cross-border online distribution.[11] When asked about the business potential of the new distribution technologies, they generally refer to the continuing economic and cultural importance of cinema exhibition and linear TV and to the necessity of closely working with, or rather actively "building," local audiences for non-national European films. VOD distribution is considered a mere addition to the more traditional windows or a potential remedy for Internet piracy and the shrinking home video market.

Laurent Danielou (Loco Film agency), an experienced French sales agent, claims that he prefers to sell all-rights packages to local distributors territory by territory. Only when there is no chance for cinematic distribution does he sell TV or online rights separately. Exactly that happened with his latest two Slovak–Czech art house titles, which he says were difficult to sell because of their locally specific stories. Selling VOD rights, he claims, is the easiest part, although there are huge differences between different online services. He often sells TV and VOD rights to HBO Europe, which is actively looking for CEE content: "But for us it is not a glory. We are quite sad, because it means we didn't find a cinematic distributor [in the CEE territories serviced by HBO Europe]." Potentially, the most lucrative VOD partner is Netflix, whose European acquisition numbers to date, however, remain very low and which

---

[9]European public funding bodies tend to give production much higher priority than distribution and promotion: In 2009, they spent only 8.4% of their budget on distribution and 3.6% on promotion schemes on average, in contrast to 69.9% spent on production. See European Commission (2014).

[10]For pan-EU statistics, see Fontaine (2019a, b); data on the Czech films on VOD platforms were compiled from the Czech VOD database Filmtoro.cz.

[11]Similarly to Poland and Greece, as shown in Marcin Adamczak's and Lydia Papadimitriou's chapters in this volume.

has a small acquisition team acting from a long distance, not expected to attend special screenings presenting national productions from the CEE to invited industry guests, so important, Danielou stresses, for closing international distribution deals.[12] It is difficult to build personal ties with them, and most of the time the sales agent is just waiting for Netflix to make a rare arbitrary choice from files he has been sending to them routinely. Although selling films to Amazon Prime is supposedly much easier for a European sales agent, Danielou remains skeptical about how many people actually see his titles from Amazon catalogues. Overall, he acknowledges that VOD revenues remain negligible: "For us, VOD is not a real market yet."[13]

The majority of Czech audiovisual online export—unlike cinematic distribution—is organized directly from Prague, without a foreign distributor or sales agent. The three major intermediaries are the Czech public service broadcaster "Česká televize" (mostly for documentaries and TV series) and the two biggest Czech home video distributors, AQS and Bontonfilm, who since 2015 have held iTunes and Google Play direct aggregation licenses and act as both domestic and international digital distributors and aggregators for Czech producers. When trading Czech films, AQS and Bontonfilm typically buy either territorial or global online rights for specific VOD services (mostly iTunes), excluding—if applicable—foreign co-producers' territories. Ondřej Kulhánek, the director of theatrical and digital distribution at Bontonfilm, claims that territorially limited licenses exclusive for iTunes and Google Play are the most common type. The distributors upload different language versions of individual titles (via an iTunes-approved encoding house taking care of the technical process of preparing and controlling the files according to the portals' requirements), fill in metadata, set prices, release dates (first a more expensive download to own and then cheaper rental) and "turn on" the titles in selected territorial catalogues. AQS' home video and VOD distribution managing director Jan Rubeš points out that practical limits for entering foreign territories via iTunes or Google Play catalogues are often set not by territorial licensing, because Czech producers usually do not expect or plan wide international sales, but by the lack of foreign language versions apart from the obligatory English. Although iTunes allows English-only localizations to be distributed to 64 territories including the Czech Republic, it still requires local language versions in the remaining territories such as France or Italy, and the financial burden on producers might not be recoverable through online sales. Rubeš follows sales numbers in individual territories and appreciates the quite significant year-over-year growth of AQS' total online revenues, but so far he has not launched any online marketing campaigns targeting foreign territories. Kulhánek adds that Bontonfilm has by far the best experience with iTunes, and it employs iTunes-enabled promotional instruments and discounts, although these focus mostly on the domestic territory.[14]

---

[12] The volume of European films produced or acquired by Netflix is expected to rise to comply with the 30% quotas introduced by the new Audiovisual Media Services Directive (Thomson 2019b).

[13] A Skype interview with Danielou Laurent (Loco Films) conducted by Petr Szczepanik, February 22, 2019.

[14] An interview with Ondřej Kulhánek conducted by Petr Szczepanik and Pavel Zahrádka, January 31, 2017; an interview with Jan Rubeš conducted by Pavel Zahrádka and Jan Hanzlík, August 23, 2018.

The bulk of the foreign sales of Czech Television content is managed by Česká televize via its sales department, which practically functions as the PSB's in-house sales agent. The department's head, Luboš Kříž, has observed significant changes that came with digitalization and the advent of VOD: the diversification and multiplication of buyers, the decrease in licensing prices and unexpected interest from new territories such as Japan and Brazil. Česká televize is focusing primarily on TV rights, selling them directly to foreign broadcasters, together with catch-up and VOD rights, omitting other intermediaries (international sales agents, Czech and foreign distributors) and limiting the scope of rights as much as possible, typically to a single territory and for three years, with an option of reselling in the same territory. While TV rights are sold exclusively, online rights tend to be non-exclusive, to allow other players in a territory to license them, and they are occasionally sold worldwide. Unlike the above-mentioned home video distributors, Česká televize focuses on VOD services that are able to pay a flat fee or at least a minimum guarantee. If a co-production agreement divides world rights between Česká televize and an independent producer, the PSB usually takes former socialist countries that it has historically exported to. According to Kříž, TV series generally sell better (in terms of TV rights) than films, which need to be grouped into packages (often mixing older and newer titles) to satisfy foreign broadcasters' programming needs.[15] But while Česká televize, taking advantage of its vast library, is the biggest exporter of Czech audiovisual content in terms of the total annual export volume (selling hundreds of titles per year mostly to broadcasters),[16] the presence of its serial content in foreign VOD catalogues seems to be much smaller when compared to independent films.[17]

The most renowned and internationally established Czech art house production company, Negativ Film, has the widest online presence in the foreign VOD catalogues mapped for this chapter: Its titles regularly reach not just the big global TVOD catalogues, but also HBO GO in Europe, smaller mainstream services such as Pantaflix in Germany and Vudu in the USA, free AVODs such as Tubi TV, public library and educational services such as Hoopla and Kanopy, and niche art house and documentary portals such as UniversCiné and Feelmakers. Negativ's sales executive Daniel Vadocký acknowledges that although he has been working with several VODs directly, for international sales he still strongly prioritizes cinematic deals, relying on foreign sales agents and above all foreign distributors with well-developed local knowledge and networks of contacts to handle not just theatrical, but also foreign TV and online distribution of his portfolio, too. An experienced international sales agent is not necessary in the neighboring CEE territories such as Slovakia or Poland but makes a big difference in large lucrative markets such as France or the USA, in terms of selecting and connecting with the right local partners, while the local foreign distributor is vital for choosing local online services as well as efficiently collecting revenues, however small they may be. The Czech producer then tends to trust the sales agent or foreign distributor without interfering with or even monitoring their

---

[15] An interview with Luboš Kříž conducted by Petr Szczepanik, October 12, 2018.

[16] Apart from Czech-made pornography, which this chapter leaves out.

[17] See www.justwatch.com.

operations beyond the obligatory financial reporting, which does not detail results for individual VOD services: "As soon as our film is bought by a foreign distributor, I completely lose track of where exactly it goes in terms of VOD." For example, *Ice Mother*, the comedy drama about unlikely love between two aging people, directed by the internationally best known Czech art house director Bohdan Sláma, the latest success from Negativ (and the Czech Republic's submission to the Oscars), was picked by the renowned sales agency The Match Factory, which sold all North American rights to the distributor FilmRise. Negativ was able to check the deal, but that is where their tracking of the process ended. FilmRise acknowledged right away that their plan for the USA was to skip theatrical distribution, publish DVDs and then go directly online (they eventually also helped with the Oscar campaign). FilmRise teamed up with the aggregator Quiver and launched a wide online release in the USA including Amazon Prime, iTunes, Google Play, Vudu and YouTube. Vadocký says he believes that FilmRise is doing their best to get the movie to as many online retailers as possible, but he also acknowledges that their strategy is rather "quantitative," pushing *Ice Mother* to the same well-proven VOD services as any other European art house title rather than tailoring the release for the film's specific qualities. According to Vadocký, revenues generated from foreign TVODs are still discouragingly small for him to engage in more active planning or monitoring of foreign online sales: "The work load required to get a film to a foreign VOD is too heavy for practically zero money. Even from the biggest portals we get monthly just one or two hundred CZK per title." For him, more important than the number of territories and VOD services is visibility in the market. Vadocký describes Netflix as "currently the best partner in purely financial terms," but quickly adds that he regrets it is so and that he prefers cultivating good relationships with Negativ's traditional cinematic partners and submitting to the Cannes Film Festival, which is notoriously at odds with Netflix. Overall, Negativ's approach is based on preserving control of international rights and tailoring foreign sales strategies for individual titles by exposing them to key decision-makers at international markets and festivals early on, ideally from the development stage.[18]

Unlike Negativ, which avoids working with domestic distributors and broadcasters in its foreign sales strategy, most producers, especially of a more commercially oriented breed, do not have their own sales executives. Instead of tailoring international marketing campaigns for each title before it is produced, they rely on one of the two biggest Czech home video distributors, Bontonfilm or AQS, to take care of both domestic and international online sales. Miloslav Šmídmajer, the owner of the Bio Illusion production house, is currently[19] one of the most active sellers of foreign online rights among independent, commercially oriented producers (he specializes in family comedies and animation). He is contracting either small international sales agents (such as London-based Amadeus Entertainment, specializing in genre films from Russia and Eastern Europe) or the Czech distributor AQS to sell his more

---

[18] An interview with Daniel Vadocký (Negativ Film), May 16, 2019.

[19] Judging from the data sample compiled from the four territories for this chapter.

attractive titles across borders. At the same time, he sells a package of his less internationally appealing titles directly via Amazon, with the help of a small and virtually
unknown Czech sales agent specializing in the Hungarian market (the agent is not
credited in foreign Amazon catalogues), with whom he shares aggregator fees and
revenues: "without the agent, I would not bother going into this." With the least
internationally attractive titles, Šmídmajer decides not to produce English language
versions at all. Outside big Western markets, he reports a rise of interest in TV and
online rights for Czech content from the Middle East, South America and above
all China, where Czech films usually end up in larger packages of cheaper content
without the option of monitoring the actual revenues.[20] But despite these signs of
progress, Šmídmajer considers foreign online sales negligible, "a joke," reaching no
more than hundreds of CZK per year per title. None of Šmídmajer's titles distributed
online across borders was able to cover even the aggregator fee.[21]

9.4   TVOD's Extensive, Bottom-Up Distribution Model

As these interviews illustrate, transnational TVOD services have been able to seam-
lessly integrate into the local industry ecosystem: They have been easier to approach
than SVODs, perfectly compatible with the traditional local intermediaries, and they
have been disrupting the established distribution practices less than Netflix. At the
same time, they also allow local independent producers to upload their films directly,
under the condition of observing basic technical and localization standards. Cross-
border TVOD distribution therefore opens a space for more diverse set of distribution
practices and intermediaries.

The most extensive and diverse portfolio of Czech films abroad is made available by iTunes and Amazon (both TVOD Amazon Video and SVOD Amazon Prime
Video).[22] There is no apparent logic behind the selection, which includes all kinds
of domestic production. The dataset compiled for this chapter does not allow for a
full-scale comparative analysis across the CEE region, but the European Audiovisual Observatory's reports indicate that Czech producers and distributors are using
transnational TVOD services more often than their counterparts in other Central and
Eastern European territories. In 2018, the number of Czech films in European TVOD
catalogues surpassed that of any other post-socialist EU country except Lithuania,
although it still represented just 0.5% of titles in European TVOD catalogues. It
also surpassed most post-socialist countries (apart from Bulgaria and Romania) and
many West European countries in terms of average country circulation (3.9 countries

---

[20]This is in line with a more general trend in the EU: China was identified as the largest non-European
market for European films (in terms of cinema admissions) in a recent EAO study (Kanzler and
Simone 2019: 157).

[21]A telephone interview with Miloslav Šmídmajer (Bio Illusion), July 12, 2019.

[22]The US and German Amazon Video catalogues include two to three times more Czech titles
than Amazon Prime Video, which is why Amazon is discussed in the TVOD section rather than as
SVOD.

and per title—as opposed to 1.1 countries per Czech title in SVOD catalogues). At the same time, the Czech iTunes catalogue contained at least ten times more local titles than in Poland, Hungary, Slovakia or any other post-socialist country in the EU, even though the Czech share was still two times less than iTunes' average share of national titles in the EU and many times lower than the national share in the EU5 (Grece 2019: 56–59, 76). Interviews indicate that the driver behind this prominent position of TVOD and iTunes in particular is not international interest in local production but the two above-mentioned Czech home video distributors' active role as local aggregators of online rights and iTunes' contractual partners (Figs. 9.1, 9.2, 9.3 and 9.4).

One of the key differences between transnational SVOD and TVOD services is their strategies for acquisition and original content. Google Play and Apple's iTunes have no original local content at all. Although Amazon has launched an aggressive local production campaign in Europe, it has not produced any original content in the CEE region and it has no visible local presence in terms of VOD representatives. For the most part, these TVODs operate as bottom-up catalogues without any specific content acquisition strategy apart from standardized quality control that has been partly outsourced to "approved" aggregators such as Quiver or Distribber. To get a movie into Amazon or iTunes' catalogue, for example, a producer does not necessarily need a distributor, which opens the door for indie and foreign titles that would not have been picked by big international distributors. The self-distribution model requires the producer to secure localization and typically to pay an upfront fee for the services of an aggregator (some of the aggregators ask for a share of revenues, too), who will take care of the ingestion, encoding and quality control. Despite this option, producers still mostly use intermediaries: A local home

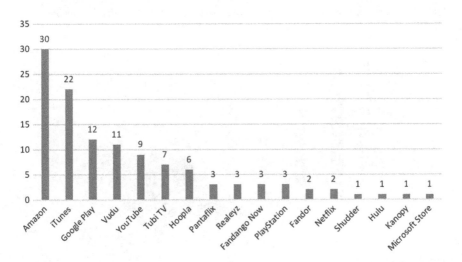

Fig. 9.1 Recent Czech feature fiction films (2011–2018) in the US Online Distribution, as of March 2019 (*Source* Data based primarily on an analysis of search results from Justwatch.com and Amazon.com)

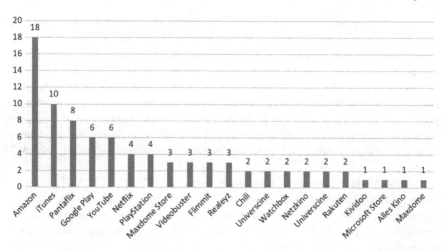

Fig. 9.2 Recent Czech feature fiction films (2011–2018) in the German Online Distribution, as of March 2019 (*Source* Data based primarily on an analysis of search results from Justwatch.com)

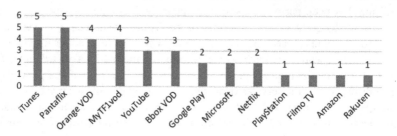

Fig. 9.3 Recent Czech feature fiction films (2011–2018) in the French Online Distribution, as of March 2019 (*Source* Justwatch.com)

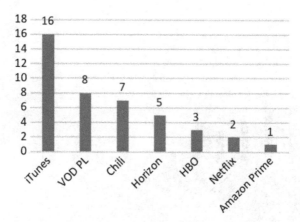

Fig. 9.4 Recent Czech feature fiction films (2011–2018) in the Polish Online Distribution, as of March 2019 (*Source* Justwatch.com)

video distributor or a foreign digital distributor, who might submit the title to several VOD services simultaneously, takes care of its editorial placement as well as giving it very modest marketing support. Different VOD services offer different financial conditions: While iTunes splits the sales 70:30 in favor of the producer, Amazon's self-distribution platform Amazon Video Direct applies a revenue-sharing program based on either a 50:50 split (for titles purchased or rented on Amazon) or per-hour revenue rates from an Amazon Prime subscription (ranging from \$0.06 to \$0.15/h depending on the total number of streaming hours). All above-mentioned VODs also rely on unique discovery algorithms which favor titles supported by strong marketing campaigns, typically US-produced blockbusters and festival winners. *IndieWire* sums up the frustrating experience of an indie film producer with the Amazon algorithm: "If I wasn't dead set on finding it, I would have given up and ordered something else" (Newman 2017). This implies that a Czech film without festival awards and proper marketing support, or at least without mobilizing its online fan base, would probably have little chance of recovering the aggregator fee that may range between \$1000 and \$1500 per title (Guerrasio 2018).

9.5 SVOD's Intensive, Top-Down Model and the Original Local Content Production

Transnational SVOD services Netflix and HBO do not have self-distribution platforms; their acquisition is much more selective, with Netflix being especially difficult to approach for local legacy media players and more disruptive to their established practices. This is even more so in the CEE region where Netflix catalogues include close to zero local content (Grece 2019: 112). At the same time, these transnational SVODs are able to offer better financial conditions, personalized marketing support and higher symbolic prestige.

Transnational SVODs—which, unlike TVODs, typically require pitching—pose a different kind of challenge to Czech producers. Negativ's sales executive Daniel Vadocký reports successful and regular negotiations with HBO Europe, whose Czech branch has co-produced several of Negativ's documentaries and bought online rights for Negativ's entire library of older titles, supposedly in a move to counter Netflix by buying out local content (as of July 2019, HBO GO's catalogues in Romania and Hungary include Negativ's 15 fiction features and a few documentaries from 1995 to 2017). But his experience with Netflix follows the well-known story of the difficulties with even contacting the right acquisition executives seated in Los Angeles, searching for the necessary help from intermediaries and then waiting helplessly for their arbitrary decision, which tends to be negative.[23]

HBO Europe is different from Netflix's European operations in terms of its long-term local presence and deep embeddedness in Central and Eastern Europe, which recently expanded into 21 European territories across the continent. HBO's first

---

[23] An interview with Daniel Vadocký (Negativ Film), May 16, 2019.

overseas branches opened in Hungary, Poland, Czech Republic and Romania in the early-to-mid-1990s; in the mid-to-late 2000s, they started acquiring and co-producing local stand-ups, documentaries and feature films. In 2010, HBO moved into in-house production of high-end series in the Czech Republic, Hungary, Poland and Romania (and more recently, it started producing original series also in its HBO Adria, HBO Nordic and HBO Espana branches). HBO Europe has been carefully cultivating its relationships with prominent local talent and legacy media players, creating a sense of trust and even admiration for its "creative freedom" approach among the regional professional communities. Since the launch of HBO GO, and especially since its recent conversion to OTT in the CEE region (in November 2017), its local originals have become a key instrument in competition with Netflix.[24] While HBO Europe aims at releasing its European originals day-and-date across all 21 countries, and while the local HBO Europe catalogues contain the most recent HBO US original titles, local HBO production does not automatically get into the catalogues of HBO US or other HBO territories outside Europe. For its most successful local title so far, the three-part miniseries *The Burning Bush* (2013), HBO Europe teamed up with the German sales agency Beta Film, one of the largest traders with film and TV rights outside the USA and a pioneer of the high-end local TV content production trend in Europe. Beta Film managed to sell *The Burning Bush* to at least 40 foreign territories, including prominent broadcasters such as Arte Germany and France, RAI and HBO Latin America, and VODs such as iTunes, Google Play, PlayStation Store, Hoopla, Sundance Now, Maxdome and Filmmit.[25] Several HBO Europe series have also made it into HBO US catalogues (e.g., HBO Czech's *Wasteland* and HBO Romania's *The Silent Valley*), which HBO Europe's executive VP of original programming and production Antony Root considers a groundbreaking success (Tizard 2018). The example of HBO Europe shows that the recent boom in original local production of transnational VOD services can significantly change the map of cross-border circulation from small media markets by opening up even the most exclusive distribution channels for them, although still only in a very limited scope.

Netflix's selection of local content is much narrower than HBO's, and the company is also much less transparent and predictable in terms of its acquisition strategy and curation. Netflix has dramatically raised its investment in original European production [to about a billion dollars in 2018, with 221 European projects planned for 2019—see Gold (2019)], but it has also become notorious for overusing the label "Netflix original." The label can refer to shows commissioned and produced by Netflix, but also to co-productions with other networks or even to exclusive international streaming rights. In the Czech Republic, Netflix has limited its selection to just one feature acquisition and one co-funded production in its first three years of local operation.[26] *The Devil's Mistress*, a biopic about a Czech interwar actress who had an

[24] An interview with the former head of HBO Czech Ondřej Zach, December 18, 2017.
[25] See the discussion with HBO Czech Republic's production executive (Czech Television 2017). See also TBI Reporter (2014).
[26] In October 2019 (i.e., beyond the time frame of this chapter), Netflix localized its interface in the Czech Republic and bought a package of about 30 older and newer Czech films, limiting their

affair with Joseph Goebbels, was the first Czech feature film acquired by Netflix for global distribution. The deal was announced half a year before Netflix launched its local service (Sedlák 2015). *Milada* is the story of a female social democratic MP executed after a communist show trial in the early 1950s, shot in English with an international cast by first-time director David Mrnka. Mrnka, who has worked in the US television industry (as a producer for *Larry King Live* and BBC World News, but not on any high-profile fiction projects), claimed that Netflix got involved during script development and acquired worldwide rights except for several territories including the Czech Republic (Czech Film Center 2017).

Although Netflix featured—until very recently—a very narrow and arbitrary selection of CEE content, it is still possible to find some regularities and significant differences across the region. In Poland, only one feature film plus one fiction and several nonfiction TV series went into global distribution via Netflix (as of February 2019). The feature film, a biopic about a Polish female gynecologist called *The Art of Loving*, shows striking similarities with the two Czech films discussed above, also stories about strong, real-life female characters against the background of the national political history. *Milada*, *The Devil's Mistress* and *The Art of Loving* are labeled with the same Netflix genre categories: "Movies based on Real Life," "Biographical Movies," "Czech/Polish Movies." None of these films was produced by a producer or a director with a strong international reputation, so it can be expected that the deals were relatively cheap for Netflix. However, a closer look at different national catalogues reveals that Netflix is not treating all the CEE markets in the same way. In Poland, it co-produced a high-budget series called *1983*, a dystopian alternative history of Poland in 2003 under continuing communist rule, directed by Agnieszka Holland, who had previously worked for HBO (including the above-mentioned Czech miniseries *The Burning Bush*). Indeed, the series seems to directly compete with HBO Europe's most prestigious projects, which also draw on national political histories and feature prominent local stars. Apart from that, Netflix has shot a serial adaptation of the globally known Polish fantasy saga *The Witcher* in English and was negotiating a historical crime series co-production with the PSB Telewizja Polska based on the Polish novel *Erynie* (Rutkowska 2019). Netflix has also acquired about 20 Polish films, mostly comedies from the 2000s, two fictions and one nonfiction TV series, and commissioned a series of "Netflix Branded Original Stand Up Specials" with Polish comedians. Most of these acquired films and TV series, however, have been available only in the Polish Netflix catalogue, and they show signs of being purchased as cheap packages from several local distributors.[27] Hungary is treated still differently from the Czech Republic and Poland: as a source of exportable art house films with strong symbolic capital. A small group of award-winning titles such as *Son of Saul*, *On Body and Soul*, *White God* and *Kills on Wheels*

---

distribution to the Czech and/or Slovak catalogue, with several exceptions being added also to the Hungarian, Romanian and/or Polish catalogues. This means that even after this leap, *Milada* and *The Devil's Mistress* remain the only Czech titles acquired by Netflix for a wide international distribution. See https://unogs.com.

[27] See https://unogs.com.

have been bought for a diverse set of Netflix catalogues, including, respectively, the USA, Japan, India and Mexico. Slovakia seems to be a blind spot, with no local content and no localization (after petitioning Netflix, Slovak fans could at least access Czech localization from February 2019).[28] Despite its fast move into the region in its 2016 "global switch on" and despite the first round of arbitrary choices described above, Netflix is showing signs of treating different CEE markets in a slightly more nuanced way: Poland as a pool of stories and talent for exportable high-end series, Hungary as a source of auteur cinema that can be of interest to Netflix's global cosmopolitan audiences, Slovakia as too small to bother and the Czech Republic as a country whose totalitarian history is more exportable than its cinema.

9.6   Conclusion

This inquiry into the practices and players involved in cross-border online distribution from CEE markets shows how diversified, unstable and locally specific the impacts of transnational VOD services are. The charts of Czech films in foreign territories change our perception of how and where CEE films travel online (outside Slovakia): Instead of France, Poland and Germany, which are the biggest importers in theatrical and TV distribution (Grece 2017a: 35, 52), the largest number of Czech films gets to the USA. They also point to the fact that the debate about the global VODs should not be concentrated on Netflix alone. While Netflix attracts the most attention, it is iTunes, Amazon and Google Play, followed by some lesser-known services such as Vudu and Pantaflix that facilitate the widest cross-border circulation of CEE content. While Netflix hails its own original content investments in Europe, it is still HBO that produces and buys more local content in the CEE region and distributes it across borders to its 21 European territories. While Netflix speaks of aggressive localization campaigns, until recently it has been one of the least localized global services with the smallest share of local content, either locally produced or acquired in the Czech Republic (see Table 9.1).

The analysis shows that it is crucial not to take the general quantitative statistics on VOD distribution at face value. A closer look at how online distribution is actually done "on the ground" reveals the emergence of a new distribution hierarchy in terms of marketing power, symbolic prestige and potential revenues. It is not enough to distinguish between SVOD, TVOD and AVOD—we need to look at individual services, their evolving business models, their algorithms, key intermediaries and different tiers of content including titles self-distributed by producers via Amazon's Video Direct. The strongly promoted and highly prestigious local HBO productions sit at the opposite end from the self-distributed, fully national (and otherwise non-exportable) productions buried in iTunes' or Amazon's catalogues. The online distribution regimes described in the above analysis can be hierarchically ordered as

---

[28] The Czech language is widely understood among the Slovak population. See VelkyObsah.info and Filmtoro.sk (2019).

Table 9.1 Comparative overview of transnational VOD services operating in the Czech Republic, as of March 28, 2019

Transnational VOD service	Business model and distribution technology	The size of local catalogue (all titles)	Original local content	Acquisitions	Localization
HBO	Pay TV/OTT SVOD	1562	29 films (fiction and documentaries) and 6 TV series	14 films (fiction and documentaries)	100%: dubbing and subtitles
Netflix	OTT SVOD	4956	1 fiction film	1 fiction film	0.5% dubbing and 9% subtitles
Amazon Video, and Amazon Prime	OTT TVOD/SVOD	999	–	3 fiction films	3% dubbing and 3% subtitles
Google Play	OTT TVOD	3598	–	36 films (fiction and documentaries)	17% dubbing and 28% subtitles
iTunes	OTT TVOD	8633	–	159 fiction films	35% dubbing and 22% subtitles

Source Data compiled from the database Filmtoro.cz (The process of localization of the Czech Netflix catalogue has sped up significantly since March 2019 [0.7% dubbed and over 16% subtitled as of August 2019, with more titles being localized later that year])

follows (from the highest level of international exposure and prestige to the lowest): (1) transnational SVODs' local productions and exclusive acquisitions with strong marketing support (such as HBO's *The Burning Bush* and Netflix's *Milada*); (2) mostly festival-oriented, often internationally co-produced art house films picked by renowned foreign sales agents (such as films produced by Negativ Film Productions and directed by Bohdan Sláma) and distributed through a wide variety of VOD services with the help of foreign local distributors; (3) mostly fully national films with limited international appeal, whose TVOD rights are sold by local home video distributors (the two Czech leaders in the home video market: Bontonfilm and AQS); and (4) even less internationally appealing, mostly commercially oriented fully national productions, self-distributed abroad by Czech producers via foreign or domestic aggregators,[29] and limited to TVOD.

---

[29]The key difference between a digital distributor and an aggregator is that the former buys and sells a license, while the latter just charges a fee for services necessary to upload a movie to a VOD catalogue.

It is likely that transnational flows from peripheral and/or small media markets in the CEE will be dependent on the changing strategies of global VOD services. With new global players and increased competition expected and with local content production initiatives anticipated to further boom, it seems that the circulation trajectories of CEE content will diversify, too. The prospect that micro-groups of audiences interested in peripheral content and scattered across the globe can be compiled just by placing the content into numerous TVOD catalogues seems utopian. More targeted production and marketing investment will be required to improve the circulation of CEE content. The legacy media players and public institutions in Central and Eastern Europe that have remained skeptical and hesitant to invest in cross-border online distribution will need take a more active approach. It remains to be seen whether the European Commission's DSM strategy will be successful by introducing content quotas, levies, prominence and transparency obligations, pushing the global giants to be more receptive to national audiovisual cultures and simultaneously to start revealing data about their catalogues, revenues and discovery algorithms. In the meantime, online distribution studies will have to keep developing methods that compensate for the secretive, black-box approach of most VOD services.[30]

References

Aguiar, L., & Waldfogel, J. (2018). Netflix: Global hegemon or facilitator of frictionless digital trade? *Journal of Cultural Economics, 42*(3), 419–445.

Alaveras, G., Gomez-Herrera, E., & Martens, B. (2018). Cross-border circulation of films and cultural diversity in the EU. *Journal of Cultural Economics*, *42*(4), 645–676.

Czech Film Center. (2017). This story really needs to get out! *Czech Film Center*, 3 November. www.filmcenter.cz/en/news/1347-this-story-really-needs-to-get-out. Accessed August 15, 2019.

Czech Television. (2017). Discussion with Tereza Polachová. *Facebook*, 31 July. https://www.facebook.com/ceskatelevize/videos/10154870705407686. Accessed November 11, 2019.

De Vinck, S., & Pauwels, C. (2015). Beyond borders and into the digital era: Future-proofing European-level film support schemes. In I. Bondebjerg, E. N. Redvall, & A. Higson (Eds.), *European cinema and television: Cultural policy and everyday life* (pp. 102–123). Basingstoke: Palgrave Macmillan.

European Commission. (2014). *Communication to the European Parliament, the Council, the European Economic and Social Committee and the Committee of the Regions —European Film in the Digital Era Bridging Cultural Diversity and Competitiveness, COM(2014) 272 final*. https://eur-lex.europa.eu/legal-content/EN/TXT/PDF/?uri=CELEX:52014DC0272&from=EN. Accessed November 11, 2019.

European Parliament. (2012). *Resolution on the online distribution of audiovisual works in the European Union (2011/2313(INI))*. https://www.europarl.europa.eu/sides/getDoc.do?pubRef=-//EP//NONSGML+TA+P7-TA-2012-0324+0+DOC+PDF+V0//EN. Accessed November 11, 2019.

Fontaine, G. (Eds.). (2019a). *Yearbook 2018/2019: Key trends*. Strasbourg: European Audiovisual Observatory.

[30]This study was supported by the European Regional Development Fund Project "Creativity and Adaptability as Conditions of the Success of Europe in an Interrelated World" (No. CZ.02.1.01/0.0/0.0/16_019/0000734).

Fontaine, G. (2019b). *Update on VOD markets and catalogues*. Strasbourg: European Audiovisual Observatory.

Gold, H. (2019). 2019 is the year the streaming wars get real. *CNN Business*, 11 January. https://edition.cnn.com/2019/01/11/media/tv-streaming-2019-netflix-disney-apple/index.html. Accessed August 15, 2019.

Grece, C. (2017a). *The circulation of EU non-national films*. Strasbourg: European Audiovisual Observatory.

Grece, C. (2017b). *The origin of films in VOD catalogues*. Strasbourg: European Audiovisual Observatory.

Grece, C. (2019). *Films in VOD catalogues: Origin, circulation and age* (2018 ed.). Strasbourg: European Audiovisual Observatory.

Grece, C., & Fontaine, G. (2017). *Trends in the EU SVOD market*. Strasbourg: European Audiovisual Observatory.

Guerrasio, J. (2018). Independent filmmakers are irate after Amazon slashed royalties by 60% on its self-distribution platform. *Business Insider*, 21 February. www.businessinsider.com/amazon-video-direct-plans-to-drastically-change-its-royalty-amount-2018-2. Accessed August 15, 2019.

Hastings, R. (2016). Keynote. *The Netherlands EU Presidency Conference "Promoting Cross-Border Circulation of European Audio-Visual Content"*, 3 March. www.youtube.com/watch?v=ZKdIT70gH6s. Accessed August 15, 2019.

Higson, A. (2018). The circulation of European films within Europe. *Comunicazioni Sociali, 3*, 306–323.

Holdaway, D., & Scaglioni, M. (2018). From distribution to circulation studies: Mapping Italian films abroad. *Comunicazioni Sociali, 3*, 341–355.

Iordache, C., Van Audenhove, L., & Loisen, J. (2018). Global media flows: A qualitative review of research methods in audio-visual flow studies. *Communication Gazette, 81*(7), 1–20.

Kanzler, M., & Simone, P. (2019). *Focus 2019: World film market trends*. Strasbourg: European Audiovisual Observatory.

Lobato, R. (2018). Rethinking international TV flows research in the age of Netflix. *Television & New Media, 19*(3), 241–256.

Newman, B. (2017). Why Netflix and Amazon algorithms are destroying the movies. *IndieWire*, 12 July. www.indiewire.com/2017/07/netflix-amazon-algorithms-destroying-the-movies-1201853974. Accessed August 15, 2019.

Nowakowska, J. (2019). O polskich subskrypcjach z serialami w tle. *Screen Lovers*, 18 February. https://screenlovers.pl/o-polskich-subskrypcjach-z-serialami-w-tle-raport-z-frontu-svod. Accessed August 15, 2019.

OD-SERV. (2018). *Households subscribing to SVOD in Europe (2013–2017)*. European Audiovisual Observatory. https://yearbook.obs.coe.int/s/document/5522/od-serv-unique-subscribers-to-ott-svod-services-in-europe-2013-2017. Accessed August 15, 2019.

Rutkowska, E. (2019). Netflix negocjuje z TVP. *Dziennik.pl*, 28 March. https://wiadomosci.dziennik.pl/media/artykuly/594516,netflix-tvp-negocjacje-serial-powiesc-krajewski.html?fbclid=IwAR3Mwy1aU2d8GShhCQcU5jm3hgPH0PZwK6FcVS8dylGa_RzgZiHldNTYYp8. Accessed August 15, 2019.

Sedlák, J. (2015). Netflix koupil práva na Renčův film Lída Baarová. *E15*, 10 August. https://www.e15.cz/magazin/netflix-koupil-prava-na-rencuv-film-lida-baarova-1217149. Accessed August 15, 2019.

SPI Olsberg. (2019). *Priority international markets for Czech producers*, Prague: APA.

Szczepanik, P. (2018). Post-socialist producer: Production culture of a small-nation media industry. *Critical Studies in Television, 13*(2), 207–226.

TBI Reporter. (2014). HBO hang hopes on Euro dramas. *TBI*, 6 October. https://tbivision.com/features/2014/10/hbo-hangs-hopes-euro-drama/337901. Accessed August 15, 2019.

Thomson, S. (2019a). CEE SVOD set to more than double. *Digital TV Europe*, 1 May. www.digitaltveurope.com/2019/05/01/cee-svod-set-to-more-than-double. Accessed August 15, 2019.

Thomson, S. (2019b). Ampere: Netflix will "aggressively ramp up" local production in Europe and Asia. *Digital TV Europe*, 8 January. www.digitaltveurope.com/2019/01/08/ampere-netflix-will-aggressively-ramp-up-local-production-in-europe-and-asia. Accessed August 15, 2019.

Tizard, W. (2018). HBO's Antony Root on creating European shows for a global audience. *Variety*, June 28. https://variety.com/2018/tv/global/hbo-antony-root-europe-1202860572. Accessed August 15, 2019.

VelkyObsah.info, & Filmtoro.sk. (2019). Netflix, make Czech localisation available in Slovakia: A petition. *Change.org*. https://chng.it/pdcxGWsh. Accessed August 15, 2019.

Vyskočil, T. (2019). Kolik lidí má u nás Netflix? *Filmtoro*. https://filmtoro.cz/blog/kolik-lidi-ma-u-nas-netflix-jaka-je-nabidka-a-kolik-filmu-ma-titulky-mame-novou-studii. Accessed August 15, 2019.

Petr Szczepanik is Associate Professor at Charles University, Prague. He has written books on the Czech media industries of the 1930s and on the state-socialist production mode. His current research focuses on (post-)socialist producer practices in Central and Eastern Europe. Some of his findings are published in *Behind the Screen: Inside European Production Culture* (Palgrave, co-edited with Patrick Vonderau, 2013). He led the EU-funded FIND project (2012–2014), which used student internships for a collective ethnography of production cultures. In 2015, he was the main author of an industry report on practices of screenplay development for the Czech Film Fund. He is now working on a study of the digitalization of the Czech audiovisual industry and the impacts of the European Commission's Digital Single Market strategy.

Chapter 10
Digital Film and Television Distribution in Greece: Between Crisis and Opportunity

Lydia Papadimitriou

10.1 Introduction

According to the EU's Digital Economy and Society Index (DESI 2018), which "tracks the progress of member states in terms of their digitisation," by 2018 Greece occupied the penultimate position as 27th out of 28 countries (DESI Greece 2018: 1). Digitization here is measured with reference to connectivity, digital skills, the use of Internet services and the integration of digital technology by both businesses and public services. Greece scores below the EU average on all indicators save the use of Internet services. The figures show that those who use the Internet do so mainly for information and entertainment—reading news online, participating in social networks, as well as accessing music, games and video on demand (DESI 2018: 6). This chapter focuses on the online circulation of professionally produced audiovisual content in Greece. It explores the platforms and institutions through which it is made available and situates these in the broader context of the country's film and television industries.

Given that a significant amount of the audiovisual content circulated and consumed in Greece is produced outside the country, a key question examined here is whether online distribution has opened up new opportunities for the country's production sector. The chapter maps out the stakeholders engaged in delivering audiovisual content online and highlights some of the ways in which residual and emerging screen media have intersected in creating the contemporary audiovisual media landscape in the country. It locates global disruptors, such as Netflix, within the structure of the Greek film and television industries, highlighting the transformations they have undergone during the last decade. Ultimately, the chapter assesses whether the opportunities offered by the new technologies have been and can be fully embraced in a small market such as that of Greece, and who have been the key beneficiaries.

L. Papadimitriou (✉)
Liverpool John Moores University, Redmonds Building, Brownlow Hill, Liverpool L3 5UG, UK
e-mail: L.Papadimitriou@ljmu.ac.uk

© The Author(s) 2020
P. Szczepanik et al. (eds.), *Digital Peripheries*, Springer Series in Media Industries,
https://doi.org/10.1007/978-3-030-44850-9_10

Before exploring the above, it is important to situate Greece as a "small market" and a "digital periphery." A country of less than 11 million, according to the 2011 census [and diminishing in population since then due to emigration and a low birth rate (Euronews 2019)], Greece is the tenth most populous country in the EU, below Belgium and above the Czech Republic (Eurostat 2019). In terms of area, it is just under 132,000 km^2, making it small to medium in the context of the EU.

Despite being at the "upper end" of the small country definition in the EU (Trappel 2014: 240), Greece is a small market and a "small media system" that shares a number of "structural peculiarities" with other similarly sized countries (Puppis 2009: 10). These include a relative shortage of resources, both in terms of capital, but also "know how, creativity and professionals in the media" (Puppis 2009: 10); a small audience and advertising market; dependence on political decisions made in larger neighboring states and a limited ability to influence global developments; and vulnerability to "foreign undertaking" (Trappel 2014: 243) with regard, especially, to the very high proportion of foreign media products in its market.

All the above help explain why small size can lead to global marginalization (unless corrective regulation or exceptional circumstances can counter this), and why, by extension, a small market can be considered as part of a "digital periphery." Small size affects the competitiveness of a market adversely both internally—in so far as it can afford "only a small number of competitors in most of its industries" (Gal 2003: 1)—and externally—as it lacks the resources to compete globally. Large markets possess the technical knowledge, economic capacity, organizational aptitude and drive for innovation that leads to the production of new technologies, consigning small markets to the position of consumers. Conversely, small markets purchase the hardware and software that they cannot develop or produce, which is desirable as it promises participation in the gains of progress that science and technology represent. When it comes to content, however, small markets are also producers— both because they can afford to be and because there is demand for local information and entertainment. However, two key interrelated aspects that differentiate content produced in a small market from content produced in a large market are resources and visibility: products from the latter can be very well-capitalized, and, by extension, they can often achieve global visibility, while those produced in a small market are more likely to be more cheaply made and consumed locally.

Distribution is the key factor that concerns visibility, and it is here that the debates about the specific possibilities afforded by *digital* distribution take place. It has already become apparent that the initial utopian promises of the "long tail," whereby the Internet would allow marginal material to be discovered by users simply due to its presence online, were unsubstantiated and naïve (Anderson 2006). Recent research has shown that a number of new gatekeepers are now controlling what circulates, and while the criteria for selection do not necessarily reflect the size of the producing market, it is clear that it is much harder for products from marginal origins to break through (Baschiera et al. 2017). In light of the above, the underlying broader question explored through the analysis that follows is whether and how the digital revolution, with regard to the circulation of audiovisual content online, can empower or disempower players in small markets. The case of Greece represents one specific iteration of this question, heuristically valuable both in its own terms and for comparative purposes.

10.2   Film and Television Industries in Greece: Structure, Policy and Debates

In order to examine whether the online circulation of audiovisual content has opened up opportunities for the production and dissemination of local/national content, it is necessary to set the scene by referring to the structure of the film and television industries in Greece, as these have traditionally controlled production and distribution. For the most part, the account below differentiates between film and television, since these two media have commanded different processes of production and distribution and have been largely represented by different public and private institutions (even though, in terms of production, there is overlap in creative and technical personnel). While digital distribution has diminished some of the conceptual distinctions between the two media, it is still widely maintained, including by Lotz (2017), who introduced the term "Internet-distributed television." Lotz's term refers to "video accessed via Netflix, Hulu, Amazon Video, HBO Now" and other such services, highlighting the fact that such content is accessed and consumed nonlinearly and (potentially) across many devices. Lotz, however, points out that "not all the video these services offer are television; many also offer feature films, which, per the difference in film's industrial formations and practices of looking, make them 'film' not 'television', or some other medium because they are Internet distributed" (2017). In Lobato's words, "Internet-distributed television" refers to "professionally produced content circulated and consumed through Web sites, online services, platforms, and applications, rather than through broadcast, cable, or satellite systems" (Lobato 2019: 5). In what follows, I examine the ways in which professionally produced audiovisual content circulates in Greece, situating recent developments within the context of the broader ecosystem of production and (online) distribution in the country.

To account for the state of the film and television industries in Greece by the year 2019, it is necessary to consider the effects of the 2009 financial crisis on the audiovisual sector. The public debt crisis and consequent austerity measures affected both the state-supported system of subsidies and the commercial system of financing production. The former depended on public funds which became scarce and largely diverted away from audiovisual production, while the latter depended largely on advertising income and/or box office revenues, both of which experienced a significant drop (Papadimitriou 2017; Iosifidis and Papathanassopoulos 2019). The effect was similar across the film and television sectors, but the ways in which it manifested itself were different.

In film production, public funding temporarily halted in the early 2010s and when it slowly but modestly resumed, the cuts had already caused significant disruption in the production flow (Papadimitriou 2017). Furthermore, a planned tax on the income from cinema tickets aimed to secure direct funding of film production was canceled in 2015, removing key resources from the main relevant institution, the Greek Film Centre (Flix 2015). Public television was even more dramatically affected as in 2013 the then-rightwing government imposed a sudden closure of the state broadcaster (Elliniki Radiofonia kai Tileorasi: ERT/Greek Radio and Television) as a speedy means to reduce costs and streamline the organization. An interim, pared down, public broadcaster took charge, until the election of a leftwing government in 2015 reversed the decision of ERT's closure, reopened the broadcaster and resumed financing of television programs and films (Iosifidis and Papathanassopoulos 2019: 7–10).

The commercial system of film and television production was impacted by the financial crisis because the general reduction in personal disposable income led to a decline in overall consumption and a consequent dramatic drop in advertising expenditures. In film, distributors who had previously invested in production, encouraged by healthy box office returns, all but stopped when the crisis and the onset of widespread piracy undermined filmgoing habits (Papadimitriou 2018). At the same time, private television channels exclusively dependent on advertising to stay afloat were unable to produce original content for broadcast and to support film production, once their income was slashed.

While financial conditions remained very difficult in 2015, the new leftwing-led government pushed forward the broader goal of facilitating the country's digitization, in terms of both infrastructure and skills, by creating the dedicated Ministry of Digital Policy, Telecommunications and Media which soon published a National Digital Policy (2016) identifying relevant priorities. Indicative of its intentions was the subsidy offered for the cost of installing high-speed Fiber-To-The-Home (FTTH) communication networks starting in June 2018, thus encouraging the adoption of next-generation access (NGA) infrastructure. Within a month, three of the four Internet providers launched commercial fiber-optic broadband networks (Gorelik 2019: 20).

As will be detailed below, this investment opened the path for a more widespread adoption of online distributed audiovisual services. Two other initiatives also led by the Ministry affected the audiovisual industry in Greece. One was the regulation of the private free-to-air television channels through the allocation of a limited number of licenses. The other was the establishment of EKOME, the National Centre for Audiovisual Media and Communication, whose aim is to "promote and foster public and private initiatives, foreign and domestic in all sectors of the audiovisual industry" (EKOME 2018a). While neither initiative directly concerns Internet-enabled distribution, both—especially the former—were highly debated. The implementation of the resulting policies provides illuminating insights into the social, political and industrial contexts in which developments in digital distribution occur and has influenced the broader media ecology that affects, among other things, the kinds and amount of national content circulating online.

The requirement that private television channels apply for, and then purchase, one of the limited numbers of licenses available (valid for ten years) is particularly relevant because it helped clarify and stabilize the landscape of legacy (terrestrial) television, which plays a significant role in the online provision of audiovisual content domestically. The process of selecting the companies that would receive the licenses was contested (both in parliament and in the press) because it indirectly implicated political and business interests. As in many European countries, private free-to-air channels began to operate in Greece in 1989 when the deregulation of national television was introduced. Benefitting from the growth of the Greek economy in the ensuing years, as well as from collusions with the political parties in power, these channels (and the interests of their magnate owners) profited significantly, while their relationship to the state was never formalized—meaning that they gave little back to the state by way of tax or relevant contributions (Iosifidis and Papathanassopoulos 2019). Calls for some regulation that would reduce, among other things, the number of channels allowed to operate in Greece—especially since the small size of its market cannot profitably sustain too many competitors—were repeatedly ignored until two factors changed the situation. One was the financial crisis that pushed many channels to the brink of bankruptcy and forced the state (that had often granted them loans with very favorable terms) to recoup funds. The other was television's digital switchover, completed in 2015, and the consequent allocation (from the EU) of a particular (and therefore limited) range of frequencies for broadcasting. It should be noted that the controversy around licenses concerned the policy implementation and not the principle itself—i.e., the number of licensed channels, the price and the manner of selection. It took three years for the matter to be resolved, and the five license-holders were eventually announced in September 2018.[1] These were the following:

- Antenna, initially a radio station, was established in 1988 by shipowner Minos Kyriakou, and it began television broadcasts a year later. Antenna is the oldest surviving Greek private channel and still run by the Kyriakou family as part of the Antenna Group that has expanded operations beyond Greece (especially in southeastern Europe).
- Skai is also originally a radio station owned by shipowner Giannis Alafouzos since 1989, and it started operations as a television station in early 1993. It was sold and renamed Alpha (see below) in 1999, but was relaunched as Skai in 2006. Alafouzos' parent company owns, among other things, one of the more established Greek newspapers, *Kathimerini*.
- Star is launched in December 1993, and the TV channel is owned by Giannis Vardinogiannis, descendant of one of the largest ship-owning families in Greece.
- Alpha is launched in September 1999 (after the channel Skai was bought by entrepreneur Dimitris Kontominas). In October 2018, just after the licensing process was completed, a more than 50% controlling stake of the parent company was purchased by the Vardinogiannis Group (which also owns the Star channel). The two channels continue to operate separately.

---

[1] The matter was initiated by Nikos Pappas when he was Minister of State in 2015 and was moved into the remit of the Ministry of Digital Policy, which he also led after it was founded. The first (badly handled) attempt at allocating the licenses took place in September 2016 and was annulled three months later. Eventually, the Greek National Council for Radio and Television, an independent supervisory and regulatory body, was constituted with cross-party participants, and the first five licenses were granted in October 2018 (CNN 2018).

- Open Beyond is bought in 2017 by Greek-Russian magnate Ivan Savvidis, and the channel had been known as Epsilon TV since 2013.

A sixth license for a channel owned by the shipowner Vangelis Marinakis (previously co-owner of the financially troubled channel Mega, which closed down in October 2018) was announced in early 2019 and is currently being processed. I will return to these companies in the following section, when exploring their Web TV presence since, as noted above, they are among the main homegrown carriers of such content.

The other extensively debated and long-in-the-making policy was the introduction of a cash rebate scheme intended to encourage investment in international productions, as well as to stimulate national productions (EKOME 2018b). As elsewhere, the scheme is aimed at all formats of audiovisual production (film, television, games), irrespective of the mode of distribution.[2] Such lack of differentiation between film and television—a consequence of the fact that both are digital media that can be distributed variously and similarly—is novel in Greece, as well as the fact that state support for production is granted not with an assessment of quality, but through a system of points based on financial criteria (Galanis 2019). These conditions have enabled new players, some of which are major stakeholders in digital distribution (such as Pay TV companies), to access state funds previously unavailable to them for production, thus offering state support for professionally created local content intended for both established (Pay TV) and new (over-the-top, or OTT) modes of circulation.

While the granting of terrestrial television licenses and the introduction of the cash rebate scheme have dominated audiovisual policy and public debates in Greece since 2015, Pay TV made the headlines in June 2016 when the introduction of an additional 10% tax on the cost of subscriptions (as a further means of amassing funds for the indebted state) was considered the key reason for the drop in subscriptions that followed (Mandravelis 2017). Pay TV represents a significant part of the Greek audiovisual media ecosystem and is especially relevant to the discussion of the online circulation of content because these companies (which are based in Greece, but often involve transnational ownership and capitalization) have been leaders in the introduction of new technologies and applications—including OTT on-demand services.

There are currently four Pay TV companies in Greece. The market leader is Cosmote, a subsidiary of Deutsche Telekom founded in 2009, with a 45% market share in 2018 (over 500,000 subscribers) (Gorelik 2019: 24). Cosmote is also the largest Internet provider by number of subscriptions (48% of the mobile and 47% of the fixed markets) (Gorelik 2019: 3). The oldest subscription TV service is Nova TV,

---

[2]The belated introduction of such a widely adopted policy across Europe was partly due to precrisis complacency, and partly to the inability to do so during the crisis since it involved public spending. While generally applauded, the generous amount set aside by the government for this scheme (€75 million over three years) has raised questions with regard to the overall direction of the government's audiovisual policy, when compared to the paltry amounts granted to the Greek Film Centre (€3.5 million annually, of which about €1.5 million can be invested in production).

currently available only via satellite, and owned by ISP Forthnet, with a 42% market share in 2018 (Gorelik 2019: 24). In 2018, with the advent of FTTH, both these companies launched separate OTT services. Two other ISPs, originating in mobile phone companies, Vodafone and Wind, entered the Pay TV market in 2017. In April 2018, Wind Hellas launched an IPTV subscription video service, Wind Vision, which also marked the introduction of the Android TV box in the Greek market, and made 60 channels, including Netflix, available to subscribers.

Pay TV in Greece (as elsewhere) is usually sold as part of a bundle that includes fixed line and broadband service, and sometimes mobile phone, too (Gorelik 2019: 19). By definition, OTT services are not dependent on line rental or a Pay TV subscription; but in one case (Cosmote Go), it is also offered for free to Pay TV subscribers, thus blurring the boundaries between the two services. By the end of 2017, Pay TV penetration in Greece was 22%—a drop of 2% from 2015 largely due to an increase in prices caused by the introduction of the 10% tax on Pay TV mentioned above. By 2018, 86% of Pay TV was via satellite (DTH) while Internet-based subscriptions (IPTV) were 14% (Gorelik 2019: 10, 24). These numbers reflect the stability of satellite technology in comparison with the low-speed broadband that was the standard until recently. With the increased adoption of faster broadband and especially FTTH, satellite connections are predicted to fall to 78% and broadband-based connections to rise to 18% by the end of 2023 (Gorelik 2019: 24).

Pay TV film and series content consists mostly of foreign fare, reflecting the overall landscape of film distribution in Greece (Papadimitriou 2018). Pay TV companies have supported Greek cinema by contributing to co-productions (in return for screening rights), but this is a very small percentage of what they show. It is mostly access to prestige (foreign) film or television series not available on Free TV (as Pay TV precedes Free TV in the value chain), and/or exclusive sports channels (depending on the package on offer) that make subscriptions attractive, rather than exclusive Greek content—although this may be about to change, as I will show below. Examples of the foreign prestige content available on Pay TV include Disney's *Star Wars* franchise (Cosmote TV) and HBO's *Game of Thrones* (Nova). Of Cosmote TV's six channels dedicated to cinema, only one shows Greek films—and these are mostly old films from the 1950s and 1960s rather than recent productions. Of its 14 documentary channels, one—Cosmote History—is dedicated to Greek history and culture and offers a mix of foreign and Greek productions (including some in-house co-productions). Nova has no dedicated channel for Greek cinema, but does promote its cinematic co-productions on its Web site.

Signs of change, in terms of the inclusion of exclusively Greek content on the Pay TV channels, emerged in 2019, as both Cosmote TV and Nova produced television series. Nova produced the low-budget but well-received comedy *Mamades sto Pagaki* (*Mothers of the Bench*), which was launched on one of its Pay TV channels in February 2019 (and was already in its second season by May 2019). Cosmote TV's series (released in summer 2019) is an eight-episode crime thriller entitled *Eteros Ego-Hamenes Psyches* (*Alter Ego-Lost Souls*), a spin-off from a controversial popular film.[3] While Nova has not announced plans to make the series available on its OTT service, Cosmote will premiere the series on its Pay TV and make it available on its OTT service the next day (Vima 2019).

As opposed to Nova's comedy series, Cosmote TV's thriller is an expensive project (by Greek standards), costing almost €100,000 per episode—35% of which is from the cash rebate scheme (Galanos 2019; Vima 2019). While these first-ever investments in the production of television series by Pay TV channels are the result of a combination of factors, including expanded state support and increased competition (partly as a result of the launch of their new OTT services), they are signs that the Greek screen media ecology is becoming more diverse and OTT digital distribution is playing a part in this.

The discussion so far has illustrated the current structure of the audiovisual industries in Greece by pointing to the key sources of funding, policies and major players that shape the field. OTT provision remains a very new phenomenon in Greece, which is still far from being able to create an autonomous virtuous cycle of production and distribution. The absence of a public debate on matters of digital distribution in Greece arguably reflects the fact that it is as yet unclear how online distribution could be monetized in the Greek context, and who would benefit from this process. While the launch of Netflix in the country in January 2016 triggered a number of press reports that presented its services and/or assessed its value for Greek audiences (Netflix 2017; Goranitis 2017), other reports on global developments in the streaming market (e.g., the upcoming launch of the Disney + streaming service), rarely if ever make references to local developments. The question of whether online distribution will help stimulate local production (and how) is almost never directly asked—with the exception of the possible investment of Netflix in the country, which I will return to below.

Furthermore, as Greek films and television series have not generally been exportable (aside from very few exceptions, including to diasporic audiences), online distribution is mostly considered just a different way for reaching the same (i.e., national) audiences, rather than reaching out to transnational markets that could bring more returns. This may partly explain why the EU's policy on the Digital Single Market (DSM) has not been widely debated. In other European contexts, such as the Czech Republic, the DSM has met with opposition from local distributors who see it as undermining their export business (especially to neighboring Slovakia) while also potentially disrupting import opportunities (e.g., by increasing the prices of premium Hollywood content) (Szczepanik 2017)—which could also affect Greek distributors. Against the background of the overall invisibility of digital distribution in Greek audiovisual policy and public discourse, in the section that follows I will examine four of Ramon Lobato's eight "elements" (2019: 8) of Internet-distributed

---

[3]Sotiris Tzafoulias' original film *Eteros Ego* (*Alter Ego*) (2016) raised controversy and was withdrawn early from cinemas due to its similarity to a real-life crime. Prior to this, it was well received by audiences and critics alike and garnered a number of festival awards in Greece. After being withdrawn from formal circulation, it was uploaded by the director for free access on YouTube. To date, it has reached almost 1.9 million viewings, a very high number for a contemporary Greek film.

television (those that relate to professionally produced content) and thus map out the OTT options currently available to Greek consumers. In doing so, I will "disaggregate the ecology of services, platforms, set-top boxes and apps" that constitute Internet-distributed television in Greece as of summer 2019 (Lobato 2019: 7), while high-lighting the challenges and opportunities for the development of a globally connected and digitally enabled local ecosystem of production–distribution–consumption.

10.3   The Distribution Ecology of Over-The-Top (OTT) Video on Demand (VOD) Provision in Greece

According to a recent marketing report, by the end of 2018, 8.66% of households (380,000 subscribers) accessed OTT content, reflecting a "quite underdeveloped" market—implicitly in comparison with other European markets (Gorelik 2019: 25). The report does not specify exactly which services this figure refers to and how the information is sourced, but given that it mentions OTT "subscribers" the figure seems to refer to SVOD services. The introduction of Netflix, the largest globally available SVOD company, in Greece in January 2016 was a major milestone for the familiarization of Greek audiences with OTT services. It was the first non-Greece-based multinational company offering an extensive catalogue of foreign films and television series at an affordable price and across different devices. Initially, Netflix provided very little content subtitled (or dubbed) into Greek and therefore targeted only fluent English language speakers, thus having limited appeal. The company, however, rapidly invested in localization, and by December 2017, 70% of the then-available content was subtitled or (less often) dubbed, and a Greek menu made navigation much easier for Greek audiences. During the launch of the localized services in December 2017 in Athens, the company's representatives made the rather exaggerated claim that "subscription levels are [proportionately] on a par to those of the American market" and publicized their goal to reach one in three broadband-enabled households by 2023 (Goranitis 2017). Netflix does not release territorialized subscriber information, but estimates about the number of subscribers to the end of 2017 have varied from 20,000–25,000 subscribers (or fewer) to over 60,000. While specific data are unavailable, it is fair to assume that localization and the increased visibility of the company will help Netflix further expand its base.

As a widely recognizable brand with a new business model for Greek audiences, Netflix is in many ways the flag-bearer in terms of OTT provision in Greece. At the time of writing, its catalogue did not include any Greek produced content (although it has included a few Greek films in the past), while the prospects for local investment by Netflix have not as yet materialized. Netflix notwithstanding the ecology of digital distribution in Greece is becoming more complex as an increasing number of players have started circulating locally produced content, with various attempts to monetize their services. The following discussion explores the way in which Lobato's first four (out of eight) elements manifest themselves in Greece.

At the top of Lobato's list is "online TV portals such as BBC iPlayer (UK), ABC iView (Australia) [...] provided by major broadcast networks and cable/satellite providers through websites and apps" that "typically include combination of new-release content, library content, and live channel feeds" (Lobato 2019: 8). All Greek television channels—public and private—have Web sites with a layout very similar to the description above. The content available is free-to-access and consists of a mix of information and entertainment programs produced in-house. There are also many trailers, as a key function of the Web sites is promotional, aiming to attract prospective viewers toward television viewings, which is the main source of the companies' income (via advertising returns, which are in turn dependent on ratings). These Web sites carry mainly information and light entertainment content (e.g., news programs and chat shows) rather than television series, but the exact proportion of these kinds of content depends on the profile of each company.

The Greek state broadcaster ERT's Web site includes live streaming of the copyright-owned sections of its three terrestrial channels, as well a select catch up service featuring recently aired programs (under the "Web TV" tab). It also provides free access to an extended digitized archive of the broadcaster's content dating back to 1974. In December 2017, the company launched ERT Hybrid, a service that enables users to access ERT's Web site on their Smart TV screens; **to-date ERT Hybrid does not provide additional content.**

ERT and most Greek terrestrial channels provide their online content for free (with some advertisements) in Greece and across Europe. The only channel that attempts to monetize access to its content outside Greece through a SVOD model is Antenna, which requires international (or rather diasporic) audiences to pay for content via local Pay TV providers in different countries. Otherwise, the content of Antenna's Web site is similar to that of the other channels (news programs, catch up and archival services) and includes a number of television series produced by Antenna. Two additional tabs, however, reveal the channel's attempts to branch out to a younger audience. The first is a portal called Netwix (a play on "Netflix"), an "autonomous" free Web channel launched in 2014 that is nonetheless part of the Antenna Group's operations (Netwix 2019). Addressed to young audiences with "exclusive content," Netwix consists of five channels/tabs (comedy, series, life, entertainment, tech and games) and claims to have streamed 40 Web series with more than 2500 episodes. The content is free but often has an advertising dimension. For example, the Web series *Kanto Fantastika* (*Do It Fantastically*), which consists of five-minute-long episodes, is an extended product placement for the soft drink Fanta. Production values of this content are generally very low, with the style often emulating amateur videos by YouTubers (from which the channel's content can also be accessed). In 2014, Antenna also launched a "strategic partnership with VICE Media, the global youth media brand and digital content studio" (Antenna Group 2019). Antenna co-produces Greek Vice content, which is then distributed via the channel's Web site (under the "Vice" tab), Vice's own portal, as well as more widely on YouTube.

Of the remaining four channels' Web sites, Skai is mostly geared toward information, while Alpha offers the largest catalogue of television series available for free. The offerings reflect the profiles of the terrestrial channels, as Skai has traditionally had high ratings for news and information programs (and for long-running reality TV shows such as *Survivor* and *Power of Love*), while Alpha has consistently invested in television series. Star and Open Beyond are roughly similar in terms of their balance between information and magazine videos, and television series. The extent to which any of these Web sites are actually used by audiences is not known, and given their lack of exclusive content, occasional difficulty in navigating, and the frustration of not knowing in advance whether something is fully available or just a trailer, it is fair to speculate that they may not be as attractive propositions as they could be. However, as will be discussed below, all these companies also have dedicated channels on YouTube that show both the number of subscribers and viewings, giving us an indication of popularity.

Lobato's second category, subscription VOD—a curated library of content for a monthly subscription—is an emerging market in Greece with only a few recent start-ups. In terms of global players, the domination of Netflix has been already noted. A number of other global companies, such as Filmbox Live and Mubi, are also accessible from Greece, but their presence is marginal. Amazon Prime is widely known, but has a smaller catalogue and much less subtitled content than Netflix and is therefore less favored. Furthermore, as Greece scores low in terms of e-shopping, the appeal of Prime as a means for speedy delivery of physical items is lost on Greek customers. Two other services listed on the European Audiovisual Observatory's Mavise database as SVOD available in Greece—Fox and National Geographic—are accessible via Pay TV subscriptions and not via standalone OTT services (European Audiovisual Observatory 2019).

Aside from these global offerings, both the private terrestrial channel Antenna and the two leading Pay TV companies, Cosmote and Nova, have launched OTT SVOD portals. Antenna launched the first such service in Greece, Ant1Next, in March 2017. Priced at €2.99 a month, it offers access only to Antenna-produced content, with the main attractions being that subscribers can watch episodes before they air on Free TV and without advertisements. Catch up of recent programs and an archive tab providing older content are also included. Self-styled as the Greek Netflix, Ant1Next is available on any Internet-enabled device and targets younger viewers. Like all of Antenna's on-demand content, it is available only in Greece via the Web site and requires a subscription via a different Pay TV company for international access.

Incentivized not only by Netflix's presence in the Greek market, but also by the expansion of FTTH networks, the two leading Pay TV providers launched the OTT services Cosmote Go (August 2018) and NovaFlix (April 2019) that do not require a Pay TV subscription. The profile of the two services is rather different: Cosmote Go offers a number of packages with 45 channels that can be variously combined, while NovaFlix attempts to emulate the Netflix model both in name and approach. Both companies offer preferential access to their OTT services for their Pay TV subscribers: Cosmote Go is provided for free to them, in addition to the services they pay for, while access to NovaFlix can be purchased at a reduced price by Nova's Pay TV subscribers. Cosmote Go's packages are organized by genre (documentaries, films, sports), each with a different monthly price, while Greek and children's films are only available to OTT subscribers who buy at least two other packages. NovaFlix's model is much simpler, offering access to a curated selection of films and television series, as well as content from US Fox TV channels, for a flat fee. As opposed to Ant1Next, which sells in-house produced (and therefore Greek) content, Cosmote and Nova's OTT services offer predominantly foreign content (reflecting the profile of their Pay TV services). While it is too early to assess their success, market forecasts project that the number of overall OTT SVOD subscribers in Greece will double by the end of 2022, reaching 13.39%, or over 650,000 households (Gorelik 2019: 25), a growth rate that presumably takes into account such local initiatives.

Transactional VOD, or "pay-per-view," Lobato's third element, refers to services that offer purchase or rental per item, with iTunes and Google Play being the top global players. While it is not possible to measure national access, all major global firms are available from Greece (including Google Play, iTunes, the Microsoft Store, and the Vodafone Video Club). Japanese global giant Rakuten became available in Greece in 2019, while UK-based FilmDoo, a service that specializes in independent and world cinema, has the most extensive catalogue of Greek films available on a non-Greek TVOD service. Pame Odeon, a portal for Greek films provided by one of Greece's largest film distribution companies, mainly provides access to its own content, but has arguably failed to make a big impact on the market.

Lobato's fourth and last element discussed here refers to hybrid TVOD/SVOD/free portals (e.g., YouTube, Youku, Tencent) that offer both free content (user uploaded and professional) and premium content (via subscription or direct purchase). Of these, YouTube is widely used in Greece for free streaming—both for amateur uploads and professional content. As noted above, all terrestrial and Pay TV channels available in Greece have YouTube channels, which provide a significantly greater amount of content than that available on their Web sites and/or via broadcast.[4] For example, public broadcaster ERT's 16-episode television adaptation of Stratis Myrivilis' anti-war novel *I Zoi en Tafo* (*Life in the Tomb*), which was first aired on the terrestrial channel in January and February 2019, is freely available on YouTube but not on ERT's Web site. The series is the first production by the public broadcaster since the 2009 crisis, and—at €100,000 per episode—one of its most expensive ever. While its critical reception was overall positive and the series was hailed as a rare example of quality Greek TV, ratings were disappointing. This is also reflected in its YouTube viewings: four months after being uploaded on the platform its viewings ranged from 106,000 (for the first episode) to 11,000 (for the last), a respectable but certainly non-blockbusting number. The fact that this prestige series is available on YouTube for free and with very few if any advertisements (and if there are, they are easy to bypass) indicates the public broadcaster's difficulty in marketizing its content and suggests a significant problem in creating a virtuous cycle between distribution and production, especially when involving quality content. It also reflects the fact that as the public broadcaster's main source of funding is state subsidy (provided mainly by a levy on electricity bills), additional monetization of content is not a high priority.

[4]Film distribution companies (such as Feelgood, Tanweer and Odeon) also have YouTube channels, but these consist only of trailers of released or soon-to-be-released films in cinemas and have no additional content (nor a large following).

In contrast, Cosmote (which runs three YouTube channels: Cosmote, Cosmote TV and Cosmote What's Up) produces original content that also serves as (self) advertising. One example is the mini-Web series *S'agapo, M'agapas* (*I Love You, You Love Me*) available on Cosmote's main YouTube channel, which consists of eight three- to four-minute-long episodes uploaded between February and March 2019 that clearly function as advertisements for Cosmote services. The Web series is a spin-off of the 2000–2002 television series of the same name (and with the same actors), which was then produced by private channel Mega, which had, in turn, been a remake of the late 1990s French Canadian original *Un Gars et une Fille*. In a period of just over three months, the number of viewings of the Web series ranged from over 1.6 million viewings (for the first couple of episodes) to over 250,000 (for the last two).

With a similar promotional aim combined with the ambition to inspire young people (especially girls) to become involved with new technologies, Cosmote produced the 50 min-long Web movie *Robogirl*. The story focuses on a young girl who crash-learns robotics in order to fix her brother's homemade prize-winning robot that she broke accidentally. During a period of five months, the film received over four million views on YouTube and rave reviews. Both these examples show that Cosmote's investment in online-only production is seen as a direct means for company promotion. While limiting the scope of what content could be thus supported, the number of viewings indicates significant audience engagement—although it is not clear whether this leads in practice to viewers choosing Cosmote products over their competitors, and whether, therefore, it directly benefits the company. It certainly helps raise its profile as a producer of innovative audiovisual content in the Greek context, however.

While the other four elements suggested by Lobato (2019) as constitutive of Internet-distributed television will not be discussed here since they refer predominantly to the informal economy, I will briefly introduce them as they are widely used in Greece, especially since the informal online economy is deemed to be particularly active in Greece (Papadimitriou 2018). These are (1) video-sharing platforms, such as Daily Motion, "which offer a range of free, ad-supported amateur and professional content, often informally uploaded" (Lobato 2019: 8); (2) informal on-demand and download services, such as BitTorrent or Popcorn Time; (3) unlicensed live, linear channel feeds; and (4) recommender and aggregator applications, such as JustWatch.

The above analysis of the four formal ways in which professionally produced audiovisual content could reach Greek audiences online (without a Pay TV subscription) by the middle of 2019 shows that, until now, there were no successful direct ways of monetizing such online services. Terrestrial channels use their Web sites mainly as hooks for attracting audiences to their main broadcast free-to-air programs, which are funded via advertising. The three SVOD services recently launched are all offshoots of larger companies, suggesting that their financial viability relies on ownership of the copyright for content (Greek for Ant1Next, and mostly foreign for Cosmote Go and Novaflix), while their success remains to be seen. The recent investment in original content by the parent companies of the latter two suggests that the commercial viability of online distribution is gaining ground, but, as discussed earlier, the new productions were funded from other sources (the companies' more established activities and from state funds via the cash rebate scheme) rather than directly from OTT revenues. TVOD provided by Greek distributors is extremely limited, while, for professional television (and film) companies, YouTube functions mainly as a means for promotion rather than direct monetization (with the exception of a few advertisements) and therefore does not drive growth.

10.4   Conclusion

In considering whether online distribution has opened up opportunities that can help stimulate audiovisual production in Greece, it has become clear that online distribution alone, and specifically OTT services, is too new and undeveloped to generate enough financial returns to trigger a virtuous circle of demand leading to more local production. The question is whether the small size of the market and, in particular, the fact that Greek content has limited scope for exportability, restricts its prospects (as has been the case with traditional film and television distribution), or whether the ease of global access that digital distribution affords opens up new opportunities for wider visibility and for healthy financial returns.

Considered as part of the broader ecology of policies, players and practices at both the local and national levels, it is very likely that online distribution will gradually play an increasingly significant role in the cycle of supply and demand for audiovisual content in Greece. It is unlikely, however, that the cycle will become sustainable and lead to high enough returns from subscriptions to OTT platforms to fund production in the way in which this has become possible (and the only means for further growth) for global services such as Netflix. The small size of the Greek market, the lack of exports and the very strong competition from global companies that make available very well capitalized and promoted content make it nearly impossible for Greek audiovisual media to liberate themselves from their position in the digital periphery. The vulnerabilities of a "small media system," including limited resources, a small audience and advertising market, and the pervasive presence of foreign media products, point to the need for regulatory intervention, without which it is difficult to sustain a healthy media ecology balancing global imports with locally produced content. But regulation has its limits too, as it functions within a globally competitive system, which, as pointed out by Puppis (2009) and Trappel (2014), depends on decisions made and practices originating elsewhere, and which serve supranational interests. The Digital Single Market and the cash rebate schemes are two such examples—the first being European in scope and not necessarily serving small markets' interests, and the latter involving different countries competing to attract foreign production (and therefore cash).

To the extent that regulators can act autonomously, their challenge is to create the conditions for a diverse and quality-oriented local production that can circulate online (although not necessarily only online) and—ideally—be relevant and popular enough to break through national boundaries and reach transnational audiences. The current mix of policy and practices suggests that more such opportunities may open up—whether or not Netflix, after all, invests in Greek-language productions. So far, only a few exceptional films from Greece have had global visibility. The Greek audiovisual industry will reposition itself outside the global digital periphery only if and when the technological, narrative and financial possibilities afforded by digital media allow it to create content and reach audiences beyond the country.

References

Anderson, C. (2006). *The long tail: Why the future of business is selling less of more*. New York: Random House.

Antenna Group. (2019). *Amplifier*. https://www.antenna-group.com/brands-and-operations/amplifier.aspx. Accessed June 3, 2019.

Baschiera, S., Di Chiara, F., & Re, V. (Eds.). (2017). Re-intermediation: Distribution, online access and gatekeeping in the digital European market. Special issue of *Cinéma&Cie, 17*(29).

Business News. (2018). Anakampsi alla kai prosarmogi gia ton klado tis diafimisis stin Ellada [Recovery and adjustment for the advertising sector in Greece]. *BusinessNews.gr*, July 18. https://www.businessnews.gr/article/114443/anakampsi-alla-kai-prosarmogi-gia-ton-klado-diafimisis-stin-ellada. Accessed June 3, 2019.

CNN. (2018). Tileoptikes adeies: I apofasi tou ESR gia ta pende kanalia [Television licences: The decision of the National Council for Radio and Television for the five channels]. *CNN Greece*, 27 September. https://www.cnn.gr/news/ellada/story/148556/tileoptikes-adeies-h-apofasi-toy-esr-gia-ta-pente-kanalia. Accessed June 3, 2019.

Cunningham, S., & Silver, J. (2013). *Screen distribution and the new King Kongs of the online world*. London: Palgrave-Macmillan.

DESI. (2018). *The digital economy & society index*. https://ec.europa.eu/digital-single-market/en/desi. Accessed June 3, 2019.

DESI Greece. (2018). https://ec.europa.eu/digital-single-market/en/scoreboard/Greece. Accessed June 3, 2019.

EKOME. (2018a). *Who we are: Establishment and mission*. https://www.ekome.media/who-we-are. Accessed June 3, 2019.

EKOME. (2018b). *Cash rebate Greece*. https://www.ekome.media/cash-rebate-greece. Accessed June 3, 2019.

Euronews. (2019). Ellada: I krisi synevale sti meiosi tou plithismou [Greece: The crisis contributed to the population reduction]. *Gr.euronews.com*, 21 January. https://gr.euronews.com/2019/01/21/ellada-i-krisi-synebale-sti-meiwsi-tou-plithysmou. Accessed June 3, 2019.

European Audiovisual Observatory. (2019). *Mavise database*. https://mavise.obs.coe.int/f/ondemand/advanced?typeofservice=3&targetedcountries=82. Accessed June 3, 2019.

Eurostat. (2019). *Population (demography, migration and projections)*. https://ec.europa.eu/eurostat/web/population-demography-migration-projections/data. Accessed June 3, 2019.

Flix. (2015). I Enosi Skinotheton Paragogon zitaei tin aposyrsi tis katargisis tou eidikou forou epi ton eisitirion [The Union of Directors producers demands the withdrawal of the cancellation of the special tax on cinema tickets]. *Flix.gr*, 13 August. https://flix.gr/news/espek-tax-tickets.html. Accessed June 3, 2019.

Gal, M. (2003). *Competition policy for small market economies*. Cambridge and London: Harvard University Press.

Galanis, M. (2019). Poies tainies kai seires pairnoun epidotisi Pappa [Which films and series receive support by Minister Pappas]. *Protothema.gr*, 16 April. https://www.protothema.gr/greece/article/882740/poies-tainies-kai-seires-pairnoun-epidotisi-pappa/. Accessed June 3, 2019.

Gorelik, D. (2019). *Greece: Mobile, broadband, TV and OTT video report.* Ovum: TMT Intelligence Informa.

Goranitis, G. (2017). To Netflix stin Ellada: Pou stohevei kai ti tha petihei [Netflix in Greece: Where does it aim and what will it achieve]. *Liberal,* 18 December. www.liberal.gr/technology/to-Netflix-stin-ellada-pou-stocheuei-kai-ti-tha-petuchei/181959. Accessed June 3, 2019.

Iosifidis, P., & Papathanassopoulos, S. (2019). Media, politics and state broadcasting in Greece. *European Journal of Communication.* https://doi.rg/10.1177/0267323119844414.

Lobato, R. (2019). *Netflix nations: The geography of digital distribution.* New York: New York University Press.

Lotz, A. (2017). *Portals: A treatise on internet-distributed television.* Ann Arbor: University of Michigan Press.

Mandravelis, V. (2017). Ten Pct Tax on Pay TV Stopped Sector's Growth in its Tracks. *Ekathimerini,* 9 May. www.ekathimerini.com/218280/article/ekathimerini/business/ten-pct-tax-on-pay-tv-stopped-sectors-growth-in-its-tracks. Accessed June 3, 2019.

Ministry of Digital Policy, Telecommunications and Media. (2016). *National digital policy 2016–2021.* https://mindigital.gr/images/GENIKOI/RALIS/PDF/Digital_Strategy_2016_2021. pdf. Accessed June 3, 2019.

Netflix. (2017). To Netflix einai pleon kai Elliniko [Netflix is now truly Greek]. https://media.netflix. com/el/press-releases/netflix-is-now-truly-greek. Accessed June 3, 2019.

Netwix. (2019). www.netwix.gr. Accessed June 3, 2019.

Papadimitriou, L. (2017). The economy and ecology of Greek Cinema since the crisis: Production, circulation, reception. In D. Tziovas (Ed.), *Greece in Crisis: The cultural politics of austerity* (pp. 135–157). London: I.B. Tauris.

Papadimitriou, L. (2018). Film distribution in Greece: Formal and informal networks of circulation since the financial crisis. *Screen, 59*(4), 484–505.

Puppis, M. (2009). Introduction: Media regulation in small states. *The International Communication Gazette, 71*(1–2), 7–17.

Szczepanik, P. (2017). Localise or die: Intermediaries in a small East-Central European on-demand market. *Cinéma&Cie, 17*(29), 33–49.

Trappel, J. (2014). Small states and European media policy. In K. Donders, C. Pauwels, & J. Loisen (Eds.), *The Palgrave handbook of European media policy* (pp. 239–253). Basingstoke: Palgrave Macmillan.

Vima. (2019). "Eteros Ego" stin othoni tis Cosmote TV ["Other Me" on Cosmote TV screen]. https://www.tovima.gr/printed_post/eteros-ego-stin-othoni-lftis-cosmote-tvcr. Accessed June 3, 2019.

Lydia Papadimitriou is Reader (Associate Professor) in film studies at Liverpool John Moores University. She has published extensively on different aspects of Greek cinema, with a recent emphasis on film festivals, co-productions, distribution and documentary. She has authored *The Greek Film Musical* (2006) and co-edited *Greek Cinema: Texts, Forms and Identities* (2011). Her co-edited volume *Contemporary Balkan Cinema: Transnational Exchanges and Global Circuits* (with Ana Grgic) is forthcoming from Edinburgh University Press. She is Principal Editor of the *Journal of Greek Media and Culture.* Her research has been published in numerous collections and journals, including *New Review of Film and Television Studies* (NRFTS), *Filmicon* and *Studies in European Cinema and Screen.*

Part IV
The Other Audiences: Convergent Viewership in Small and Peripheral Markets

Chapter 11
Finding Larger Transnational Media Markets: Media Practices of the Vietnamese Diasporic Community

Tae-Sik Kim

11.1 Introduction

International migration involves representative practices that characterize the globalized world. While migrants' mobility has changed the everyday landscapes of our world, it has also dramatically increased the transnational communication traffic between their old and new homes. Advanced communication technologies have expanded the scope of migrants' media use, allowing them to reach various media outlets around the world. Meanwhile, they have also developed ethnic media in their own diasporic communities in global urban centers (cf. Georgiou 2017). Also, media organizations in so-called multicultural societies have set their sights on this population, making available more features representing the migrants and their presence in given societies (cf. Müller and Hermes 2010). Unlike the conventional understanding of migrants in the tradition of intercultural communication studies, which highlights a positive correlation between migrants' new cultural adaptation and their uses of a new (host) society's media, the globally mobile population has opened up a variety of media landscapes on both global and local levels.

Migrant-related media studies have focused a great deal on conventional immigrant-receiving countries, such as Anglo-American and West European countries, due to the size of their migrant communities as well as their well-developed media markets. Although recent studies have begun paying attention to the diverse media flows that have originated in previously less-studied media markets such as Brazil, Turkey and India (Thussu 2006), media studies of migrant communities in emerging multicultural societies like many Central and Eastern European countries have still been limited. This chapter is based on data from two different studies on transnational media practices in the Vietnamese diasporic community in the Czech

T.-S. Kim (✉)
Faculty of Social Studies, Masaryk University, Jostova 10, 602 00 Brno, Czech Republic
e-mail: beinkid@mail.muni.cz

© The Author(s) 2020   201
P. Szczepanik et al. (eds.), *Digital Peripheries*, Springer Series in Media Industries,
https://doi.org/10.1007/978-3-030-44850-9_11

Republic. As part of a larger research project on the media practices of the diasporic community, the first phase of this study involved a series of in-depth interviews with Vietnamese young adults who were competent in multiple languages, including Czech, Vietnamese and English and thus was relatively well integrated into both the Czech and Vietnamese communities. In the second phase, the study turned its focus toward Vietnamese migrants who had arrived in the CR as independent adults. These first-generation migrants were relatively confined within their diasporic community and spent more time in their workplaces. The media practices of these different types of Vietnamese migrants reflect different migration experiences. Thus, this chapter first reviews various life contexts of the different Vietnamese populations in the CR and then discusses how they have been erased from the Czech media landscape because of their adoption of transnational media practices. This study also demonstrates how the diasporic community has failed to establish a conventional form of diasporic media but instead has found new translocal information outlets on social media.

11.2 Vietnamese in the Czech Republic

As of 2016, 58,025 Vietnamese officially lived in the CR, composing the third-largest minority after Ukrainians and Slovaks (Czech Statistical Office 2017). The Vietnamese started migrating to the CR in the late 1950s when the then-Czechoslovak Government hosted workers from other communist–ally countries. There was a short period of declining numbers of Vietnamese migrant workers during the political changes around 1989, but since then, the Vietnamese diasporic community in the CR has grown dramatically (Drbohlav et al. 2009), composing the third-largest group of immigrants overall and the largest population from Asia (Kušniráková 2014). Unlike the largest single immigrant group, Ukrainians, Vietnamese migrants consist more of business owners than employees (Drbohlav and Dzúrová 2007). Reflecting the presence of Vietnamese in the Czech economy, academic studies have focused on the economic motivations for migration and labor-related issues in the CR (e.g., Huwelmeier 2015).

Although there have been multiple studies taking the Vietnamese into account in evaluating Czech immigration policies (e.g., Drbohlav and Dzúrová 2007; Trbola and Rákoczyová 2011), only a few studies have paid extensive attention to the cultural experiences of the Vietnamese in the CR (e.g., Alamgir 2013). Instead, many studies have focused on criminal activities based in the diaspora community (e.g., Drbohlav and Janská 2009; Nožina 2010; Nožina and Kraus 2016). As the migrant population has increased and become more visible, sociological studies have recently focused on the everyday practices of the Vietnamese.

A recent study shed light on the unique family experiences of Vietnamese migrants who relied on Czech nannies in their child-rearing (Souralová 2014), reflecting not only the economic condition of the migrants who worked overtime but also the demographic composition of the Vietnamese community, which consists of a relatively large number of children (40%) (Kušniráková 2014). The language status of the Vietnamese in the CR is another topic investigated by multiple studies (e.g., Lin 2016; Sherman and Homoláč 2017). Also, recent studies on the identity of Vietnamese migrant children demonstrated the ambivalently hovering identity of these youth in the CR (Cheng and Hu 2015; Svobodová and Janská 2016). However, much about the media practices in the Vietnamese diaspora of the CR is still unclear.

The Vietnamese have been recognized as a national minority group since 2013, along with 13 other minorities in the CR (Vláda České republiky 2018). As part of the protection of national minority cultures, the Government Council for National Minorities has financially supported multiple ethnic media projects, such as print media for the Roma community and multi-language radio programs on the public Český rozhlas (Czech Radio) covering Roma, Slovak, Polish and German communities. However, there are no specifically designed channels, programs or features in the Czech public service media for the Vietnamese community. Also, the Vietnamese have not been a target audience group in the Czech commercial media market.

Despite its relatively large size, the Vietnamese community has not founded a well-formed diasporic media presence on traditional media platforms. While there have been no diasporic outlets on electronic media platforms, a couple of Vietnamese-language print magazines have come and gone. Viet Media, which once published two community magazines, *Tuần tin mới* (*New Week*) and *Thế giới trẻ* (*Youth World*), founded Vietinfo.eu, a Vietnamese-language Web portal, which is now managed by Vietinfo Group. Currently, *An ninh thế giới* (*World Security*) is regularly published in the Vietnamese language. The structures of these magazines are identical. Each issue contains news on the Vietnamese community in the CR, translated news articles on Czech society and readers' opinions. However, these community-related news features are brief; the magazines consist mainly of news articles originally published by Vietnamese domestic and diasporic media outside the CR. Along with Vietinfo, Sangu.eu has penetrated into the diasporic community by serving up-to-date information in the Vietnamese language. This small information outlet utilizes Facebook as the most effective communication platform, featuring a variety of types of multimedia-based information and ways of delivering it, such as live streaming. Currently, more than 25,000 Facebook users subscribe to its page, and its postings often receive more than 1000 reactions from the subscribers. Although the Vietnamese community in the CR has failed to establish a conventional form of diasporic media or draw attention from the Czech mainstream media, the community seems to have finally found a diasporic information outlet on the most populous new media platform.

11.3 Media Practices in Diasporic Communities

Global migrants have shaped a variety of transnational spaces by flexibly interacting with people across multiple borders, which is depicted by Appadurai (1990) in his notion of the *five scapes of globalization*. Globally, mobile people have not only expanded the *ethnoscape* by creating diasporic communities across borders but have also accelerated the shaping of the *mediascape* by consuming and transacting mediated information on a global scale. Gazing at the ever-changing global landscape around diasporic communities and media environments, migration and media studies have studied the transnational as well as diasporic media practices of global migrants. The sharing of information across borders helps migrants engage in domestic politics in their home countries (Aricat 2015). Media from migrants' country of origin is an important means to maintain native identity (Kama and Malka 2013). Transnational media consumption practices are also adopted by migrants as a strategy to cope with chronic cultural stresses they face in their new home (Kim 2016).

Some studies have revealed more dynamic transnational interactions over media by investigating migrants' media practices beyond the binational border between a country of origin and a receiving country. Migrants in Europe often use international news media from different countries (Christiansen 2004). Arab migrant women in the UK watch television dramas from countries other than their countries of origin (Georgiou 2012). When the Hong Kong film industry was dominant in Asia, Vietnamese migrant children in Australia became loyal consumers of Hong Kong movies available in their diasporic shops (Cunningham and Nguyen 2001). Asian migrants in the Netherlands consume non-homeland Asian media products on a regular basis, just as many Asian migrant youth in North America intensively consume Korean media products (Ju and Lee 2015; Yoon and Jin 2016). Their shared migratory experiences and cultural sensibilities have led them to transnational media products from Asian media markets not located in their countries of origin.

Global migrants have not only relied on media sources across borders but have also developed their own community media. Diasporic media have also been studied in large multiethnic societies, mainly in the Western world (Georgiou 2005; Matsaganis et al. 2010; Yu 2017). Like media from their country of origin, diasporic media often help migrants maintain ethnic identities (Yin 2015); play important roles in forming communities in new home countries (Shi 2005); and provide important information to migrants about how to make a living in a host society (Garapich 2008). However, there are only a very limited number of studies delving into migrants' transnational media use or diasporic media practices in countries with small media markets. One example is a study based in Ireland that demonstrates how multicultural news media have formed in the course of the transition to a multicultural society (Banks 2008). As Jõesaar et al. (2013) rightly noted in their study of Russian-language media in the small Estonian media market, the population of minorities in a small-media-market society tends to be tiny, so it draws little attention not only from domestic media organizations but also within academic circles.

11.4   Contextualizing Vietnamese Populations in the CR

As noted above, initial studies regarding Vietnamese migrant children in the CR were conducted in recent years. In the first study, the population investigated generally shared multiple demographic characteristics, like a relatively stable socioeconomic status, higher human capital and integration into both diasporic and Czech communities. During the interviews, participants often differentiated themselves from their parents' generation mainly by their multilingualism, Czech cultural literacy and global lifestyles. The children of migrants also drew a line between themselves and other young Vietnamese migrants who recently migrated to the CR on their own. They limited their interaction with the newcomers mainly because the two populations did not share many life experiences and living spaces in the CR.

Most of the first generation of Vietnamese arrived in the 1990s. Their migration trajectories are difficult to generalize; it was more common for the head of a household to come first to the CR to pave the way for his or her family to settle in the new country. They often travelled back and forth between Vietnam and the CR to bring necessary resources and family members. Most adult migrants spent a tremendous amount of time at their workplaces in order to support their families. It is now 20–30 years since their migration, and they have a reputation as hardworking migrants who have succeeded relatively well in their economic life. The Vietnamese diasporic community formed a large Vietnamese business complex called Sapa on the outskirts of Prague and established similar wholesale businesses in other cities like Brno. Backed by the huge wholesale network within the diasporic community, many Vietnamese are known as owners of small to midsized shops. It is common to see a small grocery store, called *potraviny* or *večerka*, owned by a Vietnamese merchant on every street corner. Also, many Vietnamese vendors are active in a number of border towns adjacent to Germany, Austria and Poland. While they have built exclusively Vietnamese wholesale complexes and business networks within the diaspora, their residences are quite spread out. For example, there are no specific Vietnamese residential communities in the major cities like Prague and Brno. In other words, the first generation of Vietnamese managed their community integration strategy by, on the one hand, going deep into the everyday spaces of Czech people and, on the other hand, by maintaining an exclusive "ethnic enclave economy"[1] (Werbner 2001). Nevertheless, the economic migrants spend most of their working time either in their shops or in other Vietnamese businesses like those in Sapa. Many who maintained this work pattern from the early days of their migration neither improved their Czech language skills nor built a healthy social network with Czech people. According to a criterion from conventional acculturation studies, they are a population quite separated from mainstream Czech society (Berry 1997). By and large, these middle-aged migrants who have lived in the CR for more than 20 years do not have a particular plan to go back to Vietnam, although many of them initially dreamed of eventually returning to their home country after making money in the CR.

In contrast, young adult migrants, who are often called the 1.5 generation, tend to be visible in both the Vietnamese community and Czech society. These young Vietnamese came to the CR at a young age (mostly between three and ten years old),

---

[1] There have been controversies over the concept of an ethnic enclave economy. The concept used in this paper is grounded in Werbner's (2001) definition of *ethnic enclave economy* as ethnically networked businesses that generate ethnic social space by transacting particular goods and services.

following their parents. These young adults generally shared similar life experiences in their early years in the CR; their parents worked long hours at factories, grocery stores or other Vietnamese-owned businesses; they were mostly cared for by Czech nannies or their grandparents; and they spent most of their weekday daytime hours at Czech educational institutions. For many of them, the Czech language is their first language due to these childhood experiences. However, they have also been pushed to speak Vietnamese at home by their parents, who have prioritized Vietnamese family values in their children's upbringing and discipline. Although many of their parents still work almost every day, the migrant children have spent relatively long hours with their parents since their economic condition has stabilized. As grownups, they also participate in economic activities. While some of them assist their parents in their own shops, others also work outside the diasporic community. Their multilingual skills are attractive to both Vietnamese and Czech businesses located in urban centers, which have benefited from the recent boom in tourism and rapid globalization. In our interviews, the young adults often used the term *banana*[2] as a means of characterizing their different identities. Participants in this study commonly identified themselves as "less banana" than their younger siblings, who were mostly born in the CR. Thus, our respondents placed themselves between the first generation and the second generation, which is the reason they are often called the "1.5 generation." Generally cosmopolitan in nature, they have travelled to many different countries, including Vietnam, thanks to their family's economic prosperity and various educational opportunities available in European Union Member States. However, most of them want to live in the CR or other states in Europe permanently instead of in Vietnam.

Another group of young adults in the Vietnamese community consists of recent migrants who came to the CR on their own. They generally share similar migration trajectories not with the 1.5 generation within the same age range but with the older and earlier first generation. The majority of the new migrants work at businesses owned by other Vietnamese. They are more visible in Vietnamese business complexes like Sapa than in Czech urban centers, mainly due to enclave economic practices. Thus, they rely almost exclusively on various networks within the diasporic community. It is known that they often form intimate communities with those who share the same migratory experiences in order to exchange emotional support as well as daily information. Not unlike the earlier generation of migrants, their limited language skills hinder them from seeking alternatives in Czech society. Since the opportunity and support for language acquisition are limited in the community, some of them take language courses at their own expense. The cost of private lessons, along with a shortage of time due to working long hours, prevents them from acquiring the Czech language successfully. Also, very few of them speak other European languages, which leave them few options for jobs outside the diasporic community.

---

[2]"Banana" is a widely used slur referring to Asian migrant children in a Western country, who identify themselves more with their new western home culture than with their Asian home culture.

Their future plans vary; while some of them plan to stay in the CR permanently, some define themselves as temporary economic migrants, and others are more flexible and are open to every possibility.

11.5   Crossing the Binational Border: Media Practices of the Early First Generation

In Vietnamese wholesale complexes like Sapa and on Olomoucká Street in Brno, it is very common to see owners and clerks in the shops watching television in the Vietnamese language. During downtime at a small shop or *potraviny*, one may hear Vietnamese sound emanating from a tiny screen under the counter. During the interviews, migrant children often said that Vietnamese satellite television programs worked like background music during their family mealtimes because their parents were tuned in to these channels. Such scenes characterize quite well the media practices of the first generation of Vietnamese migrants in the CR. Busy small-business owners are heavy, yet mindless, users of Vietnamese satellite television. For those who have a low competence in languages other than their mother tongue, the media from their country of origin seems to be the sole option. Although they are gradually moving from old electronic media to online social media as their main information outlet, they still spend a large amount of time with Vietnamese satellite television, mainly due to their working environments.

For those who are not very adept in exploring alternative sources of information on different media platforms like the Internet, satellite television is the most affordable as well as the most reliable media outlet. Satellite television has long been the basic, primary medium for the early migrants, who were not able to use any media based in the CR due to the language barrier. Even if some of our participants once used video players like VCRs, VCDs and DVDs to watch media products from Vietnam, they had only limited time to enjoy them. Instead, they have relied more on Vietnamese satellite channels available from both Czech Television providers and Vietnamese diasporic businesses. Although they have Internet-connected computers and smartphones at their places of work as well as at home, most still subscribe to Vietnamese satellite television at both places, mainly due to their routinized media use. Watching—or just turning on—Vietnamese television is not only an individual media practice but also a diaspora practice. Maintaining close business networks, Vietnamese often visit each other's workplaces, such as restaurants, wholesale shops and hair-and-nail shops, where the same satellite television is usually turned on.

Habitually and constantly exposed to television programs from Vietnam, the early migrants tend not to look for alternative sources. Many of those who once tried to adopt Czech media failed to become regular users, mainly due to the lack of programs that suit their interests. They have failed to find interesting programs on Czech network television, but they have also not been attracted to Czech cable channels, which are full of imported media products. The Czech-dubbed American and British media products barely entertain the early migrants, who are not comfortable with the Czech language. Rather, they are content with Vietnamese satellite television and media products with Vietnamese subtitles, which are available on the Internet.

Working in an enclave economic community, the early migrants very often obtain useful daily information from the community. Word of mouth is one of the most important information sources for those who maintain their exclusive, diasporic business networks. Vietnamese-language magazines have been published for many years, but most of them have failed to take hold in the community. Published by a few media agencies covering multiple Vietnamese communities across Europe, magazines commonly consist of news from Vietnam and other Vietnamese overseas communities, Czech domestic news relevant to the diasporic community and general news from all over the world. In other words, these magazines spend only the first few pages covering information directly associated with the community in the CR. Also, these magazines are not distributed in a systematic way but instead are displayed at stores with other commercial flyers. Many early migrants once attempted to skim some editions; but in their interviews, they did not recall well the titles of magazines and specific types of information. Generally, few respondents said that there has been a proper form of journalism in their community.

While still relying heavily on word of mouth as the primary source of information, the early migrants have recently adopted online information outlets such as Vietinfo.eu and Sangu.eu. Whereas Vietinfo.eu is an online form of the abovementioned Vietnamese-language magazines, Sangu.eu is an online blog-style community magazine that provides multimedia-based information specifically relevant to the diaspora community. Many participants who have been active on Facebook in recent years (mostly for the last two to three years) subscribe to the Facebook pages of both services. In addition, non-users of Czech media outlets often come across news and information produced by Czech media on social media. Technologically assisted translation services and social sharing features on social media finally allow them to make use of Czech news and information outlets. Having long lacked participation in the small Czech media market, the early migrants have gradually become at least passive audiences of Czech media.

11.6 Crossing the Binational Border Online: Media Practices of the Recent First Generation

As explained above, the early first generation and the recent first generation of Vietnamese migrants generally share two important life contexts: They have low competence in Czech and other foreign languages, and they are quite confined within the Vietnamese diaspora community. However, the two populations deviate from each other when it comes to media use. Working long hours at Vietnamese businesses, the young recent migrants are also ordinarily exposed to Vietnamese satellite television. As it was for the early first generation, Vietnamese satellite television has been contextualized in their work life since the beginning of their life in the CR. Unlike their predecessors, however, the relatively young migrants tend not to subscribe to the satellite service on their own. Like young people in general, they intensively use online media available on both their personal computers and mobile devices. For them, watching television means consuming television content available online. In fact, most of them adopted online media during their early years in Vietnam. They also access various transnational media products, such as Asian television shows and sports events including European football leagues and mixed-martial-arts matches, via Vietnamese Web sites. Even though they frequently use YouTube and other global media platforms to watch live streaming and video clips that interest them, it is online information in the Vietnamese language that mainly links them to these global channels.

The younger migrants prioritize connectivity in their lives, willingly spending their money on mobile data and high-speed Internet services. They rely on online social networks to obtain essential information for living in their new home. Their online social networks on Facebook, Instagram and messaging applications provide not only essential practical information on the economy, education and health but also cultural information to entertain them. They have built online diasporic communities by maintaining exclusive social networks with compatriots both in Vietnam and in the CR. Even though they currently live in the CR, they still receive information and various kinds of support from the network in Vietnam by using online communication tools. Also, online social networks allow them to continue to be involved in the initial human networks they first formed after arriving in the CR. For recent migrants, the online social network has not been one of many optional information outlets. Instead, they have shaped their migrant life by using the online social network to exchange information within the diasporic and the transnational Vietnamese communities.

11.7 Crossing Multiple Borders: Transnational Media Practices of the 1.5 Generation

Born in Vietnam and raised in the CR, the migrant children who have benefited from their family's economic stability and diverse educational opportunities in both the Czech and Vietnamese communities have expanded the scope of their transnational media practices. Their multilingual skills have allowed them to reach various media outlets ranging from Czech and Vietnamese to Western and Asian media. The 1.5 generation used to watch Czech Television shows for children and video products and satellite television from Vietnam with their parents and siblings. However, these binational media practices did not last very long. Most of them stopped watching Czech Television and Vietnamese satellite television after adopting private media practices with their personal devices such as laptops and mobile phones. As young digital natives, they have long been online users who adroitly surf new media services from all around the world. As residents in rapidly globalizing urban areas, they have nurtured cosmopolitan cultural tastes, preferring well-developed media products from the USA, the UK, Japan and South Korea (hereafter Korea). They have turned their backs on Czech and Vietnamese media partly because of the outdated styles of those media products and partly because of the lack of variety. In other words, young cosmopolitan audiences are no longer confined within the two small media markets of the CR and Vietnam because they make use of various media outlets from bigger transnational media markets.

While heavily using transnational online streaming services such as YouTube and Netflix, they also consume Korean media products intensively. It is known that there is a large fandom for K-pop music and Korean television shows in the Vietnamese community of the CR. These young transnational media fans first learned about Korean cultural products from media based in Vietnam, as well as from their family members and Vietnamese friends in the CR. The Korean media industry has been dominant in many Southeast Asian countries, including Vietnam, since the late 1990s (Peichi 2013). The cultural phenomenon has crossed borders by following the migratory trajectory of the Vietnamese overseas. Once introduced to Korean media by Vietnamese media and human networks, the migrant young adults have explored more readily available media sources by using their language skills and available technology; they watch Korean television shows and K-pop music products uploaded by users across the world on streaming services from different countries including China, Turkey, the USA and Vietnam; they consume information about the Korean entertainment industry by surfing around various Web sites and subscribing to relevant social media pages. Despite the increasing number of Korean media fans in the CR, the Czech market is still out of the Korean media's target range. Also, Korean television shows available on Netflix in the CR are much more limited than those accessible in bigger media markets, such as the USA and Japan, due to licensing issues. For this reason, many Vietnamese audiences in the CR rely heavily on illegally uploaded content on various streaming services across the world. Fans often volunteer to introduce Korean media culture and trends to their Czech peers, which is slowly generating a niche market in the CR. Following the global trend, the young Vietnamese have recently become loyal users of YouTube and Netflix, where the national origin of media products is underplayed. They often watch media products from many different countries on their streaming services. Together with Czech consumers of streaming services, the 1.5 generation has pushed the boundary of the Czech media market.

As residents of the CR, they also use the most-visited Czech Web portal, Seznam.cz, to find daily information on a regular basis. Many use the portal's e-mail service, compare prices of e-commerce products and check the news headlines on the front page of the Web site. They also spend a large amount of time on social media, where they practice more personalized information-seeking modalities. The blurring territories of online media make it difficult to simply state where 1.5 generation users are based; while being active subscribers to diasporic Facebook pages in the Czech language, such as "Přiznání Vietnamců" ("Recognition of Vietnamese") and "Viet Up," they are also involved in a variety of online networks with Czechs and people from around the world. Although they do not regularly consume Czech news media, they subscribe to the Facebook feeds of Czech news organizations. Old print media distributed in the Vietnamese community and Vietnamese news via satellite television are not taken into consideration as useful news outlets by the young migrants, but online diasporic information outlets such as Sangu.eu are well recognized by them. They are not different from other social media users who cross national and regional borders without noticing their own extensive mobilities online. The migrant children who once turned their backs on the limited media markets in the CR and their diasporic community have formed dynamic information outlets on deterritorialized social media.

11.8 Conclusion

During a couple of interviews with the old and new first generations, interviewees who knew I was originally from Korea asked me a question: "Do you know Park Hang Seo?" Of course, I know the name because the Korean football coach has become a celebrity in Korea with his achievements in Vietnam. He is the head coach of the Vietnamese national football team, which has achieved remarkable results in several inter-Asian football events. Because I was conducting open-ended interviews, I could ask the interviewees more about their media practices related to the Vietnamese national football team. They said they did their best to watch live coverage of matches while keeping informed about the team by accessing various information outlets across the border. They have, for example, subscribed to related Facebook pages and visited Vietnamese news sites more often than before. Some respondents recently bought a more extensive satellite television box from Vietnam, which covers all television channels in Vietnam. National events across the border and advanced border-crossing technologies have helped the diasporic migrants feel more synchronized with daily life in their country of origin. Likewise, transnational media practices are deeply contextualized in global migrants' lives. Moreover, the practices are neither static nor patterned but are instead continuously evolving as the migrants respond to various sociocultural changes in their countries of origin, their new home countries and their own diasporic communities, and beyond.

This chapter has reviewed how different Vietnamese migrant populations in the CR have shaped their transnational and community media practices. Those who are quite separated from mainstream Czech society have made almost no use of the Czech media market. The small Czech media market has not taken the tiny Vietnamese population into consideration as a target audience. In addition, the diasporic community has not been successful in forming its own media outlets due to the limited efforts of its business-oriented community. On the other hand, the well-educated and globalized younger generation has not been satisfied with the limited Czech, Vietnamese and diasporic media landscape. Equipped with technologies and cosmopolitan skills, the young migrants have explored the transnational, global media space. It is obvious that the Vietnamese diasporic community in CR is not premature in forming a media market comparable with those in larger multiethnic countries like the USA and Canada. It is also obvious that a small media market facing ever-increasing competition with larger transnational media markets cannot afford to cater to a small diasporic community accounting for less than 1% of the entire population. Thus, neglected diasporic audiences in small media markets seem to create a tautological dilemma.

As seen above, however, the Vietnamese migrants adopting networked media platforms like Facebook have opened up their own translocal media outlets. Advanced technological features help them to overcome such barriers as the lack of language skills and limited prerequisite knowledge. The migrant social media users often come across information outlets based on the CR. Meanwhile, they have expanded the scope of their use of Vietnamese and other transnational media outlets even further by surfing links shared on social media. In sum, the "1.5 generation" migrants are staying far away from conventional Czech and diasporic media while simultaneously finding transnationally networked Czech media outlets and Vietnamese diasporic information outlets on social media.

Because it is grounded in a limited number of interviews with Vietnamese migrants, this research needs to be further developed to cover more diverse populations in the community. Further study is expected to shed more light on the role of new media platforms in shaping transnational–translocal media practices in a diasporic community.

References

Alamgir, A. K. (2013). Race is elsewhere: State-socialist ideology and the racialisation of Vietnamese workers in Czechoslovakia. *Race & Class, 54*(4), 67–85.

Appadurai, A. (1990). Disjuncture and difference in the global cultural economy. *Theory, Culture & Society, 7*(2–3), 295–310.

Aricat, R. G. (2015). Mobile/social media use for political purposes among migrant laborers in Singapore. *Journal of Information Technology and Politics, 12*(1), 18–36.

Banks, M. (2008). Modern Ireland: Multinationals and multiculturalism. *Information, Society and Justice Journal, 2*(1), 63–93.

Berry, J. W. (1997). Immigration, acculturation, and adaptation. *Applied Psychology, 46*(1), 5–34.

Cheng, T.-H., & Hu, L.-Y. (2015). The dual identity and social integration of international immigrants in the Czech Republic: A survey research on the second generation of Chinese and Vietnamese immigrants. *Tamkang Journal of International Affairs, 19*(1), 129–197.

Christiansen, C. C. (2004). News media consumption among immigrants in Europe: The relevance of diaspora. *Ethnicities, 4*(2), 185–207.

Cunningham, S., & Nguyen, T. (2001). Popular media of Vietnamese diaspora. In S. Cunningham & J. Sinclair (Eds.), *Floating lives: The media and Asian diasporas* (pp. 91–135). New York: Rowman and Littlefield.

Czech Statistical Office. (2017). *Foreigners in the Czech Republic*. Czech Statistical Office. https://www.czso.cz/documents/10180/45709982/29002717.pdf/770a1c14-6ea7-4c47-831e-3936e3ca1ab3?version=1.2. Accessed September 18, 2018.

Drbohlav, D., & Dzúrová, D. (2007). Where are they going? Immigrant inclusion in the Czech Republic (A case study on Ukrainians, Vietnamese, and Armenians in Prague). *International Migration, 45*(2), 69–95.

Drbohlav, D., & Janská, E. (2009). Illegal economic and transit migration in the Czech Republic: A study of individual migrants' behaviour. *Europe-Asia Studies, 61*(1), 141–156.

Drbohlav, D., Lachmanová-Medová, L., Čermák, Z., Janská, E., Čermáková, D., & Dzúrová, D. (2009). The Czech Republic: On its way from emigration to immigration country. *IDEA Working Papers 11.* https://is.muni.cz/el/1423/jaro2004/SOC732/um/Drbohlav_et.al._2009._The_Czech_Republic.On_its_way_from_emigration_to_immigration_country.pdf. Accessed December 15, 2018.

Garapich, M. P. (2008). The migration industry and civil society: Polish immigrants in the United Kingdom before and after EU enlargement. *Journal of Ethnic and Migration Studies, 34*(5), 735–752.

Georgiou, M. (2005). Diasporic media across Europe: Multicultural societies and the universalism–particularism continuum. *Journal of Ethnic and Migration Studies, 31*(3), 481–498.

Georgiou, M. (2012). Watching soap opera in the diaspora: Cultural proximity or critical proximity? *Ethnic and Racial Studies, 35*(5), 868–887.

Georgiou, M. (2017). Mapping diasporic media cultures: A transnational cultural approach to exclusion. In R. Silverstone (Ed.), *Media, technology and everyday life in Europe* (pp. 51–70). London: Routledge.

Huwelmeier, G. (2015). From 'Jarmark Europa' to 'commodity city'. New marketplaces, post-socialist migrations, and cultural diversity in Central and Eastern Europe. *Central and Eastern European Migration Review, 4*(1), 27–39.

Jõesaar, A., Jufereva, M., & Rannu, S. (2013). Media for the minorities: Russian language media in Estonia 1990–2012. *Media Transformations, 9,* 118–154.

Ju, H., & Lee, S. (2015). The Korean wave and Asian Americans: The ethnic meanings of transnational Korean pop culture in the USA. *Continuum, 29*(3), 323–338.

Kama, A., & Malka, V. (2013). Identity prosthesis: Roles of homeland media in sustaining native identity. *Howard Journal of Communications, 24*(4), 370–388.

Kim, T.-S. (2016). Transnational communication practices of unaccompanied Young Korean students in the United States. *Asian and Pacific Migration Journal, 25*(2), 148–167.

Kušniráková, T. (2014). *Vietnamci v Česku a ve světě: Migrační a adaptační tendence [Vietnamese in the Czech Republic and in the world: Migratory and adaptive tendencies].* Praha: Slon.

Lin, M. S. (2016). Limits of the EU language education policy for migrants: A comparative study of the Vietnamese migrant community in the Czech Republic and the new immigrants in Taiwan. *Sustainable Multilingualism, 9,* 78–101.

Matsaganis, M. D., Katz, V. S., & Ball-Rokeach, S. J. (2010). *Understanding ethnic media: Producers, consumers, and societies.* Thousand Oaks, CA: Sage.

Müller, F., & Hermes, J. (2010). The performance of cultural citizenship: Audiences and the politics of multicultural television drama. *Critical Studies in Media Communication, 27*(2), 193–208.

Nožina, M. (2010). Crime networks in Vietnamese diasporas: The Czech Republic case. *Crime, Law and Social Change, 53*(3), 229–258.

Nožina, M., & Kraus, F. (2016). Bosses, soldiers and rice grains: Vietnamese criminal networks and criminal activities in the Czech Republic. *Europe-Asia Studies, 68*(3), 508–528.

Peichi, C. (2013). Co-creating Korean wave in Southeast Asia: Digital convergence and Asia's media regionalization. *Journal of Creative Communications, 8*(2–3), 193–208.

Sherman, T., & Homoláč, J. (2017). 'The Older I Got, It Wasn't a Problem for Me Anymore': Language brokering as a managed activity and a narrated experience among Young Vietnamese immigrants in the Czech Republic. *Multilingua, 36*(1), 1–29.

Shi, Yy. (2005). Identity construction of the Chinese diaspora, ethnic media use, community formation, and the possibility of social activism. *Continuum, 19*(1), 55–72.

Souralová, A. (2014). The Czech Nanny as a "Door to Majority" for children of Vietnamese immigrants in the Czech Republic. *Studia Migracyjne-Przeglad Polonijny, 3*(40), 171–186.

Svobodová, A., & Janská, E. (2016). Identity development among youth of Vietnamese descent in the Czech Republic. In M. L. Seeberg & E. Gozdziak (Eds.), *Contested childhoods: Growing up in migrancy* (pp. 121–137). Berlin: Springer.

Thussu, D. K. (2006). *Media on the move: Global flow and contra-flow*. London: Routledge.

Trbola, R., & Rákoczyová, M. (2011). Barriers to integration of immigrants and integration policy in the Czech Republic with focus on stakeholders and their co-operation. *Migracijske i etničke teme, 27*(1), 77–104.

Vláda České republiky. (2018). *Rada vlády pro národnostní menšiny* [Government council of national minority]. https://www.vlada.cz/en/pracovni-a-poradni-organy-vlady/rnm/historie-a-soucasnost-rady-en-16666/. Accessed December 15, 2018.

Werbner, P. (2001). Metaphors of spatiality and networks in the plural city: A critique of the ethnic Enclave economy debate. *Sociology, 35*(3), 671–693.

Yin, H. (2015). Chinese-language cyberspace, homeland media and ethnic media: A contested space for being Chinese. *New Media & Society, 17*(4), 556–572.

Yoon, K., & Jin, D. Y. (2016). The Korean wave phenomenon in Asian diasporas in Canada. *Journal of Intercultural Studies, 37*(1), 69–83.

Yu, S. S. (2017). Ethnic media as communities of practice: The cultural and institutional identities. *Journalism, 18*(10), 1309–1326.

Tae-Sik Kim is Assistant Professor at the Department of Media Studies and Journalism, Masaryk University, Brno, Czech Republic. His research concerns transnational communication, migrant studies, urban community and communication, media technologies and cultural citizenship. Grounded in anthropological concerns, he is currently working on multiple research projects ranging from the Vietnamese in the Czech Republic to the Chinese in South Korea.

Chapter 12
Configurable Culture in Wealthy and Developing Markets: A Comparative Cross-National Perspective

Aram Sinnreich

12.1 Introduction

The precipitous growth of Internet adoption around the globe over the past two decades has contributed to profound changes in our cultures and cultural markets, as well as the complex web of relationships among creators, industries and audiences. Yet, these changes take different forms from nation to nation and generation to generation; as science fiction author William Gibson famously observed, "The future is already here—it is just unevenly distributed" (Standage 2001).

One of the most important cultural developments spurred by digital networked technologies has been the emergence of a range of new expressive forms and creative practices. These new forms and practices take advantage of the unique affordances of both production and distribution platforms, specifically: (a) the "cut-and-paste" capabilities for audio, video and photographic media available on the billions of computers, tablets and smartphones in current use; (b) the prospect of a simultaneously massified and customized media experience provided by social media services such as Facebook and YouTube; (c) the "context collapse" (Marwick and boyd 2011) and blurring of the lines between interpersonal and public communication resulting from the convergence of previously discrete social networks onto a common communication infrastructure; and (d) the massive acceleration of the feedback cycle between production, reception and redistribution enabled by these media platforms.

While the cultural and industrial consequences of these changes to the communications infrastructure are diverse and far-ranging, several theorists have proposed analytical frameworks that focus on the shared dimensions of these new expressive forms and practices, as well as the collective social impact of their adoption on a broad, global scale. These include Jenkins' (2006) theory of "convergence culture," which emphasizes the new points of common interest and collaboration between

A. Sinnreich (✉)
School of Communication, American University, 4400 Massachusetts Avenue NW,
Washington D.C. 20016, USA
e-mail: aram@american.edu

© The Author(s) 2020   215
P. Szczepanik et al. (eds.), *Digital Peripheries*, Springer Series in Media Industries,
https://doi.org/10.1007/978-3-030-44850-9_12

artists, industries and audiences; Bruns' (2008) "produsage" and Ritzer and Jurgenson's (2010) "prosumption," both portmanteaus suggesting the blurring of the lines between traditional conceptions of production and consumption; and Lessig's (2008) term "remix culture," which critiques a copyright system rooted in the premise of "original" cultural expression and the resulting proprietary corporatism of the global culture industries.

In my own work (Sinnreich 2010), I have used the term "configurable culture," in order to emphasize the ways in which the logic of networked digital communications has quickly become the dominant organizational regime for cultural, social and industrial institutions around the industrialized world in the twenty-first century. A central aspect of this project has been the collection and analysis of empirical data regarding the awareness, consumption, engagement and opinions of everyday Internet users regarding new cultural forms and practices such as mashups, remixes and video game mods, as well as the role of demographics and other sociocultural factors in shaping these trends. My colleagues and I have found that attributes of respondents, such as age, income, education level, ethnicity and nationality, play a measurable role in shaping how individuals adopt configurable cultures, interact with online distribution platforms and evaluate the ethics of those behaviors and interactions (Sinnreich et al. 2009; Latonero and Sinnreich 2014).

In this chapter, I will examine the results of a recent international survey to evaluate the differences in configurable culture awareness, behavior and attitudes of Internet users across a range of different national media markets and to highlight the ways in which the divergent cultural, legal and economic factors at play in those markets influence engagement with audiovisual media. While all of the nations surveyed were English-speaking and relatively high-population (25 million or more), four of them (the USA, the UK, Canada and Australia) are designated as "advanced economies" and two (South Africa and the Philippines) are designated as "emerging markets and developing economies" by the International Monetary Fund (2018). Along similar lines, the first four countries are typically grouped as belonging to the "Global North" (despite Australia's location in the southern hemisphere), while South Africa and the Philippines are understood to be members of the "Global South" (despite the Philippines' location in the northern hemisphere) (Miraftab 2009; Misalucha 2015). These six nations are also geographically diverse, representing populations in four different global regions (North America, Europe, sub-Saharan Africa and Asia/Pacific).

Thus, while this chapter diverges from others in this volume by focusing on larger, rather than smaller media markets, it sheds light on an analogous divide— that between wealthier markets that tend to *produce* global media, and "developing" ones, which tend to be relegated to the consumption end of the spectrum. Even among English-speaking, high-population nations, there is a center and a periphery, and the differences between these markets in terms of behavior and opinions are stark and instructive.

12.2   Methods

The survey was fielded in July and August 2017, to online, English-speaking adults in six countries. After using two separate screening questions[1] to eliminate false or meaningless data, respondent numbers in each surveyed nation were as follows: the USA ($n = 510$), Australia ($n = 132$), Canada ($n = 121$), the Philippines ($n = 139$), South Africa ($n = 134$) and the UK ($n = 193$). These respondent pools were demographically diverse, in terms of gender (35.5% male, 64.5% female), income (40.7% below \$40,000 annual income, 12.6% above \$100,000) and education (20.6% with only secondary education, 65.8% with some university-level education and 12.8% with a postgraduate degree).

Initial analyses of these data demonstrated that practices and attitudes surrounding configurable culture vary considerably by age, reaffirming recent findings by Yates et al. (2015) that there is a statistically significant difference, with a large effects size, between digital media usage patterns of those under and over the age of 35. Consequently, for the purposes of this chapter, I have treated the below-35 (45.8% of respondents) and 35-and-above (54.2%) populations of each surveyed nation as analytically distinct.

12.3   Analysis

12.3.1   Awareness of Configurable Culture

There were significant divergences in awareness levels of various configurable cultural forms, across both nationalities and age groups. The vast majority of respondents said they are aware of cut-and-paste musical forms like mashups and mixtapes, though young South Africans are disproportionately unaware of mashups, and Filipinos of all ages are far less likely to have heard of mixtapes—a product that depends as much on physical as on digital distribution networks. However, Filipinos of all ages are disproportionately more likely than other respondents to have heard of anime music videos—most likely because, although this is a globally produced and consumed art form, it originated in Asia. Although there are consistent gaps in awareness between older and younger respondents across all categories, the gaps are the greatest for video mashups (with the exception of the Philippines) and video game "mods"—most likely due to the disproportionate time spent on PC gaming among younger adults (Fig. 12.1).

---

[1]"What shape is planet Earth?" and "Have you responded accurately to the questions above?"

218   A. Sinnreich

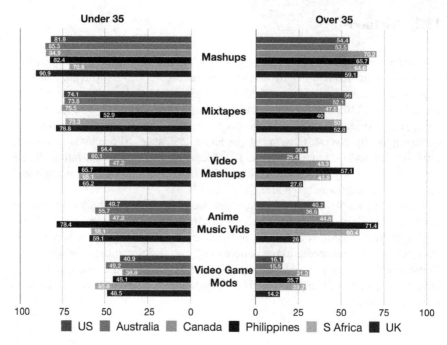

Fig. 12.1 Awareness of configurable culture, by nation and age

12.3.2 Consumption of Configurable Culture

While the majority of respondents (especially those under 35) demonstrated awareness of most configurable cultural forms, actual levels of *consumption* (captured by
the question "which of the following have you used or consumed in the last year?")
are far lower, and the gaps between young and old tend to be much greater, especially
in categories that may be understood as emblematic of online youth culture, such as
anime music videos (consumed by only 2.4% of older UK adults) and video game
mods (consumed by only 1.4% of older Australian adults). The Philippines presents
an interesting exception, however; although older respondents are consistently less
aware of these cultural forms than older ones, those who *are* aware are much more
likely to consume them. In nearly every category, Filipino adults' consumption levels
dwarf those of their contemporaries from other nations. In the case of mixtapes, older
Filipinos are nearly twice as likely to have listened to them (25.7%) than younger
Filipinos (13.7%) (Fig. 12.2).

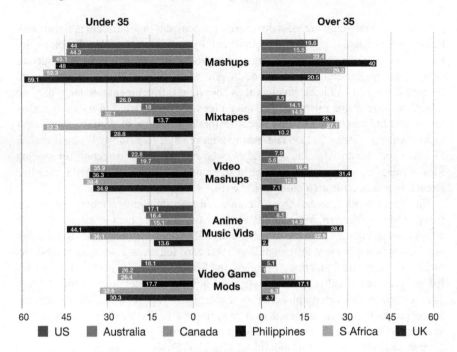

Fig. 12.2 Consumption of configurable culture, by nation and age

12.3.3 Engagement with Configurable Culture

This study distinguishes between *consumption* (discussed above) and *engagement*, which involves a mode of cultural activity that falls somewhere between the traditional modalities of production and consumption. In earlier work (e.g., Sinnreich and Latonero 2014), we distinguished between "consumption-adjacent" practices, such as creating a playlist or a custom radio station, which require relatively little expertise and effort by the user, and "production-adjacent" practices, such as producing a mashup or a remix, which have a much higher bar to entry. Of course, many other configurable cultural activities, such as making a meme or live streaming a concert, fall deeply into the gray area between these polarities and have little similarity to either traditional production or consumption modalities.

This survey queried respondents about a range of different forms of engagement with audiovisual work, from consumption-adjacent to production-adjacent. For musical works, different forms of engagement were adopted at very different rates among respondents from different countries. Americans were by far the most likely to use custom radio programming, such as the services offered by Pandora, iHeartRadio and Apple Music. While this may be due at least in part to availability (Pandora has operated only in the USA since 2017), there must be other factors as well, given that iHeartRadio also operates in Canada and Australia, and Apple Music operates in every nation surveyed.

Although Americans are most involved in the consumption-adjacent musical practices, younger Australians, South Africans and Britons, as well as older Filipinos, are
much more likely to say that they engaged in production-adjacent activities, such as
creating sample-based music. Many of the gray area practices I surveyed are viewed
from an industrial and legal standpoint as copyright infringement—in large part, no
doubt, because of the mismatch between a legal system crafted in the era of mass
media and the much broader and more flexible affordances of digital communications platforms (Patry 2011). These gray area practices are most common among
Filipinos and South Africans of all ages, who ranked first and second for sharing
files online, "stream ripping" (saving a streaming audio file as an MP3) and live
streaming a concert from a mobile phone (Fig. 12.3).

Similar patterns emerged from the question regarding engagement with video-
based media. Older American adults were by far the most heavily engaged in the
consumption-adjacent practice of using a digital video recorder (DVR) to save and
retrieve televised content (although South Africans led among younger adults). As
in the case of musical practices, Filipinos and South Africans in both age categories
led the gray area (and potentially copyright-infringing) categories of file sharing,
stream-ripping and video uploading, by exceedingly wide margins. When it came
to the production-adjacent practice of remixing video, engagement levels among
younger adults hovered around 8–10% in most nations (except for Canada, where
the rate was only 1.9%), while most older adults had little or no experience, except for

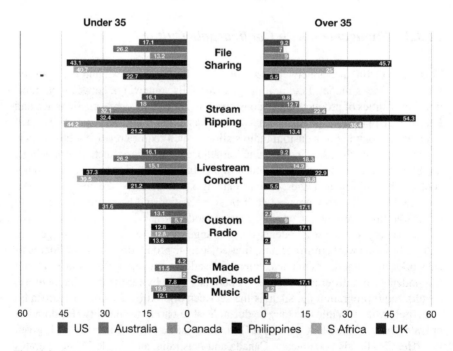

Fig. 12.3 Engagement with configurable culture (music), by nation and age

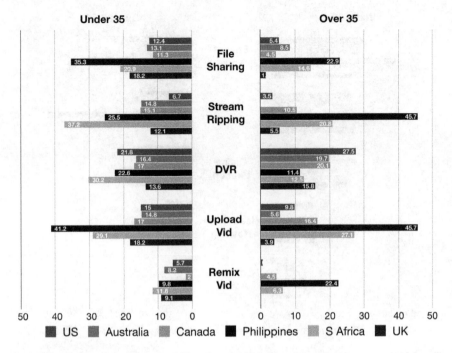

Fig. 12.4   Engagement with configurable culture (video), by nation and age

the Philippines, where nearly a quarter of older adults said they've remixed video—a staggering figure double the rate of those who said they've used a DVR.

In short, nations with higher levels of income, and stronger copyright enforcement regimes, appear to have a greater overall engagement level with audiovisual media at the consumption end of the spectrum, and nations where fewer people have access to legal sources of online content distribution tend to have a higher degree of involvement in gray area practices that skirt the lines of legality. In every nation, the production-adjacent end of the spectrum, which is characterized by making sample-based media, tends to be disproportionately a youth practice, with the notable exception of the Philippines, where older adult engagement in remixing dwarfs that of their younger compatriots (Fig. 12.4).

12.3.4   Civic Engagement via Digital Media

Engagement with audiovisual forms of configurable culture seems to dovetail with civic and political engagement via digital media. In most of the categories of online civic engagement we measured in the survey, levels of use were far higher among Filipinos and South Africans than among those from other nations. For all nations

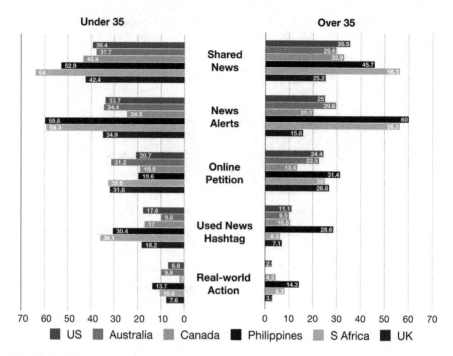

Fig. 12.5 Civic engagement via digital media, by nation and age

surveyed, the age gap for digital civic engagement was much smaller at the consumption end of the spectrum; the number of older adults who shared news stories via social media, or signed up for alerts from news Web sites and applications, was close to the number of younger adults in every country except the UK (where older adults demonstrated a much lower level of engagement with audiovisual media than their younger compatriots). The Philippines, where older adults were more likely than the young to engage in activities like stream ripping and uploading, was the one nation in which older adults were also more likely to engage in digital civic activities such as signing up for news alerts, signing online petitions and participating in real-world political action organized via the Internet. In nearly every category, Canadians were either the least or among the least civically engaged, echoing their relatively low engagement levels with audiovisual configurable culture (Fig. 12.5).

12.3.5 Opinions on Ethics and Legality

In addition to surveying respondents regarding their awareness, consumption and engagement with configurable culture, I asked them to share their opinions about the ethics and legality of configurable cultural practices such as mashups and remixes. As Raz (2009) argues, a legal system must necessarily be rooted in the ethical values embraced by the culture that gives rise to it; in his words, "legal theory attempts to capture the essential features of law, as encapsulated in the self-understanding of a culture" (p. 98). However, as I have demonstrated in previous publications (Sinnreich et al. 2018), there is an enduring gap between *what people think is ethical* and *what people believe should be legal* in the case of configurable culture; in other words, the novelty and social stigma attached to these emerging forms of expression undermine people's support for a legal system that would enable them to flourish.

This gap between ethical and legal imaginaries can be measured empirically using survey data. Specifically, one question asks, "To what extent do you consider mash-ups and remixes 'original'?" Respondents had a choice between saying that: (a) all remixes and mashups are unoriginal; (b) some are original and others are unoriginal; (c) all are original; and (d) prefer not to answer. As I have demonstrated in earlier work (Sinnreich et al. 2009), while most media consumers don't think explicitly in ethical terms, their ethical thinking is encoded in the form of aesthetic judgments regarding the "originality" of a work; hence, a mashup deemed sufficiently "original" may be seen as ethical, while one deemed "unoriginal" may be deemed unethical. This syllogism is recognized explicitly in copyright law, as well; in the USA, for instance, case law holds that "original, as the term is used in copyright, means only that the work was independently created by the author (as opposed to copied from other works), and that it possesses at least some minimal degree of creativity."[2]

Along similar lines, the survey captured respondents' legal opinions by asking, "In your opinion, how should copyright apply to mash-ups and remixes?" For this question, possible responses included: (a) all mashups and remixes made without permission of the "original" author should be illegal; (b) some uses should require permission and others should not; (c) all remixes and mashups should be made without the need for permission; and (d) prefer not to answer. In order to demonstrate the gap between ethical and legal opinion, we may compare the percentage of respondents who said, on the one hand, that configurable culture is always or sometimes original with the percentage who said that it should always or sometimes be legal.

The data show that, in keeping with my previous research, there is a consistent gap across all nations and age groups between the perception that configurable culture may sometimes or always be original, and the expectation that it may sometimes or always be legal. In other words, respondents' support for the ethical validity of configurable culture was not matched by their expectations of support from the legal system for these practices. Furthermore, younger respondents were far more likely than older ones to believe that configurable culture could be both ethical and legal. The only exception to this trend was older Filipino adults, who were more likely than their younger compatriots to say that configurable culture could be original (and therefore ethical). This makes sense in light of the data discussed above, showing that engagement with some production-adjacent configurable cultural forms—such as stream ripping, remixing and uploading—are more common among older than younger Filipinos.

---

[2] *Feist Publications v. Rural Telephone Serv. Co.*, 499 U.S. 340 (1991).

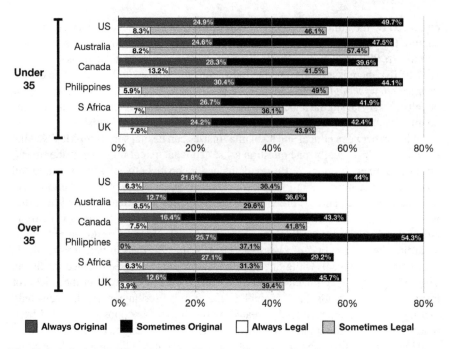

Fig. 12.6 Attitudes regarding laws and ethics of configurable culture, by nation and age

Overall, the gaps between ethical and legal opinions, and the level of support for configurable culture across and between national populations, were fairly consistent and seem to have little to do with the differences between national legal systems, or levels of awareness, consumption and engagement among the populations in question. For instance, both the USA and the Philippines have broad "fair use" rules in their copyright laws, which cover many "transformative" uses of cut-and-pasted content, but the other four nations have more restrictive "fair dealing" rules, which tend to be much more restrictive, in a configurable cultural context (Aufderheide and Jaszi 2018). Yet, attitudes about the legality of these practices were more similar between the USA and UK, and between the Philippines and South Africa (in the case of older adults) than between nations that share the same style laws. This suggests that perhaps other factors—such as cultural values—play at least as causative a role in shaping legal expectations as the actual letter of the law (Fig. 12.6).

12.4 Conclusion

In this chapter, I have analyzed survey data regarding levels of awareness, consumption, engagement and attitudes with respect to configurable cultural forms and practices, such as remixes, mashups and video game mods, as well as peer-to-peer redistributive practices, such as live streaming and file sharing. The data illuminate some differences between age groups and nations, yet also raise many questions. Patterns of ethical and legal opinions seem to have little to do with the size of individual markets, the prevailing copyright law, or the overall level of engagement with digital media among the adult population. Instead, it seems that one of the principal differentiators is between so-called advanced and developing economies. Users in wealthier nations like the USA tend to be more likely to participate on the consumption-adjacent end of the spectrum (engaging in practices such as listening to custom radio and time-shifting via DVR), while users in poorer nations like the Philippines and South Africa are far more likely to engage in production-adjacent practices like remixing, as well as gray area practices like file sharing and stream ripping. This suggests that media consumers in these markets, by virtue of their institutional relegation to being consumers of commercial content from the Global North, use digital platforms as a way to reestablish some ownership stake and participatory role in global cultural flows. Collectively, these data suggest that we must understand economics as a principal driver of adoption patterns for new media platforms and practices, with an equal or greater causative role relative to legal and cultural factors.

References

Aufderheide, P., & Jaszi, P. (2018). *Reclaiming fair use: How to put balance back in copyright*. Chicago: University of Chicago Press.

Bruns, A. (2008). *Blogs, Wikipedia, second life, and beyond: From production to produsage*. New York: Peter Lang.

International Monetary Fund. (2018). *World economic outlook: Challenges to steady growth*. https://www.imf.org/~/media/Files/Publications/WEO/2018/October/English/main-report/Text.ashx. Accessed June 22, 2019.

Jenkins, H. (2006). *Convergence culture: Where old and new media collide*. New York: NYU Press.

Latonero, M., & Sinnreich, A. (2014). The hidden demography of new media ethics. *Information, Communication & Society, 17*(5), 572–593.

Lessig, L. (2008). *Remix: Making art and commerce thrive in the hybrid economy*. London: Bloomsbury.

Marwick, A. E., & boyd, d. (2011). I tweet honestly, I tweet passionately: Twitter users, context collapse, and the imagined audience. *New Media & Society, 13*(1), 114–133.

Miraftab, F. (2009). Insurgent planning: Situating radical planning in the global south. *Planning Theory, 8*(1), 32–50.

Misalucha, C. G. (2015). The challenges facing the global south: Perspectives from the Philippines. *Bandung: Journal of the Global South, 2*(1).

Patry, W. (2011). *How to fix copyright*. Oxford: Oxford University Press.

Raz, J. (2009). *Between authority and interpretation: On the theory of law and practical reason*. Oxford: Oxford University Press.

Ritzer, G., & Jurgenson, N. (2010). Production, consumption, prosumption: The nature of capitalism in the age of the digital 'Prosumer.' *Journal of Consumer Culture, 10*(1), 13–36.

Sinnreich, A., Latonero, M., & Gluck, M. (2009). Ethics reconfigured: How today's media consumers evaluate the role of creative reappropriation. *Information, Communication & Society, 12*(8), 1242–1260.

Sinnreich, A. (2010). *Mashed up: Music, technology, and the rise of configurable culture*. Amherst, MA: University of Massachusetts Press.

Sinnreich, A., & Latonero, M. (2014). Tracking configurable culture from the margins to the mainstream. *Journal of Computer-Mediated Communication, 19*(4), 798–823.

Sinnreich, A., Forelle, M. C., & Aufderheide, P. (2018). Copyright givers and takers: Mutuality, altruism and instrumentalism in open licensing. *Communication Law and Policy, 23*(3), 197–220.

Standage, T. (2001, October 13). Peering round the corner. *The Economist*. https://www.economist.com/special-report/2001/10/13/peering-round-the-corner. Accessed June 22, 2019.

Yates, S., Kirby, J., & Lockley, E. (2015). Digital media use: Differences and inequalities in relation to class and age. *Sociological Research Online, 20*(4), 1–21.

Aram Sinnreich is Associate Professor and Chair of the Communication Studies division at American University's School of Communication. His work focuses on the intersection of culture, law and technology, with an emphasis on subjects such as emerging media and music. He is the author of three books: *Mashed Up* (2010), *The Piracy Crusade* (2013) and *The Essential Guide to Intellectual Property* (2019).

Chapter 13
Structured Film-Viewing Preferences and Practices: A Quantitative Analysis of Hierarchies in Screen and Content Selection Among Young People in Flanders

Aleit Veenstra, Philippe Meers, and Daniël Biltereyst

13.1 Introduction

A prominent voice in the analyses of contemporary audiences and their film-watching preferences is Jenkins (2006), who focuses on audience agency. In his work, Jenkins argues that contemporary media audiences live in an era of "convergence culture," which refers to "the flow of content across multiple media platforms, the cooperation between multiple media industries, and the migratory behavior of media audiences who will go almost anywhere in search of the kinds of media experiences they want" (Jenkins 2006: 2). In his view, audiences are deemed (inter)active in their choice of technology, screen and media products, and active audiences do not necessarily oppose mainstream culture. In his more recent work, Jenkins (Jenkins et al. 2013, 2016) echoes this focus on audience agency, wherein power of participation lies in the interaction between audiences, media products and media industries.

In contrast, a growing group of scholars stresses that by merely emphasizing audience agency through individual choice, the understanding of structural constraints in media consumption fades. One important body of the literature, often linked to a critical political economy perspective on audiences (Biltereyst and Meers 2011), argues that audiences perform free labor by engaging with the media products presented to them (e.g., Moisander et al. 2013), that convergence culture is used to justify reorganization leading to budget cuts and increase workload (e.g., Edge 2011) or that this

A. Veenstra (✉) · P. Meers
University of Antwerp, Stadscampus, Sint-Jacobsstraat 2, 2000 Antwerpen, Belgium
e-mail: aleit.veenstra@uantwerpen.be

P. Meers
e-mail: philippe.meers@uantwerpen.be

D. Biltereyst
Ghent University, Campus Aula, Universiteitstraat 4, 9000 Gent, Belgium
e-mail: daniel.biltereyst@ugent.be

© The Author(s) 2020
P. Szczepanik et al. (eds.), *Digital Peripheries*, Springer Series in Media Industries,
https://doi.org/10.1007/978-3-030-44850-9_13

perspective points to the limitations on the audience's choice and access by different kinds of financial or other barriers set by media industry strategies (e.g., Bird 2011; Kim 2012; Holt and Sanson 2014).

These critiques rightly point to the continuation of existing structures in media consumption, but rarely directly address audiences—a critique that also applies to Jenkins' (2006) analysis of specialized audience participation. As Couldry argues, the "only plausible way to understand the politics of convergence is to develop a better sociological and cultural analysis of what people are doing with and around media" (Couldry 2011: 498). Bil07Бilтereyst and Meers (2011) underline the usefulness of studying audiences to understanding the politics of media—a research tradition not often associated with the study of audiences. They argue that political economy can simultaneously provide an important contextualization as well as a better understanding of the audience's composition, preferences and practices.

This chapter combines the approaches of Bilтereyst and Meers (2011) and Couldry (2011) to studying audiences. We present a sociological analysis of the hierarchies that structure the feature film-watching practices and preferences of a large representative sample of audiences aged 16–18 living in Flanders (the northern Dutch-speaking region of Belgium). This is a demographic that enjoys watching movies on a regular basis (BFI 2015) and that adapts easily to new technologies such as new screens (Bennett and Robards 2014). In other words, if we want to find migratory audiences, the most likely place is among youngsters. Our analysis focuses on two traditional hierarchies in watching feature films: the country of production (or origin) and screen size. In analyzing these both as separate and related consumption preferences and practices, we anchor our understanding in a local audience, living in a specific region. Small nations may be limited in film budgets and number of productions, but advantages such as local anchorage, cultural specificity and similarity in potential audiences also apply (Hjort and Petrie 2007).[1] In this chapter, we focus upon the Flemish part of the country: With 6.2 million people living on 13.522 km^2 (Belgian Federal Government 2017), Flanders has an independent film policy. As such, it fits the definition of small nation cinema as used by Hjort and Petrie (2007).[2]

Previous research on young people in Flanders indicates that Hollywood is most popular and most appreciated, next to British cinema. European (i.e., mainly French, Italian, German and Spanish cinema) film lacks popularity and appreciation, while Flemish film is indeed frequently watched and somewhat appreciated (Meers 2002,

---

[1] The concept of national film can be problematic for multilingual/multicultural countries such as Belgium, where three linguistically different film audience communities coexist and where local governments support film production in local languages (Willems 2010).

[2] The country has three official languages: Dutch (spoken in Flanders and Brussels), French (spoken in Wallonia and Brussels) and German (spoken by a very small portion of the population living in the southeast). For Flanders, for instance, there is a government-funded body that has supported Flemish film production since 2002: *Vlaams Audiovisueel Fonds* (VAF, Flemish Audiovisual Fund). The fund aims to provide financial support, support further professionalization in audiovisual industries and assist with international exposure (Vlaams Audiovisueel Fonds 2016). The recent successive Academy Award nominations for the Flemish films *The Broken Circle Breakdown* (2012) and *Rundskop* (2011) are often cited as proof of a successful policy.

2004). In analyzing the extent to which these hierarchies between film origins remain valid and how they relate to screen use—e.g., is Hollywood still the only film to watch in the cinema and is Flemish film still associated with television viewing—we can identify structures in which contemporary media consumption takes place.

13.2 Hierarchies in Origin: Hollywood Film, European Film and National Film

The differentiation in film origin, which we understand as the country of production, is as old as the medium itself, with a long tradition of a conflictual relationship between Europe and the USA (Higson and Maltby 1999; Decherney 2013). Whereas European cinema has often been referred to as a cultural and economic patchwork quilt, Hollywood became a "metonym for the well-organised [sic] and substantially capitalized American film industry, with its international market hegemony" (Higson and Maltby 1999: 2). Hollywood's hegemony is strongly associated with a long tradition of worldwide-consumed blockbusters, with Hall (2002) even arguing that Hollywood is synonymous with blockbusters. Cucco (2009) voices a more nuanced stance in claiming that Hollywood exists beyond its most popular films, yet is best represented by these blockbusters. In addition, the profitable demographic of teens is specifically targeted by themes that appeal to them (Hay and Bailey 2002; Maltby 1999).

Hollywood thus dominates the global film market through blockbuster hits, while displaying a remarkable durability in the monopolization of international markets (Miller et al. 2001). As Scott concludes, Hollywood "is a central point of reference in the cultural economy of the modern world" (Scott 2005: 175). The resulting hegemony leads to a uniform filmic language (Elsaesser 2012) with a "narrative transparency" that characterizes Hollywood film as the most successful way of making film (Olsen 1999). While most authors recognize Hollywood's dominance, only a few speak of a continuing increase in the homogenization of film consumption. Fu and Govindaraju are two such voices in concluding that between 2002 and 2007, "the cinema markets have selected and consumed individual Hollywood movies in ways that are increasingly homogeneous" (Fu and Govindaraju 2010: 232). In a later article, Fu (2012) nuances his argument on Hollywood's market penetration, stating that Hollywood is most appreciated in countries that display a close cultural proximity to the USA (as measured through an understanding of English).

Concerns over homogenization (or unambiguous preference for Hollywood productions) in film consumption echo in the understanding of the position of European film. The European Union—and on a minor scale, the Council of Europe—for decades has responded by supporting European film distribution, providing funds for festivals that promote European content and aiding in finding an audience through the screening of non-national European films in first-run cinemas (European Commission 2017). European film is in many ways seen as the opposite of American film productions, if not in market share, then at least in (artistic) quality (Elsaesser 2005). This artistic quality is frequently attributed to the *auteurs* of European cinema: film directors with distinct styles that range from avant-garde rebellion against Hollywood to the more recent incorporation of references to Hollywood film tradition (Elsaesser 2005 [1994]). Most importantly, the auteurs of European cinema are considered to express themselves, rather than addressing an audience. As such, (European) film becomes a form of art that seeks innovation, instead of being a commercial enterprise (cf. Kersten and Verboord 2014).

This discursive dichotomy between commercial Hollywood and artistic Europe is on many levels artificial; both historically and in the contemporary landscape, European national cinemas have equally produced and continue to produce popular, mainstream, non-auteur films (Dyer and Vincendeau 1992; Bergfelder 2005). In an effort to theorize European cinema, going beyond the study of cinemas in Europe, Bergfelder (2005) concludes that (1) European film is liminal and marginal, (2) it is pan-European in its production and (3) the uniformity of the media product is compromised in its (European) distribution through dubbing and subtitling. That means that European film can indeed be labeled as such, but is strongly contextualized in how and where it is consumed. Audience research among young people in Flanders for instance, where foreign language films are subtitled, underscores this point in that the Flemish strongly disapprove of films that are not in (American) English or, second best, in their native Dutch (Meers 2004, 2002).

Another implication is the curious position of national film in Europe, for it is simultaneously national and European (Van Gorp 2010). Higson finds a solution in emphasizing the relevance of the context of consumption: "(…) a shift away from the analysis of film texts as vehicles for the articulation of nationalist sentiment and the interpellation of the implied national spectator, to an analysis of how actual audiences construct their cultural identity in relation to the various products of the national and international film and television industries, and the conditions under which this is achieved" (Higson 1989: 65). In other words, an analysis of (inter)national media products should take into account their national audiences. The usefulness of the concept of the "national" has been questioned by Higson (2002) arguing that multiple identities exist beyond and within the borders of the nation state. Diasporic film consumption is a case in point here (cf. Vandevelde et al. 2011). As such, the concept of national film can be both too limited or not limited enough (Schlesinger 2002).

13.3 Hierarchy in Screens: A Matter of Size

Next to the variability in the origin of the films, the survey also goes into the issue of how audiences watch them. There is a wide body of the literature on the increasing number of screens—large, small and smaller—on which movies can be watched and consumed. This literature goes back to differences between screening and watching films in the film venue and on television, with Sontag, for instance, declaring the decay of cinema if not watched on a silver screen: "to see a great film only on television isn't to have really seen that film. It's not only a question of the dimensions of the image: the disparity between a larger-than-you image in the theater and the little image on the box at home" (Sontag 1996: 1). Others are less deterministic, but stress the importance of screen size. Ellis (1991), for instance, demarcates between screen-related experiences with film. In a rather elitist approach, he argues that watching film on television is a mere pastime activity, whereas watching film in the cinema is a ritual. The latter includes the act of going there, watching collectively, being anonymous in the dark and attentively consuming a film. Others nuance this demarcation: While there are differences in watching film in the cinema and on television, the latter includes as many (social) conventions as the former (Silverstone 1994; Meers and Biltereyst 2012; Greer and Ferguson 2015). Emphasizing that the experience of film will vary in accordance with the size of the screen, Belton concludes that "we must begin to explore the differences among the experiences we have with images and sounds on those screens" (Belton 2014: 470). This chapter translates these experiences into audience practices in analyzing what content is accessed on what screen.

In the contemporary media landscape, there are many possibilities to access one's preferred media content, beyond the traditional screens of the cinema and television. Especially, devices connected to the Internet allow for access to an unlimited number of films. Tryon (2012) conceptualizes these new possibilities under the umbrella of mobile audiences, echoing Jenkins' (2006) "migratory audiences." We can distinguish three ideal types of audience mobility. First, platform mobility means that content can be accessed on a range of devices. Second, with spatial mobility, one can watch wherever. And lastly, one can watch whenever, which Tryon (2012) dubs temporal mobility. He grounds his analysis in advertisements, which he finds to promote personal (and by implication solitary) viewing. The individuality that comes with these viewing practices implies a more personalized media consumption experience.

Atkinson (2014), who argues for an engaged contemporary audience, also argues that today's film extends beyond the cinema screen. She underlines her argument by analyzing films specifically designed to be watched on a tablet, such as *The Silver Goat* (2012). Likewise, Odin includes the small screen as cinematic, contrary to what one might expect: "at first sight, everything seems to be the opposite of watching a film in a cinema when we watch on a mobile: small screen, poor sound and picture quality, unenclosed environment, mobility and the subordination of the viewing subject to external circumstances" (Odin 2012: 156). However, Odin (2012) concludes the opposite. With the smartphone, he argues we gain a valuable means of both making and watching film. As such, it allows for more involved film audiences.

However, in the early 2000s, the big screen also finds its way into people's homes. One of the most extensive studies on "home cinema cultures" is conducted by Klinger (2006), who introduces the concept of "new media aristocrats" to describe how technophiles create immersive film settings in the home, including big screens and extensive sound systems. Like Tryon (2012), Klinger (2006) grounds her analysis in commercials for home appliances. However, she does remark that the consumption of this type of technology implies a high (masculine) status. This makes it more of a well-esteemed exception worthy of aspiration, than an everyday means of home film consumption. In doing so, Klinger (2006) makes a crucial distinction between the possibilities for consumption (big screens and extensive sound systems) and the consumption practices themselves (few aspire to have these technologies).

The relevance of this distinction echoes in the few social scientific studies on audience practices across different devices. Macek and Zahrádka (2016), for example, find that the vast majority of Czech audiences watch film on linear television broadcast (90.4%). The younger the audiences, the more likely they are to also use other devices to watch film. However, these devices do not substitute watching film on television. Among respondents aged 18–29, 79.6% watch film via linear television broadcast, and 68.1% also watch films on other devices. A study by Greer and Ferguson (2015) yields similar results among American college students aged 18–22. Watching television on a tablet does not replace watching television on a television set. Rather, they find a positive correlation between the uses of both technologies. In other words, tablet and television set complement each other. The results are slightly different for Netflix; watching films via this streaming service is strongly associated with a tablet.[3]

In summary, we identify merits to either screen size in watching film. Traditionally, the bigger screens are considered to be better and most suitable for watching film (Ellis 1991; Klinger 2006; Belton 2014). At the same time, contemporary film content is designed for a plethora of screens (Atkinson 2014; Odin 2012), including those that facilitate mobility and content selection (Tryon 2012; Jenkins 2006). In analyzing whether today's preferences for different types of screens exist in the traditional screen hierarchies and whether these are related to film origin, we analyze individualized and mobile media consumption.

13.4   Methods

In search of remaining structures in contemporary film practices and preferences, we conducted a large-scale survey among a stratified sample of 1015 Flemish students in the two final years of their high school education (aged 16–18). The questionnaire included questions on where, how and with whom films were watched, as well as questions on film and screen preferences (Veenstra et al. 2017).[4] All surveys were digitalized using OMR software and analyzed using SPSS. Although we will present some general results from this survey, this chapter moves beyond the more traditional measures of screen use and content appreciation by focusing upon audience's engagement with a selection of concrete film titles.

---

[3]This may have changed since 2011, as Netflix became (more often) accessible via television sets.

[4]In the first half of 2015, the researcher visited 33 schools in Flanders, to supervise the completion of the questionnaires. Three more schools supervised completion themselves. The stratified sample is constructed through type and level of education. Participating schools were selected randomly. All students completed the 45-min questionnaire during school hours. Questionnaires have been digitalized using OMR software, and statistical analyses have been conducted using SPSS software.

Table 13.1 Selected film titles

Origin	More action-driven film genres	Less action-driven film genres
Hollywood	*Interstellar* (2014)	*The Wolf of Wall Street* (2013)
	Sherlock Holmes: A Game of Shadows (2011)	*Frozen* (2013)
	Django Unchained (2012)	*The Fault in Our Stars* (2014)
Flemish	*W.—Witse de Film* (2014)	*The Broken Circle Breakdown* (2012)
	Rundskop (2011)	*F. C. De Kampioenen* (2013)
	Crimi Clowns: De Movie (2013)	*Zot van A.* (2010)
European	*Tinker Tailor Soldier Spy* (2011)	*La Grande Bellezza* (2013)
	Melancholia (2011)	*The Grand Budapest Hotel* (2014)
	A Most Wanted Man (2014)	*The Intouchables* (2011)

For each of the three categories of film origins discussed earlier (Hollywood, Flemish film and European film), we selected six film titles. We questioned respondents on whether (1) they knew the films and (2) they had seen the films. If the second question was answered affirmatively, we subsequently asked them to rate the film and to indicate on which screen(s) they had seen it. It was possible to indicate multiple screens, as we intended to include repeat viewings. This list of selected films can be found in Table 13.1. All selected films were released in cinemas across Belgium and date no further back than academic year 2010–2011. This means that the youngest participating students would have been in their first year of high school when the film was released. Titles are selected from those with the highest box office successes, as published by Box Office Mojo. To assure a spread across film genres, we distinguish between the more and less action-driven film genres based on the IMDb genre classification.[5]

The resulting list is tentative; the six films per origin are not selected to analyze film industries. Even less so do the selected nine film titles per type of genre facilitate an analysis of a wide array of [often hybrid, cf. Staiger (2000)] film genres. However, our research does not aim to map film industries, nor film genres. It aims to compare film consumption across origins and screens in search of structures in practices and preferences. For such an analysis, we are confident that the films listed above present a strong and well-spread operationalization between countries of production.

Before moving on to analyzing film consumption within the frameworks of European film, national film and Hollywood film, we present a cluster analysis (Ward's method with a squared Euclidean distance interval). In this analysis, we identify possible clusters in the country of origin in our data. We based the analysis on the evaluation of films from eight different countries (measured on a five-point Likert

[5]Less action-driven includes the genres: animation, drama, youth and family, comedy and humor, historical costume, musical and music, romantic film, documentary and biography. More action-driven includes the genres: action and adventure, detective and mystery, horror, war and disaster, science fiction and fantasy, thriller and crime, western.

Table 13.2 Agglomeration schedule (baseline categories: American film [1], Flemish film [2], Belgian film in French [3], French film [4], British film [5], Spanish film [6], German film [7] and Italian film [8])

Stage	Cluster combined		Coefficients	Stage cluster first appears		Next stage
	Cluster 1	Cluster 2		Cluster 1	Cluster 2	
1	6	8	203.500	0	0	3
2	3	4	503.000	0	0	4
3	6	7	954.833	1	0	5
4	3	6	2010.400	2	3	7
5	1	5	3117.900	0	0	6
6	1	2	4552.400	5	0	7
7	1	3	10,820.000	6	4	0

scale with neutral included in the middle; the ratings can be found in Table 13.4). We operationalized European film by including the five largest European nations: France, Great Britain, Spain, Germany and Italy.[6] Belgian film in French was added to compare within the country. The cluster analysis points to a European film cluster that includes Belgian films in French, French films, Italian films, Spanish films and German films. A second cluster consists of Flemish films (or Belgian films in Dutch, if you will). Lastly, we identify a cluster that consists of American (or Hollywood) and British film, in other words: films in English. The findings are summarized in Table 13.2.

This analysis illustrates two things: (1) a first indication that structures remain in film consumption among youth in Flanders and (2) that it is a fruitful exercise to continue our analysis within the framework of European film, national (or Flemish) film and Hollywood film (which can be extended to films in British or American English). But before exploring preferences and practices within this framework, we will first present some general results on film-watching practices and preferences.

13.5   Measures of Film Consumption: Watching Film Today

In general, the survey underlined that watching film remains very popular among youth in Flanders. Nine out of ten respondents saw at least one film in the seven days prior to the questionnaire. Two-thirds saw two or more films. The activity is also thoroughly enjoyed: 84% of youth in Flanders like watching film, 13% are neutral, and only 3% do not like the activity. In similar fashion, 77% of youth like going to the cinema, 5% do not, and 18% are neutral. The silver screen is most popular for watching films; a little over half (52%) of all youth prefer the cinema over all other means to watch film. Television comes in second, at almost one-third (31%) of the

---

[6]The Brexit referendum had not yet taken place at the time of the questionnaire design.

votes. Of the new screens, only the PC/laptop is somewhat popular, with a preference rate of 12%. The projector (3%), tablet (1%) and smartphone (1%) come in last. This means that traditional screens remain most popular in accessing film.

As expected, preferences do not necessarily equate to practices. In a measure of the latter, we find that most youth watch film on television, followed by cinema. So, again, traditional screens prevail for film consumption. This time however, they switch position. In addition, we measured the way film content was accessed on each screen, taking the complexity of the contemporary media landscape into account. There are nine ways in which film can be accessed: (1) linear broadcast on television (also accessible on other screens via apps), (2) recorded from television, (3) additional film subscriptions (extra theme channels via digital television), (4) separate film subscriptions (e.g., Netflix), (5) pay per stream, (6) unpaid streaming, (7) rented DVD/Blu-ray, (8) owned DVD/Blu-ray and (9) digitally stored film. An "other" category was offered, but rarely completed. The top three ways of accessing film via different screens are summarized in Table 13.3. Here, another more traditional pattern in watching film surfaces.

Film watched on television is mostly consumed via linear access, sometimes delayed, or on owned DVD/Blu-ray disk—as also found by Macek and Zahrádka (2016) in the Czech Republic. This finding challenges the agency ascribed to contemporary audiences (Tryon 2012); most films consumed by youth in Flanders are found within the structural constraints of broadcast schedules and cinema programs. This also means that film consumption, despite the many possibilities for access, remains structured through, for example, windowing (Nelson 2014). There is one exception: the PC/laptop. While not used as frequently and by as many young people, it is a popular means of accessing film. Mostly used for individually selected unpaid streams, it is the only screen that points to the active and migratory audiences described by Jenkins (2006). The remaining smaller screens are unpopular for watching film.

Only 14% of youngsters in Flanders indicated they have access to a projector at home. This means that home cinema cultures mimicking cinema-like technology are the exception, rather than the rule (Klinger 2006). In practice, the projector also proves unpopular—much less popular than the cinema. Thus, when large screens are concerned, the one that is limited in content, time and place is more popular than the one that facilitates choice in all of these components of watching film. Moreover, film-watching practices on the projector most often concern DVD/Blu-ray. That is, selection takes place from the limited resource of purchased disks. Consequently, film consumption on large screens, like linear film consumption on television, takes place within a structure of limited supply. Again, this contradicts the understanding of contemporary audiences as mobile and underlines the importance of understanding the structures that guide media consumption.

A second conventional measure of media consumption is preference in type of film. In this chapter, we explore hierarchies in film consumption through preferences in origin. When asked to complete top three lists of favorite films (which, respectively, were *Fast & Furious*, *The Hunger Games* and *Harry Potter*), actors/actresses

Table 13.3 Most frequent ways of accessing film (per screen, largest observations in bold)

Screen	Way of watching	Every day (%)	Every other day (%)	Every week (%)	Every month (%)	Every year (%)	Never (%)
Cinema	N/A	0	1	2	**49**	45	3
Television	Linear	5	7	**41**	30	10	7
	Recorded	3	8	**39**	30	8	13
	Owned disk	1	2	7	22	**32**	37
PC/laptop	Unpaid stream	3	7	19	19	11	**41**
	Owned disk	0	1	4	13	21	**60**
	Digitally stored	1	2	8	2	15	**62**
Tablet	Linear	1	1	3	5	5	**84**
	Unpaid stream	1	1	3	6	5	**84**
	Recorded	1	1	3	5	4	**87**
Smartphone	Unpaid stream	1	2	3	5	4	**86**
	Linear	1	1	2	4	4	**89**
	Digitally stored	0	1	2	2	6	**90**
Projector	Owned disk	0	0	1	7	25	**67**
	Digitally stored	1	0	1	5	11	**82**
	Unpaid stream	0	1	1	3	11	**85**

(found to be Johnny Depp, Vin Diesel and Leonardo DiCaprio)[7] and directors (quite unanimously Steven Spielberg, Quentin Tarantino and Peter Jackson), the outcome among youth in Flanders overwhelmingly points to (the men in) Hollywood. This finding is in line with the diverse appreciation for film from various countries in Table 13.4.

Thus, Hollywood dominates in taste preferences among youth in Flanders. Yet while Hollywood might be most popular, it is not the only film country evaluated positively. Both British film (like Hollywood film in English) and Flemish film (in Dutch) score above average with a little over three points out of five. As such, Hollywood is indeed a central point of reference (Scott 2005). But it might not be as

[7]Preferences that remind the first author of her time in high school 15 years ago; posters of the same men might have been found in her room at the time.

Table 13.4 Evaluation of film origin

Origin		Mean (SD)
Hollywood	American	4.27 (0.895)
Belgian	Flemish	3.14 (1.103)
	Walloon/Brussels	2.07 (1.006)
European	British	3.31 (1.138)
	French	2.17 (1.099)
	Italian	1.87 (0.975)
	Spanish	1.86 (0.939)
	German	1.81 (0.934)

The question was how much one enjoyed watching films from a variety of originating countries from "very much so" to "not at all" on a five-point scale. The category neutral was included in the middle

hegemonic as some authors argue (Fu 2012; Fu and Govindaraju 2010). The local Flemish film proves fairly popular, especially in comparison with Belgian films in French. These are rated similar to French films. This underlines the importance of context in European film consumption (Bergfelder 2005; Hjort and Petrie 2007; Higson 2002). For Flanders, the language of film will prove significant: Films in the mother tongue are favored over (non-English) foreign language films (Meers 2004). Following this analysis, we can conclude that European film remains as (un)popular as it was at the turn of the millennium (Meers 2002)—despite efforts by the European Union to popularize its films (European Commission 2017). There is one exception: British film; in sitting comfortably in the same cluster as Hollywood, its popularity underlines the importance of language in film. However, it is not as popular as Hollywood film. As such, like Flemish film, it floats between the popular Hollywood film and the unpopular European film. The final cluster consists solely of Flemish—or national—film.

To summarize, in an age of unlimited access, film consumption preferences remain shaped along traditional hierarchical lines of origin: (1) Hollywood (which can be extended to films in British English), (2) Flemish (or "national") and (3) European film. As was the case for the variety of screens, there are important implications along the lines of political economy: If audiences stay put, rather than migrating (Jenkins 2006), media industries remain crucial in shaping media consumption (Holt and Sanson 2014). Audiences, thus, do not select just any screen or just any film. Rather, they consume film in patterns we recognize from an offline preconvergence culture era; like Greer and Ferguson (2015), we find existing media repertoires structure consumption. That brings us to the final section of this chapter: Can we find similar structuring patterns in media consumption when we combine content (origin) and screen—two aspects that are found to facilitate contemporary audience agency?

13.6 Films on Screens: Detailed Measurements of Film Consumption

In a detailed measurement of film knowledge, consumption and appreciation, our selection of eighteen film titles confirms the patterns we found earlier: Hollywood film is evaluated best, European film is evaluated worst, and cinema and television screens are most popular for watching films, followed by the PC/laptop at a distance—see Table 13.5. However, preferences somewhat diverge from practices. While Hollywood is appreciated slightly more with grades around 4 out of 5, Flemish film is as well known as the most popular titles known by the majority of students, viewed as often as Hollywood film. European film is least known and rarely viewed, sometimes by as few as 10–20 students. And when European film is viewed, ratings are low—though higher than the overall ratings for European film in the former section. *The Intouchables* (2011) is the exception here. This film is similar to Hollywood films in its popularity, as it is well known (by 74% of all students), well viewed (by 52% of all students) and highly rated with a 4.1.

To further explore the patterns between content and screen, we focus on the various screens that respondents indicated they had seen the films on.[8] This analysis further nuances our understanding of film consumption practices. We see that Hollywood film is consumed in the cinema, on television and on the PC/laptop. In short, it is popular on all common screens to watch film. The high number of students that have seen the Hollywood titles in the cinema, especially *Interstellar* (57%) and *The Fault in Our Stars* (56%), is exceptional. The only Flemish film that approaches this share in cinema attendance is *F. C. De Kampioenen* (57%). Generally, Flemish films are watched on television; the remaining film titles display audience shares between 68 and 84%. Neither of the titles in national film are accessed often via PC/laptop, tablet or smartphone.

The analysis for European film is a bit more complex, because only a few students saw the films listed. Nonetheless, we see that the PC/laptop is a popular way to access these films and more common than via a television screen and far more popular than the silver screen, for example with *A Most Wanted Man* and *The Grand Budapest Hotel*. This finding might indicate that less accessible content is indeed found by active audiences through online means. However, it concerns only very small audiences: Between 2 and 9% of the young people saw one of the European films. The exception is, again, *The Intouchables* (2011). With an audience of over half of high school students in Flanders (52%), it is comparable to Hollywood films when it comes to screen choice. Also, it is the only film regularly watched on a projector screen (33%). A likely explanation is that it is watched in school; the film was often mentioned to be screened in French class.

Thus, Hollywood film is clearly deemed suitable for all screens and shows the strongest connection to the cinema, Flemish film is predominantly watched on television, and European film is mainly accessed via the PC/laptop, followed by television.

---

[8]For this analysis, only the entries of the respondents that answered both questions are included.

Table 13.5 Watching film: film titles, known, seen, average grades and screens

Film	Know (%)	Seen (%)	Average grade (SD)—scale 1–5	N (screen)	Cinema (%)	Television (%)	PC/laptop (%)	Tablet (%)	Smartphone (%)	Projector (%)
1	51	15	3.9 (1.2)	115	57	12	35	3	2	0
2	63	29	3.7 (0.9)	229	24	66	19	2	0	3
3	47	22	4.0 (0.9)	168	21	51	30	4	0	7
4	79	45	3.8 (1.1)	362	27	43	33	3	2	7
5	87	51	3.8 (1.0)	411	21	50	43	3	1	7
6	72	38	4.1 (1.0)	605	56	21	41	3	1	3
7	40	9	3.2 (1.2)	63	27	68	8	0	0	0
8	77	36	3.2 (1.1)	275	12	79	9	0	0	5
9	54	14	3.2 (1.3)	99	12	78	11	1	1	5
10	80	47	3.5 (1.2)	368	17	81	9	1	0	3
11	82	43	3.5 (1.1)	334	57	44	10	1	1	2
12	74	43	3.2 (1.0)	325	19	84	5	0	0	2
13	20	2	3.3 (1.3)	13	8	38	62	0	0	0
14	19	3	2.8 (1.3)	17	6	59	29	0	6	0
15	28	7	3.4 (1.0)	49	20	37	47	0	0	0
16	18	3	2.6 (1.2)	14	21	36	43	0	0	0
17	34	9	3.4 (1.2)	63	21	37	40	3	0	3
18	74	52	4.1 (0.9)	404	29	47	18	1	0	33

Films are graded by ticking a box between 1 [low] and 5 [high]. Film titles are represented by numbers: Hollywood: [1] *The Interstellar*, [2] *Sherlock Holmes*, [3] *Django Unchained*, [4] *The Wolf of Wall Street*, [5] *Frozen*, [6] *The Fault in Our Stars*. Flemish film: [7] *W.—Witse de Film*, [8] *Rundskop*, [9] *Crimi Clowns: De Movie*, [10] *The Broken Circle Breakdown*, [11] *F. C. De Kampioenen*, [12] *Zot van A.* European film: [13] *Tinker Tailor Soldier Spy*, [14] *Melancholia*, [15] *A Most Wanted Man*, [16] *La Grande Bellezza*, [17] *The Grand Budapest Hotel*, [18] *The Intouchables*

Inherently, the structures that surface contest the personal and individualized media consumption practices as argued by authors such as Jenkins (2006) and Tryon (2012). Moreover, these results illustrate that watching film cannot be analyzed based on a mere choice in content and screen. For more detailed and meaningful results, a combined approach is crucial. The strong hierarchies in screen and origin point toward the continuity of structured media consumption, nuancing or even contradicting discourses on convergence culture and its alleged migratory audiences (Atkinson 2014; Bilterecyst and Meers 2011; Couldry 2011; Klinger 2006).

13.7 Conclusion

Through a variety of analyses in this chapter, a series of recurring patterns in film consumption appear. We find hierarchies in film consumption for content and screen, respectively: Hollywood and the cinema are most popular among Flemish youngsters. European films and small portable screens are least popular for movie consumption. And hierarchies solidify when measured in a detailed analysis of film titles and film-watching practices: Highly rated Hollywood films are watched in the cinema, and the less valued Flemish films are watched on television. This is in line with earlier findings from studies conducted before the alleged rise of convergence culture (Meers 2002, 2004).

But while films may be valued differently and consumed on different screens, the frequency in knowledge and consumption is rather similar between Flemish and Hollywood films. This underlines the cultural specificity and local anchorage of the national film industries and their audiences (Hjort and Petrie 2007): While there may be a highly valued and vast library of Hollywood films available via different platforms, the local Flemish film has a prominent place in the cultural consumption of contemporary young Flemish audiences. As such, film consumption is firmly embedded in the structures of the local culture. This is further confirmed by the lack of popularity of films from other European countries or even Belgian film in French, while Flemish film would be considered "European" in regions outside Flanders (Bergfelder 2005). The geographic location of film consumption therefore matters in film appreciation and should be included in analyses of preferences and practices.

If anything, the patterns and hierarchies analyzed in this chapter underline the (continuing) importance of structure in contemporary film consumption. As such, our results challenge the merits of focusing solely on audience agency, since the subjects of recent studies on audience practices and analyses of possibilities (Tryon 2012) and practices of specialized (fan) communities (Jenkins 2006), which are often taken as exemplary, are far from being common practice among general audiences. Our findings are in line with existing generalizable studies on audience practices (Macek and Zahrádka 2016; Greer and Ferguson 2015). Moreover, they underline the importance of monitoring both the diversity and continuity in (film) audience practices (Couldry 2011), as well as the political–economically informed frameworks within which these practices take place (Bilterecyst and Meers 2011).

Studying detailed audience practices, such as their acquaintance with and appreciation of specific film titles, increases our understanding of the existing hierarchies that frame consumption practices. But further context is needed in exploring hierarchical consumption patterns, both quantitatively and qualitatively, with many questions still to be answered. Why exactly do audiences make the choices they make? What kinds of new technologies and devices will change audiences' preferences and behavior? What are the social, economic, cultural and other barriers for audiences' film and media choices, preferences and practices? We hope our study contributes to a critical understanding of the classical continuum between agency and structure, when dealing with European film audiences in an era of convergence.

References

Atkinson, S. (2014). *Beyond the screen: Emerging cinema and engaging audiences*. New York, London: Bloomsbury Academic.

Belgian Federal Government. (2017). *Bevolking: Cijfers Bevolking 2010–2016*. https://statbel.fgov.be/nl/modules/publications/statistieks/bevolking/bevolking_-_cijfers_bevolking_2010_-_2012.jsp. Accessed September 9, 2017.

Belton, J. (2014). If Film is Dead, What is Cinema? *Screen, 55*(4), 460–470.

Bennett, A., & Robards, B. (2014). Introduction: Youth, cultural practice and media technologies. In A. Bennett & B. Robards (Eds.), *Mediated youth cultures: The internet, belonging and new cultural configurations* (pp. 1–7). Hampshire, New York: Palgrave Macmillan.

Bergfelder, T. (2005). National, transnational or supranational cinema? Rethinking European film studies. *Media, Culture & Society, 27*(3), 315–331.

BFI/British Film Institute. (2015). *Audiences*. London: British Film Institute. https://www.bfi.org.uk/sites/bfi.org.uk/files/downloads/bfi-audiences-2015-11.pdf. Accessed September 9, 2017.

Biltereyst, D., & Meers, P. (2011). The political economy of audiences. In J. Wasko, G. Murdock, & H. Sousa (Eds.), *The handbook of political economy of communications* (pp. 415–435). Malden, MA: Wiley-Blackwell.

Bird, E. S. (2011). Are we all producers now? Convergence and media audience practices. *Cultural Studies, 25*(4–5), 502–516.

Couldry, N. (2011). More sociology, more culture, more politics. Or, a modest proposal for 'Convergence' studies. *Cultural Studies, 25*(4–5), 487–501.

Cucco, M. (2009). The promise is great: The blockbuster and the hollywood economy. *Media, Culture & Society, 31*(2), 215–230.

Decherney, P. (2013). *Hollywood's copyright wars: From Edison to the internet*. New York: Columbia University Press.

Dyer, R., & Vincendeau, G. (1992). *Popular European cinema*. London: Routledge.

Edge, M. (2011). Convergence after the collapse: The 'Catastrophic' case of Canada. *Media, Culture & Society, 33*(8), 1266–1278.

Ellis, J. (1991). *Visible fictions: Cinema, television, video*. London: Routledge.

Elsaesser, T. (2005). *European cinema: Face to face with Hollywood*. Amsterdam: Amsterdam University Press.

Elsaesser, T. (2012). *The persistence of Hollywood*. London: Routledge.

European Commission. (2017). *Media overview: Supporting and promoting Europe's audiovisual sector*. https://ec.europa.eu/programmes/creative-europe/media_en. Accessed April 12, 2017.

Fu, W. W. (2012). National audience tastes in Hollywood film genres: Cultural distance and linguistic affinity. *Communication Research, 40*(6), 789–817.

242   A. Veenstra et al.

Fu, W. W., & Govindaraju, A. (2010). Explaining global box-office tastes in Hollywood films: Homogenization of national audiences' movie selections. *Communication Research, 37*(2), 215–238.

Greer, C. F., Ferguson D. A. (2015). Tablet computers and traditional television (TV) viewing: Is the iPad replacing TV? *Convergence: The International Journal of Research into New Media Technologies, 21*(2), 244–256.

Hall, S. (2002). Tall revenue features: the genealogy of the modern blockbuster. In S. Neale (Ed.), *Genre and contemporary Hollywood* (pp. 11–26). London: British Film Institute.

Hay, J., & Bailey, S. (2002). Cinema and the premises of youth: 'Teen Films' and their sites in the 1980s and 1990s. In S. Neale (Ed.), *Genre and contemporary Hollywood* (pp. 218–235). London: British Film Institute.

Higson, A. (1989). The concept of national cinema. *Screen, 30*(4), 36–46.

Higson, A. (2002). The limiting imagination of national cinema. In M. Hjort & S. Mackenzie (Eds.), *Cinema and nation* (pp. 63–74). London: Routledge.

Higson, A., & Maltby, R. (1999). "Film Europe" and "Film America": An introduction. In A. Higson & R. Maltby (Eds.), *"Film Europe" and "Film America": Cinema, commerce and cultural exchange, 1920–1939* (pp. 1–31). Exeter: University of Exeter Press.

Hjort, M., & Petrie, D. (2007). Introduction. In M. Hjort & D. Petrie (Eds.), *The cinema of small nations* (pp. 1–22). Edinburgh: Edinburgh University Press.

Holt, J., & Sanson, K. (2014). Introduction: Mapping connections. In J. Holt & K. Sanson (Eds.), *Connected viewing: Selling, streaming, & sharing media in the digital era* (pp. 1–16). London: Routledge.

Jenkins, H. (2006). *Convergence culture: Where old and new media collide*. New York: New York University Press.

Jenkins, H., Ford, S., & Green, J. (2013). *Spreadable media: Creating value and meaning in a networked culture*. New York: New York University Press.

Jenkins, H., Ito, M., & Boyd, D. (2016). *Participatory culture in a networked era*. Cambridge and Malden: Polity Press

Kersten, A., & Verboord, M. (2014). Dimensions of conventionality and innovation in film: The cultural classification of blockbusters, award winners, and critics' favourites. *Cultural Sociology, 8*(1), 3–24.

Kim, J. (2012). The institutionalization of YouTube: From user-generated content to professionally generated content. *Media, Culture & Society, 34*(1), 53–67.

Klinger, B. (2006). *Beyond the multiplex: Cinema, new technologies, and the home*. Berkeley: University of California Press.

Macek, J., & Zahrádka, P. (2016). Online piracy and the transformation of the audiences' practices: The case of the Czech Republic. In D. H. Hick & R. Schmücker (Eds.), *The aesthetics and ethics of copying* (pp. 335–358). London: Bloomsbury.

Maltby, R. (1999). Sticks, hicks and flaps: Classical Hollywood's generic conception of its audiences. In M. Stokes & R. Maltby (Eds.), *Identifying Hollywood's audiences: Cultural identity and the movies* (pp. 23–41). London: British Film Institute Publishing.

Meers, P. (2002). Filmpubliek en (Europese) cinema. Theoretische Verkenning en Survey bij Jongeren in Vlaanderen. *Tijdschrift voor Sociologie, 23*(3/4), 509–543.

Meers, P. (2004). 'It's the language of film!': Young film audiences on Hollywood and Europe. In R. Maltby & M. Stokes (Eds.), *Hollywood abroad: Audiences and cultural exchange* (pp. 158–175). London: British Film Institute Publishing.

Meers, P., & Biltereyst, D. (2012). Film audiences in perspective: The social practices of cinemagoing. In H. Bilandzic, G. Patriarche, & P. J. Traudt (Eds.), *The social use of media: Cultural and social scientific perspectives on audience research* (pp. 123–140). Bristol: Intellect.

Miller, T., Govil, N., McMurria, H., & Maxwell, R. (2001). *Global Hollywood*. London: British Film Institute.

Moisander, J., Könkkölä, S., & Laine, P.-M. (2013). Consumer workers as immaterial labour in the converging media markets: Three value-creation practices. *International Journal of Consumer Studies, 37*(2), 222–227.

Nelson, E. (2014). Windows into the digital world: Distributor strategies and consumer choice in an era of connected viewing. In J. Holt & K. Sanson (Eds.), *Connected viewing: Selling, streaming, & sharing media in the digital era* (pp. 62–78). London: Routledge.

Odin, R. (2012). Spectator, film and the mobile phone. In I. Christie (Ed.), *Audiences* (pp. 155–169). Amsterdam: Amsterdam University Press.

Olsen, S. R. (1999). *Hollywood planet: Global media and the competitive advantage of narrative transparency*. Mahwah: Lawrence Erlbaum.

Schlesinger, P. (2002). The sociological scope of 'National Cinema.' In M. Hjort & S. Mackenzie (Eds.), *Cinema and nation* (pp. 19–31). London: Routledge.

Scott, A. J. (2005). Cinema, culture, globalization. In *Hollywood: The place, the industry* (pp. 159–175). Princeton: Princeton University Press.

Silverstone, R. (1994). *Television and everyday life*. London: Routledge.

Sontag, S. (1996). The decay of cinema. *New York Times Magazine, 25*, 60–61.

Staiger, J. (2000). *Perverse spectators: The practices of film reception*. New York: New York University Press.

Tryon, C. (2012). 'Make any room your TV room': Digital delivery and media mobility. *Screen, 53*(3), 287–300.

Van Gorp, J. (2010). Wat is Nationaal aan Nationale Cinema? *Tijdschrift voor Communicatiewetenschap, 38*(1), 49–62.

Vandevelde, I., Smets, K., Meers, P., Winkel, R. V., & Van Bauwel, S. (2011). Bollywood and Turkish Films in Antwerp (Belgium): Two case studies on diasporic distribution and exhibition. *Javnost—The Public, 18*(3), 55–70.

Vlaams Audiovisueel Fonds. (2016). VAF/Filmfonds. https://www.vaf.be/over-het-vaf/vaffilmfonds. Accessed October 25, 2016.

Veenstra, A., Meers, P., & Biltereyst, D. (2017). Pick, play, produce: Revisiting the concept of participation through a quantitative study of film consumption practices amongst youth in Flanders (Belgium). *Tripodos, 40*, 73–90.

Willems, G. (2010). A comparative analysis of contemporary film policy in Flanders and Denmark. *Tijdschrift Voor Communicatiewetenschap, 38*(2), 172–186.

Aleit Veenstra recently received her Ph.D. in communication studies from the University of Antwerp, where she is a member of the Visual and Digital Cultures Research Center (ViDi). She worked on the project *Screen(ing) Audiences*, focusing on contemporary film audiences. She is the author of articles on popular culture, consumption and film audiences.

Philippe Meers is Professor of film and media studies, the University of Antwerp, where he chairs the Center for Mexican Studies and serves as Deputy Director of the Visual and Digital Cultures Research Center (ViDi). He has published widely on historical and contemporary film culture and audiences. With R. Maltby and D. Biltereyst, he edited *Explorations in New Cinema History* (2011), *Cinema, Audiences and Modernity* (2012) and *The Routledge Companion to New Cinema History* (2019). With I. Ilsaket and D. Biltereyst he is currently co-editing a volume on Cinemagoing in the Arab World.

Daniël Biltereyst is Professor of Film and Media Studies, Ghent University, where he leads the Centre for Cinema and Media Studies (CIMS). He is the author of over 200 essays and the co-editor of several volumes, including *Explorations in New Cinema History and Cinema* (2011), *Cinema, Audiences and Modernity* (2012), *Silencing Cinema: Film Censorship around the World* (2013), *Moralizing Cinema* (2015) and *The Routledge Companion to New Cinema History* (2019). He is finalizing *Mapping Movie Magazines* (2018) and is currently working on *Cinemagoing in the Arab World*.

Chapter 14
Uses Genres and Media Ensembles: A Conceptual Roadmap for Research of Convergent Audiences

Jakub Macek

14.1 Introduction

It is more than obvious: Television audiences have changed. We can see it in our homes. We can observe it in how we watch films and TV shows. It is evidenced in the ways we decide about, get and recirculate content. What is the difference? Simply said: multiplication and convergence. Multiplication and convergence of technological objects (and textual interfaces and platforms) coming hand-in-hand with multiplication and convergence in our TV practices as was already noted more than a decade ago by Jenkins (2006). The other chapters in this section outline it very well—as members of convergent audiences, we still watch broadcasting, but we also download and stream, we search for online content across state boundaries and we share the content with others and some of us even remix and recreate existing content. Moreover, at home we use multiple screens, and our preferences over their sizes and qualities are linked with specific content preferences and with specific situations, as we have seen in the chapter about young Flemish audiences.

For the field of audience research, this change has created a profound challenge, as it has further complicated the always troublesome notion of *watching television*. One of the crucial questions—how to assess conceptually and methodologically TV audiences' agency so our research provides satisfyingly valid and useful outcomes?—has become even more important than ever before as the story is not just about *watching* and *television* but also about many other related practices and about other technological objects.

Audience research was quite surprisingly unprepared for the new situation, although the change was well foreseen (cf. Jenkins 2006; Lotz 2007). Even when households had already started the intensive domestication of multipurpose media

J. Macek (✉)
Faculty of Social Studies, Masaryk University, Jostova 10, 602 00 Brno, Czech Republic
e-mail: jmacek@fss.muni.cz

© The Author(s) 2020
P. Szczepanik et al. (eds.), *Digital Peripheries*, Springer Series in Media Industries,
https://doi.org/10.1007/978-3-030-44850-9_14

such as wired computers, and media scholars became interested in the new phenomena, the research—when dealing with everyday audiences and their practices—
mostly focused just on one particular type of practice linked usually with a particular
type of text and a particular object. The reasons for that were obviously pragmatic.
In the "traditional TV situation," any practice was more or less firmly connected to
a single media technology, and so we did not have a strong urge to look analytically
at *dynamics* between objects, content and practices. An imperative to approach the
"media home" as a complex of interrelated phenomena was evident, for example, in
British domestication research, but even this holistic tradition mainly focused—with
some exceptions, as Haddon (2006) remarked—on particular media such as TV and
later mobile phone or the networked PC. And related proposals of double articulated
research taking the media into account both as texts and objects were considered too
complicated for data collection and analysis (Livingstone 2007).

Of course, the media in everyday life were, in terms of objects and texts, always
multiplied. In the good old television home there was always something more than
the TV set: Radios and tape recorders, hi-fis, books, journals and newspapers, land-
lines, later the VCR, video games and microcomputers. But as the colorful realm of
domestic viewership has encountered digitalization and dematerialization of content,
the relation between texts, objects and practices has become fluid. Or, in Henry Jenkins' words, convergent: content freed from its dependence on a certain proprietary
object can be and is distributed and consumed across diverse channels and interfaces
(cf. Jenkins 2006). In the case of TV, broadcasting flow has eventually lost its mighty
monopoly.

The change that has come along with the proliferation and domestication of networked digital media (namely mobile devices and wired computers) has underlined
the importance of a few simple facts. Firstly, with content being consumed across
multiple diverse screens and devices we can no longer rely on the until-recently
stable and taken-for-granted relation between texts, objects and practices. Secondly,
particular media, texts and practices do not stand alone in our everyday life: They
are neither isolated phenomena nor discrete entities, but are inevitably interrelated
and integrated in the order of our everyday routines. People treat their media-related
practices and domesticated media objects as reflexively constructed and changeable systems—with classificatory rules, with inscribed values and needs and with a
personal history of decisions, replacements and acquisitions. And thirdly, the multiplication of practices linked with watching TV content emphasizes that being an
audience member refers to multiple distinct situations filled with different types of
content, used objects and co-viewers.

In our research on post-TV audiences, we focus specifically on the problem of the
complexity and permanently shifting nature of the media-related practices of current Czech audiences—one of our main aims at Masaryk University is to frame and
understand audiences' practices as a dynamic complex firmly embedded in everyday
life. Empirically we build upon qualitative and quantitative audience research conducted in several waves since 2012 (Macek et al. 2015; Macek 2015, 2017; Macek
and Zahrádka 2016); however, in this chapter I focus not on the results themselves (as
they have already been published) but on the explication of two crucial conceptual

constructs we employ in our inquiries. These two concepts—*uses genres*, originally formulated by Bakardjieva (Bakardjieva 2005; Bakardjieva and Smith 2001), and *media ensembles*, originating from our own work (Macek 2015)—enable us to assess content-related practices while taking into an account the three aforementioned simple facts: as typified and interrelated forms of agency organized at the individual level in a more or less reflexively created system referring to socially and culturally conditioned needs and motivations of the audience members. Consequently, these two concepts provide us with the opportunity to draw an analytically comprehensible and satisfying picture of current TV and post-TV audiences—a picture that also enables us to address and outline the specificities of current small-market audiences.

14.2   Uses Genres

Calgary-based media scholar Maria Bakardjieva introduced her notion of *uses genres* in order to assess ordinary Internet users' online practices embedded in the fabric of everyday life (Bakardjieva 2005; Bakardjieva and Smith 2001). Inspired by Voloshinov's approach to language and Bakhtin's concept of speech genres, Bakardjieva proposes uses genres as both typified and situated uses of technology—according to her, we use technologies in typical, stabilized ways, and we use them in typical situational settings that refer to the immediate contexts of our everyday lives as well as to the broader social, cultural, economic and political order. The notion of uses genres inevitably resembles Berger and Luckmann's (1991 [1967]) concept of institutionalized routines—i.e., routines drawing on intersubjective agreement on "how things should be done properly." Both conceptions acknowledge that we learn what and how to do something from others and that the "proper doing" is individually variable while it is, to some degree, also normative. But, in contrast to the classics of social constructivism, Bakardjieva focuses explicitly and specifically on the uses of technological objects and their positions in everyday life and thus offers a more suitable conceptual solution for audience research.

In her approach, Bakardjieva proficiently avoids the dark risks of technological determinism as well as sweeping voluntarism. As she notes, relations between technology uses and their situational frameworks are inevitably mutual and dialectical. On the one hand, uses genres are formed by structures of everyday life because "typical social-biographical situations in which subjects find themselves give rise to specific 'little behaviour genres', including genres of technology use" (Bakardjieva and Smith 2001: 68). On the other hand, Bakardjieva sees users as active agents of technological, social and cultural processes; by using technologies, users inevitably reshape situations. And so they eventually do even with the technologies they employ: "Positing users as doers, and not simply as consumers, interpreters, adopters and so on, makes it logical to go on looking for the effects of their action on the tools they select, appropriate and implement" (Bakardjieva 2005: 34).

The concept of uses genres proved itself quite useful in Maria Bakardjieva's ethnographic study of Internet users: It enabled her to draw a complex picture of

North American users adopting and routinizing the new technology in the late 1990s and early 2000s and as such, her study represents one of the best available inquiries conducted within the tradition of critically oriented domestication research. Thanks to her conceptual work, Bakardjieva was able to analyze and reconstruct the studied practices in relation to the underlying needs of the participants and, therefore, to systematize and interpret the seemingly borderless realm of online practices.

Although the concept of uses genres has not been widely used in audience research, we have decided to employ it in our research on Czech convergent and traditional TV audiences because we have found it applicable to watching television content. In our case, i.e., in the case of media audiences, uses genres are represented by typified and situated uses of audiovisual media both as texts and as material (technological) objects. To put it simply, the concept of uses genres gives us a chance to explicitly address the fact that we watch TV content in multiple and yet typical ways, at typical times and in typical places and with the typical company of our close others, and that regularities of these "typicalities" are presumably shared by viewers with similar status, needs, cultural taste, etc. In other words, the concept helps us to find the explicit analytical sensibility necessary for grasping that "watching television" includes not only a certain agency (selection, reception or recirculation of content, and handling technological objects), certain content (films, TV series, documents) and certain objects (TV set, mobile phone, laptop, etc.) but also certain actors ("just me," "me and my partner," "with kids," etc.) and spatiotemporal coordinates (e.g., "home in the evening," "every morning during breakfast in the kitchen," or "afternoon when travelling from school"). Here, of course, comes the situated nature of uses genres—the answers for the simple questions of "with whom," "where" and "when" describe the basis of an observed situation.

And last but not least, each distinct uses genre can and should be seen as replying to diverse motivations and as satisfying specific and variable needs. As we argue in our study of pirating audiovisual content, needs linked with watching TV content are of two types:

[C]hoices of particular media made by audiences are informed by what might be called textual motivations (related to "purely textual" preferences of particular genres, narrative structures etc.) as well as by contextual motivations [...], such as those related to respondents' everyday lives (available time, need for activities shared within couples, cultural capital forming the recipient's identity and taste). (Macek and Zahrádka 2016: 341–342)

What are the typical or prevailing uses genres we can observe in relation to watching TV content? An illustrative case of a couple of our interviewees—let's call them Diana and Robert—might be helpful. Robert, in his late 30 s, and Diana, almost 30, have lived together for about a year. They have a TV antenna and broadband Internet connection at home and they subscribe to Netflix. Robert is a frequent and passionate consumer of TV series, Diana is rather a modest viewer; while he watches multiple TV series and on several occasions during his day, she usually watches only two or three times a week when they spend their time together in the evening. Their shared watching represents one of the most common uses genre—prime-time watching. In their case, it occurs in their living room, in the "main evening time," and it is usually linked with the consumption of what they consider premium content—new episodes of preferred TV series (such as *Game of Thrones* or *The Young Pope*) or, less frequently, new or well-rated movies. They do this together because they want to spend "uncomplicated private time together," as they describe it, and also because it comes with the possibility of sharing the experience and talking about it. They say that they mostly do not have any problem agreeing on what to watch; however, Diana does not understand English very well and thus she needs Czech subtitles or dubbing. So, when Netflix offers a movie or series of their choice only with English subtitles (and this happens quite often since a large part of its catalogue is not localized for Czech audiences), Robert downloads the film and subtitles from online sites.

Besides prime-time, Diana and Robert sometimes spend together binge-watching for more or less a whole Saturday or Sunday, i.e., watching many episodes in a row or watching even a whole season of a particular show. Diana admits that it is mainly Robert's call but she accepts it as a form of "total relaxation." As in the case of prime-time watching, Diana and Robert prefer to watch premium content on this occasion but in contrast to it they watch also in bed using his or her laptop.

Robert alone watches series on Netflix while having breakfast and then usually during his lunch break—he works two or three days per week from home and so he has an opportunity to do it this way. For breakfast, he usually prefers some 20–25 minutes-long formats ("something lighter," in his words), for his lunch break "something more regular" with 50 minutes-long episodes. For this type of watching, he chooses content that Diana would not watch with him because it does not fit her taste.

Diana rarely watches alone—when Robert is not at home, she turns on the TV just to have it as a background for other activities and to fill the silence. Or she watches "some older stuff," such as *Friends* or *Gilmore Girls*, which she has downloaded in dubbed versions to her laptop. When watching these, Diana does not need to fully focus, since she knows the episodes already, but listening to Czech dubbing enables her to be on Facebook and on Instagram at the same time or even do some preparation for her job.

Together they go to the cinema every two or three months—for a movie "that is worth seeing on a large screen." Sometimes just the two of them, sometimes with other couples, but they always consider it a special event linked with dinner or some drinks and socializing afterward.

As we can see in this illustrative example, Diana and Robert are typical post-TV viewers employing the TV set and laptops for their viewing habits and combining several sources of content. Importantly, their uses genres vary in many aspects, from needs they fulfill through consumed content to situational settings. Illustratively, we can draw a line between their shared and individual uses genres and conclude that the shared genres help Diana and Robert to maintain shared privacy and to negotiate their shared tastes. But even the shared uses genres (in the case of this couple's prime-time watching, binge-watching and cinema-going) are obviously distinct regarding some of their basic parameters, which indicates that these genres play different roles in their everyday personal routines.

14.3 Media Ensembles

In the case of Diana and Robert, we can also clearly see another crucial aspect of contemporary habits of viewing TV content: Uses genres are organized into systems. Each particular uses genre stands among other uses genres, and its role is defined by its position in relation to them. Visiting the cinema is positioned in contrast to ordinary everyday watching, individual genres in contrast to shared genres, and/or focused watching in contrast to watching as an ancillary part of other, and more central activities. Moreover, all these practices stand amidst a wider, more general set of media-related uses genres that include, for example, news reception, reading books and journals, using social media for online and mobile interactions, and so on. Inevitably, any valid empirical inquiry of uses genres—and of current media audiences in general—requires acknowledging this fact.

For this purpose, we work with the concept of *media ensembles* (Macek 2015). This concept, unlike the similar and widely used notion of media repertoires (e.g., Ferguson and Perse 1993; Hasebrink and Popp 2006; Kim 2016), does not put at its center the media technologies or content channels used by a social actor but instead focuses at the same time on media practices, technologies and content, i.e., on uses genres: Media ensembles are dynamic, time-varying classificatory systems that "can be characterized as individually specific sets of practices, media objects and texts—individually specific to the extent as any socially and culturally conditioned dispositives" (Macek 2015: 47).

Like the uses genres that constitute them, particular media ensembles are changeable over time. They have their histories of choices, of domestication and abandoning particular technologies, and of substituting older uses genres with new ones. But they are more than just "packages of media and related doings"—as classificatory systems, media ensembles refer to the order of one's everyday life, to its rules. They play their role in its constitution; they are one of the key classificatory axes of one's everyday world since they are usually reflexively constructed in relation both to individual needs and domestic negotiations regarding the moral economies of our households. In a completely different context—in relation to political practices—Mouffe (2005) wrote about classificatory systems and orders:

> Things could always be otherwise and therefore every order is predicated on the exclusion of other possibilities.[...] What is at a given moment considered as the "natural" order – jointly with the "common sense" which accompanies it – is the result of sedimented practices; it is never the manifestation of a deeper objectivity exterior to the practices that bring it into being. To summarize this point: every order is political and based on some form of exclusion. (Mouffe 2005: 18)

Indeed, this applies also to media ensembles. They result from the perpetual struggle over what is considered among household members as reasonably acceptable, likable and preferred in a cultural, economic, political and status-related sense. Moreover, media ensembles are political in both (private and public) meanings: They are gendered, and they stem from power relations within households, relationships and families. At the same time, media ensembles, as one of the interfaces between private and public, embody and manifest the wider, contextual power relations affecting the private sphere as well as the eventual participatory ambitions of the private individuals toward public spaces.

What in particular does the concept of media ensembles contribute to our understanding of TV watching and post-TV audiences? At the individual level, the concept pushes us to see uses genres as organized and interconnected—it explicitly draws our analytical attention to the fact that some objects and texts are employed across two or more distinct uses genres and that some uses genres rely on more than one technology or content type. Moreover, the concept enables us to systematically assess the extent and intensity of individual reception practices—and to put them in the context of other media-related practices. In the case of our illustrative couple, we can see two individual media ensembles partly overlapping at the level of shared uses genres but diverging in the extent of individual genres. Moreover, a closer look at Diana's media ensemble would reveal that she spends—unlike Robert—her leisure time reading fiction and multiple magazine titles which can be seen as the functional equivalent to Robert's breakfast/lunch viewing habits. And last but not least, each of their media ensembles is significantly shaped by Diana's reluctance to subscribe not only to Netflix but also to HBO Go; instead, she renewed her yearly subscription to *Respekt* (a Czech political weekly). Robert accepted her argument that it is a more sensible and mature choice than a subscription to another, "redundant" VOD service. In this decision, their moral economy reflecting and articulating their negotiation about shared values was manifested—and through that, the symbolic classificatory power of their intertwined media ensembles.

Media ensembles, however, are useful not only at the micro-social level as a conceptual tool for understanding and analyzing everyday media uses of one particular couple. At a population level, the concept offers the possibility to cluster audience members in line with similarities in their media ensembles—regarding their structure (in terms of involved uses genres), intensity of content reception, manifested content preferences, importance of watching films and TV series, etc. In other words, media ensembles offer a key to a more nuanced segmentation of TV audiences better suitable for the convergent, post-TV situation.

14.4   Researching the Uses Genres and Media Ensembles of Current Post-TV Audiences

The effort at the identification of typical uses genres based on empirical evidence, the reconstruction of prevailing media ensembles, and the assessment of their distribution among general audiences encounters one principal obstacle—both genres and ensembles change in time, and sometimes, as new technology or new services enter the market, they may transform quite swiftly. And this, at first sight, complicates any attempt to formulate a stable set of measuring tools that would be firmly and surely valid across time and across various cross-cut studies.

For example, since 2016 in Czechia we have observed this kind of transformation with Netflix, HBO GO and Apple TV+ opening their platforms in the country. Before 2016, the convergent segment of Czech TV audiences—making up one-third of Czech TV viewers (cf. Macek 2017; Macek and Zahrádka 2016)—relied mainly upon downloading content from unofficial online sources (mainly from download servers such as Uloz.to) and using shady streaming services (e.g., SerialyCZ.cz). After 2016, some uses genres—those newly including official VOD services—have been rearticulated into the audiences' practices, while some old practices have finally more or less disappeared since 2014 (such as those linked with visiting DVD rentals). Along with that, smart TVs enabling full online connectivity and VOD services' applications have definitely cornered the market. As a result, the valid formulation of particular measures and indicators for audience surveys necessarily differed in 2019 from the measures and indicators we used in December 2014 (Macek et al. 2015).

There are two interrelated methodological solutions enabling us to deal with this permanent flux. Firstly, there is no better tool to sketch sensitively current audience activities than qualitative inquiry—it helps to thoroughly understand the communication partners and to study them and their practices in the complex setting of their everyday lives. With a large enough sample, it also enables one to draw a preliminary map of the most common uses genres and typical media ensembles and connect them with particular needs and motivations (which is later very helpful in the interpretation of survey data). To continue with the above-mentioned example, from April 2018 to June 2019 we interviewed 80 members of Czech convergent audiences (41 women and 39 men aged 18–58, with an average age of 31 years) aiming to reconstruct their viewing habits and related practices and the interviewees' motivations for them (Jansová et al. 2019). The findings from this inquiry served to reformulate our questionnaire originally used in 2014 and to include or reword items indicating shifts in particular practices and uses and preferences of technological objects, so that the questionnaire would better fit the current situation.

Secondly, the concepts of uses genres and media ensembles implicate four dimensions of inquiry that should serve as the main grid structuring the general logic of both qualitative study and quantitative surveys. And precisely these dimensions—simply composed of what, how, with whom and when people watch—play the role of kinds of meta-tools ensuring the comparability and validity of data across different data collections.

- *The content dimension* focuses on what types of content (films, TV series or particular content genres) participants watch, how important they consider them and how often they watch them.
- *The technological dimension* refers to the technologies employed in watching and aims to identify the structure and the degree of participants' convergence, i.e., what screens, content sources and other technological artifacts are used in particular uses genres.
- *The social dimension* refers to questions regarding with whom participants watch certain content and what content they watch alone, with whom they talk about

the content they watch and how they receive information about what is worth viewing.

- *The spatiotemporal dimension* includes questions on when and where participants watch their content.

While in qualitative inquiry these dimensions may remain rather implicit (as they do not necessarily directly form the structure of an interview), in a quantitative questionnaire they directly affect formulations of items as well as the data outcome. For a 2019 survey (the results were not yet available for this book) conducted on the general Czech 18+ population, key items were formulated as follows:

- "How often do you watch films? How often do you watch TV series?" // Answer: 5-point Likert scale ranging from "Never" to "Several times a day".
- "How much do you agree or disagree with the following statements?": "I wouldn't mind at all if I can't watch films [TV series]." // Answer: 5-point Likert scale ranging from "Absolutely disagree" to "Totally agree".
- "You've said that you watch films [TV series]. What technology or technologies do you use for watching them?" // Multiple choice: "TV – via broadcasting", "TV – but with apps like Netflix, HBO GO… or from DVD, USB, other connected media or from connected PC", "PC monitor", "Laptop or tablet", "Projector", "Mobile phone" etc.
- "You've said that you watch films [TV series]. With whom do you watch them at least once a month?" // Answers: "Alone", "With my partner", "With my kids", "With my parents", "With my friends" etc.
- "You've said that you watch films [TV series] alone [with you partner] [with your kids] […]. When do you usually watch like that?" // Multiple choice: "While eating or after that", "In the evening as part of the main evening time", "In other free time I have", "As a background when I do other things", "When travelling", "At work or in a school" etc.
- "When you watch films [TV series] alone [with you partner] [with your kids] […], what technology do you use most often for such watching?" // Single-choice answers: "TV – via broadcasting", "TV – but with apps like Netflix and HBO GO, or from DVD, USB, other connected media or from connected PC", "PC monitor", "Laptop or tablet", "Projector", "Mobile phone" etc.
- "How do you get access to the films or TV series you watch?" // Multiple choice: "I buy them on DVD or other media", "I borrow them from friends on DVD or other media", "I download them from the Internet", "Someone else downloads them for me", "I watch them online for free", "I watch them on prepaid services like Netflix or HBO GO", "I buy them or rent them online (using iTunes, Google Play or similar services".

After filtering out questions irrelevant for a particular participant (e.g., participants watching films less than once per month are not considered film viewers and so they skip questions assessing films), each respondent provides in this concrete questionnaire an adequately detailed matrix of her or his uses genres and, therefore, of his or her media ensemble. Using clustering procedures, respondents are then organized into clusters drawing upon the structural similarity of their media ensembles or particular uses genres. And yes, the resulting pile of data might look a bit messy as it includes multiple variables in various mutual configurations. But in the end, it provides quite clear answers about the distribution of convergent uses genres and media ensembles in the Czech population (along with a lot of analytical joy).

14.5 Specifics of Small-Market Audiences?

The above-outlined research solution is, in its general logic, applicable to any convergent audience. Yet, two important topics remain untouched here: the topic of the specifics of small-market audiences and the topic of audiences' power (or capabilities) to resist contextual pressures embodied in strategies of official content distributors as well as in legislation. These two intertwined issues make the final point of this chapter—namely, they suggest that being a viewer in a small-and peripheral-market subordinated to global strategies comes with tactics of media consumption that very well reveal and emphasize the distinct characteristics of such a market.

As John Fiske—inspired by Michel de Certeau's critical notion of everyday life (de Certeau 1984)—remarked, popular culture is inherently a culture of resistance where the members of an audience aim to gain as much as possible for themselves from the quite little offered to them by strategic players, i.e., by content producers and distributors (Fiske 2010). People treat the commodity they receive—the content—not necessarily in line with producers' expectations or intentions but in accordance with their own cultural and other needs. They may reject it; they may interpret it subversively; they may even reconfigure or remix it. Or they may not. But in any case, if they appropriate it, they do so within the context of their everyday life, embedding it in their own meanings and rituals. As a result, through appropriation they turn commodities into their own symbolic culture—into objects of popular culture. Henry Jenkins, Fiske's disciple, further notices that in a convergent situation, this gentle resistance gains more fuel because major content producers and distributors lose their until-recently more or less total control over distribution channels, and audiences at the same time gain a broader reservoir of resistance practices and more control over their consumption (Jenkins 2006). Importantly, this cultural resistance practiced through the appropriation of cultural commodities is often not explicitly political in terms of targeting power (a system, capitalism or patriarchal dominance and oppression). Instead, in most cases this resistance is a rather utilitarian act motivated by a need to obtain a better or more befitting experience, and it often takes the form of finding alternative ways of getting and providing access to content and its interpretation and reception—alternative in relation to the intentions of the strategic players (Macek and Zahrádka 2016).

In our previous research regarding content piracy in the Czech Republic (Macek and Zahrádka 2016) and in a more recent study of the motivations of Czech convergent audiences for paying for audiovisual content (Jansová et al. 2019), we have identified several uses genres that can be understood as specific to small-market audiences. Symptomatically, all of them can be read as acts of resistance and as audience members' attempts to get more effective control over their viewership.

As we already remarked in the introduction to this book, small- and peripheral-market audiences often face situations in which they are not very well served—they are not always offered content they actually want, the most current content or content properly customized for them in terms of language localization. Small- and peripheral-markets are simply not that economically enticing for global players and so they can be neglected, omitted, left out. We see it in Diana's example: She struggled to understand English spoken movies and TV series but her VOD service did not provide most of the content with Czech subtitles. The solution for that was simple— Diana and her partner downloaded the content they wanted from an alternative online source and they found subtitles for it on a community-based server offering subtitles translated and uploaded by other users. "After all, with the subscription to the service, we have already paid for the movie," said Diana, "so it's not my fault that I have to go elsewhere to get it […] in Czech."

Downloading as a routine part of domestic watching of films and TV series in this case constitutes uses genres that bridge obstacles still typical for the Czech market with online audiovisual services—and in line with Diana's words, it is conceived by Czech viewers as a rather non-problematic solution (cf. Jansová et al. 2019). Another common tactic is streaming films and TV shows from non-authorized online platforms, and although many of these online sources were shut down in autumn 2019 in response to lawsuits filed by major content providers (and so at the time of writing this chapter it remains unclear whether this will lead to the end of non-authorized streaming in general), many participants still tend to consider downloading as one of the best solutions for alternative access to content hardly available by other means. Why? Because they do not see any other *reasonable* option, or they do not see any other option at all.

Of course, downloading and streaming content from alternative sources is not unique for the Czech or other small-market audiences. However, the Czech audiences are specific in their motivations for these activities: One of the key motivations for downloading and streaming is, along with the unsurprising intention to avoid paying, the above-illustrated need to access content which is not legally offered in the small market at all, or which is offered online without appropriate qualities (e.g., not including Czech translation, lacking localized additional information), or which is available only in domestic broadcasting. In other words, downloading and streaming have to be considered as an answer by the neglected to the neglecting.

This is further emphasized by the activities of Czech fan/media subcultures. Since the early 2000s, the most active audience members organized themselves into multiple interrelated knowledge communities that have developed their own grassroots strategies to substitute for the absence of an actual active presence of strong strategic actors in the online market for audiovisual content. They create their own translated subtitles for films and series, and they share them with other viewers through specialized Web sites (such as Titulky.com) or through general download servers. Or they directly create localized versions of audiovisual files with Czech subtitles embedded in the picture and, again, share them online via download services (e.g., Uloz.to). Moreover, responding to the lack of domestic information resources on current film and series productions, they have initiated a number of community projects (eventually even professionalized projects, such as Edna) systematically aggregating information about new titles and news from the entertainment industry. And although all that is practiced by a very small portion of the most engaged viewers, it has shaped the viewing habits of the majority of Czech convergent audiences, because they enabled the ordinary audience members to be actually convergent and to watch current international film and TV productions despite the apparent lack of interest of official content distributors to make it available for them.

14.6 Conclusion

Small-market audiences are as fluid and changeable as any other audience—and as are the major international and local content distributors' strategies and the trends in technological development. With Netflix, HBO Go and other VOD providers finally focusing on systematic localization of content, even the Czech convergent audiences will probably soon shift from downloading and streaming from non-authorized sources and the picture of their specifics drawing on data from current research will become obsolete. Nevertheless, more important for this chapter than to draw a temporal map of the specifics of particular small-market audiences is to suggest an applicable conceptual framework enabling us to assess basically any convergent audience—and, at the same time, to grasp empirically any potential specifics that might emerge across various types of current or future audiences.

The concepts of uses genres and media ensembles can play this role. As an alternative to the currently dominant notion of media repertoires, these two conceptual tools come with an explicit and intrinsic sensibility for the fact that media-related practices are structured both by the contexts of everyday life, and by broader contexts represented in cases of small-market audiences by the global market actors and their (dis)interests. This, along with their primary focus on situated practices instead of on technological tools, provides the concepts of uses genres and media ensemble with the ability to follow the ongoing changes in audience behavior not only with an emphasis on what is new but also with necessary respect to continuity of the analyzed agency—continuity in audience members' needs and motivations, in the role of watching audiovisual content in the structuring of everyday lives, and in audiences' aims to turn commodities into a vivid popular culture.

Acknowledgements This study was supported by the Technology Agency of the Czech Republic project "Research on the Impact of Current Legislation and the European Commission's Strategy for Digital Single Market on Czech Audiovisual Industry: Evaluation of the Copyright System and Preparation of Cultural Politics within the DSM" (No. TL01000306).

References

Bakardjieva, M. (2005). *Internet society: The internet in everyday life*. London: Sage.

Bakardjieva, M., & Smith, R. (2001). The internet in everyday life: Computer networking from the standpoint of the domestic user. *New Media & Society, 3*(1), 67–83.

Berger, P. L., & Luckmann, T. (1991). *The social construction of reality: A treatise in the sociology of knowledge*. London: Penguin.

de Certeau, M. (1984). *The practice of everyday life*. Berkeley: University of California Press.

Ferguson, D. A., & Perse, E. M. (1993). Media and audience influences on channel repertoire. *Journal of Broadcasting & Electronic Media, 37*(1), 31–47.

Fiske, J. (2010). *Understanding popular culture*. London: Routledge.

Haddon, L. (2006). Empirical studies using the domestication framework. In T. Berker, M. Hartmann, Y. Punie, & K. J. Ward (Eds.), *Domestication of media and technology* (pp. 103–122). Maidenhead: Open University Press.

Hasebrink, U., & Popp, J. (2006). Media repertoires as a result of selective media use: A conceptual approach to the analysis of patterns of exposure. *Communications, 31*(3), 369–387.

Jansová, I., Macek, J., Macková, A., & Žádník, Š. (2019). *Analýza podmínek pohybu českých spotřebitelů mezi zdroji s legálně a nelegálně šířeným audiovizuálním obsahem*. Brno: Masaryk University.

Jenkins, H. (2006). *Convergence culture: Where old and new media collide*. New York: New York University Press.

Kim, S. J. (2016). A repertoire approach to cross-platform media use behavior. *New Media & Society, 18*(3), 353–372.

Livingstone, S. (2007). On the material and the symbolic: Silverstone's double articulation of research traditions in new media studies. *New Media & Society, 9*(1), 16–24.

Lotz, A. (2007). *The television will be revolutionized*. New York: NYU Press.

Macek, J. (2015). *Média v pohybu: K proměně současných českých publik*. Brno: Masaryk University.

Macek, J. (2017). Traditional and convergent domestic audiences: Towards a typology of the transforming Czech viewership of films and TV series. *Iluminace, 29*(2), 7–24.

Macek, J., Macková, A., Škařupová, K., & Císařová, L. W. (2015). *Old and new media in everyday life of the Czech audiences*. Brno: Masaryk University.

Macek, J., & Zahrádka, P. (2016). Online piracy and the transformation of the audiences' practices: The case of the Czech republic. In D. H. Hick & R. Schmücker (Eds.), *The aesthetics and ethics of copying* (pp. 335–358). London: Bloomsbury.

Mouffe, C. (2005). *On the political*. London: Routledge.

Jakub Macek is Associate Professor of media studies, Masaryk University, Brno, Czech Republic. His research interests include the roles of new media in the transformation of current audiences and in political and civic participation. He was previously a member of VITOVIN, an interdisciplinary research project on the Internet and new users (2012–2015). Recently, he led the postdoctoral research project "New and Old Media in Everyday Life: Media Audiences at the Time of Transforming Media Uses" (2013–2015) and worked as a researcher at CATCH-EyoU, a Horizon 2020 project (2015–2018).

Part V
Audiovisual Policy and the Future of Copyright Economy

Chapter 15
Compensation Systems for Online Use

Christian Handke

15.1 Introduction

Digitization—the increasing application of digital information and communication technology (ICT) for a variety of purposes—has great potential to strengthen the productivity of cultural industries and to foster users' access to a vast stock of cultural and creative works. However, digitization also puts into question traded modes of rewarding those who invest in creativity. For the cultural industries, one of the major lessons of the past two decades has been that it is hard to enforce exclusive rights online. Fundamental economic reasoning implies that without clearly defined quasi-property rights, private enterprises in markets will fail to provide a socially adequate amount of new, valuable copyright works. Thus, digitization appears to raise the stakes of the underproduction-underutilization trade-off (Novos and Waldman 1984) that is at the heart of copyright in the economic perspective. The challenge is to provide sufficient incentives to those capable of creating valuable works, while not restricting access to users, or at least to strike a reasonable compromise where these two objectives are irreconcilable.

The traditional lever used (or not) by policymakers to approximate a widely acceptable solution has been copyright enforcement. The results have been mixed at best (Handke 2016). Unauthorized digital copying remains rampant and measures to enforce copyright are contentious. This chapter discusses an alternative to copyright

This chapter is based on joint work with Bodo Balazs, Joao-Pedro Quintais and Joan-Josep Vallbe at the Institute of Information Law, University of Amsterdam and financed by the Netherlands Organization for Scientific Research (NWO) from 2013 to 2015. Sections of this chapter also draw on a German-language report by the author for the German Federal Ministry of Justice and Consumer Protection (Handke 2016). The author gratefully acknowledges constructive comments from the editors on earlier drafts, which helped to improve the chapter. All mistakes are the sole responsibility of the author.

C. Handke (✉)
Erasmus University Rotterdam, Burgemeester Oudlaan 50, Rotterdam, The Netherlands
e-mail: handke@eshcc.eur.nl

© The Author(s) 2020
P. Szczepanik et al. (eds.), *Digital Peripheries*, Springer Series in Media Industries,
https://doi.org/10.1007/978-3-030-44850-9_15

261

enforcement: copyright compensation systems (CCS), which (a) provide end users with legal certainty when using widely available online resources to access and use creative works, in return for (b) a surcharge on Internet subscription, the receipts of which are disseminated among rightsholders. In a recent study on the Netherlands, Handke et al. (2016) demonstrated the potential of CCS to make markets for music recordings much more efficient. This chapter argues that CCS hold great promise in particular for cultural industries in what in this volume is referred to as countries in the "digital peripheries": Central and Eastern European (CEE) countries that were part of the Warsaw Pact and have now acceded to the European Union.

As usual, technological change and digitization have ambiguous effects. With fewer technical restrictions, it is often easier for people in small communities or remote locations to access and even actively participate in cultural life. On the other hand, so-called platform capitalism means that the dissemination of culture is run by a handful of multinational corporations, usually operating from large and highly developed economies, who do not necessarily have strong incentives to pay little attention to the specific needs of the populations of smaller countries. This chapter argues that well-designed CCS could make a major contribution to avert some of the risks associated with digitization and globalization for cultural industries in CEE countries.

15.2   The Basic Economics of Copyrights

To discuss CCS, a reiteration of the basic economic reasoning behind copyrights is merited here (for a more comprehensive treatment, see the chapter by Stepan in this volume). Copyright systems stipulate exclusive rights regarding creative works and thus enable conventional market transactions. In a nutshell, an effective copyright system endows rightsholders with exclusive control over who can use protected works. Since creative works tend to be imperfect substitutes for each other, rightsholders of valuable works enjoy some market power: They can sell copies or licenses for prices in excess of marginal costs, which may enable them to recover the initial costs of creation and even to incur profits, encouraging further investments in creativity. Higher prices are disadvantageous for potential users. What is more, markets for copyrighted works are complex—with many and highly differentiated works and great variety in consumers' preferences—and there are substantial transaction costs in operating these markets. Nevertheless, proponents of effective copyright protection argue that even most users will be better off in the long run. The question is whether the discounted future value of additional works created due to copyright exceeds the immediate drawbacks of higher prices and transaction costs (Handke 2017).

An important extension of this analysis is that there is no clear boundary between creators and users. Most creators draw on prior creations so that strong copyright protection not only fosters rewards for creators but also increases the costs of creativity (Landes and Posner 1989). Current creators must acquire licenses or work around the claims of the rightsholders of existing copyrighted works. This insight also applies to new ways of disseminating copyright works or other complementary goods and services, such as online subscription services: powerful rightsholders may appropriate much of the value of new related goods and services and exert centralized control, undermining pecuniary incentives to develop new means of making works accessible and usable (Handke 2015).

Overall, this economic analysis entails a number of important yet not entirely obvious insights regarding copyright policy. First, for a normative assessment, the effects of copyright on rightsholder revenues are not decisive, but the effects on innovation and the supply of creative works are. Second, it is not a given that stronger copyright protection always fosters creativity. Third, the optimal level of copyright protection varies with changing market conditions. Fourth, pure theorizing does not yield a general justification of copyright. More technically speaking, copyright protection is not Pareto optimal in the sense that it would make some stakeholders better off without leaving any worse off.[1] Like most public regulation, copyright does not bring us close to an optimal state as envisaged in perfectly competitive markets according to the Paretian welfare economics. That any policy aimed at improving the cultural industries fails to do so is a moot point. Instead, copyright and its alternatives need to be evaluated in comparison to their best real-world alternatives. The question is not whether any of the options is perfect, but which appears to be the best under current circumstances and to the best of our knowledge. To make that call, up-to-date empirical evidence is required.

Finally, there are three alternative means to ensure adequate rewards to those investing in creativity in the presence of digital copying technology:

First, consider so-called business model solutions: Private enterprises could develop strategies that entice users to pay for access to content or to contribute to the costs of creation in spite of the possibility of accessing creative works from unauthorized sources (an excellent overview of options is found in Varian 2005). Most promising in this respect seem to be Internet platforms that either finance themselves through advertisements (e.g., YouTube or the free version of Spotify) or that charge subscription fees to users (e.g., Spotify Prime or Netflix). The main issue with these Internet platforms is that they are subject to vast economies of scale and scope, as well as network effects. They thus tend to give rise to narrow oligopolies or quasi-monopolies. The productive efficiency of large firms (low average costs) entails the problem of centralized control and market power.[2]

Second, there is copyright enforcement, which falls into four types according to two aspects (cf. Danaher et al. 2013): On the one hand, enforcement can be directed at either private end consumers or at commercial enterprises disseminating works online without proper licenses from rightsholders; on the other, enforcement can be conducted by private agents—in particular rightsholders or their representatives—or

---

[1] Think, for instance, of individuals with a low life expectancy and thus a low discounted future value of any creative works to be generated in the future.

[2] Crowdfunding is another business solution, where potential creators seek to attract financial contributions from a broad public before finalizing production.

by public agencies. There is widespread dissatisfaction with any means to enforce copyrights (Handke 2016). This is not for lack of trying. Suppliers of creative works and public authorities have experimented with various methods to enforce copyrights in the digital realm. Technical protection measures (TPM) have aimed at preventing unauthorized copying or access to content. Other actions have included injunctions against firms whose goods and/or services are related to copyright infringements, cease and desist notices to firms or private households and notice and takedown requests directed at online platforms for hosting allegedly infringing content. However, according to the empirical literature, the methods tested so far have often been inefficient and commonly conflict with other objectives, such as privacy and freedom of speech (see Handke 2016 for a summary).

The third option is CCS, which do not rely on any enforcement of exclusive rights and case-by-case licensing, but on revenues from surcharges on more excludable goods and services (copying hardware and telecommunication services), to be distributed among rightsholders according to the metrics of use. This chapter focuses on this latter option.

15.3 Copyright Compensation Systems (CCS)

As stated above, CCS have two definitive characteristics: First, they raise revenues for rightsholders/creators from a surcharge on Internet subscriptions. Second, they provide end users with legal certainty when accessing and using creative works online. As such, CCS essentially extend the existing system of so-called copying levies to cover Internet access.

The first copying levy was introduced in Germany in 1966, and it applied to audiotapes and compact cassettes. The idea was to avoid the costs of fighting unauthorized copying on the level of millions of private households and instead raise revenues for rightsholders associated with copying. By now, copying levies are in place in virtually all European countries, as well as other major economies such as the USA and Canada, and over time, they tend to apply to new copying technologies (WIPO 2017). In major economies throughout the EU and North America, surcharges were applied to many copying technologies that became widely available in the late twentieth century, subject to territories; for instance, to music cassettes and players, to photocopiers and scanners, to CD/DVDs and burners, and more recently even personal computers and smartphones. Notable exceptions are some types of (built-in) computer memory, Internet access and "cloud" external memory services, as these have many applications other than to reproduce copyrighted works and—so the argument goes—it would seem unfair to charge all users for potential unauthorized copying. See WIPO (2017) for an overview, including the Czech Republic, Hungary, Latvia, Lithuania, Poland, Slovakia and Slovenia, among many others.

With the diffusion of peer-to-peer file sharing around the turn of the millennium, several legal scholars called for CCS (Lunney 2001; Ku 2002; Netanel 2003; Fisher 2004; Eckersley 2004; see Handke et al. 2018 for an overview). Nevertheless, to this day, there are virtually no applications of CCS. Internet access and "cloud" external memory services remain out of the scope of copying levies. No CCS has been introduced that would allow Internet users against a fee to download (or even upload) copyrighted works without specific authorization by the rightsholders.

15.3.1 The Reasoning Behind CCS

Copying levies circumvent a major problem with copyrights: it is costly to enforce copyrights on the level of a myriad of individual households or in informal parts of the economy. These costs accrue not only in resources but also in terms of privacy infringements, as copyright enforcement requires monitoring. Levies can do away with the need to monitor private behavior by shifting liability and payment to sales of excludable goods and services that are often used for unauthorized copying.

To comprehend the major advantages of CCS, an application of transaction cost economics is useful. The concept of "transaction costs" refers to all costs of conducting economic exchanges: search costs to identify potential trading partners, bargaining costs to establish mutually acceptable terms of trade, monitoring costs to establish whether trading partners stick to an agreement and enforcement costs to fight behavior that infringes on the terms of a trade. Where the full economic value—in terms of money but also the time and effort required—of transaction costs exceeds the value of a transaction, deals that would otherwise be mutually beneficial do not come about. All potential trading partners lose out. In the cultural industries, this can be a huge problem. Markets for cultural works are very complex. On the supply side, there are many different suppliers and many different works supplied. On the demand side, there are many users that appreciate diversity in the works they have access to—virtually everyone prefers access to several musical works, films or books during any month or year, for instance. With a vast number of different cultural products available, the willingness to pay (and incur transaction costs) for specific works is typically modest. What is more, the marginal costs of supplying additional users are very low, so that rightsholders could benefit from selling at low prices to at least some users. Thus, many potential transactions that would make both creators/rightsholders and users better off are averted by transaction costs in cultural industries. This has important implications for cultural diversity. Due to the inefficiency introduced by transaction costs, it is not worthwhile to even create many cultural products that would be supplied in a theoretically feasible, more efficient market without transaction costs. Works catering to smaller and less wealthy communities (say works in Czech or Latvian) are particularly susceptible to this problem.

The conventional means to lower transaction costs are standardization and bundling of transactions. There are many related practices in cultural industries. For instance, within their scope of activities, copyright management organizations (CMOs) such as GEMA and ASCAP operate as national monopolies and offer blanket licenses to near-comprehensive repertoires of works. Spotify and Netflix offer subscriptions to a vast bundle of works based on a single payment and a single contract, and they do not vary pricing on the user side subject to the intensity or diversity of use per subscriber. However, for any works not available within such a bundle, the situation may deteriorate. Users are left with a choice between staying within a bundle to which they have already acquired access and incurring additional transaction costs and prices if they venture beyond. Whatever is in a bundle becomes more competitive relative to anything outside of it. One could speak of a new type of digital divide between that which is featured or promoted on the major platforms and that which is not. CCS that establish standards for the use of anything found online for those who make a single payment would avoid much of that problem and could thus come to benefit cultural diversity.

That said, the effects of CCS are ambiguous. Copying levies will almost inevitably mean that users of goods to which a levy applies, who have little interest in unauthorized copying, are worse off. Another way to put this is that any non-copyright infringing users of copying technology are made to finance goods and services (copyrighted works) in which they have no interest.

The main objection to CCS raised by economists is that CCS would introduce standardized prices and terms of use, thus reducing the scope for private bargaining and contracting, hindering market mechanisms (Liebowitz 2003, 2005; Merges 2004; Liebowitz and Watt 2006). Handke et al. (2016, 2018) and therefore suggest voluntary participation on the user side. Then, the participation of users would provide information on-demand conditions and would guide pricing decisions and the setting of other terms associated with CCS.

Another concern with CCS is that some organization would have to be in charge of setting terms, collecting revenues and distributing them among members. These are the typical functions of copyright management organizations (CMOs, also known as copyright collectives). For an introduction to the economics of CMOs, see Handke and Towse (2008) and Handke (2014). CMOs have mixed reputations and as large, quasi-monopolies under more or less intense public regulation, they may be subject to inertia and protracted decision-making. Reasonably efficient CCS would require reasonably low operating costs of CMOs and that levies would be distributed among rightsholders according to some rather precise metric of actual use and valuation by consumers. Randomized monitoring of user behavior online could accomplish this.

It follows from this that copying levies are hardly Pareto optimal; levies do not make some stakeholders better off without putting others at a disadvantage. However, neither is copyright enforcement, as argued above. In comparison with real-world alternatives (more or less copyright enforcement), the question is whether copying levies pass the Hicks-Kaldor compensation test: Are those who gain from a levy so much better off that they would be willing to fully compensate those who lose?[3]

Furthermore, CCS relate to the emergence of Internet platforms for the dissemination of copyrighted works and their potential market power, beyond the argument

---

[3] According to standard welfare economics, it is not required that the winners actually compensate the losers. The value of their benefits just has to exceed the value of the losses for others.

developed above regarding the problems of marketing works outside of large, attractive bundles. In recent years, Internet platforms such as Spotify, Amazon, Steam and Netflix have accounted for a steadily growing share of the total markets for recorded music, books, video games and linear audiovisual entertainment (e.g., movies and television programs). Exploiting economies of scale and network effects, these firms have acquired large market shares and many worry about the market power of these multinational, profit-oriented enterprises. In contrast to CMOs, regulation of these new central agents in the cultural industries remains limited. There is considerable worry that market failure will result. Dominant Internet platforms could acquire market power and set standard prices and terms in their favor. They could collude with major rightsholders. They could also neglect smaller national markets, as it may be more cost-efficient for them to focus on major productions in large economies and sell productions suitable for international/global markets rather than dealing with a multitude of producers and productions in smaller markets. CCS could counter some of these threats by setting transparent, universally applicable standards for any enterprise disseminating copyrighted works online. With no fixed costs of licensing for such enterprises, as long as they comply with the CCS regulations on reporting the use of works on their sites, online platforms would ideally compete over who can provide the most efficient access to an attractive repertoire. There would thus be greater scope for smaller platforms specialized in domestic productions in CEE countries, too. In essence, CCS are a means to make markets for e-commerce more contestable, and to steer platforms to compete based on user services rather than on licensing strategies on the rightsholder side.

Finally, let us consider the current debate on Articles 11 and 13 in the prospective new EU Directive on Copyright in the Single Digital European Market[4]: If online platforms were to report usage data to a trusted CMO, and revenues from a copying levy would flow back to rightsholders according to that data, neither more extensive licensing of copyrights for derivative use online nor upload filters might be required. The contested Articles 11 and 13 could be revised accordingly, or perhaps even abandoned altogether.

15.3.2   The Empirical Evidence

The limited empirical evidence so far regards the USA and Western European countries and suggests that CCS could make rightsholders and users at large much better off than current markets. In a user survey conducted in the USA and Germany, Karaganis and Renkema (2012) established that about half of all inhabitants were willing to pay more than 15 Euros or dollars per month (Karaganis and Renkema 2012:

---

[4]These two articles of the Directive have different numbers in the final version of the document. We stick to the outdated numbering here, as the original numbers have been widely used in a very extensive public debate.

56–58). They referenced a number of other studies on the topic with similar results, many which are no longer available, however.

The most ambitious empirical study so far was by Handke et al. (2016). The data were produced using a specific survey technique—a discrete choice experiment using conjoint analysis—which is considered to be the most effective way to establish the value of goods or services when no data from actual markets is available (Arrow et al. 1993; Bateman et al. 2002). The authors concluded that, at least for recorded music, well-designed CCS could simultaneously make rightsholders and users much better off. This applies in particular to CCS that users could opt-out of, so that some market coordination would remain. The authors emphasized the uncertainty of survey-based data, but argued that as far as this type of data goes, the indicators regarding CCS could hardly be more positive. They thus recommended experimental adoption.

15.4 Copyright Compensation Systems in the Context of CEE Countries

Much research on copyright, digital copying and various ways of financing creativity has focused on highly developed North American and West European countries—for instance the USA, Germany, France and Italy. In comparison, many CEE countries such as the Czech Republic, Hungary, Poland, Slovakia and Slovenia share a number of characteristics that affect their domestic cultural industries.

First and foremost, these countries are comprised of small populations with relatively low average incomes by EU standards. Small domestic markets with distinct languages mean that domestic cultural industries catering to their home markets cannot exploit economies of scale and network effects to the same extent as firms in larger countries. Cultural industries in CEE nations are thus even more vulnerable to competition from abroad than cultural industries in EU Member States with larger economies. The integration of markets within the EU and globally thus threatens to inhibit the domestic production of creative content. A single digital market in the EU might even aggravate the situation, and so could the commercial decisions of large, multinational retailers of cultural products, if they were to focus on the most promising content and avoid the additional costs of actively fostering the presence of niche content in their operations. Where a broad range of creative works is available with virtually no cross-border barriers—due to technology or regulation—works with high production values could sideline domestic productions from smaller markets even more. Adequate CCS could safeguard the accessibility of culture, as well as the production of works catering to smaller communities.

Another issue concerns pricing. With relatively low average household disposable incomes and relatively high inequality in some CEE countries compared to major EU economies, many households cannot afford to spend great amounts on cultural and entertainment goods and services. Without regulatory restrictions, commercial Internet platforms will set profit-maximizing prices. They will set relatively high prices, focusing on high-value customers, thus de facto excluding many East-Central Europeans, or leaving them with illegitimate methods as the only affordable way of accessing many creative works. In such circumstances, commercial supply does not respond to the interest of large parts of the population, and the rule of law is undermined. CCS could mitigate these problems by reducing transaction costs. The prices of copying levies and CCS tend to be set domestically, often under extensive regulation from national governmental authorities and reflecting the conditions of domestic inhabitants. Governments would thus have a means at their disposal to ensure broader access to culture than unregulated markets would bring about. Therefore, CCS are particularly promising in CEE countries.

The main counterargument that applies to many CEE countries regards the quality of regulation and administration. To fully exploit the potential of CCS to reduce transaction costs and for domestic prices to reflect the majority of the population's ability to pay, one reasonably efficient organization is required to collect and distribute CCS revenues to rightsholders. Existing CMOs in countries such as the Netherlands, Germany and throughout Scandinavia are quite efficient, with operating costs lower than 10% even in the relatively costly business of monitoring use and collecting revenues from traditional, offline markets. In other parts of Europe, this is not always the case. Existing CMOs differ widely in terms of their efficiency (Rochelandet 2003). A central question for CCS is thus whether reasonably efficient CMOs can be established. However, the argument regarding the general quality of governmental services and oversight of markets cuts both ways: with low-quality regulation more generally—say, relatively ineffective anti-trust regulation or inhibition of corruption—commercial solutions generated by private businesses in markets prone to market power will not tend to reflect the public interest, either.

Furthermore, CCS could contribute to cultural policy in CEE countries. Many CMOs operate cultural deductions, where a share of CMO revenues from copying levies and other income is not distributed according to metrics of use but according to prerogatives of cultural policy. Such "social and cultural deductions" are already in place, for instance, in the Baltic states, Hungary and Poland (WIPO 2017: 14–15). A broader application of copying levies with cultural deductions could help sustain a critical level of high-quality domestic production.

In addition, many CEE countries have highly educated populations. Skillful and educated people have the potential to fully exploit opportunities for active participation in culture, for instance by creating user-generated content. The use of CCS could allow for that with minimal legal risks and may even generate pecuniary rewards for those who generate valuable content without the desire or means to operate in conventional markets, which involves the burden of obtaining conventional licensing (i.e., transaction costs).

Last but not least, CCS have implications for suppliers of related goods and services. Surcharges on Internet access, Internet services or computer hardware raise the prices of these products. Since the implementation of CCS would reduce transaction costs and thus make creative content available at lower costs, they would not necessarily conflict with digitization, however. Ideally, CCS could even foster demand for related goods and services, as they mean that attractive creative content is available for users of these related goods and services under transparent terms and with minimal legal risks. To achieve that outcome, the amount of surcharges would have to be set at a reasonably efficient level. What is more, with lower fixed costs of licensing, greater competition between Internet platforms could come to benefit users.

Overall, the specific situations of CEE countries mean that CCS are particularly promising in these countries. To be sure, CCS entail difficult compromises, like any means of organizing cultural industries, in order to strike a reasonable balance between rewarding those who invest in creativity, and placing minimal restrictions on access and participation in culture by users. Nevertheless, well-designed CCS are an option to safeguard and promote domestic culture especially in the "digital peripheries," where market failure is likely to be particularly grievous.

15.5 Conclusions

This chapter has discussed the pros and cons of CCS under some admittedly generic assumptions regarding the situation in CEE countries. Overall, it argues that CCS could foster cultural industries and access to culture, where markets seem to fail.

In essence, CCS are simply levy systems, extending the practice of copying levies in many major economies. Similar to existing levies for copying hardware, CCS entail a surcharge for Internet subscription, with the receipts being distributed among rightsholders according to some measure of the use of specific copyrighted works. The basic idea is not to enforce exclusive (copy) rights among private households but rather to compensate rightsholders for unauthorized use online. Arguably, CCS could be used in CEE countries to better achieve several objectives:

- To avoid market conditions in which many low-income households do not benefit from legal access to creative works online due to high prices. Achieving this could also reduce illegitimate dissemination of works and ensure that the preferences of low-income households influence decisions in cultural industries and in firms disseminating creative works online.
- To foster cultural diversity and the potential for niche productions by setting universal standards for online use of creative works and the compensation of creators, even for types of works neglected by multinational corporations;
- To finance cultural policy in a reasonably efficient manner based on cultural deductions of CCS revenues;
- To exploit the opportunities of digitization for skillful individuals to actively participate in culture, to generate value for themselves and others with minimal organizational costs and legal risks and even the potential for pecuniary rewards for the most successful suppliers of user-generated content.

However, CCS do require some effective CMOs and may require a great deal of political capital to resist multinationals operating in the cultural industries. It may also be hard to convince suppliers of goods and services, to which a CCS surcharge would apply, that their commercial interests would not be unduly harmed. Furthermore, there are restrictions on interventionist national policies within the EU and the framework of international free trade agreements. That said, copying levies are already common practice throughout major economies so that CCS would not require revolutionary change. Furthermore, diverse cultural industries operating throughout the EU are essential to sustain cultural diversity and national identities in Europe. CCS could help ensure that digitization is harnessed to foster diversity and to keep those at the "digital peripheries" at the table, better than copyright enforcement or unregulated markets will. It is high time that policymakers explore this option by extending the system of copying levies, and CEE countries are especially likely to benefit.

References

Arrow, K., et al. (1993). *Report of the NOAA panel on contingent valuation.* Washington, DC: National Oceanic and Atmospheric Administration.

Bateman, J. I., et al (Eds.). (2002). *Economic valuation with stated preference techniques: A manual.* Cheltenham: Edward Elgar.

Danaher, B., Smith, M. D., & Telang, R. (2013). *Piracy and copyright enforcement mechanisms.* Working paper no. 19150. Cambridge, MA: National Bureau of Economic Research.

Eckersley, P. (2004). Virtual markets for virtual goods: The mirror image of digital copyright? *Harvard Journal of Law and Technology, 18*(1), 85–166.

Fisher, W. W. (2004). *Promises to keep: Technology, law, and the future of entertainment.* Stanford: Stanford University Press.

Handke, C., & Towse, R. (2008). Economics of copyright collecting societies. *International Review of Intellectual Property and Competition Law, 38*(8), 937–957.

Handke, C. (2014). The economics of collective copyright management. In R. Watt (Ed.), *Handbook of the economics of copyright* (pp. 179–204). Cheltenham: Edward Elgar.

Handke, C. (2015). Digitization and competition in copyright industries: One step forward and two steps back? *Homo Oeconomicus, 32*(2), 209–236.

Handke, C. (2016). Urhebervergütung im digitalen Zeitalter: Der internationale Forschungsstand. Report for the German Federal Ministry of Justice and Consumer Protection. https://www.bmjv.de/SharedDocs/Downloads/DE/Service/StudienUntersuchungenFachbuecher/Studie_Urheberrecht_digitales_Zeitalter_1.pdf?__blob=publicationFile&v=2. Accessed November 11, 2019.

Handke, C. (2017). Intellectual property in the creative industries: The economic perspective. In A. Brown & C. Waelde (Eds.), *Research handbook on intellectual property and creative industries* (pp. 57–78). Cheltenham: Edward Elgar.

Handke, C., Bodó, B., & Vallbé, J.-J. (2016). Going means trouble and staying makes it double: The value of licensing recorded music online. *Journal of Cultural Economics, 40*(3), 227–259.

Handke, C., Quintais, J., & Bodó, B. (2018). Truce in the copyright war? The economics of copyright compensation systems for digital use. *Review of Economic Research on Copyright Issues, 15*(2), 23–56.

Karaganis, J., & Renkema, L. (2012). *Copy culture in the US and Germany.* New York: The American Assembly.

Ku, R. S. R. (2002). The creative destruction of copyright: Napster and the new economics of digital technology. *University of Chicago Law Review, 69*, 263–324.

Landes, W. M., & Posner, R. A. (1989). An economic analysis of copyright law. *Journal of Legal Studies, 18*(2), 325–363.

Liebowitz, S. J. (2003). Alternative copyright systems: The problems with a compulsory license. University of Texas at Dallas. https://www.utdallas.edu/~liebowit/intprop/complpff.pdf. Accessed November 11, 2019.

Liebowitz, S. J. (2005). MP3s and copyright collectives: A cure worse than the disease? In L. Takeyama, W. J. Gordon, & R. Towse (Eds.), *Developments in the economics of copyright: Research and analysis* (pp. 37–59). Cheltenham: Edward Elgar.

Liebowitz, S. J., & Watt, R. (2006). How to best ensure the remuneration for creators in the market for music? Copyright and its alternatives. *Journal of Economic Surveys, 20*(4), 513–545.

Lunney, G. S. (2001). The death of copyright: Digital technology, private copying, and the digital millennium copyright act. *Virginia Law Review, 87*, 813–920.

Merges, R. P. (2004). Compulsory licensing vs. the three "golden oldies": Property rights, contracts, and markets. *Policy Analysis, 508*, January 15. https://www.cato.org/sites/cato.org/files/pubs/pdf/pa508.pdf. Accessed November 11, 2019.

Netanel, N. W. (2003). Impose a noncommercial use levy to allow free peer-to-peer file sharing. *Harvard Journal of Law and Technology, 17*, 2–84.

Novos, I. E., & Waldman, M. (1984). The effects of increased copyright protection: An analytic approach. *Journal of Political Economy, 92*(2), 236–246.

Rochelandet, F. (2003). Are copyright collecting societies efficient? An evaluation of collective administration of copyright in Europe. In W. J. Gordon & R. Watt (Eds.), *The economics of copyright: developments in research and analysis* (pp. 176–198). Cheltenham: Edward Elgar.

Varian, H. R. (2005). Copying and copyright. *Journal of Economic Perspectives, 19*, 121–138.

WIPO. (2017). International Survey on private Copying: Law and practice 2016. World Intellectual Property Organization. https://www.wipo.int/edocs/pubdocs/en/wipo_pub_1037_2017.pdf. Accessed 11 November 2019.

Christian Handke is Associate Professor of cultural economics, Erasmus University Rotterdam. He has served as Program Coordinator of the highly ranked master's degree program in Cultural Economics and Entrepreneurship. His research focuses on cultural economics and the economics of copyright, innovation and technological change, and the record industry. He has contributed to leading specialized journals in the field, including *Information Economics & Policy* and the *Journal of Cultural Economics*. He has also consulted for a variety of public and private organizations, including the European Commission, the National Academy of Sciences (USA), Industry Canada, the UK Intellectual Property Office, the Commission of Experts for Research and Innovation (EFI) (Germany) and Fundación Autor (Spain).

Chapter 16
Sync That Tune! The Role of Collective Management of Rights in Film Production and Distribution

Rudolf Leška

16.1 Introduction

In many countries, the practice of collective bargaining between authors and users is older than copyright. The modern predecessor of collective management organizations (CMOs) was a group of dramatic authors led by Beaumarchais and informally organized in 1777 which "unionized" in 1791 under the name *Bureau de législation dramatique*—following the enactment of the first French Copyright Act of 1791 (Nérisson 2015: 176–177).

Nevertheless, outside France copyright was managed for a long time mostly individually until the late nineteenth century. In simple one-to-one relationships between authors and their publishers, it was an easy undertaking. Publishers initially did not have to engage in licensing of the works to other parties as they were mostly using them by themselves. This changed once the exclusive right of the author to the *public performance* of the work was recognized. In France, this happened in the landmark case of Bourget v. Morel (Cour d'Appel de Paris, 1849) (Albinsson 2014); in the Habsburg monarchy, this was enacted for the first time in 1841.[1] While licensing drama or opera for theatrical performances (so-called *grand rights*) might not be difficult due to the limited number of performed works, licensing the right of public performance to variety establishments, dance halls, restaurants, etc. (so-called *small rights* or *petits droits*) poses challenges to the licensing process. Users need a blanket license to a significant amount of musical works to amuse their clients. In copyright jargon and in this study, the term *user* means a person who communicates the work to the public or who is otherwise engaged in dissemination or multiplication of the work; that is, who *uses* the work. Note that from this perspective, a person who

---

[1] Kanzleidekret vom 15. Mai 1841 [Decree of the Chancery dated May 15, 1841] Nr. 537 J.G.S. [Justizgesetzsammlung].

R. Leška (✉)
University of Finance and Administration, Estonská 500, 101 00 Prague, Czech Republic
e-mail: leska@mail.vsfs.cz

© The Author(s) 2020   273
P. Szczepanik et al. (eds.), *Digital Peripheries*, Springer Series in Media Industries,
https://doi.org/10.1007/978-3-030-44850-9_16

simply *consumes* the work by watching it, reading it, listening to it or purchasing a copy of it is not considered a user.

Historically, musical authors (lyricists and composers) and their publishers joined their efforts to get paid a royalty for public performances and established the first CMO in the field of music rights—SACEM[2]—to protect their collective interests and engage in collective bargaining (Nérisson 2015: 177). This organization continues to operate to this day as the world's biggest CMO. Importantly, it also enabled the users to get a license easily and allowed for effective joint administration of copyright in a vast quantity of works. In other words, it helped to reduce transaction costs (Albinsson 2012).

Composers and lyricists have been successful in pursuing collective management of their rights in nearly every area of licensing (except for the printing and distribution of sheet music which remained the exclusive territory of publishing houses). Other authors and performing artists[3] are (generally speaking) collectively represented only for uses where the nature of such use does not allow for individual negotiation of a license at all (such as retransmission by other organizations than the original broadcaster, certain public performances, such as in hotels, restaurants and similar establishments, collection of just remuneration for private copying, etc.).

This development is analogous to the unionization of workers. But no matter how important this achievement was, it also created challenges for today's film distribution. A film producer usually clears all rights and retains exclusive licenses or is assigned the copyright to the film itself, as well as to all works and performances synchronized with the picture of the film (utilized in the film). This, however, is not the case for music. Long-established licensing practices of the music industry generally do not allow the film producer a one-time "buy out" of the copyright for music and the underlying sound recording,[4] including the rights of performing artists whose performances are embodied in the recording.

In this study, we will examine how collective management works in film, or, more broadly, in audiovisual production and distribution, and analyze the ability of collective management in music to respond to the demand for innovative film distribution and transaction costs related to music licensing.

---

[2]Société des auteurs, compositeurs et éditeurs de musique.

[3]The rights of performing artists, even if recognized in the case law of various countries since the early twentieth century, were not collectively administered in Europe until the second half of the last century. Cf. Leška (2019b).

[4]I am using the technical term *phonogram* and the US term *sound recording*, considered informal in the European milieu, interchangeably.

16.2 Peculiarities of Traditional Music Licensing in Audiovisual Production and Distribution

Music has always been crucial for filmmakers. Already in the silent era, films were designed to be performed with music and music has remained an essential element for cinematographic enjoyment (Cohen 2011). Thus, if a producer decides to make a film, having to deal with music is inevitable. It is a matter of course that a film cannot be used without the proper authorization to use the music involved, unless the musical material is from the public domain.[5]

As mentioned, while a film producer usually holds a bundle of rights in and to the film (and protected subject matter included in the film), music is an exception. Technically speaking, the music itself consists of the following three components:

- Underlying composition and, if any, text (lyrics, libretto, etc.);
- The artistic performance by performing artists (musicians, singers, narrators, conductor, choirmaster, as the case may be);
- The phonogram (sound recording).

At the moment of *production*, depending on the jurisdiction where protection is sought,[6] some or all of the following rights might be affected:

- The economic (property) right of reproduction (the protected subject matter needs to be copied to be included in the film, including copies made in the course of production)—in the licensing practice, this and synchronization are together referred to as "mechanical rights";
- The right of synchronization, i.e., synchronization of music to a motion picture[7];
- Moral rights of authors;
- Moral rights of performers.

Once the film is produced, the subsequent *distribution* usually affects all other property rights: reproduction or mechanical rights when copies of the film are made and "performance rights," known in the World Intellectual Property Organization (WIPO) and EU documents as "communication to the public." Moral rights might be also affected depending on how the distribution is done—e.g., an interruption of the broadcast by advertising might be considered harmful to the reputation of the author,

---

[5]And, as will be noted, on the global market even the simple question whether a musical work or a sound recording belongs to the public domain is often difficult to answer.

[6]In intellectual property law, the conflict-of-laws principle of *lex loci protectionis* finds its application in most national laws. In fact, I am not aware of any jurisdiction which would not follow this principle. This means that the laws of the country where IP protection is claimed by the rightsholder apply and that the claim is assessed under these laws. While this usually does not cause any problems in offline use, global online use brings new challenges to this traditional legal principle, as will be shown below.

[7]The right of synchronization (i.e., the act of incorporating music into a film) is not recognized on the international level by any of the copyright-related agreements, but it nevertheless is written into the national laws of most developed nations, sometimes only through case law, such as in the USA. Cf. 1 Melville B. Nimmer, David Nimmer, *Nimmer on Copyright* § 2.09[A] (2007).

touching upon his moral right of integrity (again, depending on the jurisdiction). As all of the above-mentioned rights are cleared differently, the case is already quite complex in an offline world even without digital distribution which brings additional challenges.

16.2.1 Licensing Author's Rights

Since the licensing of the author's rights (copyright) of the composer and lyricist has a long tradition—as old as cinema itself—the licensing situation is relatively more straightforward than with the other rights that we will deal with later.

Rights in the composition (so-called "music publishing rights") include mechanical and performance rights. The film producer usually deals only with certain mechanical rights while the performance rights are cleared through a performance rights organization (PRO). Performance rights organization is a collective management organization in charge of licensing performance rights.[8]

16.2.1.1 Mechanical Rights (Right of Reproduction and Synchronization)

If making copies of a film is necessary, the user of the film needs to deal with mechanical rights. This covers not only DVD distribution, but also situations in which copies are made for the broadcasting of the film by the broadcaster or the online offer of the film on a VOD platform—the user may clear these rights through a mechanical rights organization.

As the nature of mechanical rights dictates, these are only cleared in the country where the copy is made. During the production, this is usually the country of the producer's domicile where the film production takes place, or, to be very specific, where the post-production is done because it is usually in the course of post-production when music is copied and synchronized with the picture.

There are generally several possible licensing scenarios, depending on whether or not the author is represented by a CMO and whether the author has a deal with a music publisher. Since almost all authors of music and text and their publishers are represented by a CMO, *most* of the rights are licensed through a CMO. Although the rightsholders are usually represented by a CMO only in their home country, the global network of reciprocal agreements of authors' societies associated within CISAC[9] allows any other sister organization to license these rights on behalf of foreign authors. If an author or his publisher (to whom distribution rights were

---

[8] In some countries, like the UK and USA, mechanical and performance rights are licensed through different entities or CMOs, while in others, mostly in continental Europe, music CMOs license mechanical as well as performance rights.

[9] CISAC, the International Confederation of Authors and Composers Societies (Confédération Internationale des Sociétés d'Auteurs et Compositeurs), is an international organization associating

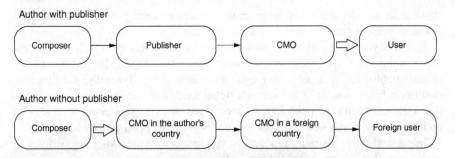

Fig. 16.1 Flow of rights from the author (composer) to the user

assigned or exclusively licensed) is not represented by a CMO, all rights to the composition are licensed by the author/publisher directly to the film producer, not only for the mere production of the film, but also for its distribution. This makes it clear why composers and lyricists (and publishers) prefer to be represented by a CMO—instead of a lump sum payoff for their rights by the producer, they will enjoy recurring royalties from every use of the film which, when aggregated, usually generates far higher income than an upfront lump sum payment ever would. Thus, direct licensing by CMOs to individual users brings to authors more remuneration but also higher transaction costs; on the other hand, the transaction costs are distributed among many players and for individual users are not high, particularly if done by blanket licensing as on the TV market (Fig. 16.1).

Even if there is a CMO representing the rights in the composition, there are traditional exceptions to collective administration of rights, such as the use of sheet music (print rights), theatrical rights known as grand rights (use in live theater) and the synchronization right. While the former two are out of our purview, the latter is important. Unless the rightsholder appoints a CMO to administer the synchronization right, which rarely happens, the producer needs to seek synchronization approval directly from the publisher or, if there is no publisher, the author. This allows the publisher or the author to better monetize the value of the synchronized music in accordance with the nature of the audiovisual work, be it a film or advertisement. Unlike in the case of collective management, the rightsholder is not bound to any published tariff and can negotiate their price freely. In some countries, such as the Czech Republic[10] and Slovakia (Kabošová 2019), the practice is to license synchronization rights for television broadcasters' in-house productions (for their use) through CMOs. This practice benefits the broadcasters who do not have to worry

---

authors' CMOs around the world. Importantly, it does not associate CMOs operating in the field of rights related to copyright.

[10]Cf. 2019 tariff for broadcasters and retransmitters published by Collective Rights Management Society for Musical Works (OSA 2019).

about using popular music in their programs (except for third-party advertisements[11] where individual granting of rights is still needed).

Practically speaking, the film producer checks with local music CMO to assess which rights the CMO can grant and which must be licensed directly by authors or their publishers, if a publishing agreement is in place. Typically, the film producer concludes—as far as the author's rights are concerned—only a synchronization agreement with the publisher. As mentioned, such an agreement is concluded on individually negotiated terms and not under the tariff published by a CMO.

Importantly, the licensing practice of synchronization licensing has evolved in such a way that the music publisher usually—besides granting the synchronization license—makes the provision of license conditional and prohibits certain forms of distribution of the film. Under these terms, the producer usually agrees—in exchange for lower synchronization remuneration—*to not distribute the film* in certain territories (such as the USA) or to disallow the exploitation of certain rights (e.g., distribution in cinemas). Depending on the construction of the contract, the producer either has to pay an additional fee (agreed in advance) for broader distribution than initially intended, or to renegotiate additional remuneration under new terms. These contractual conditions go beyond statutory copyright protection because the right to synchronize is legally consumed once the synchronized reproduction is made and this act cannot be repeated, but the law is not settled on this issue. It is disputed whether non-compliance with the synchronization terms constitutes copyright infringement or "merely" a producer's breach of contract.[12] Exceptionally, the film producer or broadcaster might be forced to change the entire soundtrack due to prohibitively expensive additional synchronization fees associated with extended distribution.

It depends on local practice whether a producer needs to have a mechanical license from a CMO in addition to the synchronization license, or whether this is cleared together with the synchronization right negotiated directly with the publisher.

16.2.1.2 Moral Rights

An intriguing issue relates to the exercise of the moral rights of authors. In certain jurisdictions with the tradition of author's rights (*droit d'auteur*), strong moral rights give authors the possibility to prevent certain uses which might be derogatory to their work or reputation. Depending on local laws, this can include the right to prevent

---

[11]Other exceptions, such as musical movies, might be applicable as well, depending on the practice of individual CMOs; few of these exceptions are harmonized globally.

[12]In Czechia, the High Court of Prague has ruled that DVD distribution of a film which exceeds contractual conditions agreed between the original producer (Czech Television in this case) and the provider of the synchronization license (OSA, a Czech CMO) infringes the synchronization right (unpublished decision in the case Radomíra Muchová vs. BONTONFILM a.s., File No. 5Co 15/2018 dated November 21, 2018). In my opinion, the court's interpretation is wrong. The case has not yet been closed, as the High Court remanded the case for a retrial. An extraordinary appeal to the Supreme Court will be possible after the new trial and a likely appeal.

some or any changes[13] to the work, such as colorization,[14] or the interruption of the film with commercial breaks.[15] In some countries, the act of synchronization is considered to be an exercise of moral rights rather than exercise of property rights as its nature lies in connecting a new work (the film) with preexisting musical work which might be ultimately a matter of taste for the composer in deciding how the music is associated with a specific film or scene.[16]

From the user's point of view, the tricky issue with moral rights is that they can only be exercised personally by the author and usually cannot be assigned, licensed or waived; furthermore, in some jurisdictions (e.g., France or Czechia) they are granted for perpetuity (exercised posthumously by the author's spouse or offspring).[17] But the physical distance between, say, a Slovak commercial broadcaster and a French author's offspring might prove too excessive for the user to seek individual permission for the interrupting of a broadcast by advertisements. In jurisdictions in which synchronization is considered to be a moral right which cannot be licensed, the authors grant in practice power of attorney to the publisher, allowing the publisher to exercise moral rights on the author's behalf. To date, there are no precedents establishing whether or not moral rights can be exercised by an attorney. For the sake of argument, it is assumed here that delegation to an attorney is possible.

It should be noted that the licensing process is substantially the same regardless of whether the producer commissions original music or not. If the author (or publisher) is represented by a CMO, the producer does not clear rights in music distribution with the author; instead, users do so with the respective CMOs (see the chart above).[18]

It is a prevailing worldwide practice that publishers and authors (composers and lyricists) share the proceeds from collective rights management equally—a practice which is usually incorporated in the distribution plans of CMOs. A concentrated

---

[13] For example, Czech law prohibits *any* changes of the work without the author's consent. The only exception is if a licensee is making minor changes which the author must under the circumstances justifiably bear; the author may even reserve such right in the contract.

[14] Cf. a French case over the broadcast of a colorized version of *The Asphalt Jungle*: Turner Entertainment Co. v. Huston, CA Versailles, Civ. Ch., No. 68, Roll 615/92 (1994), No. 16; reprinted in English: 10 ENT. L. REP. 3 (1995). Another case comes from Italy: Zinnemann v. TV Internazionale, Trib. Rome 2005 (concerning the colorization of the film *The Seventh Cross*). French and Italian courts found colorization to infringe the moral rights of the author, even if the user had a license to use the films. A similar outcome can be expected in the case of adapting music to a film without the author's consent.

[15] French and Swedish courts found it infringing to interrupt a broadcast without the author's consent; this agrees with the practice of DILIA, the CMO representing film directors in the Czech Republic. Cf. Paris Court of Appeal, November 26, 1990, Images Juridiques, January 15, 1991; Supreme Court of Sweden [Högsta domstolen], NJA [Nytt Juridiskt Arkiv] 2008, p. 308.

[16] In Czechia, the legal doctrine underwent a major shift from the original approach, in which many scholars considered synchronization right [§ 62(2) of the Czech Copyright Act] to be a moral right, to the current approach according to which most agree that it is actually a property right.

[17] Moral rights are inheritable, but in many countries they can be exercised—to certain degree—by the author's descendants (not the legal heirs).

[18] In practice, the users sometimes force authors to opt out from collective management and grant the license directly to them.

effort by competition authorities in Europe led to a loosening of this longstanding tradition for the sake of increasing competition, to the detriment of authors.

The practice of CMOs which divide the proceeds between authors and publishers has led some broadcasters to operate as music publishers as well, asking music authors to enter into publishing deals with them when commissioning music for their productions. This new practice, harmful to the standard operation of the system, has in rare exceptions also been adopted by some film producers because it allows them to get a share of the music royalties back from the film distribution if they become represented by a CMO.

16.2.2   Licensing Rights Related to Copyright (Neighboring Rights)

By rights related to copyright, or simply "related rights", I mean a variety of rights different from authors' rights but generally based on the same principles (informal protection of certain expressions). The term "related rights" is the preferred language of the international treaties and the WIPO and hence is used in this chapter instead of "neighboring rights". In the Anglo-American context, the term copyright includes both, authors' rights and related rights, which is why I try to avoid this term here in order not to blur the borders between both categories.

Related rights traditionally include the rights of performing artists and phonogram producers, but in many countries, especially in Europe, this umbrella also covers other subject matter (rights of broadcasting organizations[19] and event organizers, rights in unpublished works where the authors' rights have expired, rights of press publishers, rights of producers of audiovisual recordings, etc.). Their scope, duration and recognition differ significantly from country to country, and international harmonization is less developed than in the case of the author's rights.[20] Even in the European Union, only certain related rights are harmonized, while the Member States are free to introduce other intellectual property rights.

Considering the situation in EU countries, the use of music in film production always involves a sound recording (phonogram) and musical performances embodied therein. The film producer thus always has two options: either to record the music (soundtrack) by his own means or to obtain the rights to use an existing recording.

---

[19]Obligatory minimum rights for broadcasters in the European Union are guaranteed by the Rental and Lending Directive.

[20]International treaties, such as the Rome Convention, The Agreement on Trade-Related Aspects of Intellectual Property Rights (TRIPS), WPPT and the Beijing Treaty on Audiovisual Performances (BTAP), cover only the rights of performing artists, phonogram producers and broadcasting organizations.

16.2.2.1 Film Producer as a Phonogram Owner

In the first case, the producer contractually clears the rights with performing artists by way of an assignment or license and becomes the owner of the rights of the phonogram[21] producer (these rights are imprecisely referred to in the licensing jargon as "master rights"). Many film producers also dispose of a significant amount of sound recordings to which they own the phonogram producers' rights, which allows them to be represented by a CMO administering the rights of phonogram producers and to earn profits from the use of the phonogram (including the use of the phonogram in the film).

While the phonogram producer's rights are fully assignable anywhere in the world, this is not always the case with performers' rights. This might make cross-border trade troublesome. Performers' rights in certain European jurisdictions, mostly in central Europe,[22] are not assignable. Under the long-established principles of copyright territoriality, the individual countries recognize only such agreements which are in accordance with local rules on assignability (even if the contract itself is governed by foreign law). In other words, the assignment of rights, unlike a license, would be most likely unenforceable in jurisdictions that do not allow for such assignment. Foreign assignees (producers) often lack this information and might end up concluding agreements that do not provide them the worldwide rights clearance they might have hoped for. More sophisticated contracts address this issue by combining the assignment with an exclusive license (activated in case the assignment is void or unenforceable).

16.2.2.2 Film Producer as a Licensee

The second option is to acquire an existing license instead of investing in a new recording. Unlike the author's rights ("publishing rights"), these rights are usually *not* collectively administered. In other words, they are collectively administered only to a more limited extent and are usually cleared individually under negotiated business terms, which mean that the phonogram producer (the record label in this case) clears most of the rights with the performing artists. The label is then able to license the phonogram rights bundled with rights to artistic performances. Therefore, if a film producer seeks authorization to use a phonogram in a film, he or she needs to negotiate only with the record label who grants to the film producer not only the mechanical and synchronization license to use the phonogram with performances for the film production but also a license for the consecutive use of the film with a synchronized phonogram to the extent demanded by the film producer.

---

[21]Legally speaking, a phonogram is immaterial subject matter protected by the law; the term is sometime used interchangeably, but imprecisely, with the US term "sound recording".

[22]For example, Germany, Austria, Czechia and Slovakia.

16.2.2.3 Single Equitable Remuneration for Performers and Phonogram Producers

The collective administration of rights in phonograms and performances typically covers areas with mandatory and extended collective management, such as fair compensation for private copying, rental and lending rights or retransmission of a broadcast. In addition, countries that are signatories to the Rome Convention[23] or the WIPO Performances and Phonograms Treaty (WPPT)[24] are required to introduce *at least*[25] a system of so-called *single equitable remuneration*, which some countries rightly made subject to mandatory collective management. The understanding of the meaning of single equitable remuneration among the signatory countries is not entirely settled, but it can be said that "single" does not mean a one-time lump sum payment but rather a payment for *every* "single" use of the phonogram (Reinbothe and von Lewinski 2015: 396). While in some countries the concept cannot be put into practice outside of the system of (possibly mandatory) collective management, others leave it to collective bargaining between the stakeholders or opt for a grant of exclusive rights to performers and producers.[26] It is, of course, important for the film producer to understand where the use of the phonogram (with performances) is subject to mandatory collective administration of the remuneration system.[27] Such rights *cannot be cleared* individually by the film producer. It will be subject to rights clearance between the user (typically the broadcaster) and the respective CMO administering the rights of phonogram producers and performing artists. The most typical example is the regulation of *broadcasting*. Many countries have opted for mandatory or extended collective management of commercial recordings used in broadcasting to ease the burden on the broadcaster (both radio and TV broadcasters) who consequently does not have to negotiate individually with record labels[28] and can clear the rights under a blanket license for a royalty negotiated with the CMO or set by governmental tariff as the case may be.

Needless to say, the whole system of equitable remuneration from TV broadcasting of phonograms synchronized with films is at stake in Europe at the time of going

---

[23] Rome Convention for the Protection of Performers, Producers of Phonograms and Broadcasting Organizations (1961).

[24] WIPO Performances and Phonograms Treaty (1996).

[25] The remuneration right is considered to be a minimal right. Countries are free to adopt stricter protection by granting exclusive rights to producers and performers. Cf. Reinbothe and von Lewinski (2015: 395).

[26] Although exclusive (property) rights are considered a stricter form of protection than remuneration rights, for the performers this might not be true as they are often forced to assign or grant their rights for a lump sum payment without any right to a later royalty from the actual use of their performances (as is the case under the remuneration right scheme).

[27] This is the case in Czechia.

[28] For the system to operate smoothly, it is beneficial if the synchronization right for the broadcaster's own productions is also collectively administered. Where the broadcaster has to negotiate synchronization deals individually (e.g., in the UK or Hungary), the broadcaster's administrative and clearance costs remain high.

to press, with a pending case before the Court of Justice of the European Union.[29] In that case, the broadcaster argues that once the phonogram is synchronized with the film, it ceases to be a phonogram (it is "amalgamated" to the audiovisual recording) and no equitable remuneration is due from the TV broadcast of such a film.[30]

The system of single equitable remuneration is closely linked to the concept of the *phonogram published for commercial purposes* ("commercial recording"), which was first introduced by the Rome Convention in 1961. Under the convention, phonograms that are intended for public distribution (published on media available for purchase) are deemed "commercial recordings." The intent of the drafters was clearly not to include recordings made by the broadcasters themselves (if made for their own broadcast and not for public distribution), but many questions remain open.[31] In any case, the concept was originally meant to serve primarily radio broadcasters who were able to buy phonograms freely available on the market and then use them in their broadcasting under a blanket license without bearing the burden of negotiating an individual broadcasting license, while at the same time the phonogram producers and the artists got a guarantee of remuneration. The purposefully chosen neutral language was from the beginning meant to cover television broadcasting. The emergence of online distribution of music made it one of the key points of the WIPO Internet Treaties.[32] The WPPT has enlarged the concept to include not only phonograms published on physical media but also phonograms made available to the public online (in such a way that members of the public may access them from a place and at a time individually chosen by them). Under this broad definition, every phonogram—except those produced for internal purposes or the purposes of film, radio and TV production (i.e., not intended for divulgation online or on physical media as a separate soundtrack)—is considered a "commercial recording."[33]

The WPPT broadened the concept of single equitable remuneration to include not only broadcasting but any communication aimed at the public, which includes the making-available right for *on-demand* online use. The diverging national laws

---

[29]Pending case C-147/19, Atresmedia Corpración de Medios de Comunicación, S.A. v. AGEDI and AIE.

[30]I find this opinion clearly wrong as it does not respect the traditional rule that more layers of rights can exist next to each other (e.g., audiovisual recording, the film, the rights of performers, the rights of the author of the original novel, etc.), but the outcome at the Court of Justice is uncertain.

[31]For example, whether the commercial recording must be available to consumers or whether availability for purchase in B2B relations is sufficient to consider a phonogram to be a "commercial recording".

[32]WCT and WPPT, the outcome of WIPO's 1990s digital agenda, are referred to as the Internet Treaties.

[33]One disputed issue is whether recordings offered by so-called production music libraries should be considered "commercial recordings"; nevertheless, prevailing practice considers them to be commercial recordings as they fulfill the definition, unless such recordings are delivered to the customer in an individual and closed B2B communication, such as via a private FTP server. The advantage of production music libraries for users lies in the fact that the operator of the library bundles together the rights of authors, performers and phonogram producers (publishing and master rights), thereby easing the burden of negotiation for synchronization with the publisher and record label.

bring more uncertainties for the film producer who purchases a license for the use of a phonogram without knowing which rights in which territories are actually covered. Rights under the mandatory collective management or mandatory remuneration scheme cannot be granted by the phonogram producer and are subject to national laws. Thus, it is the ultimate user (typically the broadcaster) who has to pay for the phonogram producer's and performers' rights.

16.2.2.4 International Relations in the Field of Related Rights

The issue of licensing related rights becomes even more intricate once we start examining the international aspects. As mentioned earlier, there is less harmonization at the international level than in the case of the author's rights; many countries, including the EU Member States, adopted modern related rights legislation as late as the 1990s. When the European Community adopted the 1992 Rental and Lending Rights Directive,[34] only three EC members were granting exclusive rights to performers (as did Czechoslovakia and some other countries) (Leška 2019b). The last twenty or thirty years, during which exclusive rights for phonogram producers and performers have developed (even less in developing countries), were not sufficient for the establishment of a global network of CMOs—today there remain different CMOs in the fields of performers' rights and phonogram producers' rights. In other words, there is a lack of a coherent system of reciprocal agreements, as is the case with authors' rights. Furthermore, as the range of rights is different and the minimal rights guaranteed by the international treaties are narrower (and even these treaties allow signatories to establish significant reservations),[35] numerous loopholes exist in reciprocal agreements in the field of related rights.

Not only is there an insufficient network of reciprocal agreements, but the protection of phonograms is also not universally accepted and not every country recognizes the rights of foreign phonogram producers or performers unless international treaties require them to do so. The treaties have their own points of attachment.[36]

Signatories to the Rome Convention recognize: (a) the rights to phonograms of nationals from another convention country; or (b) produced in a convention country; or first published[37] in a convention country.[38] Importantly, if a phonogram is

---

[34] Council Directive 92/100/EEC of November 19, 1992, on rental right and lending right and on certain rights related to copyright in the field of intellectual property. It was replaced by Directive 2006/115/EC.

[35] The most prominent example is the USA, which grants the right of public communication and broadcasting of phonograms and performances only for digital uses (such as simulcasting and webcasting) and in its national laws excludes traditional broadcasting and communication in business establishments from the rights of phonogram producers and performers.

[36] Articles 4 and 5 of the Rome Convention, Article 3 of WPPT.

[37] The Rome Convention defines publication as the offering of tangible copies of a phonogram to the public.

[38] The contracting party may, however, include a reservation to not apply the criterion of publication or the criterion of fixation to a phonogram. Points of attachment for performers refer to the place

published in a non-convention country, it is protected in the convention countries provided that the simultaneous publication occurs within thirty days.[39] The USA is not a signatory to the Rome Convention, but this rule allows US record labels to receive protection in Rome Convention countries through simultaneous publication in Europe (typically the UK).[40]

Under the WPPT, signatories are obliged to recognize—with certain explicitly listed exceptions[41]—the mutual rights of the nationals of another WPPT signatory country who are defined as performers (phonogram producers) and who meet the criteria for eligibility under the Rome Convention.

The consequence for the film producer is that the mere question of whether the phonogram he or she is purchasing for the film is protected in the countries for which he or she acquires the license is a *difficult one*.[42] It is not uncommon in practice that the phonogram (performers') rights are cleared for territories or uses for which there is no need to do so, while they are not cleared where necessary, especially in the field of new media (see Sect. 16.3).

16.3 Licensing Online Film Distribution

While licensing in the offline realm is certain, or at least fairly predictable, in particular when it comes to licensing music for film distribution with CMOs, the online sphere poses more challenges to traditional licensing schemes. The crucial conflict is between the ubiquitous nature of the World Wide Web and the mandates of CMOs, which remain largely territorial.

16.3.1 Rights Affected

Services like video on demand, broadcasters' catch-up services and previews, Internet Protocol Television (IPTV), network personal video recorder (NPVR), time-shifted

---

where the performance takes place or whether the performance is fixed on a phonogram protected under the convention or is part of a broadcast protected under the convention.

[39] Art. 5(2) of the Rome Convention.

[40] Nevertheless, the Rome Convention permits reservations in this regard allowing the signatories not to protect phonograms from non-convention countries which are simultaneously published in the convention country.

[41] That is why other WPPT countries may, but do not have to, provide protection to US phonograms if they are broadcasted in their territory.

[42] As an example: any pre-1972 US recordings, including the oldest historical recordings, might continue to be protected by various US state laws until 2067 (!), while any pre-1963 or pre-1965 recordings are in the public domain in the EU and Canada, respectively.

retransmission, simulcasting, webcasting, etc., all require different licenses or licensing practices. The main difference lies in the legal distinction between three forms of distribution:

- Linear television broadcasting (usually under extended collective management of music and mandatory collective management of commercial recordings);
- Retransmission (usually under mandatory collective management);
- Nonlinear (on-demand) online services (usually under facultative collective management of music and direct licensing of sound recordings).

Once territoriality is factored in, the resulting situation becomes extraordinarily complicated as a separate license is generally required for every territory where the service is available.[43]

Linear television broadcasting, even in the online environment, is licensed in the same way as traditional broadcasting. From the copyright perspective, it is irrelevant whether it takes the form of simulcasting or webcasting. This means that where a country maintains a mandatory scheme of single equitable remuneration for phonograms, it also covers simulcasting and webcasting—but only for the territory of the specific country, forcing broadcasters to implement geoblocking measures. The revised SatCab Directive[44] tried to alleviate this problem at least within the EU single market, but failed to do so. The directive introduces the legal fiction that the use of a TV program[45] occurs only in the EU Member State of the broadcaster's principal establishment *unless* the parties to a license contract otherwise. This covers the simulcasting of programs (but not webcasting) and broadcasters' catch-up services. The directive expects that the parties will agree on *appropriate* remuneration which takes into account the availability of the service. Even if the CMOs expect each other's sister organizations to charge remuneration equal to a sum of 27 national tariffs,[46] such pricing would be prohibitive for the provision of such services. As a result, the broadcasting industry itself seems to insist on contractual clauses for mandatory geoblocking in exchange for a lower license fee. Ironically, the broadcasters themselves ask CMOs to include a geoblocking clause in the license agreement to avoid being charged fees for broader territory.

In the field of musical works, simulcasting and broadcasters' catch-up services are expressly excluded from multi-territorial licensing under the CRM Directive,[47]

---

[43] According to the Bogsch Theory, which is supported by court decisions. Cf. Ricketson (1987, 442–452).

[44] Directive (EU) 2019/789 of April 17, 2019, laying down rules on the exercise of copyright and related rights applicable to certain online transmissions of broadcasting organisations and retransmissions of television and radio programmes, and amending Council Directive 93/83/EEC.

[45] Only news and current affairs programs and fully financed in-house productions of the broadcasting organization (except sports events).

[46] It is unclear how these proceeds should be distributed among rightsholders. Is the licensing CMO obliged to distribute the proceeds to rightsholders abroad if—legally speaking—the use occurred only in the Member State where the CMO is established?

[47] Art. 32 of the Directive 2014/26/EU of February 26, 2014, on collective management of copyright and related rights and multi-territorial licensing of rights in musical works for online use in

and broadcasters must rely on the minimal rights provided by the SatCab Directive. If a broadcaster wishes to simulcast other programs or to simulcast globally (outside of the EU) without geoblocking, infringement in at least some territories is nearly unavoidable.

Retransmission taking place in a managed environment online (IPTV) is usually licensed under a mandatory collective management scheme,[48] which means that the rights cannot be licensed individually. However, if a producer enters into a contract licensing certain retransmission rights, such a contract would be unenforceable in most European jurisdictions because, under mandatory collective management, the rightsholder cannot dispose of the rights by himself.

Nonlinear (on-demand) online services are licensed in the field of music under facultative collective management (i.e., only on behalf of contractually represented authors) while in the field of phonograms (and performances embodied therein) such services are usually licensed directly by record labels, but exceptions exist.[49] Again, the problem with territoriality remains, because generally, the use takes place in every country where the service is available,[50] which means the user either seeks a multi-territorial license or adopts geoblocking technology. A user who does neither may be liable for copyright infringement.

Unfortunately for lawyers, the services are often combined. Consider a retransmission service such as Skylink. The linear retransmission must be licensed through a mandatory collective management scheme in every country where the service is available, while the ancillary nonlinear services for customers, such as NPVR or time-shifted retransmission (meaning the customer can rewind the retransmitted program), must be licensed directly with the film producers and record labels.[51] No wonder that such licenses are often missing and the users infringe the rights and risk litigation (or even criminal liability) to avoid complicated negotiation with rightsholders. A similar decision-making matrix applies to Hybrid Broadcast Broadband (HbbTV) services combining linear and nonlinear delivery of works.

16.3.2 Global Licensing Arrangements

The rightsholders are well aware of the difficulty of licensing music for online use, and since the 1990s, there have been various private initiatives trying to tackle the

---

the internal market. It is not clear why the directive regulated only authors' rights and not also phonograms when it comes to multi-territorial licensing.

[48] In the EU, such a scheme is for good reasons imposed by Art. 4 of the revised SatCab Directive.

[49] A typical exception is the licensing of catch-up and preview services to broadcasters through CMOs.

[50] One minor exception for the subscription services arises out of the Portability Regulation, Regulation (EU) 2017/1128 of June 14, 2017, on cross-border portability of online content services in the internal market. This exception applies to simulcasting as well, if the service is portable.

[51] In the case of music, the broad mandate of the music CMOs allows them to license music for such ancillary services without any additional burden.

problem.[52] The Santiago Agreement[53] of 2000, an ambitious multi-territorial licensing framework for a global license (also used for music in films) initiated by the International Confederation of Authors and Composers Societies (CISAC) and based on the existing system of reciprocal agreements, failed due to a political decision of the EU Commissioner Prodi that pushed CISAC to abandon the multi-territorial license system (the Commission considered this a restraint of trade in breach of competition rules due to the obligation to license through a CMO established in the country of the licensee's residence).

The International Federation of the Phonographic Industry (IFPI)[54] developed a similar system for licensing simulcasting, webcasting and on-demand offerings of audio and audiovisual programs, but its practical utilization remains limited due to the lack of an analogous system for licensing artistic performances (without rights in which the phonogram itself cannot be used).

This has led to the development of new business models of supranational licensing hubs often owned by CMOs and rightsholders alike, such as SOLAR,[55] PEDL,[56] ICE,[57] Mint Digital Services[58] and ARMONIA,[59] not always offering favorable terms to small users or authors. The outcome is the undesirable fragmentation of the license. While it was previously fragmented by territory, now it is fragmented by repertoire (whereby different publishers license through different entities which then provide pan-European licenses). Although these licensing hubs were originally designed for music services, some of them have been involved in licensing music for VOD services. Thus, platforms in Europe must deal with an increasing number of rightsholders and CMOs to get the license for their VOD services unless the platform wishes to stick to the repertoire of one or a few music publishers (which for films is not possible as the used film music is out of the platform's control).

Thus, the licensing of music and phonograms, in particular in the online arena, is now connected with higher transaction costs than before. The EU Commission, which did not allow private schemes to develop, is now trying to solve this problem through regulations such as the revised SatCab Directive and the CRM Directive but so far without any visible success.

---

[52] I have analyzed the historical development of and current situation in global licensing deals and licensing hubs in the field of music in Leška (2019a).

[53] Reprinted in Spada (2006).

[54] The International Federation of the Phonographic Industry is an association of major record labels; in many countries, local IFPI chapters act as CMOs in the field of phonogram producers' rights.

[55] Run by SOLAR Music Rights Management Ltd., cf. www.celas.eu.

[56] Pan-European Digital Licensing.

[57] A joint venture between PRS for Music (UK), STIM (Sweden) and GEMA (Germany).

[58] A joint venture between SESAC (USA) and SUISA (Switzerland).

[59] Associating AKM (Austria), SPAUTORES (Portugal), SUISA (Switzerland), SABAM (Belgium), ARTISJUS (Hungary), SACEM (France), SACEM (Luxembourg), SIAE (Italy) and SGAE (Spain).

16.4   The Ultimate Task: Simplifying Rights Clearance, Standardizing the Procedures

It is broadly acknowledged in the industry that it is almost impossible to clear all rights in the course of the production of a film. Not only must users deal with CMOs to get their mechanical or performing licenses to use the music, but the varied practices in the licensing of related (neighboring) rights and the fact that moral rights differ substantially from one jurisdiction to another cause some legal uncertainty—even in the offline world. Once we add the layer of global online use, the situation becomes a nearly impenetrable thicket of rights and rightsholders.

What has been achieved in the field of "offline" authors' rights over a period of decades—a settled and largely standardized way of licensing—needs to be achieved also in the field of related rights, in particular in the online arena. This needs to be done quickly, as much time has been lost in Europe due to questionable steps taken by the European Commission. There are contractual solutions that can be used, but they need the rather radical and proactive involvement of global organizations such as CISAC, SCAPR,[60] IFPI, PMA[61] and WIN,[62] who must work together on viable and efficient solutions to set an industry standard for easy and comprehensive licensing and reciprocal agreements.

The problem of complicated rights clearance of music and sound recordings is particularly pressing in the fragmented small European markets, each of which has its own established practices and where the costs of legal advice and know-how might exceed proceeds from distribution.

Yet, we must differentiate between situations where the complicated procedure of rights clearance is caused by flawed laws and where it is an expression of different cultural practices around the globe. The cultural autonomy of nations, big or small, requires that no global practice be imposed upon them without regard for their own traditions—for instance in their attitude toward the moral rights of authors and performers.[63]

References

Albinsson, S. (2012). The advent of performing rights in Europe. *Music and Politics, 6*(2), 1–22.
Albinsson, S. (2014). A costly glass of water: The Bourget v. Morel case in Parisian Courts 1847–1849. *Swedish Journal of Music Research, 96*(2), 59–70.

---

[60]The Societies' Council for the Collective Management of Performers' Rights associates national CMOs in the field of performers' rights.

[61]The Production Music Association associates production music libraries.

[62]The Worldwide Independent Network associates national independent record labels' associations.

[63]This paper was written as part of the junior project "Transformations of Individual and Collective Copyright Management" made possible by institutional support for long-term conceptual development of research at the University of Finance and Administration.

Cohen, A. J. (2011). Music as a source of emotion in film. In P. N. Juslin & J. Sloboda (Eds.), *Handbook of music and emotion: Theory, research, applications* (pp. 249–272). Oxford: Oxford University Press.

Kabošová, S. M. (2019). Úskalia synchronizácie. *Filmová hudba*. https://www.filmovahudba.eu/?page=abeceda-producenta/uskalia-syn&lng=sk. Accessed August 18, 2019.

Leška, R. (2019a). Globalization of collective rights management and the role of National CMOs. In T. E. Synodinou (Ed.), *Pluralism or universalism in international copyright law* (pp. 95–114). Alphen aan den Rijn: Kluwer Law International.

Leška, R. (2019b). Performers' rights: A Central European export. In M. T. Sundara Rajan (Ed.), *Cambridge handbook of intellectual property in central and Eastern Europe* (pp. 222–237). Cambridge: Cambridge University Press.

Nérisson, S. (2015). Collective management of copyright in France. In D. Gervais (Ed.), *Collective management of copyright and related rights* (pp. 175–204). Alphen aan den Rijn: Kluwer Law International.

OSA. (2019). Sazebník autorských odměn za vysílání a přenos vysílání 2019. https://www.osa.cz/storage/DownloadTranslation/1-2000/18-attachment-Sazebnik-OSA-Vysilani-a-prenos-2019.pdf. Accessed August 18, 2019.

Reinbothe, J., & von Lewinski, S. (2015). *The WIPO treaties on copyright: A commentary on the WCT, the WPPT, and the BTAP*. Oxford: Oxford University Press.

Ricketson, S. (1987). *The Berne convention for the protection of literary and artistic works: 1886–1986*. London: Wolters Kluwer.

Schwemer, S. F. (2019). *Licensing and access to content in the European Union*. Cambridge: Cambridge University Press.

Spada, P. (Eds.). (2006). *Gestione collettiva dell'offerta e della domanda di prodotti culturali*. Milano: Giuffrè.

Rudolf Leška is active as Attorney-Partner at the copyright boutique firm Štaidl Leška Advokáti, licensed in Czechia and Slovakia and representing the entertainment industry and advising other private clients and the public sector with media- and copyright-related transactions and litigation. Dr. Leška serves as current President of ALAI Czech Republic and is Senior Assistant Professor in media and copyright law at the University of Finance and Administration in Prague with academic research focused on theater law, collective management, moral rights and the rights of performing artists. He is an associated research fellow at the Palacký University Olomouc in the arts and creative industries research projects.

Chapter 17
Small Country, Complex Film Policy: The Case of the Czech Film Funding System

Petr Bilík

17.1 Cultural Policy as a Dispute Between Two Concepts

The cultural policy of the Czech Republic after 1989, when public administration once again became an ideological battlefield, is a locus of permanent conflict between two forces pulling in fundamentally different directions that cannot be firmly grasped in the common right–left perception of politics. The basic dispute is about the concept of the definition of public goods—the main question being, how much of a particular cultural good is needed in a society and what to do if the market fails to provide it?—and the finding of a boundary that defines the range of influence of the state and the determination of the necessity of state intervention, whether in terms of support for or regulation of specific social spheres. While the care of thousands of listed buildings or the preservation of a vast network of public libraries, which are typical for the Czech Republic and unique in the European context, has been considered a priority by all post-socialist Czech governments and under all circumstances, many other cultural sectors (e.g., theater, dance and fine art) must repeatedly strive for attention (Nekolný 2006). One of the most interesting examples, interpreted quite differently from both poles of political philosophy, is cinema, which has an extraordinary degree of dependence on public funds and institutional background.

P. Bilík (✉)
Department of Theater and Film Studies, Faculty of Arts, Palacký University, Křížkovského 10, 771 47 Olomouc, Czech Republic
e-mail: petr.bilik@upol.cz

© The Author(s) 2020
P. Szczepanik et al. (eds.), *Digital Peripheries*, Springer Series in Media Industries,
https://doi.org/10.1007/978-3-030-44850-9_17

17.2 Development of Film Policies and Funding Schemes After 1989

In the Czech environment, the interpretation of how film should be supported by the state has been influenced by several factors with historical roots. The exclusive position of film was mainly due to the following factors:

- A strong cinematic tradition established at the end of the nineteenth century;
- A developed film production sector with an average of around 30 full-length feature films per year;
- A complex system of state-supported film economy under a centralized state management;
- An extraordinary network of cinema theaters offering around 2000 cinemas to the 10 million inhabitants of the Czech regions in 1989 (Central Film Rental Institute 1990: 3–10);
- Production facilities, especially at Barrandov Studios in Prague[1];
- The iconic "Czech New Wave" movies of the 1960s and the tradition of animated cinema.

As a result of this heritage, film was considered by the majority of the stakeholders in the cultural domain (especially the audience, the politicians and, of course, the filmmakers) to be a privileged part of national culture, which must be developed as a part of the state's cultural policy. This interpretation was mainly held by filmmakers whose career culminated in the 1960s (e.g., Věra Chytilová, Jiří Krejčík).

Already at the very beginning of the transformation in 1989, the concept of film as a cultural and social necessity was rejected by a major part of the political spectrum adhering to neoliberal economic principles, according to which film should be approached as mainly a commercial good, whose production and distribution should follow the standard mechanisms of supply and demand. The view that the role of the state should be minimized was held, inter alia, by Pavel Tigrid, Minister of Culture and a famous writer.

Both these political streams were symbolically represented by prominent figures in the public sphere: While the neoliberal economic view was represented by the Minister of Finance, the Prime Minister and later President Václav Klaus, his opponent was, in particular, the Minister of Culture Pavel Dostál, who was inspired by the French model of supporting national culture and cinema and, more concretely, influenced by Jack Lang's socialist policy (Colin 2000). After the fall of the state film system,[2] the wing headed by Pavel Dostál was looking for political partners to pass a law to secure future financial subsidies for filmmaking. Their arguments for state

---

[1]Established by businessman Miloš Havel as one of the largest and most modern studios in Europe in 1931.

[2]Until 1990, there was a complex of state film studios with their own financing system based on circulation of money.

intervention in film remain valid to this day and address the lack of competitiveness of national film in Czech distribution and the global market. This is mainly due to the relatively high costs of film production and the small size of the national market and the language area.

The most important institution was and still is the Czech Film Fund (CFF),[3] which distributes funds raised from the contribution from all cinema admissions and trading rights to Czech archive films that originated during the state monopoly.[4] The producers calling for higher subsidies have pushed for additional funding to increase the budget of the CFF. The arguments are based on numerous international examples. In a situation where it seemed politically impossible to receive a share of the state budget (tax money), film professionals chose to lobby for new or higher levies from cinema admission proceeds, new forms of distribution and the commercial activities of television broadcasters. The ambition to establish a strong funding body with a mandate not only to subsidize film, but also to promote it internationally, was abandoned due to strong political resistance. For several years (especially 2004–2006), the most viable strategy was the effort to increase the income of the fund's budget. Especially the producers pointed out their vulnerability due to the high individual financial risks of investing in national cinema and the uncertainties of its international visibility.

Despite all the weaknesses of the system, Czech cinema has not disappeared. Over the last 20 years, private producers and Czech Television[5] have maintained a high number of produced films per capita, as well as an extraordinary share in both attendance and sales.[6] The Czech film industry has also made its mark by winning awards at international festivals as well, such as the Academy Award in 1996.[7]

17.2.1 Accession to the EU

With the accession of the Czech Republic to the European Union in 2004, an external authority came to defend the notion that domestic audiovisual production contributes to the creation of national identity.[8] At the same time, Czech filmmakers began to point out the external benefits of film within the so-called cultural and creative

[3]Originally known as the fund for support and development of Czech cinema.
[4]The basic principles of the Fund were brought to the discussion just after the Velvet Revolution in 1989, and the institution was set up in 1992.
[5]Since the 1990s, the national public service broadcaster has been the most important co-producer of Czech cinema.
[6]After a decline in the 1990s, the number of Czech films has stabilized at above 30 feature-length films a year with the audience share exceeding 30% in some years.
[7]For the film *Kolya* (1996), directed by Jan Svěrák.
[8]A summary is given, for example, in the Communication on Certain Legal Aspects Relating to Cinematographic Works and Other Audiovisual Works (European Commission 2002).

industries, which not only supported their case for state support in parliament, but also helped to boost the self-awareness and self-confidence of the people involved in cultural affairs. To this day, EU policy is a crucial impulse for the national film industry.

17.2.2 Finances and Funding

Although the national legislative initiative to increase the budget for film funding was unsuccessful, after joining the EU a source of financial aid was established thanks to the process of digitization of television broadcasting. In 2010, an incentives program for foreign film production in the Czech Republic was launched, due to pressure from runaway productions and from a pure economic motive.[9]

Since approximately 2007, when the government increased the budget to support the film industry,[10] the discourse has changed—the question whether or not to financially support the film industry is no longer discussed. The focus has switched to the particular design of the subsidy schemes. However, the increase of financial support, which almost tripled, raised a new set of questions. The most discussed issue was the relationship between quantity and quality. What are the objectives of financial support to the film industry and the definition of the film funding scheme in general? As in many other countries, stakeholders discussed whether film policy should pursue a popular culture approach, where film is accessible to a wide audience and funds are allocated to genre production, or if it should pursue a quality approach aiming to educate and uplift viewers and to win prestigious awards at international festivals.

Another branch of the discussion focused on maximizing the impact of film funding. First, a high percentage of scripts were developed and consequently produced, even though they did not meet the necessary quality standards to make a successful movie. This resulted in a large number of underfunded movies which met neither the goals of a commercial film industry nor those of a cultural funding rationale. As a solution, it was discussed to fund fewer projects with higher subsidies to increase the quality and hence the possibility of success.

---

[9]The economic analysis was carried out by the independent research group EEIP. The results of the report were the subject of many debates due to their bias toward seeing a positive economic impact of the film industry and the lack of considering negative (not only financial) aspects.

[10]Resulting from a promise made by Prime Minister Topolanek during the Karlovy Vary International Film Festival, when he stated: "We have promised that at least we would create an expert group immediately after our government was established and try to find the missing €15.6 million which the Czech film needs next year" (Míšková 2006).

17.3 New Law, New Conditions

The sustainability of the new system and the higher level of support depended on the reconciliation of the various political forces and finding a more permanent social and political consensus. One of the essential questions regarding such support mechanisms was how the influence of individual participants in the film industry and also outside players (e.g., political parties and their interests, who could influence which projects were considered valuable) should be eliminated to build a systematic solution. To strengthen the public acceptance of the CFF, the representatives insisted on guaranteed transparency. The trustworthiness of the institution needed to be protected from direct political influence.[11]

The law to secure film funding in the Czech Republic passed in 2012 and took effect in 2013, exactly 20 years after the CFF was first established. It took long negotiations and a notification by the European Commission to put the legal changes into practice. The essential precondition for the EU was that the funding should not distort but rather foster competition within the audiovisual industry.

The most important body in the CFF is the board of film professionals and scholars, which not only grants the subsidies to particular film projects but also acts as a steering committee where long-term strategies are discussed and decided. The members are nominated by professional organizations from the audiovisual industry or the academic sphere, and with this recommendation, they are appointed by parliament. According to the legislation, the fund is not only the administrative body for cultural film funding, but also the host of economic film funding such as automatic support, and the administration of film incentives. Last but not least, the CFF is also the guarantor of co-productions and the methodological adviser in the field of general support and promotion of the film industry.

At the same time, the CFF draws its resources from a modified ticket levy (now 1% of box office, which led to a more than 20% increase in the income from levies), as well as from the growing market segment of commercial TV stations, which have won a prominent portion of the advertising market previously dominated by Czech Television.

The CFF regularly issues thematic calls targeting authors, producers, organizers and educational institutions. The received applications are then randomly assigned to expert reviewers for evaluation. In the next step, the evaluations and the applications are studied by all board members of the Czech Film Fund and discussed in an evaluating meeting. Successful projects must offer a good relationship between (1) creative and artistic potential, (2) appropriate economic investment and (3) an elaborate production strategy. All three criteria aim at minimizing the risk of investment for each and every project. Sufficient creative and artistic parameters are also

---

[11]The main shift was initiated thanks to the discussions on financing a film project called *The Devil's Mistress* (2016) directed by Filip Renč, which caused conflict over the principles of quality assessment and Fund procedures.

a prerequisite for negotiated EU agreements and are therefore assessed as primary quality indicators in providing support.[12]

Aside from direct supply-side funding of film projects, the CFF supports the framework of the sector. The CFF sponsors a large number of activities such as workshops and consultations for producers, informational meetings during film festivals and promotional activities for new film production. Furthermore, the fund supports technical upgrades of theaters and screening equipment, film distribution and promotion, participation in festivals as well as professional training, publishing efforts and last but not least the preservation of film heritage.

17.3.1 Support Typology

The creative and production process itself is vertically divided into three phases:

- Script development;
- Complete development, where production necessities (casting, crew, location, visual concretization) are defined;
- Film production that results in a master copy.

In order to appropriately focus on different film genres and production types with different creative, technology and financial requirements, the current system is horizontally structured to support areas of animated, documentary and short films, which offer an interesting start in the professional sphere for filmmakers who still lack stature, or for student talents after graduating from film schools. Especially important is the call for feature-length debuts, which is supposed to help the growth of talents and their initiation into and connection with the professional community and to develop professional skills (e.g., their ability to create a project design, to describe a clear creative vision, to share teamwork and to establish a professional production strategy).

Support is also available to encourage a broader range of content in distribution and to familiarize the audience with art house films through promotion of selected foreign films in cinemas. At the same time, it is a diplomatic impulse for a similar, reciprocal approach to the Czech films abroad, although there are no binding contracts or arrangements for such a procedure.

17.3.2 Minority Co-production

A high value-added contribution is the fund's call to support minority co-productions leading the (mainly European) creative teams to cooperation, enhancing the exchange of know-how and encouraging networking on the basis of which domestic titles and

---

[12]The process of notification under this condition was successfully finalized in 2013.

personalities can be integrated into national schemes in other countries. The transfer of symbolic capital based on festival awards and cross-border collaborations with internationally renowned filmmakers is also important. Over the years, the system has been improved and adapted several times and finally led to the funding scheme offered by the CFF since 2016.

17.3.3   The Current Funding Scheme

In 2016, following a series of negotiations, producers, the CFF, the prime minister and the minister of culture reached an extraordinary agreement on the amendment to the audiovisual law that reinforced the position of film within the state's cultural policy and introduced an unprecedented second, symmetrical pillar to the existing parafiscal levies in the form of a mandatory contribution to film directly from the state budget.

17.4   Mapping the Czech Film Industry

In 2015, Szczepanik et al. published the first structural study of the Czech film industry which laid out a detailed map of the whole sector. The study included a number of suggestions for policymakers and funding bodies that were taken very seriously in the following year. These suggestions included a long-term monitoring system evaluating creative quality and a fixed funding scheme for script development and complete development. A very important outcome was the termination of further support for scripts that did not pass the prior assessment steps with excellent results. The changes strengthened the status of script editors and screenwriters and, within a few years, transformed the common practices of film companies, fostered trust in the relationship between the fund and the film industry, and not least helped to establish connections between the academic field and practical film production. Moreover, the extraordinary and overall respect that the study gained has become the basis for future mapping and development of new strategic planning tools. The year 2016 brought a new statute for the fund's Board and work on updating the long-term strategy which could already be based on findings that were intuitively suspected within the industry, but it was necessary to describe them statistically and further evaluate and verbalize them.

At the same time, the fund began to actively develop measures for professional education such as a script consulting incubator,[13] an international program of workshops for screenwriters and script editors that offers multi-phase sharing experience and themes in a cyclic structure. In addition to passing on experience and know-how,

---

[13] The so-called Phoenix Project.

one of the intended effects is for Czech filmmakers to think in a European dimension instead of targeting only a domestic market and audience.

17.4.1 Attracting Runaway Productions

In addition to selective support, the fund has administered a system of automatic incentives for audiovisual production since 2010, which has been implemented in the Czech Republic based on an economic rationale and to catch up with numerous neighboring countries that had introduced economic film funding earlier. The monetary incentives are perceived by politicians as a state investment, and the economic impact has been thoroughly debated and its evidence closely analyzed.[14] The approximate return on investment from automatic support through incentives was assessed by the Ministry of Culture at about 118%, which gradually grew to 150% according to CFF annual reports (2016).

After most runaway production left the Czech Republic for cheaper locations, a funding scheme was set up to attract foreign production once again. The main motivations were derived from experience abroad and from previous successful cooperation with blockbuster productions in the 1990s: The aim was to learn from the professional skills of foreign filmmakers and their staff, effectively use and modernize Czech infrastructure, gain financial benefits and to inspire the whole field of the national film industry (Aust 2009). Runaway productions receive a refund of up to 20% of eligible costs. The only condition is the fulfillment of a cultural test that guarantees cultural and value compliance with the Czech and European frameworks. Supported projects include domestic, European and American films, the latter of which are often the most expensive productions.

In 2016, when the system was simplified and optimized, the incentives were granted to a total of 50 projects in the amount of about €32.5 million, and in 2017 it was more than €35 million.[15] However, after many meetings of the institutions involved and the Ministry of Finance, the 20% refund was increased to 25% of the eligible costs in the coming years (Hungary, the strongest competitor, offers 30%) and the total budget will have to increase to almost €47 million.

---

[14]There were many experts and film industry members involved in the process of analysis (e.g., Stillking Production, scholars, the Ministry of Culture). The resulting material was published by the Ministry of Culture as "Concept of Support and Development of Czech Cinematography and the Czech Film Industry 2011–2016" (2010).

[15]€33 million and €35.8 million, according to the Czech Film Fund's Annual Reports from 2016 and 2017, respectively.

For improved complementarity of institutions supporting Czech film and better co-ordination of their activities, the Czech Film Commission[16] and the Czech Film Centre[17] were incorporated into the CFF.

17.5 Digitalization

So far this chapter has described the development of Czech film policies after 1989 and where the industry stands today. However, during the period of consolidation of funding schemes and strategies, new challenges appeared that needed political, theoretical and practical attention. The Czech film industry in general (as well as the film industries in other countries) has had to come to terms with several historical periods and types of digitalization. The beginnings of cinema digitalization, which initially took place at single-screen cinema theaters, could be observed as early as 2008. This was mostly due to the efforts of local municipalities and particular cinema theaters to prepare for an inevitable global change.[18] One year later, this trend was introduced into multiplex cinemas, while the Czech Film Fund prepared a long-term, nationwide grant scheme for the digitalization of an extensive network of cinema theaters, film productions had to deal with the change in technology independently and gradually one by one. The technology was first tested on smaller independent projects designed for online distribution,[19] in order to be successfully introduced to mainstream projects later.[20]

The production sphere was skeptical about this phenomenon, undoubtedly due to a certain amount of distrust of the image quality as well as the artistic potential of digital technology. Meanwhile, the crucial driving point of its development within the distribution sphere was the high profits earned by foreign productions and the 3D blockbuster era.

At that time, when the local film culture was threatened by decline, single-screen cinema theaters, which were under substantial pressure from the global network of multiplex theaters, profited economically and strategically from the fact that these particular titles were immediately available after their premiere. Advancing digitalization of audiovisual content was accompanied by various challenges and risks, primarily in connection with the newly established illegitimate online distribution area.

---

[16]The Czech Film Commission was incorporated into the fund, among other things because its activities logically relate to the Fund's major duty to manage film incentives.

[17]The Czech Film Centre was originally established in 2002 as a private initiative in the period when Czech cinema lost its ability to effectively promote itself abroad.

[18]Kino Central Hradec Králové, cinema theater Central Hradec Kralove.

[19]*Late Night Talks with Mother* (2001).

[20]For example, the 4K digitally compatible *Catch the Billionaire* (2009).

The Czech territory was dominated by an online platform called ulozto.cz, which offered an immense quantity of both national and foreign titles free of charge and which became much more popular than the global torrent clients of previous years. Various organizations (e.g., the Czech Anti-Piracy Union, or OSA) as well as public institutions (e.g., the Ministry of Culture) started to perceive apparent violations of the Copyright Act and financial damage to the chain of production and distribution as an essential threat to the whole system, which led to the establishment of repressive measures as one of the priorities of future cultural policy.[21] Only later was VOD distribution gradually legitimized by emerging legal servers, by the success of global VOD distribution networks and televisions, and also through the realization that viewer preference for consuming audiovisual content on TV screens and displays is for the most part irreversible.

Incentives were newly incorporated into the CFF strategic materials, and the dissemination of Czech movies through new distribution channels became a desirable aspect accompanying and widening the key goal of cinema theater distribution. The discussion, focused on the most suitable means of digital distribution of available film titles, has been essential for the CFF Board since 2016 and has remained crucial to the present day.[22] It took thirty years to establish sustainable conditions for national cinema, and this effort is hopefully in its final stage. The reforms and initiatives have resulted in mechanisms which guarantee that films in cinema distribution are prioritized and that the state cultural policy (executed mainly through the CFF) respects this principle. This is the main reason why TV series designed for global channels and digital distribution, recently a very popular phenomenon, are still excluded from the established system of financial support for national film projects. Their producers are allowed to apply only for automatic support (incentives) along with foreign productions. In fact, the line between this type of art and the classic film format designed for cinemas is getting blurred. The stakeholders acknowledge this fact and are gradually preparing to adapt to it. Even the definition of "cinema distribution" and its rules are subject to reform.[23]

Unfortunately, the international availability of Czech national film production is not sufficient. Meaningful profit is often expected only within the Czech and Slovak territories, and sometimes the Polish area because of the insignificant language differences and low cultural barriers as well as familiar cast. The successful spread of Czech films within a network of foreign cinema theaters is so rare that it is not usually part of project budgets and most production companies connected with local distribution do not even target this goal. Even co-production titles are often released only on TV. Cross-border cinema theater release of new movies is almost out of the question. The recent Czech position in transactional video on demand (TVOD)

---

[21] Only some particular films had to be removed from uloz.to due to the legal regulations. Uloz.to is still active and has a strong influence on audience behavior and the audiovisual industry.

[22] The support of Filmtoro which offers all available film titles in Czech, with Czech dubbing or subtitles.

[23] While some TV or Internet series consider cinema premier, the minimal number of cinema screenings as a condition necessary to fulfill grant application eligibility criteria was lowered to 10.

distribution, where many Czech films are available, is more optimistic as opposed to subscription video on demand (SVOD) networks, where you can find only a few Czech film titles apart from European HBO GO. From a financial point of view, digital film distribution in other territories is still considered complementary. From this perspective, the concept of the European Digital Single Market (a EU proposal from 2015–2018) is rather a double-edged sword for the Czech film industry: The common markets could be opened up more effectively, but in the present situation the confidence in their own competitiveness is low and local distributors are not persuaded by claims about mutual cultural enrichment within the EU territory and the belief in the ability of European production to fight the American domination. The fear of losing the advantage of territoriality and possible disruption of the fragile support system is so overwhelming that it complicates other aspects of the issue as well as the challenges and possibilities of completely new solutions.[24]

17.6 The Lack of Analysis and Future Hopes

In spite of this, in 2016 the CFF decided to financially support a research project mapping the preparedness of the Czech territory to accept new conditions, and various other academic papers have also been taken into consideration since. Also, APA, the main Association of Czech Producers, is concentrating on future implementation and is trying to identify the most suitable way to incorporate Czech film productions into modern international digital networks and to widen their possible international impact. It seems that a thorough legal and economic analysis of the possible implementation of DSM is what the Czech territory and audiovisual sphere are still lacking in order to be able to articulate a clear approach and make a qualified decision on their standpoint with regard to any future discussions. Despite the complex and detailed ideas offered by European bodies, the Czech debate over the DSM issue is for most institutions and relevant stakeholders in its beginning stages.

Perhaps a few years of stabilization accompanied by another international success are the necessary conditions for this field of Czech national culture to attract global attention and to gain new self-confidence to be more active and open in this process. Right now, we can identify several impulses which could lead to success.[25] However, the coming years could contain a certain risk factor: Europe and the DSM could develop at such a pace that Czech politicians would be seriously challenged to establish an appropriate course of cultural policy.

---

[24]In October 2019, Netflix introduced its Czech localization with 150 Czech film titles. Possible effects of further development are yet to be seen.

[25]Recently, *The Painted Bird* (2019) was accepted by festivals in Venice and Toronto. The short animated films *Daughter* (2019) and *The Fruits of Clouds* (2017) were also extraordinarily successful.

References

Central Film Rental Institute. (1990). Závěrečný účet roku 1989. *Zpravodaj ÚPF*, No. 3.
Colin, J.-P. (2000). *Le Mystère Lang*. Chêne-Bourg: Georg.
Czech Film Fund. (2016). Výroční zpráva 2016. https://fondkinematografie.cz/assets/media/files/
    H/VZ/vyrocni_zprava_2016.pdf. Accessed November 28, 2019.
European Commission. (2002). Communication from the commission to the council, the Euro-
    pean parliament, the economic and social committee and the committee of the regions on
    certain legal aspects relating to cinematographic and other audiovisual works, COM(2001)
    534 final. https://eur-lex.europa.eu/legal-content/EN/TXT/PDF/?uri=CELEX:52001DC0534&
    from=EN. Accessed November 6, 2019.
Ministry of Culture of the Czech Republic. (2010). Concept of support and development of Czech
    cinematography and the Czech film industry 2011–2016. www.mkcr.cz/koncepce-podpory-
    a-rozvoje-ceske-kinematografie-a-filmoveho-prumyslu-2011-2016-536.html?searchString=
    koncepce%20podpory. Accessed November 10, 2019.
Míšková, V. (2006). Filmaři jednali s politiky o kinematografii. *Novinky*, July 1. https://www.
    novinky.cz/odlozna/89591-filmari-jednali-s-politiky-o-kinematografii.html. Accessed Novem-
    ber 10, 2019.
Nekolný, B. (2006). *Divadelní systémy a kulturní politika*. Praha: Divadelní ústav.
Szczepanik, P., Kotišová, J., Macek, J., Motal, J., & Pjajčíková, E. (2015). *A study of feature film
    development in the Czech Republic*. Prague: Czech Film Fund.

Petr Bilík is Assistant Professor at the Department of Film and Theater Studies, Palacký University Olomouc. He specializes in Czech and Central European film culture and the management of
cultural and creative industries. From 2015 to 2018, he was a member of the Board of the State
Cinematography Fund and helmed two projects based on mapping regional and national creative
industries. He is experienced in the field of production and the festival distribution of audiovisual content, having served as a commissioning editor at Czech TV, the head of Academia Film
Olomouc and founder and head of the PAF film festival.

CPSIA information can be obtained
at www.ICGtesting.com
Printed in the USA
LVHW051807300820
664584LV00002B/115